AMERICAN ARTS GALLERY

Compliments of J. Laughton
Johnston

YALE UNIVERSITY ART GALLERY

VICTORIANS 60° NORTH

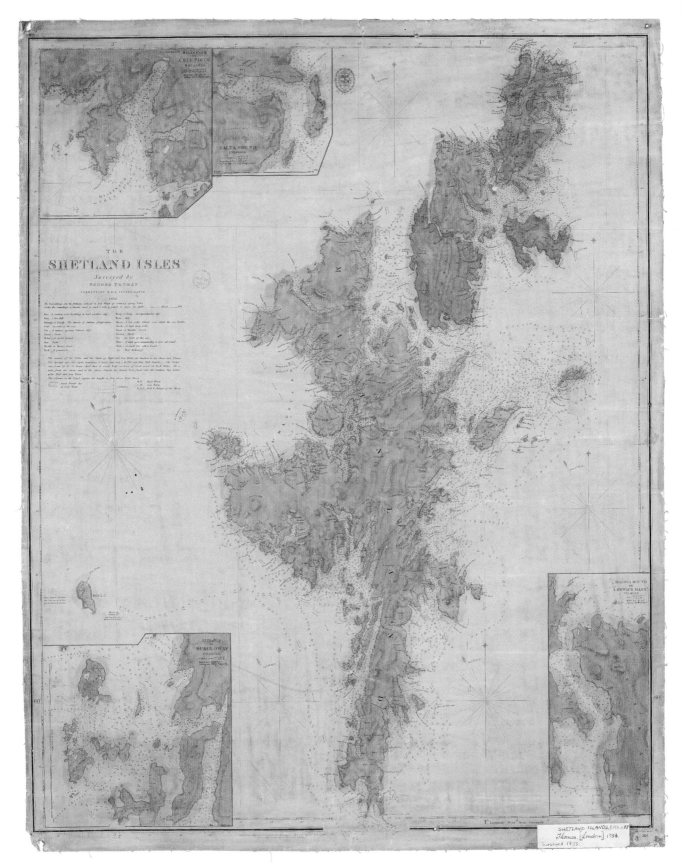

The Shetland Isles, Hydrographic Office, Surveyed 1833.

VICTORIANS 60° NORTH

The story of the Edmondstons and Saxbys of Shetland

The Shetland Times Ltd.
Lerwick
2007

First published by The Shetland Times Ltd., 2007.

ISBN 978-1-904746-25-6

A CIP catalogue record for this book is available from the British Library.

Books by the same author:

The Natural History of Shetland, 1980 (with R. J. Berry)
A Naturalist's Shetland, 1999
Scotland's Nature in Trust, 2001
Beinn Eighe: The Mountain above the wood, 2003 (with R. Balharry)
A Dream of Silver, 2006

Printed and published by
The Shetland Times Ltd.,
Gremista, Lerwick, Shetland,
ZE1 0PX, Scotland.

"There is no history, only biography"

Ralph Waldo Emerson 1803-1882

To Joy

without whom this book would not have been written

CONTENTS

PREFACE

This story began on the arid slopes of a bare, rocky headland on the most northerly inhabited island of the British Isles in 1837. The botanical discoveries there of Tom Edmondston, an eleven-year-old, sent ripples through the botanical circles of this country that reached the very top and ensured his fame for all the days of his short life. Among the plants he recorded was one that occurs only on that headland and on the slopes of a hill only a short distance away. In 1969, knowing about his discoveries but very little about Tom himself, I – much less of a botanist than the child – found myself on the headland admiring his fragile, white-petalled flower. Then I remembered that although the flower had been recorded also not far away, it had not been seen there since 1894. I left the headland, crossed the road, made my way up the slopes of the hill and there stumbled on the flowers not seen for 75 years. That latter event established a personal interest in Tom that I have never quite been able to throw off.

In 1996, while researching and writing *A Naturalist's Shetland*, I came across Tom again and found that his father, Dr Laurence Edmondston, had been a very good amateur naturalist and might have been a very good professional naturalist had he not gone into medicine. Then I found that Laurence's brother, Dr Arthur Edmondston, had also been a good amateur naturalist and like his brother, had published several ornithological papers and even written a book on Shetland at the dawn of 19th century. But that was not all; Tom's sister had married another doctor, Dr Henry Saxby, who wrote the first book on the birds of Shetland: the seeds of an account of these men and their accomplishments were sown.

In 1999, I met Joy Sandison, the great-granddaughter of Tom's sister, Jessie M. E., who had just given the house on Unst where Tom was brought up to the National Trust for Scotland. I told her of my latent ideas for an account of the natural history achievements of the family. She told me a bit more about the family and the fact that her great-grandmother, whom she had known as a child, had been Shetland's most prolific author, particularly of stories for boys, but also a journalist and a feminist of her day. It seemed that I would have to include her in the family story. Joy encouraged me and offered her support. I began to dig a little deeper. Laurence and Arthur had three other brothers, one inherited the Buness Estate on Unst and another emigrated to Charleston in 1799.

Next, I met Laurence's great-great-grandson, David Edmondston of Buness, the home of Laurence's brother who had been the laird of the Buness Estate and financial backer of young Tom the botanist. David gave me access to the uncatalogued family archives which contained numerous letters between members of the family and between the family and many others, including Charles Darwin. David and Joy then agreed that I should write the story of the family, not just about their achievements, but of their personal lives revealed by their letters, publications and other sources, principally the Shetland County Archives.

This is the story that I have written.

To distinguish personal comments and letters, from publications and official records, the former are *italicised*.

To allow the story to flow without distraction, text references have been placed at the end of the book.

Throughout the story, sums of money are quoted. In order to put their relative value into perspective their present (2007) monetary equivalents follow immediately in brackets (). These are approximations and should only be taken as a guide.

ACKNOWLEDGEMENTS

Many people assisted me with the writing of this book, from guidance in research to comments on the text. First and foremost, I must thank Miss Ida D. J. Sandison whose support, encouragement, knowledge of the family and whose sponsorship, in grateful memory of her Saxby forebears, made this book possible. I am also indebted to her for access to her family papers and other memorabilia that she has left to the Museum of Scotland.

Secondly, I am hugely indebted to David and Jennifer Edmondston for access to hitherto unpublished family archives at Buness and their generosity in allowing me to quote from so many private family letters. Courageously, they and Miss Sandison all agreed to an account of the family being written without any preconditions on the contents.

Other members of the family who provided information and support and to whom I am very grateful include, Elizabeth Edmondston in England and Laurence Edmondston Coffin, Eleanor S. Boulware and Mary Seabrook in Washington and South Carolina.

I must also acknowledge the financial assistance of the National Trust for Scotland that allowed me several visits to archival sources in London, Cambridge and Edinburgh; the Shetland Amenity Trust, for providing the wherewithal to obtain the illustrations; and the Shetland Arts Trust that made possible a visit to the American Edmondstons and the Edmondston-Alston Museum in Charleston. I would like to thank the museum staff there for their warm welcome and particularly Betty J. Saunders and Mary Edna Sullivan for their help and comments on early drafts of the American side of the story. In Charleston too, I received help from the South Carolina Historical Society. I need also to thank David Kater and Julian Holland in Australia for so freely providing me with information on Captain Henry Kater.

In Shetland, I am extremely grateful to John and Wendy Scott for access to relevant Gardie House papers; for encyclopaedic guidance at the Shetland County Archives from the Archivist Brian Smith and his assistant Angus Johnson; for the patient help of the staff of the Shetland County Library including Douglas Garden, and for the help of Tommy Watt at the Shetland County Museum. Several Shetlanders very kindly gave of their knowledge and recollections concerning the Edmondston and Saxby families and their times. These included Douglas Sinclair, Wendy Gear, Mary Ellen Odie, Walter Scott, Jonathan Wills and the late Mae Sutherland. Tony Gott of Bayanne (and his website) was extremely helpful in tracing family connections. Of all the expert assistance I received in 'uncovering' archival papers, none was more helpful or comprehensive than that which was given by John Ballantyne who, as well as correcting errors, pointed me in the direction of many relevant pieces of information that I would otherwise have missed. I cannot thank him enough.

Jonathan Wills, Brian Smith, John Ballantyne and Wendy Scott, all read and commented on early or late versions of the draft and I thank them for their patience and valuable contributions to the finished article.

I am also grateful for the help, in Edinburgh, of Irene Mackay at the Museum of Scotland, National Archives, National Library of Scotland, National Portrait Gallery, Edinburgh University and the Royal College of Surgeons; in London, of the Public Records Office at Kew, Greenwich Maritime Museum and Friends Library; in Cambridge, of the Cambridge University Library and the Scott Polar Research Institute; in Australia, of the MacLeay Museum of the University of Sydney;

and finally in America, I would like to thank the South Carolina Department of Archives and History, and the North Carolina Office of Archives and History for allowing me to quote liberally from the *Journal of a Secesh Lady* by Catherine Devereux.

Despite all the assistance above I am not a professional historian and any errors remaining are entirely mine.

The evocative cover is by Maggie Riegler, thank you Maggie.

Finally, I wish to thank Patricia for her love and for her forbearance over five years of research and writing.

PART I &

THE BROTHERS EDMONDSTON

CHAPTER ONE

BEGINNINGS

"My ever dear Miss Mally   *Lunna June 10th 1774*

Short very short will this letter be and very ill wrote as my time is so little. We got to Hascosay last night around 7oclock. I being not very well, the men were prevailed on to stay all night. About 10oclock your big boat came by. I was greatly staggard how to do. But it being very calm and the tide nearly gone & on the night I was prevaild on to stay. Jenny Hay too would have been disappointed. However this morning I repented I did not go with her as they have made a very fine passage I dare say. All here are very well so I hope to get to Lerwick this night or tomorrow. I would have got this night but no boat here – You was saying you was to go to Fetlar soon. You must not go soon. I heard in Hascosay that your aunt was better, and for certain two of Johnie Hunters children were either in the fever or had very lately come out of it. Now my dearest for Gods sake do not go in the way of the fever I beg of you. As you value your own health and if you have any regard for the happiness of him whose greatest pleasure is your welfare, keep out of the way. The Misses [?] are here. So God bless you. I'll write you more fully soon I hope. I am with unalterable love

                My ever dear Miss Mally
                Your ever faithfull & affecte
                Laurence Edmondston
       We got a fine passage here, came about 11 oclock."[1]

So wrote Dr Laurence Edmondston (1740-1814) to Mally Sanderson (1751-1831), from Lunna at the north-east tip of the Shetland mainland after a night on the island of Hascosay that lies to the north sandwiched between the larger islands of Yell and Fetlar, a kilometre to the west and east of it respectively. About 6 km to the north of Hascosay lay the island of Unst, Mally's home and the most northerly inhabited island in the British Isles. Laurence had just returned from Unst to his father's home on Hascosay by a small open boat the previous evening and was on his way to his own home and medical practice in Lerwick, one of the two principal fishing towns of Shetland that lay a further 50 km to the south. As there were no roads and the 75 by 25 km archipelago consisted of but one main island and dozens of others – varying from the size of Yell and Unst that contained a thousand or two souls to tiny islands that might only contain one family – getting from one place to another, apart from haphazard journeys across peat-covered hills by Shetland pony when one could catch one, was most reliable by boat.

The sea dominates the lives of Shetlanders. It is their marine boundary, their principal natural resource, main road and side roads, access to Scotland and Europe and, too often, their winding sheet. Laurence reassured Mally that his passage had been fine. This was June, the time of the

Mally Edmondston (Sanderson).

simmer dim when the nights were never entirely dark, when the sun shone till late in the evening and arose so early that man and beast scarcely slept. On such a calm night, Shetland is as pink and secure as a nursery and as romantic as a Victorian painting. Forgotten for a moment, are the harsh dark days of winter when boats are drawn up and tied down with boulders, when doors and windows are barred, and sheep and ponies cower behind the most meagre shelter. Forgotten too, are the sudden summer gales, more dangerous for their unexpectedness, than those of winter.

That night in 1774 it was calm, so the tenant-fishermen rowed Laurence across a silent swell as smooth as silk, dotted with tubby little black and white seabirds that tore brief holes in its surface as the boat passed, or flew in long strings across its path. Somewhere on their passage they would have disturbed a large, mysterious and solitary seabird, compulsively dipping its head in the water as if checking what lay beneath and slipping like a knife through the sea surface as they approached, to reappear what would have seemed like minutes later more than 100 metres away. The only sounds, apart from the brief cry of birds, were the plash of the oars, the complaining creak of the boards as the boat was pulled forward and the odd comment, out of the side of the mouth or over the shoulder, from one of the four rowers to another. Laurence was now 34 and had reasonable prospects as a surgeon in Lerwick. He could not offer Mally, 11 years his junior and the descendant of an old Shetland landowning family – whose roots went back several centuries to Norse immigrants – quite the home and life in which she had been raised. But he was a solid, professional citizen with a good reputation as a doctor and he too could trace his roots in Shetland to some blue-blooded, if later, settlers: the Edmondstons. They, like several of the landowning, merchant and professional families in Shetland – Cheyne, Gifford, Hay, Murray, Sinclair and Wishart – were Scottish incomers who had immigrated over the years after Shetland became part of Scotland in the 15th century. Though neither knew it at the time, their marriage was to bring Mally's mother's property, the Buness estate, into the Edmondston family where it would remain for the next two and half centuries. The marriage would also give rise to two succeeding generations of ambitious and talented men and women of the Edmondston clan who would leave their mark on Shetland and the world.

Laurence wrote his love letter to Mally after staying the night in the Haa of Hascosay, the home of his parents, Martha (born 1720) and Arthur Edmondston (born 1720 – died 1798) (see family trees from page 286), a two-storey, tiled roof and stone building with flagstone floor and wooden linings. Laurence was the eldest of nine. His father was a merchant[2] and the owner of half of the island: the other half belonging to his father's brother, William Edmondston (1715-1786), a surgeon-apothecary making his living almost 500 km away in Leith, the port for Edinburgh, and the first of five generations of doctors in the family covering a period of 200 years. Relatively primitive though it was, the Haa was still superior to the cottages of Arthur's dozen or so island tenants who shared one end of their extended thatched dwellings with their animals and cooked on an open fire at the other with a hole above their heads. The Haa, with the Edmondston coat of arms – a shield bearing a cross between three crescents surmounted by a camel's head and neck – carved in stone above

Interior of tenant's cottage.

its main doorway, stood stark above a low, treeless landscape, exposed to all the winds and close to Housa Wick, a sandy shore whose regular bounty of seaborne timber gave the island its name: Hascosay, the island of driftwood. This was Hascosay's only attribute as it lacked a sheltered anchorage and was predominantly peat-covered leaving very limited areas for arable culture.

The fears that Laurence had expressed for Mally's health, should she travel to Fetlar as she planned, were very real. They both had had firsthand experience of the many diseases then prevalent; Mally had already lost three of her sisters[3] while Laurence had lost many more patients. This was the time when measles, whooping cough, scarlet fever and influenza could be fatal, when virtually all that could be done for victims was to keep them hot or cold, as current treatment or old wives' tale dictated, and watch them die: death often being a relief for all. One of the most feared of the non-fatal diseases was leprosy, or what was thought to be leprosy. People were terrified of catching this disfiguring ailment. A future son of Laurence's (Dr Arthur Edmondston of Lerwick) was to think it was a form of elephantiasis, although it was probably a form of scurvy. He recorded that the people were so afraid of it that "… when this affection was very prevalent, the unfortunate individuals who were seized with it, were removed to small [isolated] huts erected for the purpose, and there received a scanty allowance of provisions daily, until the disease put a period to their miserable existence."[4]

There were very few surgeons in Shetland at this time of transition in medicine when the barber-surgeon was giving way to the professionally trained general practitioner, when it was common for many people to die from disease, particularly as infants. In 1720, the smallpox epidemic "… was so fatal, that it was distinguished by the appellation of mortal pox." In some years "… smallpox alone carried off, at each time, about a fourth part of the inhabitants … In the island of Foula [the most remote and most spectacular of the Shetland islands], the mortality was so great, that there were scarcely people left to bury the dead."[5] Smallpox had appeared in 18th century

Waverley Market and North Bridge.

Shetland several times before Laurence wrote his letter pleading with Mally not to travel, the last time just five years previously. This was a horrendous century for Shetlanders, never knowing when the dreadful disease might settle in their family and carry off their loved ones, infants, children, adults and lovers alike.

Laurence's professional experience with smallpox went back to 1758 when he began his five year apprenticeship with his uncle William in Leith, when Mally was still a child.[6] As part of his medical training he had attended the University of Edinburgh with around one thousand other students. To get to the University from Leith, Laurence, twice daily, had to skirt around the construction of the North Bridge, one of the grandest single building projects Edinburgh had ever seen. By the end of his life it would link Auld Reekie with the still expanding and meticulously ordered streets and buildings of the New Town, where a grandson, one hundred years later, would take up his winter residence.

Laurence's uncle, William, had been elected to the Royal College of Surgeons in 1753 and was now a respected surgeon and held in high regard, not least by his fellow Shetlanders. Besides his nephew, he took on other sons of Shetland landowners as surgeon-apprentices, including another Laurence (1734-1820), son of Robert Hunter of Lunna and Gideon Gifford (1748-1811) of Busta.[7] Their four year indenture cost £25 (£1000 in today's terms); the last two years of which they were expected to attend university. It included bed, board and washing and William Edmondston was bound to:

"… instruct, learn and teach … his whole bussiness and proffession of Surgery and Pharmacy to the utmost of his power and skill and … not hide nor conceal any part or practick thereof from him but shall honestly and carefully lead him into the knowledge of all the Secrete Art of his said profession …"[8]

The year that Laurence began his training with his uncle, an islander wrote to William in Leith for advice on the treatment of smallpox. William replied with the following instructions on inoculation:

"… make a small incision with a lancet … then put in about the bigness of a barley corn or little more of cotton … in which the poxy matter has well absorbed … then a sticking plaster and afterwards a compress and bandage. The poxy matter must be keeped into the wound for 24 hours at least."[9]

This was a relatively new and, as yet, not entirely safe procedure and it was to be another 40 years before the Englishman, Edward Jenner (1749-1823), developed a safe vaccine. William went on to recommend a diet and care that included keeping the patient warm and indoors, but this treatment "… was confined entirely to the higher ranks, or such as could afford to pay the operator for his time and attendance. Not more than ten or twelve persons were inoculated at this time."[10]

In his letter to Mally, written at Lunna, Laurence mentioned his companion Jenny Hay, whose family had immigrated in the early 1700s. Jenny may have been the young daughter of William Hay (1723-1804), a tacksman (factor) and fish merchant on the island of Yell, one of those to whom Laurence's uncle had provided medical advice on the treatment of gout; beginning a close relationship between the families that would be continued by Laurence, his sons and grandsons.

On the 16th February, 1767, Laurence had written from Leith to seek advice from William Hay:

"… if I don't come to Shetland I must be destitute, and as you are not a stranger to my circumstances you know I have not substance to push my fortune abroad …"[11]

It is clear that Laurence is fretting about his financial situation, a cloud he was to live under for most of his life. However, after completing his apprenticeship Laurence managed to return Shetland as a surgeon. Determined to bring the latest medical thinking to Shetland, one of the first things he did was to carry out very many more inoculations. As a surgeon (before a surgeon generally became called a doctor), Laurence made his living by obtaining subscribers among the relatively well off or charging them *pro rata* for his services; from the poor he took nothing or only what they could afford. Mally's family, like other landed and successful merchant Shetland families, were subscribers to Dr Laurence and, when need arose, he stayed with them until his patient(s) recovered. After all, they were paying him for his services and travel was not quick or easy: it was a good 24 hour's row or a day's sail from Lerwick to Uyea Sound at the south end of Unst, then a 9 km walk or pony-ride to Buness, often in inclement weather. So it was that Mally, when still a girl, and along with several hundred others, was inoculated by the man who would become her husband. While Laurence's uncle had recommended that the treatment for smallpox should consist of sweating the patient under blankets in a stuffy room with the fire roaring and the doors and windows closed, his nephew:

William Hay (1723-1804).

"... relaxed from the hot regimen then generally practised, and substituted the antiphlogistic* in its stead. He informed me [Dr Arthur Edmondston, his son] that the people of the lower classes were soon convinced of the great advantages to be derived from inoculation, and, resigning every prejudice to the voice of reason, both young and old presented themselves for inoculation, and experienced its benefits."[12]

*in the 18th century phlogiston was believed to be an element given off on combustion: Laurence was recommending fresh air!

On the journey from Unst to Hascosay, Laurence and his crew may well have crossed the path of a *sixern* on its way home from fishing. This was a relatively new design of boat in Laurence's time, developed for line-fishing at the *far haaf* (deep sea), for ling, tusk, cod, halibut and skate. These were un-decked, open boats, rowed, or sailed with a lug, up to and beyond 50 km offshore, reaching 80 km in the last years of the fishery. The fishermen operated from the most convenient shore nearest the fishing ground and at these stations, where the men lived in small stone huts for the summer fishing season, they split, salted and dried the fish. These stations were often at some distance from the fishermen's small tenanted farms, which meant much of the summer farm work was left to the women and children.

For anyone who has not been far out to sea, and overnight, in a small open boat, and even for Laurence who did much of his travelling by boat, it is difficult to imagine the skills and the hardships involved in such a fishery. The ocean swell would often hide the land and only when they were briefly perched on top of a wave would the fishermen have caught a glimpse, in good visibility, of the very tops of the islands on the horizon. It was a long journey out and only when the 9 km of lines, baited with 1000 hooks, were run out could the fishermen rest for a few hours before they had to haul all those kilometres of cold, wet, heavy and salty cord back on board, unhooking maybe 400 ling, or as much as five tons of fish, as they came over the side and then, if there was no wind, there was the long row back to the shore. Such exposure burns the face while the work exhausts the muscles of the arms and back and the cold wet cord tears the flesh of the hand.

In clear weather they navigated by triangulation on prominent landmarks or *meids*, and when out of view of landmarks they checked the composition of the sea floor with a greased weight. Frequently, due to distance offshore and poor visibility, the men lost all sense of where the land lay, but over the generations they had learned a skill that was handed down from one generation to the next. In every seventh wave underlying the chaotic movement of the sea, whatever the wind direction, they sensed the mother wave, or *moder dy*, a constant surge of the sea towards the land that, time after time, brought them safely home.

Sixareens at fishermen's summer base at Fethaland.

Apart from the fishing, there were few other openings for a young man in Shetland to gain a cash income in those days. Their reputation as hardy seamen and their location at the most northern extremity of Britain made them ideal crews for the whalers, from Peterhead and Dundee and as far south as London, that stopped regularly in the spring at Lerwick on their way north to Greenland and the Davis Straits. The other seaborne employment opportunity of the time was not the first choice of Shetlanders. In fact, in most cases, this opportunity was no choice at all! Just as the whaling firms sought out Shetlanders for their ships, so did the press gangs target them for the British Navy. At the end of the Anglo-French Seven Years War in 1763, when Laurence was 23, it was estimated that some 900 Shetlanders were paid off from the navy, out of a total population of around 16,000, and during the American War of Independence (1776-1783) it is estimated that there were at least 2000 Shetlanders in the Royal Navy. In fact, somewhere between a third and a half of all adult men were at sea during this period. In some cases Shetlanders were 'pressed' straight off the whaling ships as they returned from Greenland. The loss of a working man was a potentially fatal blow to an ordinary Shetland family who depended on him for their very bread. He was also a loss to the laird who railed against the whaling and the press gang.

As if the hardships of the fishing and disease and fever were not enough for the ordinary inhabitants of Shetland at this time, there were often years when the fish were not to be found or there was outright failure of their crops. Starvation of both the people and their animals occurred several times in the 1700s. Laurence, however, was privileged in the face of these adversities. As a surgeon he was immune from the press gang, and as the son of a laird and merchant he never had to put his life at risk at the fishing and, because his family had reserves of capital to fall back on in times of want, he never starved.

Laurence and Mally were married at her family home, the Haa of Buness, in 1775. They chose to be married in February, a time when few boats venture out, and any fishing is carried out from the rocks of the shore, when the last blade of grass has been consumed by sheep and ponies, and when the tottering cow in the byre has forgotten there is a world beyond the door. In other words, at a time when the domestic stock and the resources of the land are almost exhausted and when the people have to rely on their stores of cured meat and dried grain. It was not a month for travelling far in the northern isles, but then the guests were principally Mally's Unst relatives and Laurence's from nearby Hascosay and Yell. Although Laurence had little property at the time of his wedding he was heir to his father's modest share of the island of Hascosay and he was related to several Edmondstons who had other land on the island and on Yell. The marriage was one of love, but it was also a traditional uniting of interests and a securing of obligations that happened regularly between the landowning families.

Laurence and his Edmondston contemporaries owed their property and place in Shetland society to their ancestor, Andrew (1559-1632) – the first Edmondston to settle in the islands around 1589 – and to the powerful and influential position he secured for himself. The name Shetland does not have the same ring of magic as the Indies or El Dorado that one might think would attract adventurers and settlers, secular and religious, in the 16th century: adventurers such as Laurence Bruce of Cultmalindie (in Perthshire), a half-brother of Earl Robert Stewart of Orkney and Shetland, himself the illegitimate son of James V and half-brother of Mary Queen of Scots. So, what brought Andrew to these apparently remote northern isles in the 17th century?

Buness 1817, purportedly by J. B. Biot with wigwam in which he protected his instruments.

The answer lies in the marriage, in 1469, of Princess Margaret of Denmark to James III of Scotland, that ended nearly 700 years of Norse rule in the North Isles that had begun with the arrival of the Vikings in Shetland in 800AD. The Scandinavian crown could not afford Margaret's dowry in cash, so pawned the islands to the Scottish crown, with its rents and taxes instead, in the understanding that when it could find the cash it would redeem the pledge. This never happened and Orkney and Shetland have remained part of Scotland ever since, and, just as the Vikings had been land hungry in the 9th century, so too were the Scots in the 15th and 16th centuries and Andrew was one of the many Scots who saw his opportunity. Edmondston family tradition has it that "He was a clergyman who fled from persecution",[13] but there is no evidence for this.

Andrew's birth coincided with the Scottish Reformation when the Bishop of Orkney became responsible for the appointment of the reformed ministers in Orkney and Shetland. In 1568 he passed this power to Earl Robert Stewart who had been granted the lease of Orkney and Shetland by Mary Queen of Scots. These appointments were sinecures, gifted most probably as rewards for service – sometimes illegally where the individual was not qualified to act as minister. In 1589, Andrew Edmondston appeared as a notary and servitor in Shetland – one who is authorised to perform certain legal formalities such as drawing up and certifying documents and contracts – indirectly to Earl Robert himself.[14] Shortly afterwards, in the 1590s, Andrew was appointed minister of Walls, a parish in West Mainland, and then became minister for the island of Yell.[15]

Andrew's position was worth a very comfortable £60 (£2400) annually and included the tenants' tithe or teind (1/10th of the crop), payable to the minister in kind. Andrew also had an income from his position as collector of taxes for the Governor, or Foude.[16] Other obligations on the tenants from which he benefited included three days work to him in his own fields (the glebe) or assistance in the cutting and transport of his fuel (peat) from the hill. This relatively good income allowed Andrew, like other ministers in his position, to purchase land and by the time of his death in 1632 he had become a relatively wealthy and influential figure in the north isles of Shetland, passing on his accumulated property down through the generations. Along with Andrew, perhaps on his coat-tails, came John and Robert Edmondston who were possibly his nephews. Those three were the antecedents of several Edmondston families who had settled in Yell and Hascosay by the time of Laurence and Mally.[17]

Mally could equally well trace a long lineage on her mother's side of the family, for Ursula Henderson's (1724-1786) Norse ancestors at Buness went back to the 16th century. But her father, Thomas Sanderson (1725-1800), came from the Scottish mainland. His sister, Mary Sanderson (1710-1798), had married the Rev. William Archibald (1702-1785) in 1728 and they had settled in Unst where he had taken up the ministry.[18] It may well have been on a visit to his sister that Thomas first met and then married Mally's mother in 1747.

A few days after Laurence and Mally's wedding, and when they and all the guests had recovered, a happy, house-hunting Laurence wrote to his young friend, James Hay (1750-1831), son of William and an up-and-coming entrepreneur with less regard for the legal niceties of business than his father.

> "*Dear Jamie, I have the pleasure to inform you that I have now enlisted in Hymen's train, and, as something for a house must be looked for I would be obliged if you could furnish me in the following articles, viz the teeking* [thatching] *I spoke to you about, – and if you have anything fit for towels … spare me what you can …I sent your father some strengthening plaster.*"[19]

James Hay (1750-1831).

Mally had lived all her life up to now on Unst where Buness stood a few hundred yards from the shores of Balta Sound, an inlet sheltered by the sandy island of Balta at its mouth. But Balta Sound was no remote backwater chanced on by accident. Travelling west across the North Sea from Scandinavia, Shetland is the threshold to the vast spaces of the North Atlantic. Bergen, at 320 km, is the same distance away from Shetland as Aberdeen. North-west from Shetland it is the same distance to Faroe and continuing in that direction it is but another 500 km to Iceland. Following a great circle route westward from Shetland at 60° north, the first landfall is Cape Farewell, the southern tip of Greenland, 2500 km away. From the point of view of Scandinavia in the 9th century, Shetland was the ideal stepping stone to

Scotland, Ireland, England and the North Atlantic islands, then on to Greenland and North America. Balta Sound is the most northerly safe anchorage in Britain and later became one of the final stopping-off points and the first returning point for Arctic explorers, and for whalers to and from Greenland and the Davis Straits, for traders to northern Russia, as well as for fishermen landing, curing and exporting their catch. Shetland, on the northern rim of Britain, was the strategic centre of a European wheel of exploration, conquest and exploitation.

Lerwick

Mally was therefore well used to the bustle of a relatively busy port and to the comings and goings of seamen and travellers of many nationalities. She was, however, not used to living in a house on a narrow street, cheek by jowl with neighbours. Nevertheless, she made the transition from eldest daughter of the Haa at 24, to wife, with relative ease and confidence and, mercifully, had the strength to face the emotional roller-coaster of the first few years of her marriage that tested her resilience to the limit. Almost immediately she was settled in Lerwick, she was able to announce to both their parents the joyful news that their first grandchild would be born in November. Then in July, when she had been carrying for five months, came calamity. One of her younger sisters, the 14-year-old Jean, who happened to be staying with them in Lerwick, fell ill and died. Mally had already lost three younger sisters before her marriage and was familiar with the terrible intimacy of death, but nevertheless, Jean had been in her care. This must have been a shattering blow and difficult to cope with when she herself was so near giving birth. Laurence, on the other hand, could only feel helpless, unable to save Mally's sister or relieve her grief. It was a blessed relief to all therefore, when their first child, Arthur (1775-1841), named after his paternal grandfather, was born without complication on 10th November.

The following spring, Mally lost yet another sister, aged 18, but not long after fell pregnant again. For the next ten years she fell pregnant almost every other year, giving birth to seven more

children – Thomas (1777) who died in infancy, a second Thomas (1779-1858) named after his maternal grandfather, Janet (1780-?), Henry (1781-1831), Charles (1782-1861), Mary (1785-1853) and Ursula (1786-1813). Unhappily for Mally, after having given birth successfully to eight children, the fifth of her six younger sisters died in December 1786, leaving her but one brother, Charles, and one sister, Barbara (1753-1831), from her original eight siblings. Happily, for her parents, Barbara had settled in Unst where she married her cousin, James Archibald, son of the Rev. William Archibald. By 1790 therefore, out of the ten children born to Mally's parents at Buness, only three remained, one of whom was the only son, and heir to the Buness estate. Meanwhile, the first children of Mally and Laurence were growing up.

Lerwick from Fort Charlotte by John Irvine.

Even though Shetland might be thought one of the remotest parts of Scotland, the children of the better off – the landowner, merchant or professional – at the end of the 18th century got a solid education, but of course, it cost money. As far as ordinary Shetland children were concerned, they would have to wait until 1827 when all twelve Shetland parishes had schools before they began to get a basic education. Arthur, Laurence's first born, was a very intelligent child who showed a great interest in everything around him and from an early stage developed a particular aptitude in natural history. The Happyhansel School in Walls in West Mainland was considered to be the best school in Shetland at the time and the only one to teach Latin. It had received its delightful name (happy gift) because it was originally endowed with four and a half acres of land.[20] Walls was a small fishing village only about 20 km from Lerwick as the crow flies, but a hard day's journey by foot and boat, so Laurence sent Arthur to board with Archibald Greig (c1757-1831), the headmaster.[21] One of Archibald's children was James (1785-1852) and Arthur knew him only as an infant, but some thirty years later they would meet again in very different circumstances. In the meantime, following successful results at school, in 1793 Arthur, to his parent's delight, went off to Edinburgh University and indenture to a surgeon when he was nineteen, just as his father had done 36 years previously and his grand-uncle 50 years previously.

The year Arthur went to Edinburgh an incident occurred that, like his first meeting with James Greig, would later come back to haunt him. In September 1793, the Rev. James Barclay (1742-1794), a brother-in-law of Mally's sister Barbara and now the minister for Unst (after his father-in-law, the Rev. William Archibald), arrived unexpectedly at Laurence and Mally's home in Lerwick with his servant and "*with an obstinate dysenteric affection*"[22]. He stayed and, despite being nursed by Laurence for what must have seemed four very long months, he died on the 17th January, 1794. During this time Laurence's servant, and Mally herself, caught the dysentery. The servant died but, fortunately, Mally survived. After the Rev. Barclay's death, leaving his wife and children in Unst without income, Arthur later noted:

> "*My grandfather* [Thomas Sanderson of Buness, as the landowner and benefactor of the minister and his manse] *helped to make up every deficiency* … [Mrs Barclay benefiting from a slender annuity from the Widow's Fund] *He built her a house and gave her a farm free of rent. His grandson and successor followed his example: and the family resided on it until the youngest child was provided for.*" [23]

In a letter to James Hay in 1800, Thomas Sanderson expressed a very poor opinion of the two Barclay sons and the daughter, "*I have had enough of their ingratitude and loosed plenty of money supporting them and their parents …*"[24]

While Thomas Sanderson saw himself as generous and compassionate towards the Barclays, they saw it very differently, later describing the collapse of the manse around their ears for lack of maintenance by the then landowner – Thomas Sanderson![25] The result of this spat of blame and ingratitude was a great bitterness between the families that lasted a long time, nursed by Thomas Sanderson's grandsons, Arthur Edmondston and his brother Thomas. Arthur thought that the Barclay sons, John and Thomas, blamed *his* father, Dr Laurence of Lerwick, for *their* father's death, whereas he saw his father's efforts in nursing the dying Reverend, over a prolonged period in his own home, as equally generous and compassionate as that of Thomas Sanderson in providing accommodation for the family.[26] Some 30 years later the spat was reopened by Arthur and only healed by his nephew after his death.

The year after Arthur went to Edinburgh his mother, Mally, who, after eight years, assumed that Ursula would be her last child, unexpectedly fell pregnant for the ninth time. In February 1795, 20 years after they had married, when Mally was 44 and Laurence 55, they had a fifth boy whom they christened Laurence (1795-1879), after his father.

Then occurred an event that was to forever change the life of one of Mally's sons. Charles, Mally's only brother and heir to the Buness estate, died in his late 30s, and Mally, as the eldest sister, became the heir. As long as her father was alive, of course, she need not think of taking over the estate. He, however, was now approaching 70 and no longer had a son to help him run it. At this point Laurence was 50 and had a well-established medical practice in Lerwick. Although he could have done with the extra income, it was too late now to assist his father-in-law, had he been asked or even wanted to. An heir then, had to be sought among the grandsons and he had to be trained up to take over the estate. By primogeniture, Arthur, the eldest, should have succeeded to Buness. Arthur, however, was in Edinburgh in the middle of his medical training and when he was approached by his parents regarding the future of Buness, he declined the inheritance. After all, he was heir, after his father, to his grandfather's and namesake's piece of property on Hascosay already, albeit of much less value than Buness. Besides, he had a wide range of interests and wanted to devote his time to study and publication which he regarded as far more important. The inheritance of Buness was therefore settled on Thomas, Mally and Laurence's second son, who was now a youth. Thomas was not gifted like his elder brother, he was, however, very enthusiastic at his new prospects and travelled eagerly from Lerwick to Buness to take up residence with his grandparents and learn about estate management, the fish trade and other merchant ventures in which his grandfather, Thomas Sanderson, was involved.

CHAPTER TWO

FIRST STEPS

"From the first moment I saw you as a child of 2 or 3 years (I at that time a man) in this house in your mother's arms my heart yearned towards you with more than a brother's love."

Thomas Edmondston (1779-1858)

Arthur's Edinburgh

When Arthur arrived in Edinburgh in 1794 to begin his medical training it was in the evening years of the Scottish Enlightenment. While David Hume (1711-1776) the philosopher had died in the 1770s and Adam Smith (1723-1790) the economist in 1790, the brilliant geologist James Hutton (1726-1797) was still a resident and his equally illustrious countryman Joseph Black (1728-1799) was still a Professor of Chemistry, and the University was still a magnet for students from England, Europe and the United States. However, by the time Arthur came to do his studies in the late 18th century, Edinburgh had also become the world leader in pioneering the training of the general practitioner, so that Arthur, after taking a medical degree at the University and a diploma in surgery at the Royal College of Surgeons, graduated with the skills, not only of surgeon and apothecary but of a general physician. In addition, the medical qualification in Edinburgh now required much greater rigour and application than it had when his great-uncle, William Edmondston, had studied in the first half of the century. Edinburgh's medical training reputation was so good that it had become the model for the other medical schools in Scotland, in Glasgow, St Andrews and Aberdeen and at this time it was the only place where the qualification could be guaranteed to be reliable, hence the reason that every member of the Edmondston family and many other notable students who took up medicine studied here.[1]

In Arthur's time, work had begun on the new University that was to replace the original 16th century buildings, although it was not to be finished for quite a number of years. Edinburgh's New Town had also expanded since his father's day west to Charlotte Square, one side of which was just being completed, while construction had begun on the Mound, linking Princes Street with the upper end of the old

Edinburgh New Town from the North.

15

Edinburgh High Street. The New Town, however, was still, at this stage, on the very verge of the countryside. Sir Henry Cockburn (1779-1854) (Solicitor General) remarked at the turn of the century that "*I have stood in Queen Street, or the opening at the north-west corner of Charlotte Square, and listened to the ceaseless rural corn-craiks, nestling happily in the dewy grass.*"[2] It was all very impressive to Arthur from Shetland, perhaps more so than it had been for his father or his great-uncle. Arthur, however, was a very different man to them; he was better educated, academic and ambitious. Not only did he attend university in Edinburgh but sometime during his studies he travelled to France to attend lectures at the University of Paris.[3] His conservative political beliefs that he brought with him from Shetland must have been considerably shaken by this newly republican city and he returned with many liberal ideas that sat uneasily alongside his innate reactionary views: contradictions that remained with him for the rest of his life.

With whoever he served his apprenticeship in Edinburgh, Arthur did not have a high opinion of his outmoded medical skills, commenting later in his *Biographical Notices of Pharmacopola and Presbyter* (1830):

> "Our master had a genteel and an extensive practice; and although naturally clever and clear-sighted, was purely empirical in his views. He rarely, I may say never, perused a medical or surgical work; and he was not only unacquainted with, but he despised the doctrines of modern medicine. His pharmacopoeia consisted of a few nostrums, applied to almost every case, among some of which, chemical incongruities were but too apparent. He carried his personal disinclination to study even to the pursuits of his pupils, restricting their academical studies to the fewest possible numbers and variety of classes, and never approving of private lectures. He discountenanced anatomical dissection, that fundamental and indispensable source of all medical and surgical intelligence, because it took up too much time."

Edinburgh might be a hotbed of medical progress but there were still some who were stuck in the past!

Of very much the same age as Arthur and indentured to a Dr John Cheyne in Leith, was another medical student, Robert Jameson (1774-1854). Cheyne, as it happened, was Arthur's uncle; the son-in-law of William Edmondston, the surgeon-apothecary. Jameson's father was a soap-boiler in Leith who came from Shetland,[4] and like Arthur, Jameson had interests other than medicine. In his case they were in geology and natural history to which he gave such passionate devotion that he soon decided to drop medicine in favour of those interests. Earlier in the same year that Arthur went to Edinburgh, Jameson spent a three-month field trip in Shetland studying its geology, which he published as an *Outline of Mineralogy of the Shetland Islands and Arran* (1798): the first account of the complex geology of Shetland. The year after Arthur graduated, in 1804, Jameson, at the age of 30, became Professor of Natural History at Edinburgh University where he remained throughout his life, making an international reputation, influencing several brilliant British naturalists and attracting talented students from all over the world. Subsequently, Arthur, his brothers Thomas, Henry and Laurence, and one of Laurence's sons, all made Jameson's acquaintance and sought his advice and help.

Before he graduated, Arthur joined the army as a surgeon with the Argyleshire Fencibles for a short period, after which, in 1802, he produced the first of his many academic publications: *An account of an ophthalmia which appeared in the Second Regiment of the Argyleshire Fencibles in the month of February, March and April 1802.* This first account in English of what was termed the Egyptian ophthalmia was an auspicious beginning to a promising academic career. The following year he graduated as a doctor from Edinburgh University, his final dissertation being on cholera, a disease that had not yet arrived in Europe but the study of which was to prove useful to him thirty years later.

But, while Arthur was gaining respect and success in the medical profession at the turn of the 19th century, there was much happening in his family back at home in Shetland. His grandfather, Arthur Edmondston of Hascosay, having lived all his life on the island, died in his late 80s – a ripe old age even now – leaving his portion of the island to Laurence, Arthur's father. Arthur's next younger brother, Thomas, was now permanently resident at Buness assisting his grandfather and gradually taking over the running of the estate. Then the next brother, Henry, in his turn went south to Edinburgh in 1799 at the age of 18 to begin *his* medical studies,[5] later settling as a surgeon in relative anonymity in Newcastle. However, it was the action of the fourth brother that took them all by surprise. Charles had seen Thomas

Robert Jameson by Frederick Schenck.

become the laird of Buness and knew that Arthur would inherit the Hascosay property. Perhaps he did not wish to stay in Shetland nor have any desire to take up medicine but, in that same year that Henry went to Edinburgh, Charles decided to emigrate. He travelled south to Liverpool and from there left for Charleston in Carolina to seek his fortune.

The journey from Lerwick to the Scottish mainland, Peterhead, Aberdeen or Leith was not one to be taken lightly at this time. It could be a risky business and could take several days. There was no regular service and in the winter months there were few boats. In fact, when the weather was poor there might be delays for days, even weeks. The next part of Charles' journey was a long trek by carriage to Glasgow and then by sea to Liverpool and then a voyage of up to six weeks across the Atlantic.

With Arthur away in Edinburgh this left Mally and Laurence, in the last year of the 18th century, with only their three girls, Janet 19, Mary 14, Ursula 13, and the 4-year-old Laurence junior. Losing all his elder brothers from home in such a short period left the young Laurence to be brought up in Lerwick by three much older sisters, a mother in her 50s and a father in his 60s, and could only have resulted in some emotional confusion for him. True, he saw Thomas from time to time and, before Laurence was ten, Arthur returned to Lerwick to take up the practice of their father, but because the age gap was so great – Thomas was now 20 and Arthur 24 – his elder brothers must have seemed more like uncles to him.

At this point, Thomas seems to have become the apple of his grandfather's eye. In a letter to James Hay, now a merchant in Lerwick, in January 1800, the ageing Thomas Sanderson revealed his deteriorating state of health and his complete trust in his youthful grandson and apprentice.

> "*I am much obliged to your friendly ... and attention to Tam Edmondston, which I take in better part as shown to myself. I hope you and him may have friendly correspondence and transactions after I am removed to a better world than this has been of a long time ... I will be obliged you advance a few pounds I formerly mentioned twixt 6 and 8 £ sterling* [£240-320 in today's terms[6]]*, chiefly in silver, as little gold or notes as can be, which deliver to T. Edmondston and take his receipt for it. Any things he may demand for himself give, with freedom and pass the value to my debit.*"[7]

Thomas Sanderson went on to ask James Hay to send him some oatmeal as the Unst oats crop had been a failure, and 15 or 20 yards of cotton shirting. In his reply James Hay referred to young Thomas as "*a pretty lad*" and asked the old man if *he* could oblige "*... by putting 5 or 600, or a boat's cargo, of your winter ling to the Stones, to be so dry by the middle of March as transport here for the service of the Greenland ships.*"[8] James Hay was asking Thomas Sanderson to have the fish dried on the beach stones so that he could sell them on as provisions to the whalers in the spring when they stopped in Lerwick for crew and victuals on their way north to the Davis Straits.

That year, Thomas Sanderson died and Buness estate passed to his grandson, Thomas Edmondston. At this time, Laurence's financial situation was even more precarious than usual, not surprising considering he was putting a second son through university, had three daughters and a son to house and feed, and that he had had to provide another son with enough to get him to America and established in some employment or other. His delicate position was made clear in a letter from James Hay to his father, William Hay, in June 1800, when James sought subsequent approval for having lent his friend Laurence £14 (£560) to pay for his father-in-law's – Thomas Sanderson – funeral.[9]

It must have been a sad time for Laurence and Mally, with the death of her father and the departure of so many sons from home. Nevertheless, they could imagine that their first son, Arthur, would shortly take over Laurence's medical duties in Lerwick and at least they had the girls and their youngest son at home. Mally must also have had some quiet maternal satisfaction in that it was *her* son, Thomas, at the tender age of 21, who had succeeded to her family home. They could imagine too that their two eldest sons, now financially secure in Lerwick and Unst, would soon take wives and that they would not have long to wait for grandchildren.

The Island Home

In 1792, a couple of years before Arthur had gone to Edinburgh, an Unst landowner, Thomas Mouat of Garth (c1750-1819), who lived in Belmont, a fine Georgian house he had built in the south end of the island and, purportedly, the Rev. James Barclay – the same who died in the Lerwick house of Dr Laurence Edmondston – reported on the state of Unst in *The Statistical Account of Scotland*:

> "The whole number of the inhabitants … in 1775, was 1368 … and at present, [in 1791] amounts to 1988 … There is no parochial school … Fishing is an important branch of industry of these islanders. By the sale of the ling, cod and tusk [they] pay their rents. These are salted and dried, and in this state exported to Barcelona, Ancona, Lisbon, Leith and Hamburgh … The minimum number of men employed in fishing is about 350, who go out in 70 boats … Almost every woman in the island manufactures fine woollen stockings … much valued for softness and warmth … Considerable quantities of them are sent every year to Edinburgh … The property of the island is at present divided among 37 heritors. Of these 26 are resident. The principal heritors are, in order of the extent of their property, Mr Mouat of Garth, Mr Sanderson of Buness, Mr Scot of Greenwall, and Sir Thomas Dundas of Kerse … Within these two years, a considerable part of the lands in the island have been sold by the former proprietors, who were before resident heritors …"

This was the island society into which Thomas settled at Buness.

From being an undistinguished youth and the second son of a surgeon in Lerwick, overnight Thomas had become the second biggest landowner on Unst responsible for many tenants, a fish merchant and trader, and was, potentially, a very influential figure and, most certainly, a very eligible bachelor.

The island of Unst is approximately 20 km north-south and 6 km east-west. Its large population at the time was a mark of the natural fertility of its soils and that of the surrounding sea. However, it has several extensive areas of rough moorland which held the common grazings or *scattalds* on which the tenants grazed their stock of cattle, ponies, sheep, pigs and geese, cut peat for fuel and vegetation for roofing, and had done for as long as anyone could remember.

Thomas, despite the brevity of his experience in estate management, proved to be a canny business man and he quickly settled into running Buness more profitably than had his

Thomas Edmondston (1779-1858) as a young man.

grandfather. He continued in the fish trade, purchasing 3990 ling weighing 193½ cwt for £174.00 (£7300) in 1804 either for export or for supplying merchants like James Hay for the whalers or passing merchant ships. Thomas thrived despite the fact that Shetland's foreign fish trade was hit badly in the 10 years following Napoleon's self-promotion to Emperor in 1805 and the continuing threat to shipping from the French navy, even though Nelson had struck him a heavy blow at Trafalgar that year.

Though Thomas bought fish from other merchants he also bought fish directly from his tenants at the two Buness *far-haaf* stations on Unst. From Burra Firth, a long, deep inlet with cliff-bound shores, in the north of the island, his tenant-fishermen pulled out into some of the most fearsome waters around the British Isles. Here, at the last outposts of the islands, the tides can sweep around the rocks of Muckle Flugga and Outstack like a river in spate. The other, and most inaccessible of the Buness *far-haaf* stations, was on the shores of Wood Wick on the west coast, entirely exposed to the Atlantic swell. Here, the approach to the beach was through and over a sea of boulders and rocks, each one capable of destroying or capsizing a boat should there be a misjudgement or a retreating wave to leave it stranded across their sharp and lethal backs. It is a place where no one would dream of landing a boat unless the only alternative was running onto the surrounding cliffs. How the fishermen ran in their fully loaded ocean-going boats through these boulders onto the beach in the best of weather, never mind the many days when the prevailing westerly winds kicked up a following sea to make steering a nightmare, is frightening to consider. In Thomas' time, it was estimated that in Shetland as a whole there were some 459 *sixerns* at the *far-haaf*, crewed by almost 3000 men. He himself might have had half-a-dozen boats operating from each station and later he also employed men in the near-shore *saithe* fishing.

A young friend of Thomas', Dr Basil Spence (1800-1877), a man from a landed Yell family who had married the heiress of Uyea, an island at the south end of Unst, later commented on the rise of his prosperity, saying that Thomas had told him:

> "When he [Thomas] succeeded to the 'bit of property of Buness [he] could barely realize £50 [£2000] a year from it'. But getting from Mr Bolt a tack [lease] on favourable terms of Lord Dundas' lands in Unst, supplying vessels, 'Archangelmen', especially at that time putting into Baltasound harbour, and managing well his business generally he prospered …"[10]

Dr Basil Spence in later years.

The trade to Archangel in northern Russia that called in at Balta Sound carried sophisticated European goods outward bound and tar, timber and furs on the return voyage.

This account by Spence was a little flattering as the estate had at least been sufficiently profitable for Thomas' grandfather to have bought several plots of land prior to Thomas' succession. But such was Thomas' energy and business acumen that between 1803 and 1817 he was able to increase the extent of Buness property by 400 acres of arable land.[11] He also had sufficient funds from the rents, the victualling of ships and the fishing in 1815 to be able to afford to invest £700 (£34,300) in the purchase of a substantial piece of property in Lerwick – Braewick House, its kail yard and waste ground, from the Street to the Hillhead above, along with houses, shops, workshops and other buildings. The purchase was described by William Hay as the "… most eligible property in Lerwick."[12] There is no doubt but that Thomas was rapidly finding his feet and prospering: he was also growing in confidence and influence.

If the Shetland landowner, merchant and professional classes held the financial and secular powers in the late 18th century, the Church, through the parish minister, bestrode the moral ground and played an influential role in setting the moral parameters of the time. From the pulpit the minister could put anyone in their place, though he was usually careful what he said about the laird and it was not uncommon in the 17th and 18th centuries for 'sinners' to have to submit themselves to public admonishment and humiliation in front of the congregation.

Although the landowner was, naturally, reluctant to part with the cash for the minister's stipend, or for repairs to the manse and the church for which he was responsible, the minister was not too badly off and knew who buttered his bread. The Rev. James Barclay had reported in the 1790s that:

"The whole income of the minister, consisting of the old money, stipend, an augmentation obtained in 1785, and payable in butter, ling, wool and lambs: a glebe of 12 merks of excellent land; an annuity allowed, consequence of an agreement by the heritors [landowners], and three days work by the parishioners, may be estimated at L. 108 Sterling a-year [£9500]. The manse is rather in a ruinous condition, but the present minister preferred the annuity above mentioned to a new manse."

In comparison by 1801 an average family of a tenant farmer and fisherman lived in a cottage of two rooms and few, if any, windows. Directly off the entrance was the byre in which the cattle were kept in winter. This intimate connection was an extra source of warmth in the winter, but the associated dirt was also a source of disease. Most of the cottages, grouped in townships, had earth floors and a hole in the roof to let out the smoke from the fire. The walls were built of stone and clay and the roof consisted of a layer of thin turf covered by a thatch of straw. Enclosing the land of the townships was a hill-dyke that kept the grazing animals on the common grazing or *scattald* from entering the arable land within. The *inby* arable land was not fenced but parcelled out in narrow strips or *rigs* on which the tenant farmers, or crofters, grew potatoes, bere and oats for their subsistence and which they hand dug with the traditional Shetland spade.

Food for the ordinary Shetlander consisted chiefly of bread, oatcakes, milk and fish. Fresh meat was usually only available in the autumn and the early part of winter as there was limited fodder to keep many animals alive through to the spring. Fish of several varieties was nearly always

Tenant's cottage.

available in the summer and the winter diet was supplemented by *piltocks* (colley) and *sillocks* (their immature form) that could be caught off the rocks or from boats inshore. The people, including the lairds, were at the mercy of the elements. In a good year the farmer-fishermen could supply most of their wants, but years of poor weather or disease, sometimes consecutively, could rapidly reduce them to starvation and beggary, when they had to depend on the goodwill of the laird, charity, or the importation of grain for their very survival. Although they may have lived on the same spot for generations, they had no security of tenure and their attitude to the landowner was one of subservience and suspicion. Even when offered some security through leases, they were reluctant to take them.

By the late 18th century the land was divided up among numerous landowners, most of whom had modest landholdings and only a few of whom owned relatively large estates. *Their* housing conditions were of course superior to their tenants, many living in two-storey, flagstone and wood-floored houses with fireplaces and chimneys in every room, like Buness or the Haa on Hascosay. They tilled the best land, could afford more efficient and up-to-date equipment and often, like the minister, had three days or more free labour from each tenant. By and large, the landowners, rich merchants and the professionals were naturally conservative people and their families frequently intermarried, forming an intimately linked network of ties and obligations that in effect, controlled Shetland politics, society, property, production and profit. That is not to say that there were not benevolent landowners in Shetland, or that many were not devout Christians who took their responsibilities for those less well off very seriously, but that was the order of things. This, then, was the island and society into which Thomas the laird settled and prospered at Buness, where he became an antagonist of fellow landowner, William Mouat of Garth, at the south end of the island and the friend of a more geographically distant neighbour, Sir Arthur Nicolson of Fetlar.

Laurence the budding naturalist

There was another side to Thomas the laird, however, very different to the character who grew from landowning entrepreneur to political self-satisfaction. From his youth he had retained a boyish and adventurous spirit and now that he was financially secure he indulged himself. With his right-hand man and general factotum, Peter Sutherland (1796-1858) – a six foot Shetlander of many practical talents – he liked nothing more than to take his open boat and a crew of his tenants and go seal hunting or fowling. Equally, he enjoyed an evening with a few of his cronies and his favourite fiddler and, tight as he was with his money in business affairs, he could be quite benevolent, even indulgent, as far as his family was concerned.

Many years later, a nephew (another Thomas Edmondston 1847-1923) described Thomas' seal hunting activities, at the same time betraying his own inherited assumptions of the place of tenants in society which later would lead him to oppose reforms.

"My uncle, the laird of Buness, used to be a mighty seal-hunter. It was before the days of the modern "arms of precision", long before breech-loaders were in common use, and even before the Enfield or Minié rifles were invented. In those days the muzzle-loading rifle was found to be not a trustworthy weapon; he therefore used a very thick-metalled fowling-piece, which was deadly up to sixty or eighty yards. He had a splendid boat, which he named the *Haaf-fish*, about seventeen feet of keel, a capital sea-boat, equally good for sailing and rowing, safe, therefore, in bad weather and rough sea, and at the same time handy to manage when rapid movements might be required, such as landing in narrow creeks, or on slippery shelving rocks, or shallow beaches with a surf on. His crew was composed of four picked men from amongst his fishermen tenants, and his henchman [Peter Sutherland], who was as much a friend and adviser as servant, a man of great natural sagacity, intelligence, and fertility of resource, and of prodigious bodily strength. All of them were first-class boatsmen, expert pilots, familiar with every rock and reef and tideway on the coast and amongst the islands, and withal steady, bright and intelligent fellows. … He would be absent for a week, sometimes more, if the weather should turn out unfavourable … The first day would be spent amongst the nearest islands; and in the evening he would land, and spend the night in the hospitable mansion of one of his brother lairds, where he was always a welcome guest, his boatmen at the same time making good their quarters at very small cost in the nearest fishermen's cottages. … In some seasons he would bag … as many as forty or fifty [seals]. In ten years, during which he kept a careful record of the number he shot, he secured close upon three hundred of both species … The most he shot in one day was eleven, ten of which he secured. Not a bad day's sport."[13]

Unsurprisingly, as soon as he was old enough, Thomas' brother, Laurence junior, began spending an increasing amount of time away from Lerwick with his elder brother at Buness, as otherwise he was closeted in the little fishing town with elderly parents and older sisters. Laurence was a kind of amalgam of three of his elder brothers. He shared with Thomas a love of the outdoors, he was also gifted with Arthur's intelligence and academic curiosity, and shared a thoughtful and sensitive nature with Charles, but on the other hand, he lacked their self-confidence and strength of character. Being so much older than Laurence, Thomas looked upon him in a very different way than is usual for an elder brother. In a letter to Laurence some 36 years later, he told him:

"*From the first moment I saw you as a child of 2 or 3 years (I at that time a man)* [18] *in this house* [Buness] *in your mother's arms my heart yearned towards you with more than a brother's love.*"[14]

Laurence's formative years with Thomas brought about an almost entirely dependent relationship with him that was to last for as long as they lived. In some ways Thomas became a father to Laurence and it was he who provided the opportunity for Laurence to develop his passion for natural history, particularly for birds. Freed from Mally's apron strings and his old father, Laurence accompanied Thomas on his boating trips. From the men he learned the local names of the seabirds, seals and cetaceans they met around the gentle shores of Balta Island, under the precipitous seabird cliffs of Herma Ness or in the dark caves of Saxa Vord. From Thomas the zealous hunter, he also learned to shoot: an important attribute for a budding naturalist in the 19th century.

But Laurence was not just content to enjoy the company of his brother and his men, nor was he entirely satisfied with the excitement of chasing, shooting and capturing game, fun as that was in an open boat with the sting of salt spray in his face and the cry of seabirds filling his head. He soon found that Thomas and his crew could not answer all of his many questions and so he began to take notes himself of the plumage differences between the many birds they met and the seasonal changes in their presence or absence. He also began to enjoy spending time on his own, when he could watch the birds without the disturbance and impatience of the others and to speculate on the relationship between them. He realised that, very occasionally, there were individuals he could not give a name to. He was not alone; there was much confusion at that time regarding the juvenile plumage of many birds. Among the three breeding species of large gulls for example – the great black-backed, lesser black-backed and herring gull – few could identify which speckled juvenile belonged to which and some thought they might even be different species from the adults. In Laurence's time there were no binoculars and as soon as he approached close enough to begin to distinguish subtleties of plumage his quarry would be off. Hence, he was grateful that he had become a good shot and could examine specimens in the hand. Next, Laurence taught himself, as best he could, to skin his specimens so that he could preserve them and build a working collection.

Both at Lerwick and at Balta Sound, Shetland's thriving fishing industry attracted thousands of gulls. They could do so much damage to fish laid out to dry on the stony shores that boys were employed to keep them off. When he was at home, Laurence spent many days walking around the Lerwick foreshore or sitting quietly on the beach among his brother's drying fish on Balta observing the birds. By his early teens he had noted that no one knew the proper names of two of the wintering gulls. The larger gull, its immature form speckled like the immature of most others, was called the Iceland *scorie* by Shetlanders. *Scorie* being the name they gave to all young gulls, and they reckoned Iceland was where it came from as the whalers among them had seen them on their trips to Greenland. The very similar but slightly smaller gull Laurence thought might be a different species, so he called them the greater and lesser Iceland gulls. The fishworkers and the beachboys became quite used to the sight of him on Balta squatting among the fish, sometimes with his brother's gun, peering at the gulls and scribbling in his notebook. One day in 1809 he managed to shoot a specimen of the larger gull and it became the first British record, later to be named the glaucous gull. It was to be another ten years before he managed to shoot the other, slightly smaller gull and it became known as the Iceland gull, a second new record for the British Isles.

When the opportunity arose, Laurence tried to discuss natural history with his eldest brother Arthur – who, when he was home, often spent his spare time away from Lerwick on Hascosay – whom he discovered had far more

Glaucous gull by William MacGillivray.

24

knowledge than Thomas about birds. Unfortunately, Arthur did not suffer the company of little boys with much pleasure nor did he have much of an opinion of Thomas and perhaps critically, as Laurence's knowledge grew, he could see that Arthur was not such an acute observer as himself. However, Arthur's ornithological knowledge was the best Laurence could get in his early years for Thomas was really more interested in the excitement of the chase and the kill than in the niceties of plumage or behaviour. He *was*, though, fascinated and impressed by others with greater knowledge than himself, the tourist, the traveller or the naturalist who from earliest times homed in on Shetland like migrant birds, for the islands were the last stepping stone of Europe before the leap into the North Atlantic: a curiosity, geographically, geologically, zoologically and culturally.

One of the first natural history travellers to Shetland of the 19th century, who coincided with the blossoming of the young Laurence's interest in wildlife, was a printer and naturalist called Patrick Neill (1776-1851), author of *A tour through some of the islands of Orkney and Shetland* (1806). Neill's home was in Canonmills, a little village half a mile down the hill and through the fields to the north of Edinburgh's New Town and his business among many other projects was responsible for printing the *Encyclopedia Britannica*. When Neill visited in 1804 Laurence was nine and much as he was impressed, he found that Neill could not tell him very much more about the birds of Shetland than his uncle Arthur. Laurence also met the Rev. Dr John Fleming (1785-1857), who came to Shetland in 1807 on a commission to survey minerals. Fleming was an all-round naturalist, who, on invitation, took up the post of minister on Bressay, the island opposite Lerwick. But the person who inspired Laurence most, through his great enthusiasm and knowledge, was the Englishman, William Bullock (c1773-1849), when he visited in 1812, by which time Laurence was 17.

William Bullock, one of many, slightly eccentric, British travellers of the 19th century, was an antiquarian, naturalist and collector who founded a Museum of Natural Curiosities in Sheffield in the late 18th century. This collection then moved first to Liverpool and then to London in 1812, becoming the London Museum. In 1819 the collection, including many birds and animals, was auctioned and parts were purchased for Edinburgh University

Patrick Neill.

25

by Robert Jameson. In the 1820s, this material would be the source of much fascination and inspiration for Laurence and later, in the 1830s, for his eldest son. However, they were a few of the lucky ones, as Jameson could be a very difficult character, guarded the collection jealously and was even known to bar some of the most famous from it. Eventually, through constant addition by Jameson, the amount of material was so great – second only to the British Museum in London – that it became the basis for what is now the National Museum of Scotland in Chambers Street.

When Laurence first met Bullock, the latter was in the North Isles on a collecting tour for his museum. One of his main goals was to seek to obtain a specimen of one of the last great auks from Papa Westray in Orkney. On this trip he was unsuccessful and so he travelled on to Shetland becoming one of the first of many distinguished naturalists and scientists who were to be invited by Laurence's brother Thomas to stay at Buness during their visits to the most northerly isles of Britain.

The well-travelled, sophisticated and knowledgeable Bullock made a lasting impact on the young Laurence. They made expeditions together across Unst's moorlands and around its shores where the latter proudly showed Bullock his favourite bird haunts. He also shyly showed him specimens of birds that he had shot and inexpertly skinned. In return, Bullock, an experienced preserver of his own specimens, gave Laurence some tips in the art of taxidermy. One of Laurence's prize specimens that he proudly presented to Bullock was a large white owl that he had shot and skinned the previous year. To Laurence's surprise and delight Bullock offered to purchase the bird.[15] It was in fact a snowy owl, a bird that breeds on the tundra in more northern latitudes, and yet another new record for Britain. Over the next few years Laurence corresponded regularly with Bullock and sent him several more specimens of birds for his museum. Sadly, on the later sale of Bullock's museum, Laurence's contributions to his collection were lost. Nevertheless, the visit of Bullock set Laurence on the right path and stimulated him to take even more time and care in his natural history observations.

Snowy Owl by William Yarrell.

CHAPTER THREE

THE RUBICONS OF ARTHUR AND CHARLES

"… to consider all mankind engaged in the just defence of their natural rights as brethren, and to contribute, by every means in its power, to their assistance and support …"

Aims of the Iberian Patriotic Society

The Pen As Sword

Six years after publishing his dissertation on cholera, in 1808, even at this early stage in his life – he was only 33 – Arthur had established himself as a medical academic of note with the publication of a second, and book-length account of the contagious nature of ophthalmia: *A Treatise on the Varieties and Consequences of Ophthalmia* (1806). In this ground-breaking treatise Arthur divided the inflammations of the eye into those externally observable and those that can be described only by the patient, anticipating an approach that became the standard some 30 years later. Meanwhile, he had been attending the Royal College of Surgeons to which he was elected in 1805. He also became an Honorary Member of the Royal Physical Society.

Arthur now faced a difficult decision. Should he stay in Edinburgh and take up a practice there, perhaps even further his medical career by becoming an academic at the University or the College of Surgeons, or should he return to be a general practitioner in Shetland? There is no doubt he had the qualification, capability and self-belief to succeed in academia, but there were other sides to this complex man. His feet were very firmly planted in his native soil, he prized the opportunities, like his young brother Laurence, to be out on its moors and shores watching and studying the birds and, like Laurence, he wanted to know more about their habits and relationships. As he wrestled in Leith with a decision that would shape his life, he might have recalled summer days of a year or two ago when he had spent time on his grandfather's island of Hascosay.

There, he would have watched with pleasure, the shy little dunlin with its chestnut jacket and its white waistcoat stained with black – as if it had been carelessly muddied among the mossy pools in which it lived – and wondered if this was the same bird as the identically sized one with the grey jacket and clean waistcoat that he saw in the autumn and winter? On one of those days he heard a mellifluous trill from a long-beaked bird. He might have thought at first glance that it was a curlew, but the call was sweeter and, while the bird's plumage appeared to be the same as the curlew, it seemed smaller, the bill definitely shorter and less curved and there was a very distinct dark and light striping of the head that was absent on the curlew. It was a whimbrel, the curlew's northern cousin and on that day Arthur was the first in Shetland to identify and record it. In recall, in the dirty narrow streets of old Edinburgh, such memories drew him back to the islands like a magnet.

Whimbrel by William Yarrell.

Arthur was also fascinated by the romantic history of his home and he harboured ambitions to write about it. The last book on Shetland to be written by a Shetlander – *An Historical Description of the Zetland Islands* (1733, although not published until 1786) by Thomas Gifford of Busta – was now over 70 years old. Arthur recognised that he could not follow his real interests from afar and resolved, therefore, to forgo potential fame in the big city for its certainty in the small pond of his home islands. The man that returned to Lerwick, though still only in his early 30s, was self-confident, verging on the dogmatic, with a confusion of radical and conservative beliefs. But, like his father, he was a caring and skilful practitioner who rarely charged the poor, a benevolence that also encompassed a strong conviction for justice, for himself and for others less fortunate.

Back in Lerwick, in 1808, in the face of the downturn in trade and the general air of depression due to the recent successes of Napoleon – in defeating Austria and Prussia and forcing the retreat of the Russians – but uplifted by the efforts of the Spanish in support of the British contingent there, Arthur and five other leading gentlemen of Shetland, in a noble and patriotic fervour, founded the Iberian Patriotic Society:

"… [to] commemorate the glorious exertions of the Spaniards in the cause of liberty and patriotism, against the unprincipled usurpations of France … [to] … cherish patriotism, as the chief virtue of a citizen, to consider all mankind engaged in the just defence of their natural rights as brethren, and to contribute, by every means in its power, to their assistance and support … to embrace whatever tends to maintain the independence, or conduces to the improvement of their native country [i.e. Shetland]."

Lerwick, head of Morrison's pier, 1879, by Charles McEwan.

On the formation of the Society, Arthur, never one to do anything by halves, at once took the responsibility upon himself to publish the *History and Laws of the Iberian Patriotic Society*,[1] a pamphlet of 16 pages consisting of an extremely long list of the laws of procedure of business designed to guide the smooth running of the Society. These reflected Arthur's growing certainty in his innate superiority. Under Order of Business, Rule VI he instructed that, "No member, unless he be the proposer of a motion, shall speak, without the express permission of the President." It was, of course, no coincidence that Arthur was the president and it was, perhaps, no surprise that the Society was short-lived!

Arthur surpassed himself the following year with the publication of *A View of the Ancient and Present State of Zetland* (1809), a book of much more ambitious scope than Gifford's of the previous century. Several accounts of Shetland had been published by visitors including Patrick Neill's travelogue of 1806. Then there were the Parish accounts, such as that by Thomas Mouat of Garth for the *Statistical Account* (1792). However, some of these works were not reliable and Arthur thought he could write a much better work.

He was right. His two-volume work was an outstanding contribution to the corpus of knowledge of Shetland of his time. It is far more comprehensive than any of the previous accounts and remarkably detailed and accurate, if a little long-winded, on almost every aspect of these remote northern islands and the changes that were occurring to its society. In the preface to the second volume Arthur set the tone for all his future work, explaining to his readers that his descriptions were from personal observations and reassuring them, in his own inimitable way, that "... although ... some slight inaccuracies may have crept in, the reader may rely on the correctness of my statements"[2]. There is no doubting Arthur's self belief! But, by and large, readers *could* rely on his observations and analysis. He described his home town of Lerwick at the turn of the 19th century:

"It contains, at present, about three hundred houses, some of which are handsome. They are built of breccia, quarried above the town; and many of them have their doors and windows ornamented with freestone. The houses, however, have been set down without regard to any plan, and generally with their ends to the sea. The principal street, or rather row, which extends from one end of the town to the other, is in many places well paved with large flag: it is, however, of very unequal dimensions, and in some parts does not exceed six feet in breadth. The houses which are placed on the rising ground towards the hill [Hillhead], and which have neat gardens attached to them, produce an agreeable effect; and they contribute much to ornament the town. Those which are built on the side next to the water, and which are fortified by a kind of hollow wharf projecting into the sea, form where they occur, a double street, and afford shelter from the north and east winds, but they give the town a singular appearance. Viewed from the bay, at high water, it resembles an irregular fortification, these bulwarks, appearing like so many bastions ... There is a respectable looking building, called the town-house, in which there are apartments for the different purposes of court-room, custom house, mason-lodge, and prison. This, and a neat church, is the only buildings of a public nature of which Lerwick is possessed."[3]

The houses on the seafront that Arthur referred to were *lodberries* (loading rocks). The wharf on their seaward side not only provided protection from the sea but allowed cargo, and sometimes contraband, to be unloaded. Their construction, however, in some cases obliterated the foreshore where people kept their boats, or at least impeded public access to it. The flagstoned 'row' between the *lodberries* and the next line of houses behind them, at the foot of the hill, became known simply as the 'Street'.

In his book, Arthur expressed strong views on the way the over-populated land was traditionally managed; views that upset both his brother Thomas, the laird at Buness, and other Shetland landowners. Arthur had read his Thomas Malthus (1776-1834) – *An Essay on the Principle of Population* (1798) – and he put the blame for the over-population of Shetland squarely on the landowners and, long before the infamous 'clearances' reached Shetland, warned against the injustice of taking such action.

> "It appears that this country, in its present state, can barely furnish the means of subsistence to a population equal to two thirds of the actual amount … But although this fact be admitted, yet as the landholders have themselves been chiefly instrumental in encouraging the system which led to the present superabundant population, it would be both cruel and unjust, to introduce any plan of management on the Zetland estates, which might lead to a compulsory removal of the tenants from their farms."[4]

Arthur was railing against a relationship between a number of owners and their tenants that had developed fairly recently.

Early in the 18th century there had been a period of fever and famine when many of the Scottish lairds in Shetland went bankrupt: though not the Edmondstons of Hascosay and Hendersons of Buness. These lairds were dependent on rents for their income but this source dried up as more and more of their tenanted small farms became unused. Local merchants then took over many of the bankrupt estates and the fishing industry. Many of the tenants fished to supplement their income and diet, but now some of the new landowners, and the few remaining traditional landowners, set up fishing stations with their own cash and obliged their tenants to sell their fish only to them or their proxy. In other words, for some, fishing to the laird became a condition of tenure. Those landowners provided the means to buy and maintain the boats and fishing gear, or took out shares in them and very often their tenants could only get their other necessities of life from their shops. Little money changed hands between them as most payments were in kind. Perhaps, when the population was small and the ties between the landowner and tenant closer, the system worked, but now with a larger population and harsher economic circumstances and under the pressure of inevitable hard times when the season yielded poor returns, many tenants regularly found themselves in debt at the end of the season settlement. This form of tenure, known as the 'truck system', was a kind of debt-bondage that continued throughout the lifetime of the five Edmondston brothers, eventually stirring up such controversy that towards the end of the century the British government set up a commission to investigate it.

The problem for the tenant was exacerbated by the custom of the lairds of encouraging the splitting up of small farms and the creation of new ones, so as to provide more fishermen and more income for themselves. The majority of the farms were only of a handful of acres and were too small to provide subsistence. Although the landlords provided the materials for the new farm building, or '*outsets*', the often poor and stony hill ground had to be broken in before the soil was fit to produce anything. The result was that, as Arthur had pointed out in his book, the population rose but there was less food produced to support them.

It was the fishing tenures and the tenants' lack of security, Arthur suggested, that were the impediments to agricultural improvement: the answer, he believed, lay in organising the fishing and improving the farming:

"… the chief and natural source of wealth to this country [so that it]… may be conducted as to yield, with less risk and expense to the individuals engaged in them, a large increase … Good enclosures, larger farms, more efficient implements of agriculture, leases, attention to the cultivation of plants which yield winter fodder to cattle and sheep, regular cover for both in winter time, and a judicious distribution of the ground into arable and pasture land, would be of incalculable benefit to Zetland."

It was a radical and far-sighted view for one with pretensions of aristocratic, landowning blood, for it was clear that Arthur meant that such improvements should be for the tenants and not just the landowners. Another 'injustice' aired by Arthur was impressment into the navy. In Orkney, by special arrangement with the government, there were no impressments, yet Shetland suffered badly in the 18th and very early 19th centuries before impressments ceased in 1810.

"The merchants of Lerwick are constantly complaining of a disinclination on the part of the heritors to unite with them in petitioning Government to relieve their country from this vexatious oppression, and to offer to contribute a regular quota of men, proportioned to their population in its stead. The heritors, on the other hand, urge, that regular fishing tenants are exempted, both by custom and law, from impress; that the Greenland [whaling] trade is prejudicial to the morals of the people, and they wish to put a termination to so injurious a system."

There was a large element of self-interest here by the landowners, in that any tenant who went to Greenland or was impressed, was lost to them from the fishing.

Another hobbyhorse of Arthur's was the church. He could not thole public humiliation of sinners. As usual, he took the liberal line, in this case in the matter of the punishment for sexual activity outwith marriage:

"The fair frail delinquents, for a single discovered imprudence, instead of being secretly reproved, in the mild spirit of Christian gentleness, and having their imperfections shaded with the veil of forgetfulness, were indiscriminately stigmatized, and repeatedly subjected to the sneers of a whole congregation. Repentance under such circumstances could be but temporary."

Ten years later, did he but know it, 'deviation from chastity' was going to come pretty close to home and he was going to be very glad that the practice of public condemnation had ceased, at least in Lerwick.

Arthur's book then, was not simply descriptive, it was a platform for his deeply held and sometimes contradictory views. For some, notably Thomas' neighbour, William Mouat of Garth, an able spokesman for the landowners, Arthur was a dangerous radical. In correspondence between the two Arthur had suggested that in Shetland some 4000 families of the lower order were cheated and abused by 50 families of superior rank – under the fishing tenure and debt-bondage land management system. Mouat replied that this "… *is as unfounded in fact as the language in which it is conveyed is coarse and inapplicable*"[5]. He went on to accuse Arthur of disseminating the democratic principles of France, a dangerous heresy for the establishment who not only feared public disorder, even revolution in Britain, but feared – incredible though it may seem today – even the possibility of an invasion from France. After all, it was only a few years since the French Revolution.

Unfortunately for Arthur, he had two major literary faults. He was long-winded and he could not refrain from expounding on subjects on which he had little knowledge. Both faults left him open to attack. In one paragraph he would repeat unfounded hearsay and in the next would analyse and explain a complex situation with great clarity. In the *Edinburgh Review* an anonymous reviewer scoffed unmercifully at Arthur's verbosity:

"Upon the whole, the book is bad: and though it does state some facts that ought to be generally known, bears evident marks not only of haste and carelessness, but of absolute and utter ignorance of the subjects it affects to discuss."[6]

This criticism was somewhat unfair and a little ironic, since the review itself ran to 20 pages!

One Shetland bird of legend that intrigued local naturalists and which Arthur discussed, was the *immer-gös*: the same mysterious bird that his father, Dr Laurence of Lerwick, may have seen many years ago on his way to Hascosay from his tryst with Mally on Unst. This bird is a large and solitary marine diver and, although regularly seen on the sea, was never seen ashore; its nest never found. Curiously, the *immer-gös*, although different in plumage, was virtually the same size as the better known great northern diver, a northern bird species that regularly frequented Shetland's inshore waters in the spring and summer months. Such is their adaptation to an aquatic life that if disturbed by a boat these birds seek their escape by diving beneath the surface, or sometimes running on top of it, rather than taking to the air, which requires of them a much greater effort. They do not plunge beneath the surface in haste or panic, but simply slip out of sight. Such is their predilection for diving rather than flying that in Arthur's time it was thought that they could not fly. As if these peculiarities were not enough, divers have the most unearthly call and, as a result, in every human culture where they occur they are the subject of myth and legend. In Shetland it was thought that the *immer-gös* might build its nest on the sea! Since the *immer-gös* did not appear to be able to fly it was alternatively suggested that it might swim all the way to Shetland from its breeding haunts somewhere in the far north.

In his book Arthur discussed the *immer-gös* and correctly disputed some of the accepted wisdom of the time:

Great northern diver and young (the Immer goose) by William Yarrell.

"As imber geese are seen in Zetland at all times, we are led to infer, either that they breed in this country, or possess the means of easy removal to another. To leave a place where food abounds, to swim across the northern ocean, and to fish during the passage … occupying several months … in several hundred fathoms of water, would … be a perversion of instinct … It therefore appears to me, that the colymbus immer can fly, but that it uses its wings only at particular seasons of the year."

However, he was unable to explain where it nested.

Arthur was quite rightly angered by the anonymous and harsh review of his book in the *Edinburgh Review* – probably by William Mouat of Garth, laird and nephew of the late Thomas Mouat – but not as angry as he was about a second anonymous critique entitled *Strictures of Orcadensis* that appeared in the *Scots Magazine* (1810). This one he took very much to heart and deduced – rightly or wrongly – from the pseudonym, *Dr Falmaing*, that the author was the Rev. Dr John Fleming, then minister of the island of Bressay opposite Lerwick. Now Fleming was no ordinary minister, he was a keen and know-ledgeable zoologist and mineralogist who had graduated from Edinburgh in 1805, possibly as one of the first students of Robert Jameson and the first of many who would be inspired by Jameson to visit the northern isles. A few years later he became the Professor of Natural Philosophy at the University of Aberdeen and then Professor of Natural Science at the New Free Church College Edinburgh. Fleming's criticism of Arthur's account of the zoology of Shetland had to be taken seriously. Neverthe-less, Arthur instinctively took up the challenge and in 1810 published a *Reply to the strictures of Orcadensis* in several magazines and as a privately printed pamphlet in which he all but named his critic in typical flighting language. Despite all the criticism of Arthur's zoological observations it is now recognised that he did lay some natural history myths *and* he added a creditable 21 or so new species of birds to the Shetland list.

Arthur's next venture into print was in 1810 when he wrote a paper on his *Observations on the Natural and Medical Histories of the Zetland Sheep* in which he noted, among other things that, in very bad weather Shetland sheep stand in a flock facing inwards and eat the wool off each other's backs – quite true! The following year Arthur, with his usual self-conviction, privately published a short story, *Henry's return: A Zetlandic Tale*, and a rather

Rev. Dr John Fleming by David Octavious Hill and Robert Adamson.

33

Arctic Skuas by William Yarrell.

bad poem of six stanzas. The latter was written, from the viewpoint of an imaginary sweetheart, about an officer of the marines who had just died in Lerwick. The poem was doggerel and quite forgettable.

His next publication was further thoughts on the strange marine diver that he had mentioned in his book: *Observations on the Natural History of the Colymbus immer* (1811). Both this paper and the previous one were published by the Wernerian Society in Edinburgh, of which Arthur was one of the first members. This Society had been established by Robert Jameson in 1808 as the Edinburgh equivalent of the Linnean Society of London and Jameson named it in honour of his geology teacher, Abraham Gottlob Werner (1750-1817), whose lectures he had attended in Germany in 1800. The Society attracted many eminent scientists to its pages and was immensely influential. Jameson was its president throughout his life, supported by Patrick Neill as its secretary.

Arthur tried to have other papers published by Jameson in the Wernerian Society papers and from 1815-1819 carried out a regular, hectoring and one-sided correspondence with Jameson, who turned them all down.[7] However, in 1821, Jameson relented and published *Observations of the Natural History of some Species of the Genus Larus, or Gull Tribe* in the Edinburgh *Philosophical Journal* (which he co-founded). In this paper Arthur hypothesised, wrongly as it later proved, that the two colour morphs of the arctic gull (now known as the arctic skua) – a northern summer visitor and parasitic seabird – which he had studied on his grandfather's island of Hascosay, actually represented two different species. Arthur was also planning an *Ornithologia* or *Zoologia Zetlandoica* and wanted Jameson to correct the proofs. Jameson knew Arthur too well however, and demurred. In the event the work was never completed.[8]

By the age of 40, Arthur had become a man of property with a town house and land and a summer house just outside the town limits, a confirmed bachelor and an upstanding citizen of Lerwick. His substantial reputation rested on an extraordinary range of publications and a successful career as a doctor. Unfortunately, his success combined with an apparently indestructible self-belief encouraged his worst faults to flourish. His relationship with his family suffered and he antagonised just about everyone else with whom he came into conflict. This was just at the time when he decided to enter public life and dispense his own justice from the bench.

Charleston and the last Hurrah

Charles had left for America in 1799, around the time Arthur had been away serving in the army, Thomas establishing himself at Buness and Henry leaving for his medical apprenticeship. His departure from home was probably the most emotional of all these partings for Mally and Laurence, for Charles was leaving for the New World and the chances were that they would never see him again: which they did not. He had no skills to take with him bar his education and his father would only have been able to give him a limited amount of funds to tide him over. Charles was not physically big, neither stocky like Thomas, nor naturally tall and slim like Laurence, but he was wiry and resilient. What he took with him was the courage and confidence of youth and it was an indication of his determined and independent character that he may have left home just before his seventeenth birthday. He did not go alone, however. Accompanying him was his friend John Ross (b1773).[9] Ross was the only son of the last of the Ross family of Skerpa in Unst, whose once extensive property had all but gone – coincidentally, some of it becoming part of the Buness estate when it was purchased by Thomas in 1843.

It is not known if there was any particular reason for the choice of Charleston in the southern United States as a destination. Perhaps that was John Ross' destination, or there was a contact there, or the coincidence of name tickled Charles' curiosity, or it was just to be a starting point. The only known and tenuous connection Charles had with that part of America was that many other Scots went to the Carolinas during the infamous 'clearances' of the late 1700s, although most went to the Cape Fear area about 240 km to the north of Charleston and perhaps that is where Charles was originally heading.

The colonial cities that sprang up on the east coast of North America in the 1700s were established where they were most accessible to shipping, as trade was their *raison d'être*. At the time, Charleston, at Oyster Point on the mouth of the Ashley River, in what became South Carolina, supported a population of around 12,000. The city was established in 1670 and was named after Charles II and it became one of the centres in North America for the importation of slaves. Between 1700 and 1775 more than 40 per cent of the slaves from the British African colonies came into America through Charleston[10], many to cultivate rice that was introduced to the area in the 1690s and became the staple crop for the next 100 years or so. This is where Charles arrived less than 20 years after the War of Independence (1775-1781) – or as he would have come to call it, the Revolutionary War – on the 25th August, 1799.

The transition from Shetland, with a 15˚-20˚C maximum in summer to Charleston with a 30˚C+ summer average and high humidity took a bit of getting used to. The burning overhead sun was merciless on one more accustomed to turning his face to it in gratitude for its appearance. In Shetland there were very few trees, and those that survived their early years were twisted and bent by the wind. In his new home in Charleston, Charles found himself seeking the shade of palms and strolling among the extravagant and aromatic blooms of azaleas and dogwoods and many other exotic shrubs and trees with which he was unfamiliar. One of the first things he did, when he could afford it, was to purchase lighter clothes, particularly night attire. It was a curious kind of freedom, to sleep almost naked under a single sheet having spent his nights thus far wrapped up in a flannel nightshirt under layers of blankets, supplemented in the winter with heated stones or stoneware bottles!

Charles arrived, not as a colonist, but as a welcome settler to an independent and enormous country. Not only was that country relatively new, but the bulk of it was yet unexplored by Europeans. It was only seven years prior to Charles' arrival that Alexander Mackenzie (c1755-1820) had crossed Canada and one year since Lewis and Clark and the Corps of Discovery had crossed the new America.

As with the other great coastal trading cities of North America, there was no existing aristocratic structure and it was the wealthy merchants and plantation owners who established themselves as the patricians of these new world societies. The goal of such standing quickly became Charles' ambition on arriving in Charleston. He was from a seaport too, albeit much humbler, and the sight of the many trading vessels in Charleston harbour unloading sophisticated goods from Europe and loading up rice, indigo and tobacco, excited his imagination and he determined to make good. His friend John Ross, on the other hand, was a practical Shetlander, a man of action, and he soon found a position on one of the many ships trading up and down the coast.[11]

In 1787, the US had temporarily suspended the slave trade. In 1803, of all the states in America, only South Carolina reopened it and in the next four years, until it was finally prohibited entirely in 1807, brought in 40,000 slaves, the largest traffic in slaves that Charleston had ever seen. During this period, on the 25th April, 1805, at the age of just 23, Charles purchased a slave named Clarinda as a house servant. Two years later he was registered in the Charleston Directory as a trustee of an apothecary that dispensed drugs to the poor and the following year he was registered as a merchant and as a member of the Saint Andrew's Society of the City of Charleston, to which he belonged for the next fifty-two years. The Society was originally established in 1729 for "the purpose of cultivation and maintaining a good understanding and acquaintance with one another." After the Revolutionary War the Society established a school for the education of white children of indigent parents that continued until the establishment of state support for education.

At the very same time that his brother Arthur was facing the Rubicon of his career – would it be better served in Edinburgh or in Shetland? – Charles was facing *his* in Charleston, but the choice concerning *his* ambitions was moral in nature. There is no doubt that his native country's attitude to slavery was ambivalent. While the Court of Session in Edinburgh had given a black slave from

View of Charleston from the Harbour by S. Bernard. Charles Edmondston's house is partially hidden by a small schooner to the right of the tall house.

Jamaica his freedom from his Scottish owner in 1778, just a few years before Charles was born, the profitability and success of the tobacco trade in Glasgow depended at this time upon slavery in the southern states of America. When the adventurous Charles first arrived in Charleston he had only been 17 years of age and had drunk in all the excitement and exoticism of this new world without giving it much thought, but he could not fulfil his ambitions and indulge his entrepreneurial flair in Charleston, or the southern states as a whole, without accepting black slavery. Very quickly he had grasped that there was an opening for him here and he did not want to leave. Now, perhaps, he searched his conscience and his decision was to stay and to accept the culture of black slavery. Charles, like his mother, was an episcopalian and his church in America reassured him that slavery was beneficial to the black people from Africa, bringing them the consolation of Christianity and the certainty of salvation that, they convinced themselves, the slaves otherwise would not have had. It was to this church and its good causes that Charles resolved to devote some of his time and money. Charles had come into this culture from a very different one and he was too astute not to see its contradictions: it was a very deliberate choice.

Following the early death of his first wife, Charles married Mary Pratt (1789-1872) of Chesterton, Massachusetts, the daughter of a sea captain, on Christmas day in 1810. The captain may well have been the skipper of a ship carrying goods belonging to Charles as he was, by now, involved in the maritime trade. Charles and Mary proceeded to have thirteen children, only two of whom did not survive into adulthood. Their first child was born in 1812, the year Charles took the oath and became a naturalised American, and the last was born 21 years later.

In the year that Charles ceased to be British, America became embroiled in the war between Britain and France. Seven years previously, in December 1805, Napoleon had destroyed the armies of Russia and Austria at the battle of Austerlitz and had come to dominate Europe. However, his losses at Trafalgar had forced him to relinquish to the British any influence he might have had on the high seas. The Americans took advantage of this reversal of fortunes and in the absence of French vessels began shipping its own exports to France and shipping French goods abroad. The British reacted as if America was an ally of France by taking American ships and sometimes impressing the sailors into the British Navy. The dispute between the two came to a head in 1812 when, exasperated by what was seen as British aggression and the loss of their Atlantic trade, America declared war on Britain. Fighting, in this second War of Independence, took place on the east coast of America and across the Canadian border. One spectacular and successful act of the British that enraged America was an incursion in August 1814 into Chesapeake, the taking of Washington and the burning of the White House. The British forces then pressed on for Baltimore in September, at that time the fourth largest city in America. There, however, they met a large defensive force and after a siege of the city had to retreat. One of the British killed in this action – "the forlorn hope" – was another Arthur Edmondston, a cousin to Charles in Charleston and the son of his father's brother[12], aboard HMS *Melpomene*. Three months later the war was over.

When the news of his cousin's death reached Charles, he could only shake his head in sorrow. How could it be that his British cousin could give his life fighting against *his* democratic country and *his* beliefs? Had Charles read a pamphlet published by his brother Arthur – *Observations on the causes and probable consequences of the war in which Great Britain and the United States of America are at present engaged* – just the year before, in 1813, he might have understood the strength of feeling in his old country. Arthur's pamphlet was a bitter denunciation of America's friendship with France, noting that there had long been "… a spirit of envy and hostility towards Great Britain and an unworthy and unnatural subservience to the views of France." He advised that America was just trying to take advantage of Britain's distraction by France and that the government should send a strong force to quell the Americans. It was a long, dense, patriotic rant, totally out of touch with reality and an indication of the direction in which the argumentative Arthur was going.

CHAPTER FOUR

LITERATURE AND SCIENCE

"Dr Edmondston … improves much on acquaintance … [his brothers] all men of talent … one of the oldest Shetland families had produced in one generation … an accomplished chemist [Henry], an eye-specialist [Arthur], a London merchant prince [Laurence], and the most progressive of the islands' landowners [Thomas]."

Henry Kater (1777-1835)

The Amateur and the Professional

In 1812, Napoleon occupied Moscow, Charles became an American citizen and Laurence junior, who had spent most of the previous five years in Unst, left Shetland, at the age of 17, just as his brother Charles had done, for a life in commerce. His destination – just a little closer to home, though equally exotic in its day – was London. Meanwhile, Thomas the laird was flourishing at Buness; Dr Henry was in Newcastle; Dr Arthur, their parents, Laurence 72 and Mally 61, and the three sisters were all in Lerwick and all seemed to be well in the Edmondston family. In May of the following year, however, one of the sisters, Ursula, died, unmarried at 27, in Edinburgh.

Ursula seems to have been Arthur's favourite sister and perhaps the only one of his siblings with whom he was close. He was so broken-hearted by her death that, from a corner of a heart that he so rarely showed, he produced a loving, touching and bathetic memoriam of six stanzas so typical of the age and only a slight improvement on his first public poetic effort. The first stanza was:

> "O God! – and art thou dead,
> Thou darling sister of my heart!
> Sweet Ursula! – art thou lowly laid,
> By death's unsparing dart!
> And shall I ne'er behold thy face,
> That beam'd with every female grace?
> That face – so lovely, sweet, and mild,
> It spoke thee Virtue's purest child."[1]

The following year Mally became a widow when Laurence passed away at the age of 73. Her once large household now consisted only of herself and her two grown-up daughters who were never to marry. Her only grandchild, the first child of Charles and Mary, was several thousand kilometres away on the other side of the Atlantic and the only son close by was Dr Arthur, who published no poem on his father's death.

That year, the budding versifier met a real poet and one of Scotland's greatest literary figures of the 19th century, Sir Walter Scott (1771-1832). Scott was visiting Shetland as a guest aboard the yacht of the Commissioners of the Northern Lights on a tour of the lighthouses of Scotland. At that time, the lawyer was known only as an editor of literary works and as the author of long romantic poems, notably *The Lay of the Last Minstrel* (1805) and *The Lady of the Lake* (1810), while *Waverley*, the first of his 30 novels, had just been published anonymously. From the notes he gathered on this trip to Shetland Scott later wrote *The Pirate* (1822). In terms of the purpose of the voyage, however, the most important person aboard the yacht was the Board of Commissioners' engineer, Robert Stevenson (1772-1850) – the grandfather of another famous Scottish novelist, Robert Louis Stevenson (1850-1894) – who was there to survey sites for new lighthouses.

In early August 1814, the Commissioners' yacht anchored in Bressay Sound and Scott noted in his diary that Lerwick, now with 21 lodberries along the shore was:

Sir Walter Scott by Colvin Smith.

> "…a poor looking place, the streets flagged instead of being causewayed, for there are no wheel-carriages. The streets full of drunken riotous sailors, from the [Greenland] whale vessels … The Zetlanders themselves do not get drunk, but go straight home to their houses, and reserve their hilarity for the winter season, when they spend their wages in dancing and drinking … We parade Lerwick [and] are introduced to Dr Edmondstone, author of a History of Shetland."[2]

The drunken behaviour of the Greenland whalers while in Lerwick was quite a headache for the local citizens. During the Napoleonic wars there had been a garrison of soldiers at Fort Charlotte in the town, who had been able to

Lerwick with Tolbooth 1879 by Charles McEwan.

keep them under control, but after 1815 there was only one solitary artilleryman present and he could do nothing, that is, until a certain Dr Arthur Edmondston became involved a few years later.

In *The Pirate*, Scott acknowledged Arthur's book – *A View of the Ancient and Present State of Zetland* (1809) – as the source of some of his background information, even recommending it to his readers. But what Scott did not tell Arthur was that he was so taken by him that he had modelled one of his novel's characters on him! Arthur had become by then, in the words of a local historian, "self-opinionated, dogmatic, quarrelsome, litigious, a heavy drinker [in a heavy-drinking age] and fond of spouting his own verse"![3]

Claud Halcro, Arthur's alter ego in *The Pirate*, is a slightly pompous, name-dropping, bottle-loving, self-centred man who believed himself a poet and descended from an ancient line. In the novel he is described and speaks:

> "His [Claud's] laughing eye kindled with a sort of enthusiasm, which the ordinary folks of this world might have called crazed, while he dashed into the subject [of how he had once met the great poet John Dryden] which he best loved to talk about … [Claud speaks] 'Even old Dryden himself, glorious old John, could have said little about a girl that was always of one mind – as well as write verses upon a mill-pond. It is your tides and your roosts, and your currents and eddies, that come and go, and ebb and flow, (by Heaven! I run into rhyme when I so much as think upon them,) … Did you never hear my Adieu to the Lass of Northmaven … whom I call Mary for the sound's sake, as I call myself Hacon after my great ancestor Hacon Goldemund, or Haco with the golden mouth who came to the island with Harold Harfager … she was the cause of my leaving the isles of Hialtland, (better so called than Shetland, or Zetland even,) … I held out till my cousin Laurence Linklutter, died, and left me the bit of an island yonder … it is as barren as Parnassus itself … and [I] have a bed and a bottle for a friend, as you shall know, boys, if you go back with me when this merriment is over.'"

It is a sad irony for Arthur that his very great respect for Scott was returned with such stinging mockery. There is doubt that Claud is Arthur! There is reference to his stubbornness in clinging to *Zetland*, an old name for Shetland; to his conceit of aristocratic ancestry; to his inheritance of the blanket-bog covered island of Hascosay from his father Laurence; to his verse and to his growing love of the bottle. Once Scott's novel was published in 1822, if Arthur did not realise he had been lampooned, everyone else did and the name Claud Halcro stuck to him. Fourteen years later, during a general election, when he published an attack on a well-known Shetland candidate, an immediate and witty reply was published anonymously, entitled *Epistle to Zetlandicus by Claude Halcrow*.

Scott was also responsible in *The Pirate* for romanticising Shetland's Viking past – just as he was doing to Scotland's Celtic past too – a view that Arthur did not uphold. Such was the reverence for this novel in Shetland that the name of Scott's old udaller character, Magnus Troill, became adopted for a Shetland trading schooner in the 1830s.

Men of Science

The geology of Unst, first described by Robert Jameson in 1798, plays a critical role in the Edmondston family history. Elements of it secured the fortunes of Thomas the laird and a little later it was found to support a unique flora that inspired and eventually led to another Thomas Edmondston (1825-1846), voyaging halfway round the globe.

For the first-time visitor to Unst, landing at the south end of the island after a short crossing from the island of Yell – most of which is covered in blanket bog like much of the rest of the hill land of Shetland Mainland – the landscape is quite unlike anything previously experienced. As with the rest of the islands there are no signs of trees or shrubs and the tallest vegetation barely covers one's ankles. But what catches and holds the eye are the ochreous bones of the landscape – by way of scattered knobs of boulders and rocks that protrude above an otherwise smooth skin of green grasses, sedges and dark stubby heather – that dominates the eastern and southern part of the island. These bones are just the surface manifestation of what was once part of the ocean floor. Some 500 million years ago, this area of the Earth was caught in the collision between the two immense continents of Gondwana and Laurentia that created the Caledonian mountains. In this mighty encounter, the floor of the ocean that had separated the continents was here, on Unst, thrust up onto the land. These rocks were then eroded and re-buried for many millions of years under younger sediments, before once more re-surfacing as the yellow-brown serpentine rocks. While buried, they were metamorphosed under enormous heat and pressure, creating many different minerals, some with familiar names like garnet and talc, but most, to the uninitiated, with strange and esoteric names, such as biotite, chlorite, staurolite, kyanite, sillimanite, chloritoid, hornblende, epidote, diopside, microcline, serpentine and one named chromite that was to be discovered on Thomas' land in 1817.

In 1814, the year Scott met Arthur in Lerwick, Samuel Hibbert (1782-1848), an Englishman with a penchant for sesquipedalian natural history rambles, began the course in medicine at

Baltasound by Henry Saxby.

Edinburgh University. One of his many interests was geology and he therefore, like many in this story, attended Robert Jameson's lectures. A few years later, persuaded by the professor, he extended his rambles to Shetland, an area whose geology Jameson knew well. In the two years, 1817-1818, just after Wellington's (1769-1852) famous victory – much celebrated by Thomas the laird who was to become a correspondent of the 'Iron Duke' and later Prime Minister – Hibbert and several outstanding scientists of international repute spent a number of weeks on Unst. One was a Frenchman, Jean Baptiste Biot (1774-1862), and the other three were Englishmen, all of whom became acquainted with Buness and grateful for the generous hospitality of Thomas Edmondston.

At the time, across the North Sea in Paris, the French government had decided to make the circumference of the Earth the basis for their new metric system of measurement. However, it was known that the Earth was not a perfect globe, so French scientists were directed to establish its irregularities. The eminent French scientist Jean Baptiste Biot, Professor of physics, member of the Academy of Sciences and a Chevalier, took up the challenge. Biot's approach to measuring the curvature of the Earth involved measuring the Earth's gravity by pendulum along a meticulously surveyed and lengthy arc of the meridian or line of longitude: the results of which were later written up as *Recueil d'observations geodiques, astronomiques et physiques executes en Espagne et Écosse* (1821). A critical factor in his attempt to establish the curvature of the Earth is that the longer the arc the more accurate would be the result and that is what brought him eventually to Shetland.

With special dispensation from the British government during the Napoleonic wars, Biot had been working near Valencia and in the Balearic Islands in the Mediterranean. The longest arc of longitude along which he had been able to achieve a series of gravitational measurements was from the Balearic Islands to Dunkirk: a distance of roughly 12 degrees of latitude. Two years after Waterloo and the defeat of Napoleon, Biot came to Leith, with the support of the Royal Society and the British government, to extend his length of measurements a further six degrees. There he heard that the British Trigonometric Survey was about to depart for Shetland. This presented Biot with the possibility of extending the arc of his meridian from the Mediterranean by a further four degrees of latitude, giving him a total length of almost 22 degrees or a quarter of the distance between the equator and the North Pole: an opportunity he could not miss. So, with the full support of the British survey team, he sailed from Leith for Shetland on the survey brig *Investigator*, along with all his instruments, on the 9th July, 1817.[4]

Biot's observations in Shetland were not just those of a scientist. He also had the acute eye of the seasoned traveller and he kept a personal journal of the landscapes and cultures he encountered and the individuals he met and with whom he stayed. Nine none too

Jean Baptiste Biot.

comfortable days at sea after leaving Leith, he and the survey team came in sight of Shetland, crouching under clouds and surrounded by a "swell and a perpetual tempest,"[5] very different islands from those on which he had camped in his research in the Mediterranean, but then, nobody comes to Shetland for the sun! Biot went on to say how warm was the hospitality in comparison with the desolate land and cold temperatures and how much generous assistance he received, firstly from a certain learned and well travelled doctor in Lerwick.

"Above all we received much essential advice from Dr [Arthur] Edmondston, a well informed physician, who has published a very good description of the Shetland Islands and who remembered with pleasure having attended in Paris one of the courses of our colleague, M Dumeril. He gave us letters to one of his brothers [Thomas] who lived in the little island of Unst, the northernmost of the whole archipelago."

Initially, Biot had intended to set up his instruments in Fort Charlotte in Lerwick, but Arthur's offer of his brother's support in Unst with the opportunity of extending the arc of the meridian by another half degree was too good to turn down. So, with the rest of the English survey team on the *Investigator* they sailed on. When they got to Balta Sound the rest of the surveyors chose to camp on the island of Balta at the mouth of the Sound, but Biot made it known that the island was not convenient for his experiments, so he landed on the shores of Balta Sound and sought help from the only house he could see.

Entrance to Balta Sound looking towards Keen of Hamar from Balta by Henry Saxby.

"Happily it was that of Mr [Thomas] Edmondston, whose brother had been so affable in Lerwick. We experienced here the same kindness … The portable observatory was set up in Mr Edmondston's garden … When I was left on my own I was able to appreciate how lucky I was to be living with Mr Edmondston. The benevolence of this excellent man seemed to grow with the difficulty of my position. I could not operate the repeating circle alone, it requires two people, one to follow the star and the other to note the reading of the level. Mr Edmondston, who was as interested as I was myself, suggested to me the idea of using for this latter part of the observation a young carpenter who had already given us proof of his intelligence in setting up the observatory and who, besides, like all the Scottish peasants and even those of the islands, could read, write and count very well."

Based at Buness, Biot took sightings of the stars to give himself an exact fix of his position that he required before taking his gravitational measurements by way of his pendulum. Biot spent two months on Unst, spoke highly of Thomas and all the kindnesses he received and of the way of life in such a harsh environment. Had he stayed on Balta Island with the others he admitted he would have left with all the prejudices of a stranger.

Although it had taken him nine days on the *Investigator* to travel to Shetland from Leith in July, his return journey in October was a two-day surf-ride driven by a northerly gale. The friendship between the Edmondstons and Biot continued long after Biot's departure. They corresponded and Thomas visited him in Paris, and when the second child of Thomas' younger brother Laurence was born he was christened Biot in his honour. Biot went on to publish widely and prolifically in all fields of science, became a commander of the Legion of Honour and, in 1840, an admirer named the rock-forming mineral biotite after him.

When Biot had been in Spain in 1806 he had worked with another Frenchman, the physicist and Director of the Paris Observatory, Francois Arago (1786-1853), who later became Secretary of the Bureau des Longitudes. Arago, despite the war, was himself working in close collaboration with an Englishman, Captain Henry Kater (1777-1835), who in 1815 became a Fellow of the Royal Society and in 1817 won the Copley Medal for his design work and application of the reversible pendulum. When the *Investigator* expedition returned to London in 1817 it was found that some of the work carried out by the team on Balta Island had been compromised by the presence of a carrying-clamp that had been left attached to the pendulum apparatus during the gravity deter-minations. In May 1818, Sir Joseph Banks (1743-1820), the British naturalist and then President of the Royal Society, had just succeeded in reconstituting the British Board of Longitude with redefined objectives including finding the north-west-passage and fixing the magnetic poles. One of those whom he appointed to stipendiary positions on the board was Captain Kater. It was to Captain Kater that the Royal Society then turned as an expert on the pendulum, knowledgeable of the work of and probably a personal acquaintance of Biot and asked him to go to Shetland to continue Biot's work and repeat the experiments of the previous year.

Kater was a man of private means whose German parents had settled in England and made their fortune in sugar refining in Bristol and his upbringing and personal wealth ensured a taste for good living. He had gained his commission in the 12th Regiment of Foot and through the technical requirements of survey work with the British army in India found his life's vocation in improving and refining the measuring instruments required for this task. The exacting and dedicated nature of his work reflected his precise and rather aloof character. He was also known for his temper. On the 6th July, 1818, he arrived in Lerwick from Leith as the leader of the expedition aboard the brig HMS *Nimrod* with "a letter I had been given to Dr [Arthur] Edmondston":[6] perhaps from Biot. Lerwick, the accommodation and the climate did not appeal to him, but he did appreciate the fresh local fish.

Kater took his letter to Arthur who had just been elected Lerwick's Chief Magistrate, "… a very chatty, intelligent, well-informed gentleman …" Though Kater was only amused at the "… variety and extent of Edmondston's knowledge", he was very impressed with Arthur's book (*A View of the Zetland Island*s) and his views on topics such as the need to balance the population with the natural resources. He was also impressed by Arthur's visions for local industries and his very modern enthusiasm for old buildings and horror at the "barbarous economy" that led to the destruction of old buildings for their stone. So impressed was Kater that he invited Arthur for dinner aboard the *Nimrod*. His initial impression of Arthur, however, did not survive the dinner, perhaps unsurprisingly, as they were both men of strong opinions. Also, while Kater was a Tory, Arthur was a radical Whig. Kater's description of Arthur in 1818 was very revealing:

Henry Kater by George Richmond.

"Vanity is apparent in all that Dr Edmondston says. He is a striking instance of the ill-effects of living where one has no equal. The chief magistrate and the best informed man of the place, his opinion is probably considered as decisive (sic) and hence he has acquired a dogmatical manner and a want of bienséance of good society, for which his talents, which are certainly great, can by no means compensate. He is a poet, and repeated some pretty things which he had written – violent in politics, and indeed apparently in everything."

Having said that, Kater later said of Arthur and, rather hyperbolically, of his brothers:

"Dr Edmondston … improves much on acquaintance … [his brothers] all men of talent … one of the oldest Shetland families had produced in one generation … an accomplished chemist [Henry], an eye-specialist [Arthur], a London merchant prince [Laurence], and the most progressive of the islands' landowners [Thomas]."

On his side, Arthur later and presciently said of Kater:

"I found him a pleasant intelligent man. Buness will be celebrated as the classical spot in which were performed the experiments that … the Newtonian pendulum [was used res]pecting [the establishment of] the figure of the Earth."[7]

After a few days in Lerwick, Kater went on to Balta Sound with the *Nimrod* to repeat the pendulum experiments. There, Thomas the laird was rowed out to him and bestowed on him the same kindness he had showed to Biot the previous year.

"A quiet, intelligent, farmer-like man … At ten o'clock I landed on a pier-head, constructed of masses of serpentine. Mr Edmondston again met me and conducted me to his dwelling which is on the sloping declivity which runs down to the bay. On seeing the outside of the house [Buness], I confess I felt chilled. It appeared like a very poor cottage in England. The windows were about eighteen inches by two feet … a number of ruinous-looking sheds were scattered about … [however, the accommodation for him consisted of] … a snug comfortable parlour with a cheerful peat fire, and my kind host, taking me upstairs conducted me to an excellent drawing room and a small bedroom contiguous and begged me to consider them as mine."[8]

Kater then began setting up the experiments using the same stone and location that Biot had used before him just in front of the house. Typically, the cloudy weather of Shetland in July did not make it easy for him to fix his exact position by the sun or stars. When he was not working Kater found time to discuss the economy of Unst with Thomas and the latter revealed that he was much more than just a "farmer-like man". One of his proposed projects, in which Kater and Franks, his assistant, very nearly invested, was to run a small fishing vessel, or mother-ship, of about 50-60 tons which would have on-board facilities for salting fish and from which small open boats would operate to catch the fish. This system, Thomas surmised, would get around the dangers of the *sixerns* having to venture so far out to sea without support and would allow the fishermen to stay out in most weathers. Luckily they did not invest their money as this idea had been tried some years earlier in the 1770s without success (and would be tried again) due to the problems of the *sixerns* keeping in touch with their mother ship and the very real danger of smashing themselves up against her in the violent swells of the open sea. Did Thomas not also consider the dreadful conditions and dangers the fishermen would have had to face, if they had had to spend a week rather than just a couple of days in an open boat, far out in the North Sea or the Atlantic?

Thomas had another scheme and showed Kater his fish-curing establishment on Balta Island:

"The chief art consists in the drying. The fish of Newfoundland are dried on boards, but they are not so fine as those of Shetland, which are dried on the stones of the beach and the air consequently admitted under them … We have talked a great deal of our fishing and seemed to have agreed positively to make a trial next year. Mr Edmondston is to conduct it, and Franks and myself are to use our best exertions among the merchants of London to find a market. Mr Edmondston suggested a plan which, if it could be effected, would be very lucrative. The Navy, having one banian [supposedly meat free] day a week on which they are fed with salted pork, which is frequently indifferent. His idea was to enter into a contract with Government to supply them with salted fish, which would be a great saving and much better food for the men."[9]

By this time Thomas had developed a *saithe* fishery from Skaw, the most northerly beach in Unst from where boats rowed out to the "*Skaw strings*" – fast tidal currents which the fish favoured. These fish were dried and many exported to Leith adding to the Buness estate income, though as Kater had noticed, Thomas did not seem to spend much money on repairing his buildings. Thomas' relations with his tenants and their outlook on life from a less privileged position, was also recorded by Kater.

"The poor of this country appear to live in the most miserable manner, but yet seem perfectly happy and respectable. Their huts are generally furnished with skate and piltocks hung out to dry, and a heap of peats piled up near the cottage … All his servants seem greatly attached to him. The Major Domo is named Magnus [Magnus Winwick 1793-1864]. He is the chief of Mr Edmondston's fishing [at Fiskawick, Burra Firth]. Many an evening when the fog would not allow us to go out he has amused us by dancing to our host's fiddle (an excellent Cremona bye the bye which he got in exchange for a new one, from a Dutch vessel)."

Kater left Balta Sound on the 26th July to the cheers of his host's boat crew. His last words on Shetland were remarkably similar to Biot's the year before, acknowledging his host's geniality and generosity.

"God bless them all, say I from my soul. Often in more polished and more heartless society shall I think of them and of that kindness which is all sufficient to constitute my happiness."

Kater's scientific work, as well as the development of the reversible pendulum, included the addition of a mirror to the compass that allowed the observer to read the scale while observing the object and the setting of standards of precision on weights and measures. For his contributions to science Kater was elected to many of the leading scientific societies in Europe and America. Later, he emigrated to Australia.

Thomas was so impressed by Biot and Kater and so enjoyed their company that he erected a stone that still stands on the very spot in his garden on which they had placed their instruments and on it he had inscribed:

"To this stone were attached the clock and pendulum employed by the celebrated French philosopher BIOT, and on the one on which it rests stood his repeating circle.
The distinguished English philosopher KATER placed his repeating circle on this stone also.
The former was sent by the Institute of France in the summer of 1817, and the latter by the Royal Society of London in the summer of 1818, to determine by their experiments and observations the figure of the Earth.
These memorials remain as a pleasing and lasting remembrance of the splendid talents and great worth and amiable manner of these eminent men by their friend.
THOMAS EDMONDSTON, 21st October, 1818."[10]

The Goldmine

Besides the fishing resources of Unst, Thomas also showed Kater some of the mineral resources including "… serpentine, granite, gneiss, micacious shistus (sic) and asbestos." On enquiring about chromite, or chromate of iron as it was called, Kater was led by Thomas to a vein

Samuel Hibbert.

of this mineral – one of the most interesting and profitable ores of Shetland – which had just been discovered the previous year, 1817, by the third man of science to visit Shetland and Unst in this period, Samuel Hibbert. The chromate was found within the ancient, ocean mantle rocks that had been thrown onto the land so many million years ago. Surprisingly, the ore had not been spotted by either Jameson on his geological survey in 1794 or by John Fleming on his economic mineralogical survey in 1807.

Hibbert had originally begun studying medicine in Edinburgh in 1814 and, like so many other of Jameson's students, he had changed direction, graduating in geology in 1817. Hibbert was one of those individuals who stand out in a crowd. He was a big, shambling man with brown hair and blue eyes, whose capacious pockets were invariably weighed down with mineralogical specimens and who was often accompanied by his dog, Silly. He was capable of walking prodigious distances and never seemed to mind whether he slept in the manse or the byre. On his first visit in 1817, Hibbert had left Leith on the Lerwick Packet just a month after Biot's departure, and had spent six weeks that summer on a ramble around the islands. After he returned south, Dr Arthur Edmondston, who was considering writing a new book on Shetland, wrote to him requesting a meeting if he came back so that he could "… *render my topographical and geological chapters more accurate and recondite.*"[11]

On his last day in Unst, Hibbert discovered commercial quantities of chromate on the hills just to the north of Buness, some of it on Thomas' land. Chromate of iron was used at that time to produce a range of exquisite pigments: with lead it formed orange, with mercury it produced vermillion and with zinc and bismuth various yellows. It had great value therefore in the art world and in commercial ceramic production and it was also to be used in hardening steel. At the time, chromate of iron was imported from America and Unst was the only European source, hence it became much in demand and at good prices.

Jameson persuaded Hibbert to return to Shetland in 1818 after a winter's study at Edinburgh and he then spent a second six months on another rambling geological survey of all the islands, returning to Edinburgh later that year with 4000 geological specimens. On this visit he stayed first with Arthur in Lerwick but when he departed on one of his tours he forgot his dog and shirt, which Arthur was obliged to send on to him, though Arthur "… *could find no trace of his wanderings* [for several days] *and was at a loss to think upon what parallel his property would find him.*" Like Biot and Kater, Hibbert was a keen observer and fluent with the pen, leaving vivid and horrific descriptions of a whale drive in Hamna Voe in Yell; his admiration for the skills of the *haaf* fishermen; the meanness of the peasant's cottages and accounts of his rambles over the magnificent scenery of Shetland including a day in the fog in the wilds of North Roe in North Mainland with a compass in one hand, a hammer in the other and a bottle of Cape Madeira in one of his many pockets.

At this point in his life, approaching 40, Thomas, thanks to his inheritance but also to his own business efforts, was enjoying the good life, the food and the wine. But he was ambitious to be seriously wealthy and to firmly cement his place alongside the other notable landowners and merchants at the pinnacle of Shetland society. To him, the discovery of chromate was akin to the discovery of a goldmine. Knowing that it also occurred elsewhere on Unst he was desperate to keep the discovery to himself for as long as possible so that he might get a head start on the other Unst landowners – such as William Mouat (d1836) of Garth, the nephew of Thomas Mouat and inheritor of the estate – and corner the market before they entered it. Almost from the very beginning there were disputes between the various landowners concerning the ownership and extraction of the chromate, which is not surprising, considering its value. When, 20 years later the disputes came to a head, Thomas recorded in a private pamphlet:

"In 1817, Doctor Hibbert came to this country on a Geological and Mineralogical tour, and I, as well as many others, had the pleasure of becoming intimately acquainted with him during his stay. In 1818, he again returned to prosecute the same enquiries. He came to my house early in the summer of that year, and it was not till then that he communicated to any one, as far as I know, that he had discovered the mineral chromate of iron, the former season. I believe I was the first chromate proprietor who went out with him in search of this mineral … We found many surface specimens, and the Doctor said there must be some mines or quarries of it; that it was of much value, and he would endeavour to find this <u>treasure</u> in <u>quantity</u> [Thomas' underlining!]. He remained about a fortnight at this time, making diligent search for it in quantity, but without success …"[12]

A letter from Hibbert to Jameson in Edinburgh in June 1818 confirmed Thomas' account:

"*I shall feel obliged if you will give this discovery for the sake of the proprietors of the land that publicity which the importance of it may seem to require and in the manner you may think proper. Hagdale and Crucifield where the metal occurs form a common land belonging to 8 proprietors, but until the value of this mineral is fully ascertained I have declined communicating the discovery to any of these gentlemen except to Mr Edmondston of Buness. I am unwilling to raise expectations …*"[13]

Thomas' account was contained in his *Letter to Chromate proprietors* (1839) following a dispute and litigation with other proprietors. He was careful to say in this letter that the first samples he had taken were from a vein of the mineral on his private property and not taken from surface finds on the *scattalds*, of which he was to be accused. The point being that at that time very few *scattalds*, or common grazings, outwith the small farms and enclosures, had been divided up among the landowners. Each landowner had only a share according to the amount of enclosed land they owned and, up to now, they were not particularly interested in them since they were but poor hill grazings. The eventual division of the *scattalds* by the lairds was carried out, both to give them sole rights of property and to allow them to initiate agricultural improvements. In Unst the divisions were made in relation to the finding of chromate and were some of the very first carried out in Shetland.[14]

Quite naturally, what Thomas did not reveal 20 years later to the other chromate proprietors, was how he had taken immediate steps to try and secure the most benefit for himself. A couple of days after he had been in Unst in June 1818, Hibbert was staying once again with Arthur in Lerwick where he received a letter from Thomas. In the letter Thomas claimed, unjustly, to have found the most commercial sites himself and sought confirmation from Hibbert that they were on his private land. The letter was brought to Lerwick clandestinely by Peter Sutherland who carried more samples with him. "*These few crude ideas, hurriedly written, must be seen by no eye but your own, and as no person knows the object of his* [Peter's] *journey but yourself and me, the matter will be perfectly secret.*"[15] Hibbert was somewhat alarmed by Thomas' claims and his attempts to use him for his own ends. His friends, on hearing of Thomas' shenanigans, advised Hibbert to keep copies of all his correspondence with Thomas!

Hibbert then passed the chromate samples on to Jameson in Edinburgh to have them analysed. On the 29th July, 1818, Thomas received a letter from Hibbert quoting one *he* had received from Jameson: "*I have just received your specimens, and am happy to find the appearance so very favourable. The ore is excellent, fully as good as that from North America, and will supply the European market.*"[16] In his later 1839 letter to the other proprietors Thomas revealed how little time he wasted in exploiting the ore:

"On receiving such favourable intelligence regarding my chromate, I quarried several tons of it, and about a month after receipt of Dr Hibbert's letter, he came the second time that season to Buness, and was both surprised and delighted to witness the first mine of chromate he had ever seen in his life, or that ever had been seen in Great Britain."[17]

With this discovery of chromate the financial future was looking very healthy for Thomas, but now he needed somebody he could trust to find markets for the ore on the mainland.

SANCTIMONY

"Mind what I told you about Tea drinking … snuff taking … exercise … fresh air and so forth …"

Dr Laurence Edmondston (1795-1879)

The Promise

Laurence, the youngest brother, had a retiring and introspective disposition and was courteous and genial with friends and colleagues. He was very well read, morally upright with a simple belief in God and was described as being as humble as a lamb. He was an undemonstrative man of nervous disposition[1] whose conscience always worried him. When he arrived in London in 1812, with letters of introduction and funding from Thomas – his father having died four years previously – he sought, unsuccessfully, to establish himself as a merchant trader like his brother Charles. He then travelled on the continent to Germany and later to Paris to visit Biot. Laurence, among his other gifts, found that he had a facility in languages. Somewhere along the way, in his Shetland education and on his travels on the continent, he picked up French, German, Spanish and Dutch and with this talent, once back in London, he found employment as a corresponding clerk with a merchant named McBriar.

Between 1812 and 1821 he made several brief journeys home, but on the 24th June, 1818, he wrote a reply to a letter from his brother Thomas that suggested he had been tardy in keeping in touch. The letter also suggested that Thomas had been hurt by a tone of flippancy in Laurence's communications. The letter reveals some less positive aspects of Laurence's character. Although described as a humble man, beneath this he hid an innate sense of intellectual superiority. There was also a certain stiffness in his manners and, most troublingly for his future, a growing dependence, financial and emotional, on his much older brother. Laurence opened his letter by saying that he was hurt that Thomas should think he had forgotten him and went on:

"In all cases in which my friends have wantonly misunderstood me and ascribed mere irony and playfulness of remark to resentment or indifference, I had yet rallied in the conviction that of your confidence I was at least assured that whatever ambiguities might arise in my conduct, your long personal experience of my character … and my continual asseverations of the permanence of my principles would always lead you to bestow on them the most favourable interpretation … how mortifying for me to find my expectations so fallacious in the very first instance of their trial … how can my correspondence retain the same familiarity or … when the doubt of their construction is continually fettering my ideas. When I acceded to Mr

McBriar's proposal of adding my name to his firm, I had taken a mature and systematic view of existing circumstances … [which will require me to have] a reputation for caution and intelligence and an undeviating regularity in fulfilling our engagements."[2]

Laurence went on to tell Thomas that he intended to disengage himself from Mr McBriar as he found his judgements poor. "*I thank God that as difficulties have increased I have found my mind rising superior to them.*" He went on to reveal his thirst for knowledge across a wide range of interests, and a desire to put that knowledge to use. His many questions and suggestions indicated that he had taken a great interest in the running of the estate. He asked Thomas, "*… have you again attempted to rear some hardy trees?*" Then he suggested ways Thomas could improve the house and gardens and how an ass would be useful in eating weeds other animals would not … what about oxen and cabbages and new breeds etc.? He asked after the fishing profits, the boats and the skippers, by name. Aware of the opportunities to increase the size of the estate, he encouraged Thomas to purchase old arable land, never mind its condition, as such land entitled the owner to additional *scattald* when and if it will be divided. Finally he mentioned that he had had a letter from Charles who hoped soon to make a visit to Europe, and from Henry who was getting on with his medical profession in Newcastle.

This early in his career Henry appeared to be following Arthur's footsteps for around this time he published two papers that indicated he was more than just a practicing surgeon. One was entitled *Observations on cowpox and on the necessity of adopting legislative measures for enforcing vaccination*. This paper contained remarks on a letter on vaccination he had written to the Prime Minister (1812-1827), the Right Hon. Earl of Liverpool. The other was entitled *Hints on Hydrophobia*. Henry also wrote a very cordial letter to Robert Jameson in August 1818 that indicated both that he knew the latter and his family well, and that, just like his brothers, he had wider interests than medicine. However, whatever ideas he had, they seemed to peter out and there were no more publications from him.

The events of the year 1818 were critical in Laurence's life. Funded largely by Thomas, he had failed in his efforts to go into business on his own account and, at 23, now realised that he must look for something else. Before he took any further steps, however, Thomas suddenly found himself in a position to 'employ' him in the business of chromate. Under his direction Laurence initially consulted both Jameson and Hibbert regarding the uses and value of chromate and then for the next three years he perambulated the country looking for markets for Thomas.[3]

Thomas the laird, at 40, was now a confirmed bachelor like his elder brother Arthur in Lerwick and living alone in the large Haa, looked after by his domestic staff including the young housekeeper, Sinclair Bruce (1795-1877). He and Laurence were very close, in the sense that they professed loyalty to each other like father and son, but, whereas the son trusted the father to make the best decisions for him, the father made decisions for the son that he asserted were the best for the son, when in fact they suited him the better. So Laurence took up the challenge of laying the groundwork for years of future profit for Thomas without question. Then the completely unexpected happened.

On the 24th August, 1819, Sinclair Bruce produced a baby girl of whom Thomas was the father! The child was named Ursula (1819-1898), after their maternal grandmother and perhaps in memory of the sister of the five brothers, who had died six years earlier. Sinclair Bruce's large family were tenants of Thomas', from the township of Burrafirth on the Buness estate. It was not unusual for people in Thomas' position to have illegitimate children; it had happened in the family before and would happen again. What *was* very unusual, however, was that Thomas acknowledged paternity and, although he did not marry Sinclair Bruce, nor make her mistress of the house, he kept both mother and daughter, openly, at Buness. This brought down public admonishment from the pulpit which Thomas, because of his powerful position, ignored. Initially, it also set tongues wagging in Shetland society, but as such 'indiscretions' were not uncommon in those days eventually the local establishment came to accept the situation. Thirty years later, however, Ursula's presence in the household still had the potential to scandalise a visitor from high society in London. Had Thomas still been a young, eligible bachelor his decision to acknowledge Ursula might have been very different, but he was middle-aged and had nothing to lose. He was also as proud as any father and very fond of her. Six months later he ensured, through the first of several wills, that when he died she would be left with a comfortable annuity of £90 (£4700).[4] Although he named no heirs, he charged Laurence and his friend Arthur Nicolson (c1792-1863, who succeeded to a baronetcy in 1825) of Lochend and Fetlar to see to her education and to care for her during her minority.

Purportedly Dr Arthur Edmondston but possibly Dr Laurence Edmondston (1785-1879) by John Irvine, begun in 1831 finished in NS in 1870s; note that Dr Arthur Edmondston in 1831 was 56, broken and bankrupt.

Mally, now almost 70, must have been torn between shame and delight at the news of the birth of a granddaughter in Buness. Arthur would simply have shrugged, but Laurence, in Edinburgh, was shattered by the news. It felt like a betrayal and nearly destroyed the special relationship between him and Thomas. He went home to confront him, but found that Thomas, having taken away with one hand, was prepared to make an offer with the other.

Thomas suffered from ill-health in later life and the first symptoms were already present when Ursula was born. He may well have had an inherent long term illness, but he was also suffering from living too well. Laurence confirmed this just three years later when he wrote to Thomas from Edinburgh, expressing concern about his health and his ability to look after himself, "*Mind what I*

53

told you about Tea drinking … snuff taking … exercise …fresh air and so forth …"[5] Tea at that time was considered particularly unhealthy for those of an indolent disposition leading to all sorts of problems of digestion.

The year of Ursula's birth, aware of the fragility of his health, Thomas – according to Laurence some 20 years later – made him an offer he could not refuse. He, Thomas, "… promised and engaged that in the event of [Laurence] going to reside and settle in Unst in Shetland, as a medical practitioner, and as [Thomas'] medical attendant …he would make him generally his heir and executor …" Additionally, if Laurence did not take up any other post, Thomas promised to support him with an annual allowance.[6] Thomas had reassured Laurence that this would be put in writing and, although he wrote a will stipulating Ursula's annuity, he put in nothing about their arrangement. Like a son, with implicit trust, Laurence accepted the offer without question. He arranged to matriculate at Edinburgh University two years later in 1821, at the relatively late age of 26, in the steps of his brothers Arthur and Henry, his father Laurence and his grand-uncle William.

Medicine was clearly not Laurence's first choice of career, but his brother's proposal of an annual allowance offered him a secure future, whether or not he found enough subscribers in the north isles of his home; he had not forgotten his father's financial struggles. The offer also presented him with the opportunity to pursue his natural history studies that he had all but neglected these past few years away from home. Most important of all, however, was the prospect of inheriting Buness. He could just imagine all the possibilities for radical management that might open up in owning the estate and the time the income would give him to study so many subjects.

In that year he wrote twice to Thomas from Edinburgh. Thomas' offer had taken the stormy wind out of his sails and he had found, despite his unease, that he was bowled over by the infant Ursula. He wrote asking after, "*my own little darling*" and "*dreaming of the dear creature*".[7] He sent "*a small scent bottle to keep Sinclair from nervous fancies*" and two picture books for "*my own sweet little darling*".[8] He talked of coming home and drawing up the settlement, and of independence and brotherly love and, by the by, he mentioned meeting a prospective buyer who wanted two tons of chromate at £10 (£520) per ton. He also wrote about his plans for the immediate future. "*I shall have my hands full instantly with Surgery, Midwifery, dissection, Infirmary etc., woe on it – it is a dirty business in the meantime – never mind*."[9] It was just a hint that he was not particularly looking forward to his studies.

Over the top

In 1818, Arthur had sufficient funds to help two of his late father's sisters to purchase property on the outskirts of Lerwick. Generous, as he then was to his relations, he had a reputation with his peers for bad temper, contempt and an over-fondness for the bottle. Despite these failings and his radical views he was elected Senior Baillie (Chief Magistrate), pipping the Lerwick merchant Charles Ogilvy (1761-1827) into second place.

One of the first acts he carried out after his election was to ameliorate the problems – noted by Sir Walter Scott on his visit four years previously – caused by the crews of the merchant ships and whalers when they came ashore to carouse in Lerwick. Arthur, as the Chief Magistrate, after consultation with the Sheriff Substitute, arranged for a circular to be given to all the masters to ensure that those who came ashore had permission and that they would be back on board by 8pm. He also created a band of special constables to deal with any offender. Thomas Fea (1767-1841),

Lerwick 1850 by John Irvine.

the Collector of Customs, was of the opinion, however, that special constables did not have the power to arrest the sailors and that they had to be taken in front of a Justice of the Peace. He did not just express this opinion but actually interfered in the work of the constables. So began Arthur's lifelong battles with those who had the temerity to challenge his authority or opinion, whether they be a neighbour, minor official, politician, Procurator Fiscal or the Lord Advocate himself.

Fea's interference infuriated Arthur and he called on him to desist. Not only did Fea ignore the Chief Magistrate, but, according to Arthur, publicly said "That he [Arthur] was a damned scoundrel, and that he [Fea] would pull his nose the first time he met him"! Arthur's reaction was to be a benchmark for all future challenges, he completely overreacted to what he saw as an outrage against his person and his authority as Magistrate. He sat down at his desk with a glass or two of wine and wrote a Summons of Damages against Fea seeking the outrageous sum of £1000 sterling (equivalent to £50,000)![10] There is no record of his success but the extent of the damages sought was typical of Arthur's vanity.

The previous year he had petitioned against Francis Heddell junior in Lerwick, whose impressive list of official titles included Surveyor of Taxes, Comptroller of Customs, Keeper of the Public records and Clerk to the Sheriff and Admiralty Courts.[11] The charge was that Heddell had unlawfully removed Arthur's boat from the beach. The beach in question was in Lerwick and lay between two *lodberries* on the lower side of the Street and opposite the house of Francis Heddell senior on the upper side of the street. By 1814 there were some 21 lodberries on the seafront of Lerwick and subsequently there was less shoreline accessible to the public. Arthur held that the beach, from which Heddell had removed his boat, was public and that from time immemorial Shetlanders had had the right to pull up their boats there. Heddell, however, stated that it belonged to him and he had the right to refuse access or charge for its use. In the absence of roads, with the

55

main form of communication being by sea and with an abundance of inshore fishing, Arthur saw Heddell's act as a very serious threat to his citizen's rights.

The Heddell family, like the Edmondstons, was well established in the upper echelons of Lerwick society. Another family on the way up was the Greigs. Archibald Greig had been Arthur's teacher at Walls and his son, James Greig, whom he had known as an infant, was now the Procurator Fiscal in Lerwick and had been since 1808.

The basis of the 'foreshore' dispute that arose between Arthur Edmondston, Heddell and subsequently Greig – that was the beginning of a lifelong antipathy between Arthur and the latter and, later, a successful summons by him against Arthur for defamation – lay in the very design and layout of early Lerwick. The *lodberries*, on the lower side of the street, were designed for the convenience of trading with the sailing ships that came into Bressay Sound so that small boats could carry goods to and from them to the ships. Around 1801, a merchant called John Morrison had begun building a lodberry below his house in Lerwick adjacent to the beach in front of the house of Francis Heddell (senior) – the very beach from which Heddell (junior) later removed Arthur's boat. Heddell (senior) had objected and taken Morrison to court. He had complained that when the building and its pier were completed, and if Morrison's neighbour on the other side of the beach did the same, the shore would become inaccessible to the public, and to himself of course. An interdict had been awarded against Morrison preventing further building, notwithstanding other lodberries having been built on the foreshore without the authorities – the Procurator Fiscal, Greig, among them – objecting. Morrison had challenged the interdict but it cost him dear: financial ruin and death, by a broken heart according to Arthur. In upholding the interdict the authorities had pointed out that many of the lodberries had been built for the purposes of smuggling, which was true, although the days of smuggling were all but over. What had not escaped Arthur's notice in all of this was that Cecilia Heddell, the sister of Heddell (junior) – who now lived in the house of his recently deceased father and who had tried to claim the beach as his own property when he evicted Arthur's boat – was the wife of James Greig. In other words, the Procurator Fiscal, who had taken Heddell's (senior) side against Morrison, was his son-in-law and brother-in-law of the man against whom Arthur was petitioning regarding the removal of his boat! On top of that, while Heddell (senior), on the one hand had had Morrison's building stopped because it might deny public access to the beach – when the construction of several other lodberries had already been allowed – on the other, Heddell (junior) was claiming (against Arthur) that the beach was not public but his private property. Arthur saw that his protagonists were trying to have it both ways and he smelled a rat. He could not contain his righteous wrath.

The dispute became more complicated after Arthur won his case against Heddell (junior) for use of the beach. Not content with

Well-appointed cottage in Unst by Henry Saxby.

winning his case, Arthur – because he was so infuriated about what had happened, unjustly, to Morrison – and unbeknown to Greig, the Procurator Fiscal, wrote an official letter, in his capacity of Chief Magistrate, to Sir William Rae, Scotland's Lord Advocate, complaining about the lack of impartiality of the tribunal, i.e. Greig. He got no reply to this – he later alleged – so followed it up with a private letter, to which he got no reply either – he also later alleged.

The following year, in 1819, Heddell (junior) came up with the sasine (document of legal possession of property) for his property to which, in his own handwriting, he had added the beach. Greig supported him. Arthur now smelled corruption. Then, in 1821, Greig got wind of Arthur's approach to the Lord Advocate.[12] He accused him of improprieties and abuse of his position as Chief Magistrate, hastily penning a rather nervous and obsequious letter to Sir William Rae in his own defence.

> *"My Lord, It is with utmost reluctance that I presume to trouble your Lordship, but confiding in your high and honourable character and in your well known condescension and impartiality, I am almost persuaded that your Lordship will not be offended at my boldness. I have just accidentally heard that Dr Arthur Edmondston Surgeon here has given out that he has already preferred … certain charges against me for some fancied improprieties on my part as a public officer … he is a person who quarrels and interferes with almost every body … when I inform you that there is hardly a Public man here whom he has not outraged and quarrelled with or written against some public board or Functionary for causes which turned out to be the most groundless and capricious – What his charges against me are I am at a loss to imagine …"*[13]

That same year the pair squared up for several more skirmishes. First, Arthur served two summonses, one against both Heddell (junior) and Greig for encroachment on his summer house at Sound, just outside Lerwick, and the other against Greig for demolition of a wall encroaching on common ground.[14] Arthur, as usual, went public with his opinions and Greig then charged him with libel and won the case.[15] Their summer houses were in fact adjacent at Bankfield and Westhall and the result of their disputes over the boundary were the construction of two parallel walls that remain to this day. The gap between the walls became a footpath for locals which they named 'Contention Lane'![16]

All the testosterone released into Arthur's blood must have awakened his dormant libido, for in the middle of all this scrapping, in December 1822, at the age of 47, Arthur, the confirmed bachelor, like his brother Thomas the laird, became a father of an illegitimate child. His housekeeper, Ellie Georgeson, gave birth to a son whom they named Thomas. It was a field day for all the Lerwick gossips and all those who had felt the lash of Arthur's tongue; the old humbug and hypocrite! Like Thomas, Arthur doted on his baby, and had it only survived, Arthur's perspective on life might have undergone a transformation. But it was not to be, little Thomas took ill and died an infant in his father's arms.[17] Although he was getting himself into deep water before he lost his infant son, that event seemed to turn Arthur's mind and quite blinded his already clouded judgement. From here on, the demon drink, pursuit of lost causes, and a series of defences against allegations of non-payments of debts and even violence against others, became a way of life for Arthur, of which the events of the following year were just a foretaste.

Arthur invited one of his few friends and drinking cronies, William Jameson, a fishery officer, for lunch at his home in Lerwick. They had a good meal, a lively conversation and a few drinks. It was all so convivial that Jameson stayed on through the afternoon until the evening meal. They continued drinking through supper and eventually, warming to a dispute, their arguments became heated. In their, by now, inebriated state their verbal disagreement became a clumsy physical conflict. Arthur, sensing that he might come to harm and perhaps, in his befuddlement, that his reputation and position as Chief Magistrate might be compromised, sent Laura Irvine, his new housekeeper, out for help. It did not arrive in time, however, to prevent him receiving an injury from the drunken Jameson. When his perennial adversary, the Procurator Fiscal, Greig, heard about the brawl, he saw a wonderful opportunity to further ridicule Arthur and cited the two of them for assault.[18] Each of them and the housekeeper were then required to make statements, the contents of which, although differing slightly, described nothing but pure farce. Arthur's official statement was a desperate attempt, from a recently sobered up citizen, to express innocent outrage. The recorder noted from him that:

"… they dined, drank some toddy after dinner and took tea … after supper as they were sitting leisurely over a glass of toddy (for the Declarent [Arthur] had felt somewhat uneasy all that day) a difference of opinion arose on certain religious points … Mr Jameson then proceeded to threaten the declarent with immediate violence if he attempted to persuade him to concur in his opinions … the Declarent proposed that they should go to bed as it was late … Mr Jameson then became more furious and asked if the declarent meant to insult him … the declarent said to his Servant "Girl, Light the Gentleman out" then went up to his room took off his Coat, waistcoat and Neckcloth, with a view of going instantly to bed … Mr Jameson then came to the foot of the bed room stair, and called to the Servant in a very authoritative tone, to go and demand of her Master if that was his order. Declared that being apprehensive that Mr Jameson might come up to his bedroom the declarent came down Stairs to see if he could meet with any person whom he might send for Constables. Declares that he saw nobody, and being nearly naked he returned into the house soon after and desired the Servant to go immediately for Magnus Mouat the Sheriff Official. Declares that the girl did so, and Mr Jameson followed the declarent upstairs. That apprehensive of some serious attack from the declarent's knowledge of Mr Jameson's character when under the influence of Spirits, the Declarent went into the next room and taking his fowling piece in his hand (which had been imperfectly charged above six weeks before to shoot a bat and which from the loss of the priming could not fire), said to him "You shall not insult or murder me in my own house with impunity" or words to that effect. Declared that Mr Jameson then sprung unexpectedly upon the declarent and seized the fowling piece. Declared that as the Declarent's intention was merely to intimidate Mr Jameson and save himself, he made no determined opposition to his getting the piece, but immediately after he got possession of it he struck the declarent a violent blow on the left eye and temple, which stunned and knocked him over the stone stair. Declares that although almost stupefied by the blow the declarent recollects his head striking against the different steps of the stair as he descended to the foot of it. Declares that the declarent then fell into a kind of swoon, and felt as if there were people entering the house by the windows and beating him on the back and shoulders. Declares that on hearing the door open some time after the declarent said 'Laura, is that you'. Declares that he was soon after carried to bed cold and shivering."[19]

Laura Irvine's statement broadly supported Arthur's and Mr Jameson did not deny there had been violence between them.[20] Magnanimously, after Greig told them to sort this out between them, Arthur said:

"Although I am at this moment suffering, and am likely to suffer during the remainder of my life from the effects of the barbarous treatment which I met with on that occasion, yet it is not my intention to sue for compensating damages …"

All he asked for was an apology and, being the man he was, he even drafted the apology he expected Jameson to give him.

"I confess with the deepest regret and contrition that being in Dr Edmondston's house on the night of the 18th instant, I insulted and personally maltreated Dr Edmondston without having received any provocation from him, and I entreat his forgiveness for a conduct so unjustifiable on my part."[21]

This affray did not dampen Arthur's intention to pursue Greig for alleged corruption over his dispute with Heddell, with which he got nowhere. Having not had any reply from his letters to the Lord Advocate several years previously, Arthur took his usual course in these disputes and, despite being a magistrate, not only penned, but published, a 30 page pamphlet, *A Letter to Sir William Rae, baronet, Lord Advocate of Scotland, on the conduct of James Greig, procurator fiscal for the Zetland Islands* (1823). Like Don Quixote, his motives, he thought, were the best intentioned but, alas, he was taking on the baron's castle not an innocent windmill. In his virtuous pursuit of justice Arthur did not hold back, but directly libelled the Procurator Fiscal, even casting aspersions at the Lord Advocate's behaviour!

"Is the support of such a man [James Greig], or, at any rate, the disinclination to enquire into his conduct, an object so worthy in itself of your lordship's serious attention, or calculated to yield you such lasting reputation as the gratitude of a whole country, and the reflected satisfaction to your mind that you had done everything in your power to check abuses, and to secure the equal administration of justice? And why should government be inculpated in maintaining such a system of unmeaning corruption, when not even the wildest radical can assert that any parliamentary influence could result from its practice?"

Arthur had gone too far! Greig could not possibly leave such a public libel unchallenged. In 1824 he raised an action of £2000 (£100,000) damages against Arthur.[22] The latter countered by suing Greig for £3000 (£150,000) damages for recording "letters of inhibition against him …", locking up "the pursuer's [Arthur's] personal funds by using arrestments in the hands of every person indebted … to the pursuer …" and for harassment.[23]

These self-inflicted wounds, however, did nothing to diminish Arthur's various other enthusiasms. That same year he was presented with a silver salver from the Highland and Agricultural Society of Scotland:

"... for having planted the greatest number of trees on the largest extent of ground, between the 1st February 1822 and 1st November 1824, of any proprietor or tenant in Zetland ... The plantations [are] at the residences of Mr George R. Tait [Helendale] and of Mr Joseph Leask [Bankfield], in sheltered situations near Lerwick ... chiefly of sycamore."[24]

The few trees planted in Shetland at this time were principally planted as small policies around large houses. Arthur showed great foresight, setting an example that many were to follow over the years, notably his youngest brother Laurence in Unst several years later. His brother Thomas had already attempted some tree planting at Buness but his efforts had been unsuccessful. Arthur's plantings, on the other hand, survived and are still standing nearly 200 years later!

Rev. Samuel Dunn sketch, photographed by J. D. Rattar.

When not in court, another of Arthur's enthusiasms was attacking humbugs wherever he found them and in 1825 his sharp eye spotted a report to the Methodist Church by an evangelical visitor to Shetland. The early and middle part of the 19th century was a busy time for evangelists. The Presbyterian Church was finding itself under pressure from visiting Congregationalists, Baptists, Methodists and even Quakers, of which the first three became well established in Shetland. The leading Methodist divine in England in 1822 was Dr Adam Clarke (1760-1832). He was persuaded by a lone Shetland Methodist, John Nicholson (1792-1828), to send a mission to Shetland and in that year he sent the Rev. John Raby (1790-1858) and the Rev. Samuel Dunn (1797-1858). It was Dunn's reports on the state of Christianity in Shetland, the progress of his work and the exaggerated hardships associated with it to the Wesleyan base in England that, on the surface, angered Arthur and impelled him to write and publish *A view of the conduct of the Wesleyan preachers in the Zetland Islands (By a calm observer)* (1825). He was, in fact, joining in a more general attack on Dunn in defence of the Rev. John Turnbull (1775-1867) of Tingwall and he was possibly the author of an earlier pamphlet published that year in Leith – *Notes on the Rev. Samuel Dunn's Observations on the Rev. John Turnbull's Address* (1825). His, *A view of the conduct of ...* became so popular that a second edition quickly followed the first![25]

In his pamphlet the good doctor quoted an extract from Samuel Dunn's diary of 25th November, 1822, in which Dunn described his 50 km journey back to Lerwick after preaching in Sandness, in West Mainland:

"So I borrowed a little equuleus about 40 inches high, and began about ten o'clock to ascend a steep hill about a mile and a half high."

After pointing out the superfluous use of the word 'little' – the Latin word means 'little horse' – Arthur launched into one of his typically scathing broadsides. On this occasion he attacked Samuel Dunn's wildly exaggerated estimation of the height of the hill the poor Shetland pony had to climb with the preacher on its back.

"Every school boy knows that, the height of a hill is the altitude of its summit above the level of the sea. The height of the hill therefore … … was just above 7920 feet [1.26 km] … or between eighteen or nineteen hundred feet higher than Mons Cenis, one of the Alps … … if he (Dunn) subtracts 7000 feet [1.12 km] from the height of Sandness hill, he will bring the result pretty near the truth. And this fact should be made public, for the quiet of all the little equulei in that part of Zetland which may in future be employed to transport itinerant Methodist preachers over it."

He went on to quote the next part of Dunn's 'terrible' journey from his diary:

"…the rain descended, the floods came, and the winds blew. My umbrella was blown away out of my hands about half a mile, and broken in pieces. In crossing two or three burns or rivers, I and my pony were nearly carried away to the sea. It was truly fortunate …"

Arthur pointed out the wonder:

"that Mr D. was able, during this hurricane, to retain his seat, and to keep his eyes steadily fixed on the scattered fragments of his umbrella, when removed to the distance of half a mile from him."

Then he upbraided Dunn for not thanking his many hosts for their support and kindness; for example the meal he had with Mr Ogilvy, a minister in Lerwick, where he partook of "… quite an English table. Boiled beef, roasted mutton, fish, soup, excellent vegetables, minced and apple pies and cream &c &c." Life was clearly not entirely Spartan for an evangelist! Arthur concluded his 31 page demolition of Dunn with his usual flair:

"It may appear to some, that I have enlarged too much in exposing the contemptible puerilities with which the immediately preceding communication are filled. But I deemed it essential in a discussion of this kind, to ferret ignorance out of its most secret lurking places, and to hold up to view in their naked deformity, the jesuistical attempts of such men to impose on the public. It requires, however, but little penetration to discover, that the real design of blazoning forth of an account of self-imposed privations, and of ideal dangers, is to enhance the merit of their services in the eyes of their employers, and to wheedle the good people of England out of their money, to build unnecessary chapels, and to favour their darling work of proselytism."

In the absence of many other public entertainments this pamphlet of Arthur's was eagerly sought after.

In *his* description of Arthur, Dunn on the other hand, was a little more diplomatic. He was "… a Bachelor about 50, very intelligent on most subjects, but likely to get too warm in disputing".[26] Several of Lerwick's residents, particularly those of the cloth and of the law, would have heartedly agreed with him. On the other hand, Dunn had to admit that Arthur was a conscientious doctor. On another occasion, according to his diary, Dunn had collapsed under the strain of a long walk in the worst of Shetland's weather:

> "I went to Dunrossness for a week, where I preached two or three times every day besides meeting the classes. In walking back, I had to face a strong north wind and rain, which was the means of completely laying me aside. I was obliged to take to my bed, where I remained for nearly a month. For three days I was to all appearances very near death and little hope was entertained of my recovery. I was attended by Dr Edmondston, who is very skilful in his profession, and paid me every attention. He says my disorder was occasioned by too great exertion; that nature was quite exhausted; and that I was like an old worn-out man."[27]

Given his penchant for exaggeration it is a little difficult to believe Dunn really was at death's door, nevertheless, his comments reflect well on Arthur's medical professionalism. Dr Adam Clarke, who had sent Dunn north, came himself in 1826 and again in 1828. On this latter visit he went to Unst and visited Buness. Although Arthur attacked Dunn and did not believe that Methodism would take root in Shetland – he could not have been more wrong – he was an admirer of Dr Clarke and persuaded him to publish two of his Shetland sermons in his collected works.[28]

In the meantime, in 1826, the upright but fallible Arthur, at the age of 51, became the father of a second child, Mary. The mother was his new housekeeper, Laura Irvine, who was clearly not just a passing fancy for she gave birth to Charlotte, another daughter, four years later in 1830. Like Thomas, Arthur did not disown the children nor did he marry the mother, but he did give them his surname. This period of Arthur's life, between his earliest court case in pursuit of Francis Heddell in 1818 and the birth of Charlotte, found him in and out of the courts on over 20 occasions. On more than half of these he was under summons or complaint for non-payments of debts and the rest were cases he pursued for non-payments or encroachments on his property or his rights. It was to be the summons from the Procurator Fiscal, just before the birth of Charlotte, however, that would prove the most serious for him.

CHAPTER SIX

FOUR DIFFERENT PATHS

"… I would not like to lose time unnecessarily as Edmondston is carrying on like smoke and will preoccupy all the markets before we can come into the field."

William Mouat of Garth (1785-1836)

Charles the Entrepreneur

With Arthur trying to establish himself as a man of the enlightenment in Lerwick while openly living with his housekeeper and mistress, Thomas securing the financial future of the Buness estate, Henry in Newcastle and Laurence in London, Charles, by 1816, had become a merchant at Crafts's Wharf in Charleston and in 1819 a director of the bank of South Carolina, a position he held until 1831. Although he kept in touch with his family back in Shetland he was now an American, even a Southerner, in every sense.

Charles Edmondston and Mary Edmondston (Pratt).

In 1822, by which time he was 40, he had become a business agent for plantation owners, had his own 'Edmondston' Wharf and resided in fashionable Church Street, following several moves within Charleston over the previous 15 years. He was now a very successful and respected entrepreneur, a loving husband and the father of five children. He had achieved his business success by riding an American financial boom that coincided with a similar, albeit relatively modest, boom in Shetland, and by exploiting the opportunities for trade, particularly the relatively new and very profitable cotton crop of the hinterland. In addition Charles was a promoter of textile manufacturing, a ship-owner and a moving force in the local Episcopalian church. He also felt himself regarded as a bit of an upstart by the established wealthy *aristocratic* plantation owners. Charles, though, could look on his position with some satisfaction, from nothing and entirely through his own endeavours, he had achieved as much, if not more, than he had ever dreamed of. Unlike his older brothers in Shetland, Charles appears to have been a humble man in many ways, ever grateful for all the good things of his life; a man untainted by hubris, but still ambitious.

On the other hand, his friend John Ross, who had accompanied him to Charleston from Shetland, was not so ambitious and was content to settle down as a seaman on the east coast trade. However, they remained close friends and Ross frequently dropped in to see Charles when he was in port. But, when Charles bought a yacht he persuaded Ross to skipper it for him, having no seamanship skills himself. Ross then took the family up and down the coast on leisure trips and when he was no longer able to sail the yacht he became part of Charles' household with a room of his own until he died.

In addition to buying a yacht, Charles was now able to lay out the substantial sum of $4500 ($80,000) to buy a plot of land in Charleston for his dream house.[1] The site was on the old Fort Mechanic, built in 1795 during the American conflict with France. The Fort, of earthworks and logs, was reputedly named for the free labour expended upon it by the city's artisans – carpenters, blacksmiths, furniture makers etc. It was on marshy ground behind the low Atlantic shore and was frequently inundated by the sea, especially during the hurricane season. To combat this, a high, stone esplanade, named the Battery, had been erected. The protected land then became a prime building site being situated directly in the path of cooling sea breezes and well away from the noise and bustle of the wharfs and warehouses. It also afforded extensive and unhindered views of Charleston Harbour – now America's major cotton and rice port – and the ocean on which Charles had floated his fortune. At times he could see up to 300 sailing ships lying offshore awaiting berths.

What better place for a shipping merchant to overlook his trade *and* upstage the rich and fashionable of Charleston! Here, Charles built a mansion in 1825 to house his growing family, now of eight children. It was to be the first house on the Battery and the envy of Charleston society. All that lay between it and the far horizon was a low-lying artificially created island at the mouth of Charleston Harbour on which a fortification, called Fort Sumter, would later be built. To the rear of the house Charles had a large extension built for his house slaves. After any initial doubts about the morality of slavery, Charles now fully accepted the status quo. It was not something he could have ignored and, kind though he may have thought he was to his own slaves, he would have been uncomfortably reminded of the dubiety of the practice almost daily, as he passed through the slave market on the Battery.

Number 21 East Battery was completed around the same time as his new office on Exchange Street. The house was built in the late Federal style with large and spacious adjoining rooms that

View along the East Battery by S. Bernard. Charles Edmondston's house in 1831 is the second house with the blue-roofed veranda on which may be Mary and two children.

could be opened into each other by means of folding doors, providing coolness in the summer and suitable spaces for entertaining on the grand scale. It was composed of three floors with piazzas, or covered verandas, along the length of the south side of the house on the ground and first floors. These shaded the house on that side and offered a cool outdoors spot to sit in the hot Charleston summers. In this house, in elegance and luxury, Charles and Mary had four more children. However, although Charles now seemed firmly established, all was not well under the optimistic surface of Charleston.

In 1829:

" … Charleston shipped out its greatest rice crop and the second largest cotton export ever, 214,000 bales, but that same year the Chamber of Commerce reported: Charleston has for several years past retrograded … Her landed estate has within eight years depreciated in value one half. Industry and business talent … have sought employment elsewhere."[2]

These were ominous signs heralding a downturn in trade. And neither was the social fabric of the city entirely healthy. Although the last uprising of slaves in South Carolina had been as far back

Spode Dinner Service in 21 East Battery.

as 1739 at the Stono River Bridge about twenty miles southwest of Charleston, there was an underlying nervousness among the whites that it might happen again: a fear justified in nearby Virginia a couple of years later, in 1831, when Nat Turner (1800-1831) and his followers killed 55 whites. In Charleston there were many mysterious fires, most of which were blamed on black arsonists. Following an unusual number of these the city augmented its Guards and instructed them to enforce control over the city's Negroes. It was a nervous city, built on the back of black slaves on the plantations. It was also a very cultured city with theatre, opera, art and a number of museums. The ships of Charles and other merchants, in addition to carrying the staple exports, carried the sons of wealthy citizens to Europe for their education and returned with sophisticated goods for American homes. Having come from a relatively modest and little known background, Charles was now able to take his place among the wealthy citizens of Charleston society and entertain them on their own terms. One of the European extravagances that he had shipped over for his splendid new house on the Battery was a 144-piece dinner service made by Spode in England, each piece of which was decorated by an elaborate letter E for Edmondston. Family tradition has it that this was an extraordinary wedding present from a former suitor of Mary. The Spode pattern, however, was not designed until well after their wedding in 1810.[3] Charles also allowed himself another extravagance, perhaps to demonstrate to those at home just how far he had come. In 1828 he sent a gift of a modern American rifle, inlaid in silver, to his brother Thomas in Unst, for the latter's fiftieth birthday.

This period in the 1820s when Charles was making serious money was also a time of growing discord between the northern and southern states of America. On the one hand was the question of slavery to which the southern states were almost entirely committed, since slaves were the labour force that produced and harvested the staple plantation crops of cotton, rice and tobacco: commodities on which their wealth depended. On the other were the protective tariffs on imported goods, imposed by the Federal Government, that were beneficial to the North and West but financially damaging to the South. These disagreements led to factionalism among the States and to some local politicians of South Carolina demanding the right to nullify Federal laws with which they disagreed: a recipe for political anarchy among the States. Those in support of nullification became known as the Nullifiers, of whom many later became secessionists; those against became known as the Unionists. To a great extent, the former were Democrats and the latter Republicans.

It was into this fracturing society in sub-tropical America in 1825 that their fifth son and Mary's ninth confinement, was born on 7th September. He was named Thomas (1825-1874) after his uncle and his paternal great-grandfather.

Laurence in the footsteps

Meanwhile, back in Scotland in the autumn of 1821, Laurence began his medical studies at the new Edinburgh University. The new University buildings were still not completed, nevertheless, student numbers had grown to around 2000, attracted by the University's growing reputation, particularly its medical school. By now the road to the port of Leith was one of the great thoroughfares of the city and while construction had spread northwards, obliterating fields and swallowing up villages such as Broughton, the village of Neill the printer at Canonmills, less than a mile beyond, still retained its mill loch and character right on the city's periphery.

In December Laurence wrote to Thomas:

"We are enjoying the putrid half of the woman that was hanged lately at Montrose for the murder of her husband. Two poor fellows expiate their crimes tomorrow on Leith Sands – they too will figure on our mortuary tables."[4]

In a letter the following year he could not hide the fact that he would rather be doing something else:

"Vexations – this moment a call to the hospital – to assist to multiply the subjects of human misery – the little personage little knows what a world of confusion and annoyance it is about entering."[5]

For the moment, however, he accepted the course of his life, on the understanding that at some time in the future he would become the laird of Buness and that he would not always need an income from medicine. In the meantime he urgently needed to seek subscribers for his future medical practice in Unst, Yell and Fetlar, reckoning that he would be lucky to get as much as £60 (£2750) per year.[6]

In November, after a brief return to Shetland, Laurence wrote to tell Thomas of the return trip from Shetland on the *Coldstream*, an 87-ton sloop that ran several times a year between Lerwick and Leith. His comments illustrated just how uncomfortable and hazardous the journey could be. He thought the *Coldstream* unseaworthy:

"… in every respect … she was very deeply laden … the least straining deluged her with water … her mainsail was rendered totally unsafe … unfit indeed either to take advantage of a favourable wind or work off with the contrary … for it was worn out with age … I was soon useless the very day after leaving Lerwick. The decks were so open that our beds were constantly filled with water."[7]

Laurence's fears were well founded for exactly a year later, in November 1822, she was lost with all hands on just that very passage.

Barely four months into his studies, Laurence was becoming increasingly concerned about his financial dependence on Thomas and was beginning to doubt the wisdom of his decision. In a letter to Thomas in December 1821, he wrote to tell him that he had a *"… savage* [desire for] *independence"*,[8] and to apologise for all the expense he was costing Thomas – his travel, clothes, lectures, etc. – and yet he was giving nothing in return. That was not true, but it was the way Laurence saw it, as he sought reassurance from his brother. In fact, while immersed in his medical studies at the University and busy writing up his ornithological notes for publication, Laurence was still very active for Thomas in the chromate market.

Economic expansion in Shetland

Laurence spent his days in Edinburgh in the early 1820s at lectures and up to his elbows in blood, and his evenings studying texts; Henry continued quietly in his medical practice in Newcastle; Thomas prospered in Unst; Charles continued his steady climb to similar prosperity in Charleston and Arthur divided his time between his medical practice, his magisterial duties, litigation – accusing and defending, composing letters and pamphlets, and drinking. Meanwhile, Shetland's economy was looking up and its population increasing. Cod fishing, by Shetlanders themselves, had commenced only ten years previously and was proving very successful. One of the main grounds, 50 kilometres west-south-west of the island of Foula, that had been discovered and lost again 30 years previously, was rediscovered by accident. In his *Observations on the Nature and Extent of the Cod Fishery* (1820), Arthur described how, in 1817, John Petrie's boat had been blown off course in a gale and when the wind dropped and he had become becalmed he decided to put the fishing lines out. In 36 hours he and his crew caught 900 cod! The Foula Bank was to remain the main fishing ground for smaller vessels for the rest of the century.[9] Arthur, though, warned that he thought that the Shetland cod grounds were not large and could easily be exhausted: how right he was!

WilliamHay (1787-1858).

In 1820, in response to the success of the cod and the herring fisheries, Thomas the laird's friend, William Hay (1787-1858), the son of James Hay (and grandson of his namesake, William Hay 1723-1804 who had been the friend of his grandfather), built a new dock in Lerwick as a centre for fishing and curing, and for the building of brigantines and barques from 200-300 tons. The smuggling that the Hay family had been involved in had now been taken over by outsiders and the family business was now strictly legitimate: between 1816 and 1823 some 10,000 to 12,000 gallons of gin along with tea and tobacco were estimated to have been smuggled into the remote parts of the islands. So large were the quantities that it was reckoned by some to have had a serious effect on Shetland's legal economy. Smuggling on such a large scale, however, died out as the Shetland economy improved in the 1820s and legal trade increased, especially in fishing. The Greenland whalers that picked up crews and supplies in Shetland were also doing very well at this time and this too benefited the local economy. In 1818 some 34 whaling ships called at Lerwick and in 1819 there were 43. On the land too, modernisation was creeping in and the first 'improvements' were being made to estates and some of the first 'acts of removal' – the forcible eviction of small farm tenants to allow the old run rig arable system to be replaced by large farms with enclosures – were being carried out by landowners.

Such was the confidence in the Shetland economy that the following year William Hay and *his* father-in-law, Charles Ogilvy (1761-1827), established the Shetland Bank. These entrepreneurial merchant families and a few others now became the main movers of Shetland society replacing many of the old landowning families of whom only a handful survived: families such as Mouat of Garth, Bruce of Symbister and Sumburgh, Nicolson of Lochend and, of course, Thomas Edmondston of Buness. However, crucially, the foundations of this financial confidence, on which the economic developments depended, lacked capital.

In 1821, the Rev. James Ingram (1776-1879), moved to his new post in Unst, from Fetlar and North Yell – which position he had gained in 1803 when his predecessor drowned while travelling between Lerwick and Fetlar. The Rev. Ingram was not unfamiliar with Unst and the Edmondston family, for before he took over the parish he had been the tutor to the children of the then minister, the Rev. James Barclay – the same who had died at William and Mally's house in Lerwick almost 30 years previously. The Rev. James Ingram then married Mary (1776-1859), daughter of the Rev. Barclay. He and his son, the Rev. John Ingram (1808-1892), who succeeded him as minister in Unst, then held that ministry until the latter's death 12 years after his father, a period of 70 years. The Ingrams were a formidable pair, father and son, and instrumental in the 'disruption' of the Church of Scotland in Unst in 1843 when they came up against the laird, Thomas Edmondston. Mary Barclay's two brothers, Thomas (1792-1873) and John (1778-1841), were also soon to play an important role in the lives of several of the Edmondstons, the former to become another thorn in the side of Arthur and later a supporter of his nephew.

By 1823, Thomas Edmondston, through a fair amount of travelling and trading by Laurence as well as through his own efforts, had established the beginnings of a very lucrative trade in the export of chromate at Baltasound, well ahead of all the other landowners who had shares in one of the *scattalds* where the chromate was to be found. The most important of these was William Mouat of Garth who had no trust in Thomas and was aggravated that he might be losing out on the money to be made. Mouat wrote to his lawyer in Edinburgh on the need to get their skates on if they, too, were to benefit.

"*... as to the latter* [Thomas Edmondston] *I expect nothing from him that any species of Chicanery can keep us out of ... A Doctor Hibbert who was here upon a Mineralogical tour ... and who has written a huge quarto about Shetland which perhaps you have seen, discovered a very rare and valuable Mineral here in Unst, under the circumstances, as the property described in the enclosed memorial, which I have drawn up hurriedly in order to overtake a vessel which sails for the south tomorrow morning – and upon which I shall be much obliged to you to get me a practical (or practicable) opinion as soon as you conveniently can ... I would not like to lose time unnecessarily as Edmondston is carrying on like smoke and will preoccupy all the markets before we can come into the field.*"[10]

The *scattalds* had not yet been divided between the landowners so Thomas, keen to exploit the chromate there, approached Mouat of Garth and they came to an agreement to work the chromate found there through a Trust on behalf of all the proprietors. Thomas proposed that Mouat should be the trustee so as to assure everyone that they would get their fair share of the sales. Mouat accepted and remained the trustee until his death in 1836. About this time a large deposit of chromate was found at a place called Hagdale on the Buness estate and Thomas was able to open up a quarry. The trust accounts show that between 1823 and 1829 approximately £6500 (£357,500) net was made on the sale of chromate.[11] It was a lucrative trade and this figure may not have included £3000 (£165,000) from sales on private land, principally Buness estate. Thomas was making a great deal of money in this period, but he was a very canny business man. In several letters between him, Mouat and his friend Arthur Nicolson on Fetlar, it is clear that while Thomas was making money hand over fist he was also borrowing at the same time, to invest in more land and property and he was in no hurry to pay it back. To Arthur Nicolson in 1821 he wrote:

"*I herewith enclose you a transfer on Sir William Forbes & Company for £120* [£6240] *sterling as an* <u>*instalment*</u> *on our account current, and next season will I hope wipe off* <u>*old scores*</u>. *If, however, I am wrong in my calculation, I know the* <u>*lenity*</u> *of my creditor.*"[12]

Thomas was banking that his friendship with Nicolson would spare him any penalty if he reneged on the date of repayment. He pretended some naiveté in his financial calculations but, in reality, he was too astute to be wrong and Nicolson knew it. Then, when the payment was due the following year, once again using the cloak of friendship, Thomas had the audacity to write:

"*… & as I am on this subject* [money], *I wish even to be farther obliged to you – I have at this very moment the prospect of extending my property in this quarter a little, but feel the want of that* "*necessary evil*" *money; would it be perfectly agreeable to you to add £200* [£10,500] *– to the £200* [£10,500] *– I already have?*"[13]

Thomas also added as an aside in this letter that he had not crossed "*… the door of my room for three weeks …*"[14] an indication of his increasingly fragile health that he intended would soon have the care and attention of Laurence.

The Immer-gös

As if Laurence had not enough to do in the early 1820s, chasing up markets for the chromate, studying medicine, getting vaccine matter for Arthur, editing an article of Thomas' for publication in the *Philosophical Journal* and writing one himself for the *Edinburgh Magazine*, he somehow found time to pursue his first love of natural history.

In March 1822, he wrote to Thomas promising to send a book with large letters for the two-year-old Ursula, asking him in return to send some skins of black guillemots, in all states of plumage. As a casual aside, he mentioned that he had already sent some skins to Thomas Bewick (1753-1828), the gifted British natural history artist and wood engraver. He also promised that: "*I shall write a paper on the species (Immer) proving among other things its identity with the Northern Diver – an opinion I have long entertained*"[15], which he did, not long afterwards.

Laurence had got to know Professor Jameson through the marketing of the chromate, prior to attending university and, of course, Jameson was acquainted with his brother Arthur. It was not surprising therefore, that Jameson gave him access to his museum. At this juncture it contained over 74,000 geological and zoological specimens and was the envy of every other university. The man solely responsible for the museum at the time, and temporary assistant to Jameson, becoming his permanent assistant and secretary the following year, was William MacGillivray (1796-1852). When Laurence had arrived in Edinburgh to take up medicine, MacGillivray had already dropped out of that study five years previously to concentrate on zoology.[16]

MacGillivray was a plain, unassuming, Calvinistic, but sensitive young man from Aberdeen who had spent most of his childhood on the west coast island of Harris. He was very independently minded, if not stubborn, and found the mundane administrative post he held, under the strict and possessive Jameson, trying in the extreme. His chief interest was ornithology, though he was thoroughly knowledgeable across the whole range of Scotland's natural history. MacGillivray and Laurence were virtually the same age, shared a childhood fascination with wildlife, particularly birds, had both been brought up on islands and, despite their social differences, became close friends and remained so for the rest of their lives.

Through Jameson and MacGillivray, Laurence was introduced to the world of the Wernerian Society and to many other distinguished naturalists of the day who contributed to the Society papers, including Hibbert and Fleming, both of whom he had probably already met, William Scoresby junior (1789-1857) – the Arctic whaling captain turned scientist and explorer who had often been into Balta Sound, and Dr Thomas Stewart Traill (1781-1862) – an Orcadian amateur naturalist who had studied medicine in Edinburgh under Jameson, probably in Arthur Edmondston's time and who went on to become Professor of Jurisprudence at the University; while members included William Jackson Hooker (1785-1865) – the botanist, then Professor at Glasgow University and the naval Arctic explorer Captain Edward Parry (1790-1855) – whom Laurence would meet again in Unst.

The opportunity to mix among these people and to discuss the latest thinking in natural history made the chores of attending medical classes, distasteful dissections and births, almost acceptable. It also made it quite difficult for him, for here were people, specifically Jameson, Hibbert and MacGillivray, who had dropped medicine for natural history, a course Laurence might ideally have chosen for

William MacGillivray self portrait.

himself, but for his contract with Thomas and, perhaps, some timidity in his character. During this highly productive period at the University he produced, over two short years, a string of papers on Shetland's birds for the Wernerian Society: the same Society in which his brother Arthur had been published ten years previously. One of the first was *Observations on the Snowy Owl* (1822) and as he was a corresponding member of the Society his papers were read to it by the secretary, Patrick Neill, the printer whom he had met almost 20 years previously in Shetland: it was a small world.

The research and observation behind the papers that Laurence wrote for the Wernerian had been painstakingly carried out by him since childhood, some written down and some still in his head. Since leaving Shetland in 1812 he had found precious little time to devote to natural history study in the field, especially in Shetland, although he had had the opportunity to read many books and papers. One of the studies that he and Arthur had pursued, a popular one of the time, was the identification of species, particularly the understanding of plumage differences – those between species, immature and adult, between seasons and sometimes between sexes. From this study Laurence had learned that identification of a species must be from a specimen in the hand. He was adamant that a stuffed specimen was not adequately representative of the living bird and should never be given a specific name – a tendency of some naturalists. Laurence's request that Thomas despatch him skins of the black-guillemot was so that he could demonstrate their distinct winter and summer plumages, grey in the former and black and white in the latter season. Laurence's ornithological observations were very acute, much more so than Arthur's. He was able to point out, for example, that what was called the 'black-billed auk' was in fact the young of the razorbill, and what was known as the 'speckled diver' was in fact the young of the red-throated diver, or *rain-gös*.[17] Both of these were generally accepted at the time as separate species in their own right.

Like Arthur before him, Laurence was intrigued by the divers, the family in which the *rain-gös* and the *immer-gös* belong. Many a time he had raised his head, drawn by the *rain-gös*' cry *'we're a' weet we're a' weet, war wadder war wadder'* (we're all wet, worse weather), as it flew steadfastly from its nest by a lochan on the hill like an arrow to the sea. In Laurence's time, the *immer-gös*, in its grey and speckled, rather drab plumage, was still thought by Arthur and others to be a different species from the great northern diver, with its black head and intricately chequered black and white back.

Laurence now added to his brother's observation, in his own paper on the bird – *Observations on the Immer Goose of Zetland* (1822) – to the Wernerian Society:

"There are few birds to which anomalous and perverted instincts have been more ascribed than to the Columbus Immer [*immer-gös*]. It has been represented as incapable of flying … [of] crossing boisterous oceans merely by swimming … as hatching its eggs under its wing, or forming its nest on the surface of the water. And nothing more clearly demonstrates the necessity of investigating patiently the habits of birds in their native retreats, than the fact of the singular improbabilities that have so long been mingled with our information of a species which, from its number and general diffusion, ought long since to have been correctly known."

In his paper, Laurence was the first to correctly deduce that the *immer-gös* and the great northern diver were actually the same species and that the former was the immature of the latter.

Laurence regarded the beasts of the natural world as God's creatures, but equally, he saw them as put there for man's use and he could be as harshly pragmatic about their despatch as he was touched by their beauty and sensitive to their place in the world. His paper on the *immer-gös* continued:

> "The plumage on the body is so full, and the skin so thick, that small shot makes little impression when the back of the bird is not turned to the sportsman; and it is therefore the practice of the experienced to wait for this favourable situation, or to take aim chiefly at the head or neck. It dives with great celerity on the flash of the pan … It is exceedingly tenacious of life and I have seen it even when mortally wounded, with its head literally shattered and the brain perforated in various directions, still struggle to escape, with almost undiminished vigour and sagacity; and as it seemed impossible to kill it speedily, without unfitting it for being a specimen, the sportsman, relenting at its torments, has been compelled to put an end to them, by beheading it."

Another of Laurence's Wernerian papers at this time – *Remarks on the Larus Parasiticus or Arctic Gull* (1822) – that illustrated the depth of his interest and the care that he took over his ornithological observations and researches was on the 'arctic gull', the same bird on which his brother Arthur had published a paper in the Wernerian Society only a year previously. The arctic skua is yet another northern species restricted in the British Isles to the north and west of Scotland. It is a most elegant and swift predator named '*parasiticus*' because of its habit of obtaining its sustenance almost entirely from other birds, particularly terns, and forcing them to give up the food they are carrying in their bills.

It is a very unusual species in yet another way. As Arthur had pointed out, there are two distinct adult plumage patterns (or morphs) – one almost completely dark brown and one with a lighter brown back accompanied by a creamy breast. In Laurence's day it was believed that either the two morphs were different species, or at least, they were different sexes. The former belief was promulgated by Arthur who had first come to the correct conclusion that the colour of the bird was unrelated to its sex. Laurence too, shot several birds of the different colour morphs and dissected them, confirming that the colour differences were not related to sex.

The last of Laurence's major contributions to the ornithology of Shetland was a *List of the Birds observed in the Zetland Islands* (1822), again written for the Wernerian Society. Arthur had included a list of 80 species in his book of 1809, of which 21 were first records for Shetland. Laurence now added a further 34 species including four new records for the British Isles. Between them, the brothers were responsible for recording 80 per cent of all the new species for Shetland between 1800 and 1853. Over two short years, between 1821 and 1823, Laurence wrote 10 very detailed and accomplished papers on half-a-dozen bird species that received wide attention throughout the academic world. It was an outstanding achievement and by the end of that period he had eclipsed his eldest brother in the field of Shetland's ornithology.

Membership of the Wernerian Society threw up some strange and exotic connections for Laurence. Just prior to his attendance at the University and his first published papers – in 1819, three papers were read to the Wernerian Society by Jameson's former student, T. S. Traill. The papers were on the Jacketed Monkey, a new species of *Felis* and an account of an otter, all from Guyana in South America.[18] In each, Traill thanked a friend for supplying the specimens. In the second paper he commented:

"The specimen from which this description is drawn, was brought from Demerary by my friend Charles Edmonstone*, Esq. Who during a residence of near forty years in that part of America, has devoted a considerable portion of his time to do the practical study of Zoology … The recent skin has been very well stuffed by the person who killed the animal – prepared under Mr Edmondstone's eye …"

*not to be confused with Laurence's brother Charles in Charleston

In January 1823, Traill published a fourth paper describing the jaguar of which he again noted that several skins came from Charles Edmonstone in Guyana. The significance of this paper is that Laurence, if he had missed the previous three, would not have missed this one as he had papers of his own read just before it. Significantly, at the next meeting of the Society in March 1823 – at the end of his own paper *Notice of a Specimen of the Larus eburneus, or Ivory Gull, shot in Zetland; and further Remarks on the Iceland Gull* – Laurence noted of a specimen of his Lesser Iceland Gull, "This interesting specimen I met with in the rich zoological cabinet of my highly respected friend Charles Edmonstone, Esq. of Cardross Park." It seems that Traill's references to Charles Edmondstone had led Laurence to his distant relative. In fact it was not Charles Edmondstone who had stuffed the specimens and Traill was careful not to implicitly suggest this, it was either Charles Waterton (1782-1865) an eccentric English squire, naturalist and traveller, or a man called John Edmondstone.

Laurence's distant relative, Charles Edmonstone had been a wealthy timber merchant in Guyana and was known for giving shelter to the homeless at his remote plantation of Mbiri Creek, including freed black slaves. John Edmondstone, who took Charles' surname, was one of those to whom he provided refuge.[19] Waterton's great gift to science was the development of the art of the taxidermy and when he was in Guyana at Charles Edmonstone's plantation he taught his skills to John Edmondstone. When Charles Edmonstone retired and returned home to Scotland around 1817, bringing with him an incredible collection of stuffed zoological specimens, John Edmondstone came back with him: this was before slavery was abolished in Britain in 1833. Once in Britain, John took up the best trade he knew and set up in Lothian Street – a popular street for lodging houses for the students of Edinburgh University – with his wife and family. There, he did a good trade in taxidermy, taught the technique and sold his specimens. In 1825 John sold two swallows, one water ouzel and one chaffinch to MacGillivray for the Museum. Laurence knew John Edmondstone and no doubt picked up a few tips in the art of taxidermy.

In 1826 John Edmondstone taught another student neighbour in Lothian Street, Charles Darwin, for an hour a day for two months at a cost of one guinea, who later said of him in a letter to his sister *"A negro lived in Edinburgh, who had travelled with Waterton, and gained his livelihood by stuffing birds which he did excellently. He gave lessons for payment and I used to sit with him, for he was a very pleasant and intelligent man."*[20] Darwin was only 17 years old at the time and John Edmondstone was possibly the first person he had met who could describe to him the exotic world of tropical forests from personal experience, especially the birds: an environment that Darwin could only dream of at that time. There can be no doubt also that John Edmondstone was the first black man with whom Darwin conversed on any subject in detail, never mind one so near to his heart and that this "pleasant and intelligent" man greatly influenced Darwin's attitude towards all the non-white people he was to meet on his travels and later also to influence his thinking in *The Descent of Man* (1871).

CHAPTER SEVEN

NEW HOMES

"Let us always bear in mind, that rank and wealth are, at best, casual and fleeting, and that the only enduring superiority, and the only rank worthy of being envied, which one man possesses over another, is derived from the union of worth with intellectual talent."

Dr Arthur Edmondston (1775-1841)

Homeward Bound

As soon as Laurence had finished at the University he ceased writing papers for the Wernerian Society and, although he still had further medical studies to come, went straight back into marketing the chromate for Thomas. Between November 1823 and April 1824, at least 79 tons of chromate was gathered from the hills behind Buness and shipped to Glasgow via Lerwick for between £8.13s and £9.13s per ton[1] (£470-£530). In other words, probably less than ten proprietors between them made at least £380,000 in just six months, with the largest landowners, Thomas and Mouat of Garth, making the most! Thomas shipped the ore in barrels from Balta Sound either via the *Norna*, a schooner of around 100 tons belonging to the Leith and Shetland Shipping Company, or the *Fidelity* of 126 tons that belonged to Hay & Ogilvy. On the 16th March, 1824 Thomas wrote to William Hay to tell him that he had just shipped 20 barrels of chromate on the *Norna*. He went on brusquely, on the one hand to complain about the attitude of the skipper of the *Fidelity*, saying: "*... his conduct towards me in more instances than one has been so wantonly disrespectful ...*"[2] and threatened not to send any more goods with her; while, on the other, looked to buy more barrels and

sought advice on shipping and destination. In his reply, William Hay showed himself to be a friend, business adviser and diplomat. He offered Thomas dry casks rather than barrels and advised him, like others, to send his chromate direct to Liverpool. He also pointed out that if he did not use the *Fidelity* all the trade would go to the opposition, finally suggesting that "*... you must be somewhat mistaken about the man* [skipper] *... as those who know him best seem to like him well – at any rate placed so few above him as you are ... *[his behaviour]* is not worthy of your notice*." Thomas, the man of wealth and substance was becoming impatient of his 'inferiors'.

Hagdale chromate quarry, remains.

A year or so before his altercation with the skipper of the *Fidelity* one of Thomas' tenants complained to him about an incident that had occurred on the shore between him and the tenants of another laird, Leisk of Uyea, at the southern tip of Unst. As the laird, Thomas was expected to stand up for his tenants when need be, so he wrote to Thomas Leisk (1762-1837) on his tenant's behalf.

"The bearer of this, John Bruce with two other men found a piece of wood which they salved, & thereafter some … men [tenants of Leisk] raised it off from them by force – they have been plaguing me about it & I now refer them to [you]."[3]

A piece of wood on the shore was no mere flotsam and jetsam to a Shetlander. Tenants, in addition to their grazing, peat-cutting and other rights on the *scattald* and rights to gather seaweed from the shore, also had rights to collect drifting timber, prized on islands with no trees. Prized too, where the people were intrinsically poor, were cordage, sails, block and tackle, bolts, screws, tools, grease, paint, oil, chests or linen, or anything useful that could be picked up from wrecks or casually at sea or on the beach. It may have been that John Bruce was a relation of Sinclair, Thomas' housekeeper, that forced him to put pen to paper, but in the event it was rather half-hearted and he ducked a confrontation.

When wrecks did occur, the rights to a share of salvage were complicated and did not involve the tenants, except for what they could carry away and conceal. The tenants only had certain rights to larger items that drifted or were driven onto the shore, but so did others: the others being the owner of the shore and the Earl of Zetland, Lord Dundas. Occasionally large whales would drift ashore but the common smaller whale of the time – pods of which appeared regularly in shallower waters and could be trapped in a voe by small boats and driven ashore – was the pilot or '*caain*' whale. In the case of whales it was not the meat that was valued so much as the blubber. Lighting was by means of oil lamps and blubber provided a bulk supply in a fairly short time, albeit with some effort and risk. Tradition, enforced by the establishment, said that the spoils were to be split three ways; one third to the Earl, one third to the owner and one third to the tenants. Arthur Edmondston, not surprisingly, had other views, that he had expounded in his book (1809). He had described the case of the men of Sandsting in West Mainland, who had driven some pilot whales ashore.

'Driving bottle-nosed whales 1891' by R. H. Carter.

"In August or September 1784, several fishermen … fell in with a great number of whales at sea, and with great labour and difficulty drove them into Sella-voe, where with guns, spits and scythes, they killed and brought on shore twenty-three of them. The largest one was scarcely twenty-three feet long and the smallest only six … The greatest part of the whales were landed on a beach belonging to the glebe, and the others on a beach belonging to the estate of Sir John Mitchell [1733-1783] of Westshore … the fishermen underwent great fatigue, and ran the risk of their lives, in endeavouring to kill and capture the whales. One boat was completely destroyed and another damaged."[4]

Mitchell – actually, a distant relative of Arthur – claimed all the whales. He employed the tenants to cut up the whales and transport them to where the blubber was auctioned, but the tenants were not allowed to bid. They appealed to Lord Dundas who over-ruled Mitchell and apportioned them their one-third share. After some discussion of this case Arthur stated:

"The claim of the heritor, therefore, to an actual share of the whales, either on the principle that they have been killed through the medium of their property, or that the ground has been injured by their presence, appears to be founded in mistake, and to be unsupported by reason … [the tenants] hazard the destruction of their boats, and endanger their lives in the pursuit, for not one man in five hundred of them can swim, and they have an obvious right to a larger share of the produce of their enterprise … let the heritors receive one part, and the captors two parts; and this is surely as ample a proportion to the former, as either justice or liberality countenance."[5]

The rights of the Earl of Zetland and the proprietors, however, remained in place until almost the end of the century when a successful legal challenge was made by the tenants of Hoswick in South Mainland.

Meanwhile, Laurence in the closing months of 1824 was still busy travelling the country seeking markets for the chromate in London, Liverpool, Manchester, Birmingham, Bristol and Glasgow. When he was in Edinburgh he dined regularly with Jameson, who informed him that there had been discoveries of large amounts of chromate in Bergen. In a hasty letter to Thomas in 1824, Laurence told him, "… *be quick Thomas*"[6] before the market goes. Jameson also informed him that someone in Glasgow was taking out a patent for a new application of chrome ore that would increase the demand and Laurence told Thomas that he could get business that would clear £1000 (£55,000) for him before carriage. The next month, from Edinburgh, he wrote that he had just returned from London and had sold 127 tons of chromate.[7] In that letter he revealed that he was also dabbling in a little trade himself. While arranging for the *Norna* to go to Shetland to fetch chromate, he looked to gain some profit by shipping coal back to Shetland on the otherwise empty boat.

In September 1824, Laurence went to Dublin where Robert MacBrair (b1775), a shipping merchant (curiously, it was a Mr McBriar for whom Laurence had worked previously in London) was staying at the home of his second wife. MacBrair was a Glasgow merchant who lived in Paisley and whose first wife had died in 1818. A daughter from that first marriage was the 23-year-old Eliza. This was not an ad hoc journey for Laurence, for, on the 8th October, he and Eliza were married. Laurence's new father-in-law was a wealthy man who had had the portrait of Eliza's grandfather – the Rev. David Johnston (b1756), a founder of Edinburgh's Blind Asylum – painted by Sir Henry Raeburn (1756-1823): Eliza MacBrair therefore came of an excellent and highly respected family. That autumn, while fretting over being delayed in Edinburgh on his way home and tormented by timidity and his dependence on Thomas, Laurence laid bare his soul to him in an extraordinary outpouring, revealing all his hopes and fears:

"What is the loss of a few weeks in emolument … [in Edinburgh compared] … to my practice in Unst – perhaps about £5 [£275] – for a month's toil and anxiety about the sick! £60 [£3300] a year is all I can expect … where are all my laudable prospects of professional eminence – how can I dream of M.D. or natural History or anything but subsistence? … my constitution is not robust – my temperament is irritable nervous and unequal – I am generally – morbidly alive to (I am ashamed to confess it) the opinion of the world – even of those I despise."[8]

Laurence was terrified that Thomas might think that, because he was now married, Thomas would lose his affections. Since Laurence was totally dependent on Thomas' support, financially and emotionally, his mind was in turmoil and he could not think rationally. He wrote to reassure Thomas, while virtually betraying his new wife, that his marriage was not a prudent step, that nobody could replace his brother's love and that he would never be happier than he had been under his brother's paternal roof. In bizarre statements for a newly married man, he told Thomas:

"I did not enter into this relation anticipating greater happiness from it than I enjoyed before – it was merely fulfilling a previous engagement …'[9] [and] *'my best friend and benefactor – oh – nothing – nothing can compensate for the want of your society."*[10]

One can only hope that Eliza never read this letter.

In the month following his wedding Laurence made one of his last perambulations around England marketing the chromate, leaving Eliza with her father in Paisley and not even informing his friends and colleagues in Edinburgh that he was married! At the end of the year he took his bride, the refined Eliza, to Buness, the home of Thomas, his housekeeper and the five-year-old Ursula. It was not a happy introduction to Shetland for Eliza, for the boat carrying the chest with her trousseau sank in Lerwick in a storm. The chest was eventually recovered and the boxes with her sodden

Bressay Sound with boats by John Irvine.

clothes and gifts returned.[11] Later she was able to laugh at this event, but at the time, the only redeeming pleasure would have been the reception she had from the 73-year-old Mally, who at last had a daughter-in-law in Shetland and the prospect of legitimate grandchildren.

Neither could the following few years have been easy for Eliza, for Laurence had to return to Edinburgh to complete his studies at the Royal College of Surgeons leaving her, pregnant with their first child, in a remote, cold and strange household. It was November in Shetland, when a cold, damp wind blows across the waves of Balta Sound, and the last flowers of the garden are blackened by equinoctial gales. There was no shelter from trees, no golden autumnal colours, no close, friendly neighbours to have tea with and to gossip with, no soirees with songs and performances at the piano and none of the domestic refinements that she had so grown used to at Paisley. There was only the rustic, 47-year-old farmer and landowner, Thomas, with his fiddle, his claret and his cronies, Ursula and Sinclair. What would her sophisticated acquaintances have said if they knew she was under the same roof as an illegitimate daughter of the master of the house? Whatever, Eliza, like her mother-in-law, was made of sterner stuff.

Laurence returned from Shetland to Edinburgh to study surgery in the second half of the 1820s to find that his friend, William MacGillivray, had resigned from his post with Professor Jameson. Through him and the Wernerian Society, Laurence then brushed shoulders with two gifted men who were in Edinburgh for a few years around this time, who both also became close friends and pupils in some ways, of MacGillivray. One of those was already highly distinguished, the other would eclipse even him in the years to come. The first was the French-American, John James Audubon (1785-1851); the second was Charles Darwin (1809-1882).

Audubon had come to Edinburgh from America via T. S. Traill in Liverpool, who gave him an introduction to Patrick Neill. He had come to Britain and on to Edinburgh seeking a publisher for his paintings of American birds. In Edinburgh, he was given MacGillivray's name as someone who could help him with editing the text and with the technical illustrations. Audubon, a great naturalist, had not been to university and he needed someone like MacGillivray who was an excellent draughtsman as well as an academically trained zoologist. During those few years in the late 1820s in Edinburgh, MacGillivray virtually educated Audubon in zoology, helped him with the *Birds of America* and wrote much of the text for his *Ornithological Biography or an account of the habits of the birds of the United States of America* (1831-39).

Just after Laurence completed his medical training and returned to Shetland at the end of the 1820s, MacGillivray was appointed curator to the museum of the Royal College of Surgeons. Then, for the next two decades he devoted himself to producing – not only the text of his own great publication on the birds of Britain and many other scientific papers on the natural history of Scotland – but his own very beautiful bird, plant and animal illustrations. Darwin, who spent two years at that time in Edinburgh, attending Jameson's lectures, spoke highly and fondly of MacGillivray and some 30 years later, during the writing of *On the Origin of Species*, he corresponded with Laurence; among other queries, seeking similarities in the colonisation of Shetland by its flora and fauna with other islands with which he was familiar, most famously the Galapagos.

Laurence was nearing the end of his medical training in Edinburgh when he, unknowingly, made a connection that would literally come back to visit him, or rather Eliza, at Buness, some ten years later. He had written to Thomas early in his training about his experiences dissecting the bodies of murderers, "*the putrid half of the woman*" from Montrose and the "*two poor fellows*" to be hanged on Leith sands.[12] Bodies for dissection at the Royal College of Surgeons were hard to come by and the availability of those recently hanged for murder was rather limited, there was therefore a lucrative, illegal trade in grave robbery. However, even that posed difficulties in fulfilling the insatiable demand. Two Edinburgh citizens then took the prevailing paucity of cadavers to its logical conclusion and began to supply the market, particularly the anatomy lecturer, Robert Knox (1791-1862), with fresh ones to order. These two were the infamous William Burke (1792-1829) and William Hare (d.c.1860). They were caught after their sixteenth murder when Hare turned King's evidence and Burke was hanged. Laurence took part in the dissection of the latter on the mortuary slab in Edinburgh in 1829. He proved to have a macabre taste in curios for he took a piece of Burke's skin back to Unst that year after finishing his medical studies.[13] Hare was supposed to have fled Scotland after the trial, but not before he, inadvertently, came very close to retrieving that piece of his erstwhile partner.

Arthur, the Library, hubris and eviction

In 1826, Arthur, in Lerwick, had become the father of his second illegitimate child, Mary, by his housekeeper, Laura Irvine. Happily, Mary was a healthy infant and once again Arthur acknowledged his paternity and gave her his surname. Arthur had recently turned to the scriptures for poetic inspiration and privately published a versified and 'improved' passage from the Book of Daniel to make it available for the benefit of others: it was a mistake, the result was apocryphal! Now, struggling with his conscience and his dignity, following the birth of Mary, he turned again to the Bible for solace and chastisement. This time publishing a sermon and his own version of the Lord's Prayer:

> "Deeply impressed with a sense of our own frailty and unworthiness, may we approach with contrite hearts, the footstool of thy mercy and implore assistance from above ... Teach us O thou fountain of wisdom to look upon this world as a scene of probationary pilgrimage, and may our hearts never be seduced from thy service by the love of its deceitful vanities ... Fill our hearts O God! With a spirit of charity and love to all our brethren of mankind ... Fit and prepare us O father of mercies! For that awful change to which we are fast hastening and from which, as the sinful descendants of Adam, we cannot escape ... Amen."[14]

Had Arthur read Robert Burn's *Holy Willie's Prayer*? Surely not, or he would not have left himself so open to ridicule by Lerwick's populace: they had a field day at his expense. But despite his internal turmoil, in public Arthur held his head up high. Refusing to stumble over his mistakes, he now threw himself into further good works. This time it was the establishment of the first General Zetland Library (1828) of which he was also the first president, an act for which he was never given the recognition he deserved. There had been a Lerwick Subscription Library set up in 1809, but the entrance fee at £2.2s (£95) and the annual subscription at 12s (£27) was far too expensive for most. The new library proposed by Arthur, on the other hand, set the entrance fee at 10s (£22) and the annual subscription at 6s (£13) making it more affordable for the ordinary person.

On the occasion of the public meeting organised to set up the library Arthur gave an extemporised speech on education that was so successful that: "... [I was] requested repeatedly, by different individuals, to furnish them with a copy of the observations which I [Arthur] made ..." Modestly, he stated:

"My answer has uniformly been and must still be, that I cannot comply, literally at least ... having never composed a speech before it was delivered, and being directed always, in my extemporaneous compositions, by the impressions and associations of the moment ... Omissions and inaccuracies can hardly fail to be perceived by [those who were] witness of it; but retrospective emendations would take from it its only recommendations – simplicity and fidelity."[15]

Arthur then proceeded to remember enough of his speech to produce 16 pages of advice for the education of Shetland youth along the lines of "... having mastered Eutropius in the way recommended, the pupil might proceed to the Commentaries of Caesar; and then to Ovid, Virgil ..." In a subsequent paragraph, despite his previous spiritual humility and his well-known belief in the importance of lineage, Arthur revealed his credo:

"Let us always bear in mind, that rank and wealth are, at best, casual and fleeting, and that the only enduring superiority, and the only rank worthy of being envied, which one man possesses over another, is derived from the union of worth with intellectual talent."

Dr Arthur Edmondston (1775-1842) by John Irvine, begun in 1831, finished in NZ in 1870s.

Unfortunately, Arthur did not spell out what 'worth' was. If it was a record of achievement for the civic good, then he could rightly feel that he had it. Alas, it was not long before Arthur's 'intellectual talent' once more got the better of his 'worth', nor was it to be long before he was to repudiate the statement that 'intellectual talent' was superior to 'rank' for on the horizon were events that would test his credo to destruction. Before all that, however, came the crushing news of the success of James Greig's libel case against him and his most public downfall to date. Arthur was required to pay Greig damages of £300 sterling (£17,100). Arthur was also being pursued by several other creditors – including Robert Bruce of Symbister[16] and William Hay, John Ogilvy (1800-1840) and Charles Ogilvy (1802-1844), sons of the recently deceased Charles Ogilvy and partners of the Shetland Banking Company – for two bonds of £350 (£19,950) he had taken out in 1820 and 1823 respectively.[17] The result was bankruptcy and on 25th March, 1829, the trustees for his creditors had Arthur's property seized. He lost his Lerwick house and adjoining buildings, his summer retreat at the time, a four-roomed wooden house at Trigdale (Helendale) to the south of Lerwick where he had planted his trees only a few years before, and several acres of land in that area.[18]

Arthur was now forced to move into a small apartment rented from Her Majesty's Ordinance in Fort Charlotte where his second daughter by Laura Irvine, Charlotte, was born in 1830. And, as if all this was not humiliation enough, to rub salt in Arthur's wounds, at the auction of his property, Greig bought one of his Lerwick houses that he had been forced to sell. The pain of the loss of his property and position in the town where he had lived for more than 25 years and where he had been a respected doctor and magistrate was acute. But it was not as agonising as that of the following year when he lost to his creditors, the Manor House, Booth, Shore and Strand on Hascosay.[19] Sometime before, in 1812, the other parts of the Edmondston property on Hascosay that had been passed down through the lines of his grandfather's sibling, William the surgeon in Edinburgh, had been sold to Sir Arthur Nicolson. So his was the last piece of Hascosay that had belonged to the Edmondstons for 200 years. It was a blow that might have felled a lesser man or at least driven him into retirement and obscurity: not Arthur. There were still wrongs to right and a way to fall.

One of the many influences that small islands like Shetland have on their sons and daughters is a binding allegiance. The landscape and way of life is unique, the population relatively small and society intimate. Everyone knows everyone else and departing the islands is like departing an extended family. Such was the case for the two sons of the Rev. James Barclay, minister for Unst before the Ingrams. Both John and Thomas Barclay, like most of the sons of the establishment, were sent south for further education, one becoming a doctor and the other a minister like his father. Shetland's pull, however, brought them back when they had completed their studies in the 1820s, Thomas Barclay becoming a Lerwick minister and John another of Lerwick's doctors. Arthur had a poor opinion of them both and was not pleased at their return. Apparently, Thomas Barclay had really wanted his father's old parish of Unst and had suspicions that the two main landowners, Thomas of Buness and William Mouat of Garth, had spoken out against him. Thomas told his brother Arthur that the Rev. James Barclay senior had once chastised him violently – when he was quite young and before he had become the laird – and that he was opposed to all Barclays in Unst!

One day in 1830, Arthur and Thomas Barclay met on the Street and got into a conversation that quickly degenerated into a dispute. Thomas Barclay accused Arthur of speaking out intemperately against him "…on a political subject, [and Arthur] made use of harsh expressions [to him] …" Communications were exchanged and Arthur, as was his usual tactic, tried to have a letter on the subject published in an Edinburgh paper. He failed, probably because the letter was libellous, and he was therefore "… compelled to publish in a separate pamphlet the whole correspondence." The pamphlet was entitled *Biographical Notices of Pharmacopola and Presbyter, Published anonymously by an Eye-Witness* (1830), with an introduction by someone who identified themselves only by the initials A.E.; as if nobody might guess the name of the author! It was a scurrilous attack on the Barclay family and John and Thomas in particular, who were referred to as J.B. and T.B. Everyone guessed, of course, to whom these initials referred, but that was half the fun of such publications.

Arthur accused the Barclay family of ingratitude for what his father, brother and grandfather had done for them after the Rev. James Barclay had been nursed and died in his father's home in Lerwick. He explained in his pamphlet how J.B. (John Barclay) had come to his notice when they were both studying medicine and in the process presented that wonderful cameo of one of Edinburgh's least radical practitioners of medicine described earlier. Arthur went on:

"J.B. came to Edinburgh in 1796, to qualify himself as a surgeon; and he was soon after apprenticed to the surgeon to whom I was then under an indenture. As I had been two sessions at the College before his appearance, he may be said to have served his noviciate under me."

After some further promotion of his own medical talents and enquiring mind, Arthur turned again to his fellow student J.B.

" ... whether he had an innate abhorrence of any thing like severe mental exertion, I cannot well say; but he cordially embraced the empirical system, and scrupulously observed the most rigid of its tenets ... read little, and reflected less ..."

Having cast as many more aspersions as he could think of, Arthur turned his acerbic wit on John's brother Thomas, who was destined for the church.

"He early evinced an inordinate passion for theatrical representations, and once performed the part of Douglas in Lerwick, with a company of strolling players."

And if that were not enough to undermine his fitness for the cloth, Arthur noted that he also served for a time as a reporter on *The Times*!

"These pursuits, it must be admitted were not the best calculated to advance his knowledge in theology."

However, Arthur's opinion of Thomas Barclay was not shared by others and Thomas did become the parish minister in Lerwick and later went on to become Principal of Glasgow University. Before then, however, Thomas Barclay was going to get his own back on Arthur.

In 1832, a couple of years after Arthur had been forced by his economic circumstances to move into a small apartment of three rooms and a kitchen in the barracks at Fort Charlotte in Lerwick, he and his housekeeper/mistress Laura Irvine fell out with one of his neighbours, Alexander Riach, "... my turbulent and deceitful neighbour ... low base, ill bred son of an Aberdonian Garter ...", a purser in the Royal Navy, and accused Riach's "intemperate strumpet...",[20] of a servant, Marion Fraser, of defamation of character.[21] Fraser replied the next day with a complaint to the Procurator Fiscal, James Greig, that "... without any cause whatsoever, [Arthur and Laura Irvine] conceived a deadly malice, hatred and ill will against ... and actually beat, bruised and otherwise maltreated [Marion Fraser]"[22]

As a result Arthur was fined £10 (£590). However, the matter did not rest there and Arthur was fined a further five guineas (£290) the following April for assault and battery on Fraser,[23] and in May, Riach was bound over to keep the peach towards Arthur, whom the latter accused of provocation on more than one occasion. However, it would not be long before they were no longer neighbours.

PART II

DISTANT
COUSINS

CHAPTER EIGHT

HEIRS, TRAVELLERS AND PREACHERS

"And what a day of storms was on the morrow, the wind whistled through the shrouds, the sea even, in this quiet harbour, rolled and roared as if impatient to burst the bounds of land, and as the sun went down the gale increased and blew with a tenfold fury."

Edward Charlton (1814-1872)

Laurence and family

Two weeks after the birth of Charles and Mary's fifth son, Thomas (1825-1874), in Charleston, almost 6500 km away on the other side of the Atlantic and 30 degrees further north, on the 20th September, in the Haa at Buness, Laurence's wife Eliza, gave birth to another Thomas (1825-1846). It was to be the first of Eliza's eleven confinements.

In Charleston the temperature was still topping 30°C but at Buness it was barely half that. Nevertheless, September could be a pleasant month in Shetland, especially if it had been a good *far haaf* season and the rents and shops' bills were paid. The *sixerns* would now be turning to inshore fishing for ling, others would be hauled up for the winter and their crews taking to their smaller *fourareens*. Stacks of peat – cut by the men early in the season, dried and brought down from the *scattald* by the women by pony or in *kishies* on their own backs – would be standing at the side of every cottage. Hay, for winter feed, would already be stacked by the byres, but in the *rigs* groups of neighbours from the township would still be cutting bere or oats in some fields, while in others they would be bringing in the scattered *stooks* to build into large *skroos* by the already built haystacks. The gates in the hill-dyke would still be closed and the cattle out on the *scattald*, but with only the potatoes to lift and thoughts of the long winter still distant, there would be a feeling of gentle satisfaction. For the tenants, there was plenty more work to come but it would be mainly in and around the cottage and byre. For Thomas, the rents would be in the bank along with a good return from the chromate, which could now be stockpiled until the weather settled again in the spring and boats could safely make the passage to the north isles and Balta Sound. Then, of course, there was the child, another Thomas, whom Laurence saw as a future heir to Buness.

There was much celebration in the family as Tom, as he was to become known, was the first male to be born in Buness for almost 100 years and Mally, at 74, at last had a grandson in her old family home. A few weeks after Tom's birth – just as long as the post took to come from Charleston – all at Buness heard of the delightful coincidence of the birth of Yankee Tom, as *he* was later to become known. In naming his first son Thomas, Laurence was acknowledging his trust in his brother and the support he had received since he was a youth.

Surgeons Square.

All was not as it seemed, however. Two years later, in 1827, while Laurence was finishing his medical training in Edinburgh as part of his agreement with Thomas and Eliza and Tom were still living at Buness, unbeknown to him, Thomas wrote a will.[1] Though verbally he had promised Laurence the inheritance and had promised to put it in writing for him, the will identified Thomas' illegitimate daughter Ursula *and* Laurence as joint executors and heirs, and only if Ursula produced no heirs would the estate go to Laurence in its entirety. In the will, Thomas acknowledged his American nephew Yankee Tom, leaving him £200 (£11,400) and £100 (£5700) each to his brothers Arthur and Henry, as well as free rent and annuities to his mother, his sister Mary, who never left Unst, and Sinclair Bruce. He also planned to leave a small annuity to his right-hand man, Peter Sutherland. In the meantime, Laurence's family lived under his roof which they thought one day would be theirs.

The previous year, in 1826, Laurence was awarded the Silver Medal of the Zoological Society of London for his efforts in the protection of a tiny population of a large, dark and menacing seabird that, literally, had only a toehold in the British Isles. The common name of this bird is the great skua but locally it is known as the *bonxie* (from the Old Norse *bunksi* or thickset person). The breeding site for this bird was on Herma Ness, a *scattald* grazed by the tenants of the Buness estate and the main threats to its survival were the Victorian 'sportsmen' and egg collectors. The *bonxie*, often acting in partnership with its mate, will dive on human intruders to its nesting territory and may even hit them hard with trailing feet or wings. For the sportsmen, this 'courage' was an added and attractive challenge. Only Laurence's protective action, repeated by John Scott of the island of Foula, ensured the survival and expansion of this bird in the British Isles. Today, thanks to them, Shetland holds almost 50 per cent of the world population of this seabird.

Great Skua by William Yarrell.

Laurence finally completed his medical studies in 1830 and returned to settle in Unst and take up his medical practice at the age of 35, when Tom was five and his younger brother,

Biot, three, and when they all still lived in Buness with Thomas, Sinclair Bruce and Ursula, now eleven. Sadly, just as Laurence began *his* medical career his mother, Mally, died at 80 and his brother Henry died in Newcastle at the relatively young age of 50. Although Laurence and his sisters had kept in some contact with Henry ten years previously, there seems to have been little contact with him in his final years.

Laurence returned to Shetland with some trepidation. Even though Thomas had promised him an annuity, he had only a limited number of wealthy subscribers and he still did not know how he was going to support his family. Adding to his unease and frustration was the fact that he could no longer spend the time he used to observing his beloved wildlife: how he must have envied his friend, MacGillivray, who had had the courage to switch from medicine to natural history.

In 1828, so that the principal rooms might look out over Balta and perhaps to accommodate Laurence's growing family, Thomas had built an extension on the east gable of Buness.[2] In July of that year, on his second visit to Shetland, Dr Adam Clarke, the leading Methodist in England who had sent Samuel Dunn to Shetland as a missionary in 1822, visited the Edmondstons at Buness. In the evening a service was held by the invitation of Thomas the laird in Buness, when 150 people attended and filled the ground floor rooms to bursting. Thomas opened a large bible and chose the text at random: "Arise, shine, for thy light is come, and the glory of the Lord is risen upon thee". Dr Clarke[3] then proceeded to extemporise on it for an hour and a quarter without hesitation. Whether or not Thomas agreed with Clarke's religious position he was amazed "for he said [to Dr Clarke] he could not have thought that such a subject could be thus treated at so short a notice." The following day Thomas invited his party for a visit to the chromate quarry at Hagdale. They were told that 200 tons were exported per annum at £4.10s (£256) per ton, half the price it was making a few years earlier, but still giving him an annual income at that time of around £900 (circa £51,200). The Rev. James Everett (1784-1872), who kept a diary of the voyage, recorded the generous dinner they enjoyed later at Buness:

> "The inmates of the domain consisted of Mr Edmondston [Thomas] himself, – a bachelor, – a maiden sister [Mary*], – Mr L. Edmondston, his good lady [Eliza] … and three or four lovely children … We had a genuine English dinner. Among the more prominent eatables and drinkables in these barren regions presented to the palate, may be named, smoked hung beef, roasted and

Dr Adam Clarke.

89

embedded in cabbage, – curried chicken, accompanied with boiled rice, half a Zetland sheep, roasted, little larger than a well-grown lamb, – potatoes, – Ling, – Peas' Soup, – Rhubarb Pie – Custards etc.; – Whiskey, wines, etc …"[4]

*The brothers' sister Mary now lived at Marypark, a small house Thomas had built for her at Baltasound.

The children they met were Tom (3), Biot (1) and of course Ursula (9). It is indicative of Ursula's position in the household that, even as an illegitimate daughter, she was allowed into society. Everett's choice of words suggest that either he was unaware that Ursula was not Eliza's child or that he chose to be diplomatic.

Thomas was so moved by Dr Clarke's perorations that he resolved to do something concrete for him. Hearing that he was seeking land on which to build a Methodist chapel, Thomas visited him a day or so later on the *Henry* and, having a mind to the value of his chromate, made him an offer.

"Dr Clarke, you shall have as much ground as you want; even an acre, if you please, with the reservation of the minerals; and should it ever cease to be a place of worship, that the land shall revert to the original owner, he giving the fair value of the premises as they may be found; the value to be estimated by two indifferent persons chosen by each party."[5]

It was a generous gift which Dr Clarke took up with alacrity at the time, but upon which he never acted.

All was not as well at Buness as it seemed to the visitors, however. Even though Thomas had built on an extension there was not room for two families, or perhaps two mistresses of the household, Sinclair and Eliza. In addition, the latter was not reconciled to living in the same house as her illegitimate niece. The curious, if not unhealthy, relationship between Laurence and his elder brother was also under strain and they took to communicating serious matters by letter. It was inevitable that Laurence and his growing family would have to live elsewhere and plans were therefore made for a permanent residence for them close by Buness.

Laurence was in a quandary. Thomas had offered him an annual "*benefaction*", as he called it. Desperately wanting to keep as much independence from him as possible, Laurence had at first refused this, believing he and his family could survive on his income from subscribers if they lived "*parsimoniously*". However, with some bitterness, he wrote to Thomas in 1831 that because of the –

"… *unjust and treacherous conduct towards me of many in this island who first induced me to settle in it then, without cause introduced medical competition and became hostile to me …*"[6]

– it had made it necessary for him to take the offer of his brother's financial help. The medical competition that Laurence spoke of was in the form of Thomas' friend, Dr Basil Spence, who had taken up a practice covering Unst, before later moving to Lerwick: Laurence was becoming paranoiac. He believed that other former subscribers had deliberately established Dr Spence's practice and that his brother Thomas had forgotten his promise to support him, although he had just told him that he thought he could manage without it. As it was, Thomas was not in a hurry to press the annuity on him.

In an extraordinary response to Laurence a few years later, Thomas revealed a self-awareness of his faults and the most singular relationship between the two brothers. The letter revealed the most fundamental fears and anxieties of Laurence, painting a picture of a man who, although he was much-travelled, privileged and accomplished, and who on the surface appeared enlightened and erudite, was emotionally fragile and completely lacking in self-confidence.

> "*If the ground has been cut from under your feet* [writes Thomas] *by unlooked for opposition in your profession, thus diminishing or in a great measure destroying your hopes of independence, this is no fault of yours nor has it been brought about by any incompetence, misconduct, misdemeanour on my part ... the great error in all you have written on the peculiar subject under discussion* [the annuity] *is, that you wish to make a man, or more properly* myself *what I ought to be, not satisfied with what unfortunately* I am *... From the first moment I saw you as a child of 2 or 3 in this house in your mother's arms my heart yearned towards you with more than a brother's love ... There were five brothers of us, you the youngest. It is as I have said about 17 years since you returned to this country, a man ... but you were received by your oldest brother* before you had offended him *... getting the shelter of his roof ...*"[7]

Laurence partly blamed his father for the financial situation he was in, having received no inheritance which might have secured him financially. Thomas went on in his letter to explain to Laurence that their father's funds had been much reduced by helping his eldest sons, "*... thus depriving you of your proportion ...* [while I] *never diminished his funds a shilling in my life*", conveniently forgetting that he was the one who had inherited the Buness estate and had therefore no need of funds from his father. He also conveniently forgot that Laurence had done much for him in establishing a market for the chromate that was making him a small fortune and that it was he who had encouraged Laurence to come to Unst in the first place.

Laurence felt like a rejected son – of Thomas – burning with unrequited love. In *his* letter he had poured out the hurt it was causing him that he was going to have to live in a separate house from him. In his reply, an exasperated Thomas began, "*For Heaven's sake my dear brother ...*" going on to remind him that he was a married man and had to live separately! This letter of 39 foolscap pages concluded with Thomas expressing his love for Laurence's family and reminding him how he had looked after them during Laurence's absence when he was in Edinburgh completing his medical training.[8]

The year after Laurence returned to Buness and the same year he found that he faced medical competition on Unst, his brother Arthur, despite his impoverished circumstances, continued *his* production of private publications with a pamphlet entitled – *A brief inquiry into the nature and causes of the cholera which has prevailed, and at present prevails, in the Russian armies* (1831) in which he concluded that the army must have picked up the cholera campaigning in Turkey; unaware that cholera had already arrived in Britain that very year. His second publication of that year, in his Mr Hyde mode this time, was a general attack on the directors of General Zetland Library which he himself had been instrumental in establishing. As was often the case with Arthur's pamphlets it was not entirely clear what the actual point was he was trying to make, although there is no doubt he had it in for them! Arthur described the proceedings at a directors' meeting that followed an encounter with of one of them in the Street:

"The first speaker had not finished, when another Director rose, and asked me [Arthur] in a confident, but hurried manner, whether it was correct in me, to tell a Director in the street, instead of selecting a private parlour for that purpose, that I intended to expose them all in biographical sketches; and he added repeatedly, with a significant nod, 'Begin with your own biography, Doctor, and be sure to leave room for marginal notes.' And, in corroboration of the truth of this gossip, he stated, that I had said in a shop that I would trample them (the Directors) under my feet, as I had done 'the Barclays'."*[9]

*This last sentence being a reference to his character assassination of John and Thomas Barclay the previous year.

In January of that year, back in Buness, Eliza gave birth to their third child, Jane Mary (1831), but she only lived until April. The following year she gave birth to Mary (1832-1898) and the next year, Laurence and Eliza moved out of Buness into the new house nearby, but not before they met a couple of travellers from the south.

Sportsmen, cholera and the *Haaf* Disaster of 1832

The two visitors to Shetland in 1832 both recorded vivid descriptions of their adventures. The first was an ironmaster, George Clayton Atkinson (1808-1877)[10] and the second, Edward Charlton (1814-1872)[11], a student, later to become a well-known doctor in the north-east of England. Atkinson came in May, Charlton in July and both met up with the Edmondstons in Lerwick and Unst. Each, in his way, symbolised the itinerant Victorian tourists who sought out the remote and romantic parts of Scotland. The former was an unrepentant 'sportsman' while the latter had broader interests in natural history, Norse culture and antiquities.

Atkinson, on his way north with two companions, first called on his friend William MacGillivray in Edinburgh, "… a man of more information and that of greater variety, than any other man I know, and as modest as men of true merit generally are …" MacGillivray was then still curator of the Museum at the Royal College of Surgeons and gave Atkinson a letter of introduction

The topsail schooner Magnus Troill *by P. Henderson.*

to Laurence in Unst. Atkinson procured another letter of introduction from Patrick Neill in Canonmills and in this letter Neill informed Laurence of a terrible scourge that was abroad in Edinburgh. This was the first epidemic of cholera in Britain, a disease that had been working its way westward from India via trading ships, arriving in England in 1831 and in Edinburgh at the end of January 1832.

In Leith, Atkinson and his friends joined a topsail schooner of 134 tons, the *Magnus Troill* – the one named after Scott's character in *The Pirate* – which was the regular vessel for Shetland. They left Leith on the 18th May and due to weather of 'complacent serenity' did not get to Peterhead, only 200 km to the north, until the morning of the 21st. After that the wind picked up a little and to amuse themselves they got out their rifles and shot a few seabirds on the water and on the wing.

When Atkinson and company arrived in Bressay Sound they were eager to get ashore and get on with their sporting activities and were therefore very indignant to find that the vessel was to be quarantined for five days because of the cholera outbreak in Edinburgh. Eventually they got off and ten days later, on the 3rd June, they arrived in Unst and met up with Laurence and Thomas at Buness. Atkinson's comments on both brothers were quite perceptive:

> "This gentleman [Laurence] with his wife and three children, live with the squire, as he would be called in England, who is a burly good-natured man of between fifty and sixty and heartily welcomed us to his house: the first objects which presented themselves on our entrance indicated pursuits congenial to some of our own; for over the chimney piece hung three heavy but well-appointed guns, which looked like rifles but which we afterwards found had been changed from that to smooth-bores: interspersed with these, were the usual accompaniments of flasks, cleaning rods, belts etc., but what we contemplated with much greater interest [were] several gigantic seal skulls with holes in them …"

Over the next four days Atkinson and his companions made outings on their own. The first was to a loch where "… we attained an island in the middle, on which the Red throated diver or Rain Goose [*rain-gös*] breeds, for the eggs of which we found our visit too early." The second was to the seabird cliffs of Herma Ness by boat with both Laurence and Thomas, where "we fired Mr Edmondston's gun at them [guillemot, puffin and kittiwake] once or twice, ate some bread and cheese, drank some whiskey, and then returned to Burra Firth."

In the evenings they talked of many things including Thomas' travels to London and his meeting and conversation with the most distinguished man of the time, whom he had come to regard as his hero; the Duke of Wellington, then the Prime Minister (1828-1830).

> "After various endeavours to satisfy himself [Thomas] by public views of him [Wellington], & wishing to possess some more exclusive knowledge of him, he determined to write & request an interview, candidly adding in his note that he had no business to bring before his grace, but entertained such a sincere esteem for his character as a soldier & as a Statesman,

Duke of Wellington presented by him to Thomas Edmondston.

93

that he was very desirous of being enabled to exchange a few words with him before his departure for a most remote part of Great Britain."

Wellington tried to brush off his ardent fan but Thomas persevered and to Atkinson's astonishment Thomas got an appointment to call at Downing Street the following day at noon. According to Thomas, they conversed about Shetland, its population and trade and Wellington concluded the visit with "I knew a countryman of yours in India, an excellent officer and a good man" and bowed Thomas from the room. Thomas later sent Wellington some mineral specimens from Shetland and visited him at his home where Wellington gave him a signed portrait. They continued a correspondence for some time, of which Thomas was very proud. The association with this man undoubtedly increased the genial Thomas' belief in his own self-importance.

Most of Atkinson's discussions with Thomas, however, were about their mutual interest in shooting. Thomas had shown him the two pairs of the rare *bonxies* nesting on Herma Ness and in his journal, Atkinson noted, and deplored, that a previous sporting visitor, one Robert Dunn (1797-1859), after obtaining information from gentlemen such as Thomas on the localities for the *bonxies*, had "as nearly as he could, extirpated the rare kinds. It is un-necessary to say he was not a gentleman." But then went on to describe *his* own reaction to finding *bonxies* elsewhere, outwith the company of Thomas or Laurence: "… we had no sooner reached the region [Ronas Hill] of their nests, than one of them sailed fearlessly within a score of yards of our heads & met its doom immediately."! Atkinson recorded that Thomas was a great sportsman and, in the way sportsmen are impressed by the size and number of their quarry, noted:

"… as the islands present but little game … he [Thomas] confines himself to the more noble diversions of Whale and Seal shooting, in both which pursuits he is the most skilful man in Shetland – in fact the only one who takes any trouble about it: last year he killed forty two seals; two of which were Haaf fish, as the Shetlanders call the great, or Bearded seal, and one of them weighed upwards of 900 lbs …"

The *haaf* fish Atkinson refers to are grey or Atlantic seals that are numerous in the exposed waters of Shetland. The other 40 seals that Thomas had shot were the smaller harbour seals, also numerous in the islands, but that prefer the more sheltered inshore waters.

Thomas also regaled Atkinson with the story of how once, by shooting the leading animal, he had diverted a school of pilot whales that had come into Balta Sound onto the shore of his land when it looked as if they would be driven by their pursuers onto another landowner's shore! By doing this and obtaining his one-third share as landowner, Thomas

Robert Dunn at Ronas Hill from The Ornithological Guide to the islands of Orkney and Shetland.

claimed he had made £50 (£2950) on the one shot: an indication of just how valuable was the landowner's claim to beached whales!

Atkinson and his two companions returned south to Leith on the *Magnus Troill* in June. On her return journey northwards on the 7th July, she carried Edward Charlton, a young man who had just completed his first year of medical studies. He described her only accommodation: "The main cabin, about 12ft. by 8ft., had to contain as constant residents, not less than nine gentlemen, and at dinner, ladies and all, we mustered twenty-one." Four days later, in heavy mist, they arrived off Sumburgh Head, the most southerly point of Shetland, and there Charlton got his first sight of Shetland fishermen manning the elegant six-oared *yoal* that was designed for fishing in those treacherous tidal waters. Charlton recorded his first impressions:

> "… on a sudden, as I was leaning over the bow, two yawls full of strange-looking mortals, broke through the mist, pulled astern of the ship without hailing, and disappeared in the driving fog … I shall never forget the impression their strange garb made upon me. Dressed in their skin coats and breeches, with their nether limbs encased in high boots, they rather resembled the pictures we have seen of some of the Esquimaux tribes, though having since had an opportunity of comparing these strange garments, I must confess those of Shetland to be decidedly inferior in point of manufacture … the long fair hair of the Shetlanders, escaping in coils down upon their shoulders from beneath their large pendant caps of variegated worsted … [their] boats, extremely sharp at both ends, with an extraordinary spring fore and aft …"

Later that day, when the *Magnus Troill* entered Bressay Sound, Charlton and the rest of the passengers and crew found themselves quarantined like Atkinson before them. Then it was discovered that a passenger in the forecastle was ill and Charlton became witness to the terror there was of the cholera, even by medical men. The captain sent to Dr Spence in Lerwick the following day, but *he* excused himself, saying it was not necessary to come. The next day, Dr R. C. Cowie, author of *Shetland: Descriptive and Historical* (1871), although not a medical doctor, and Dr John Barclay came on board but the man's condition had worsened. "The great Barclay a little round dull heavily paunchy creature descended the ladder looked for a few minutes at the countenance of poor Robertson then turned again to the hatchway and scrambled up again on deck with most wondrous agility"; such description suggesting that perhaps Arthur had had some reasons after all for his antipathy to the man! The crew of the *Magnus Troill*, meanwhile, slept on deck for fear of catching cholera, if that is what it was. Charlton, very nobly, stayed with the patient and the three doctors made another visit, "… one of whom ventured no further than the gangway, the second looked down the fore-hatchway upon the face of the dying wretch, and but one, Dr Cowie (the non-medical one!) [the medical one was Dr Isaac Cowie (1804-1847)] descended to his bedside."

The passenger died that evening and upon hearing the news the Lerwick magistrates held a council, ordered the vessel to raise a yellow flag, placed her under martial law and condemned all on board to another ten days' quarantine. The doctors refused to come aboard to open the body, "… nor would the magistrates allow the only man of talent in Lerwick, Dr Arthur Edmondston, to perform the necessary duty" and verify the cause of death. Without, therefore, finding out if the man had actually died of cholera, the corpse was sewn up in heavy canvas with stones for weights and dropped into the sea.

Charlton was then to experience just how quickly and fatally the weather can change in Shetland, even in July, at the height of summer. On Monday when the passenger died it had been a day "… unruffled by a breath of wind", but during the night the wind got up:

"And what a day of storms was on the morrow, the wind whistled through the shrouds, the sea even, in this quiet harbour, rolled and roared as if impatient to burst the bounds of land, and as the sun went down the gale increased and blew with a tenfold fury."

The 17th July, 1832, was not the first day that a Shetland *haaf* crew in their *sixern* were to be lost at sea in a gale, but it was the first time such a tragedy was to engulf so many families at one time. Nearly all the *haaf* boats on the east side of Shetland were caught out by the suddenness of the deterioration in the weather and the day was to be known for a long time to come as the day of '*da grit gale*'. Charlton pieced together the whole story and described what happened around the *Magnus Troill* that day as she strained at her anchor in Bressay Sound while the wind howled through the rigging. It was to be one of the most moving accounts of the dangers of *haaf* fishing and the skills of the fishermen ever written; an industry upon which the tenant-fishermen were dependent and upon which merchants, and landowners like Thomas, relied as a source of much of their wealth.

"Suddenly, a [*haaf*] boat was seen approaching 'The Swan' cutter, then alongside us. For a moment it was visible topping the foaming waves, and then disappeared on the other side of the cutter … Immediately after communicating with the boat the cutter slipped her cable, and carrying all the sail she dared, swept out of the south entrance of the harbour … we soon learned that sixty boats of six men each were missing from the eastern shore of Shetland … By means of the telescope we could see that the whole town was in a state of commotion … Presently a Dutch herring buss sailed in with two boats' crews she had rescued. Another Dutchman passed them, which was hailed, 'Six boats' crews on board and many seen bottom upwards …' A few more Dutch herring busses came in with some boats' crews on board … Wednesday, July 18 dawned, and the storm was unabated … One of the first objects that met my eye on issuing from the cabin was a six-oared boat driving gallantly through the north entrance of the harbour. She had saved the crew of another boat that had been swamped alongside her … It was a really beautiful and anxious sight to watch these poor fellows, of whom eight were lying at the bottom of the boat, one managed the helm and the other three trimmed the sail, as the boat dashed on through the heavy surf. As every white squall approached dashing up the spray like sleet into the air, we saw the sail lowered and then cautiously raised again … An old skipper and his crew of young lads … did not reach Fair Isle till the Saturday, [sailing] on one tack for thirty-six hours … ere they came in sight of that island … they were almost lifted out of the boat by the inhabitants of Fair Isle. Those poor fellows had taken with them no other provision than their customary scanty stock of meal and water for three days, and this they had consumed upon the Thursday morning, having been out from the Monday previous on the open sea."

The gale lasted for several days and some of the *haaf* boats were blown almost all the way to Norway. But the most extraordinary story of that great tragedy:

A gaff-rigged trader perhaps beating into Balta Sound by Henry Saxby.

"… was the account brought by the *Norna** of an American outward-bound vessel, which had hailed them when running before the wind, to the effect that she had five boat's crew [of a *sixern*] on board."

*104 ton topsail schooner that ran between Leith and Shetland.

These five men, the sixth having been lost while climbing to safety up the side of the American vessel when the *sixern* smashed down upon him, then crossed the Atlantic and did not return to Shetland until six months later, in January 1833. For all those six long months the families of the crew did not know who the man was who was lost and could only wait and hope that he was not theirs.

When the reckoning came at the end of that terrible event there were found to be 18 boats, including five from Unst, and their crews lost; 105 fishermen drowned. In many cases small communities lost the best of their men, grandfathers, fathers, brothers and sons, without whom their families could not support themselves. Four were recorded as "much in debt"; 30 recorded as leaving dependants "destitute, very poor", or "aged in poverty"; five left relations "in tolerable circumstances"; 40 "not married".[12]

97

After these dramatic events Charlton perambulated around Shetland noting its natural history and collecting geological and archaeological specimens. In Unst he "Called at Buness and met there with Dr [Laurence] Edmondston, a well-informed man, but who appears sadly out of his element there": an indication of the frustration of a gifted man who had hoped for better things when he returned to Unst. After three months in Shetland, Charlton had a stormy passage himself on the *Magnus Troil* on his return journey to Leith. Two years later he returned for a second visit, but one that was rather dull when compared to the first.[13]

After a decade or more of rising prosperity, the 1830s was a period of difficulty and change for the fishing industry and the Shetland people when the lack of capital began to show. It began with several poor years for the cod and *haaf* fishery that dragged small businesses under and concentrated those that survived in fewer hands, benefiting the larger businesses such as Hay & Ogilvy. After that first great *haaf* disaster, the company unsuccessfully adopted the mother-ship approach that was tried before, in the 1790s, and that had also been advocated by Thomas the laird. Coinciding with the poor fishing were poor years at the Greenland whaling. Then, to cap these problems, there followed several years of poor harvests from 1835 to 1838.

A saving grace at the time was the herring industry that reached a peak in the middle of the decade. Of the 200 or so small and half-decked herring boats, half belonged to Hay & Ogilvy who exported the fish to Spain and to the West Indies to feed the slaves on the plantations there. However, the Spanish put a tax on the herring imports, reducing that market, and then insisted that fish could only be delivered to Spain by Spanish vessels. This coincided, in 1833, with the abolition of slavery in the British Isles and the colonies, causing the collapse of the West Indies market. Finally, in 1840, there was a disastrous herring season and debts that the Shetland Bank had incurred to the Royal Bank of Scotland forced the latter to withdraw its credit and stop payments. In 1842, the Shetland Bank and Hay & Ogilvy, the largest and most successful businesses in Shetland, went under and the former half, the friend of Thomas, William Hay, was declared bankrupt. Although there was destitution in Lerwick and Scalloway where many fish workers were concentrated, those in the country areas, who could grow some of their own food, fared better.

On the positive side, and on a national level, in 1832 the first of the Reform Acts enfranchised the industrial cities, although it only extended the vote to those with property. Nevertheless, the aristocrats who dominated parliament, and many landowners, including Thomas, deplored this very limited democratic development. The first parliamentary election under the Reform Act followed in Shetland in 1835 and in that year also began the first proper postal service between Lerwick and Peterhead, with Hay & Ogilvy's *Fidelity* making a regular nine-day round trip. A year later another vessel belonging to another company took over the run and she, with her two cabins, was the first on the North Isles' route to be adapted especially for passengers. Then, in 1838, came the penultimate improvement to the service between Shetland and the Scottish mainland with the very first, albeit summer only, steam service provided by the paddle-steamer *Sovereign*. It was not until 1861, however, that there was a screw-driven steamer capable of providing a year-round service.

In 1837, Queen Victoria began her long reign and shortly afterwards a Shetlander, Arthur Anderson (1792-1869), presented her with fine and beautiful examples of Shetland's now-famous knitwear, which up to then was hardly known outwith the islands. In that same year, Anderson, one of Shetland's most notable sons and its greatest benefactor, who had petitioned hard for the introduction of the *Sovereign*, turned his attention, after many years' absence from the islands, to

Sovereign *photographed by G. Robertson.*

setting up the, ultimately unsuccessful, Shetland Fishery Company on the island of Vaila in West Mainland that was intended to provide an alternative market for the *haaf* fishermen. The year previously Anderson had also set up the first Liberal-supporting paper in Shetland, the *Shetland Journal*. Anderson, who was born just outside Lerwick and who had started his working life as a beachboy among drying fish, eventually worked his way up from midshipman in the British Navy to become a co-founder of the Peninsular and Oriental Company (P&O). He was later to come to political blows with Arthur.

CHAPTER NINE

FATHER, SON AND MORE VISITORS

"Dr Edmondston brought his two sons on board to see our remaining Reindeer. The eldest is a particularly intelligent boy, passionately fond of Natural History."

Dr William Dawson Hooker (d1840)

Halligarth

In the autumn of 1832, Laurence and family moved into Halligarth, a small two-storey, dormer-windowed house that Thomas had built for them not much more than a stone's throw from Buness. Thomas also provided finance for Laurence to establish a garden, for the new building sat unadorned in the middle of the small arable fields on the periphery of the home farm. What he did not do, however, was pass over the deeds of the property to Laurence, although he did not charge him rent. Laurence was not particularly concerned by this at the time because, of course, he understood that Thomas would one day leave the whole estate to him anyway. If anyone had misgivings it was Eliza. Thomas' motivations for holding onto the deeds were fairly straightforward; as a landowner he was reluctant to part with any property and it gave him some control over Laurence whom he appeared to regard as not fully mature. Halligarth was to be the home of Laurence and his family for almost 50 years, a home of both great happiness and tragedy and where the children received from their parents, particularly their father, a very unusual and radical upbringing for the age.

Despite his depressed state, in having to leave the house of his brother, their deteriorating relationship and his precarious financial situation, Laurence brought a great deal of enthusiasm to the family's new home. Both Thomas and Arthur were very aware of the benefits of shelter that could be gained around a house and garden in almost treeless Shetland. They had both planted trees around their own houses, the former, with the encouragement of Laurence, but unsuccessfully, and the latter spectacularly successfully. Laurence had been involved in Thomas' selection of trees and he now applied the experience to Halligarth. Not that everyone thought that Shetland necessarily needed trees. J. B. Biot, reflecting on the tranquillity he had found in Shetland, had noted: "If they had only trees and sun, no residence could be more delicious, but if they had trees and sun, all the world would wish to be there, and there would be tranquillity no longer."[1]

Many years later, a daughter of Laurence's described the Halligarth of her childhood:

"The house stood on a gentle slope, overlooking [Balta Sound] … Behind rose a tiny range of hills, whose varied peaks resemble those of the Cheviots. The house was … small and unpretending … but nevertheless, a stranger would have his attention attracted to it before all

Halligarth by Henry Saxby.

others, because its lawn and garden were surrounded by more than a hundred species of shrubs and trees … Every tree was planted by the Naturalist [Laurence] himself … He watched their growth with the fostering care of a parent …"[2]

In addition to an avenue of shrubs and trees that he planted in front of the house, fully exposed to the Shetland sea winds, Laurence took the precaution of planting a half-acre copse within the shelter of a 2 metre high stone dyke. In this situation the trees – particularly sycamore – flourished, forming a dome rising from the height of the wall around its circumference to a peak at its centre that, some 170 years later still survives as one of the most northerly pieces of woodland in the British Isles. Laurence extended his horticultural experiments into agriculture. Unfortunately, though not through lack of scientific approach, these experiments were failures as a means to supplement their income, principally because the fields were too small and Laurence entirely lacked a practical or commercial approach such as would have been taken by his hard-headed brothers, Thomas or Charles.

At Buness, Thomas, following the trends of agricultural progress, began enclosing regularly-sized fields, of six or seven acres, by dykes. He strongly disapproved of Laurence's agricultural experiments, his opinions surfacing a decade later in 1847, when the brothers had one of their, seemingly annual, disputes over the annuity. Thomas, even though he had promised it in 1818, sometimes either forgot to pay it or deliberately did not pay it, so that Laurence was obliged to go begging to him. Thomas then took these opportunities to remind Laurence of his extravagant and wasteful use of the allowance, especially in his agriculture experiments. The two, although they still lived a mere five minutes walk from each other, continued to discuss their major disagreements by letter: on Thomas' side these were very lengthy. On one occasion they had had a discussion on which crops should be grown. Thomas had said that the only test of success should be the result, but:

> "*This however gave rise to your* [Laurence's] *usual charge against me* [Thomas] *of not approving of your style of culture of your ground … whenever the subject of farming arises between us I am always found fault with for not approving of your procedure …*"[3]

Thomas went on to say that *he* had used a tried and tested method of cultivation for 40 years which Laurence had never tried. It irritated him that Laurence thought *his* results were superior. He pointed out that all Laurence's quarrying and trenching for drainage had been done on land that had been worked for generations, so it was impossible to say which method was the better. Then he twisted the knife by suggesting that Laurence's allowance was simply being used to line the pockets of others, by which he meant all the labour Laurence employed to carry out his agricultural 'experiments'. It irked Thomas that the cash he was giving his younger brother, even though he had promised it as part of the agreement, was being 'wasted'.

None of this, however, touched the growing family at Halligarth, to which Jessie (1834-1841), David (1837-1884) and Isabella (1839-1923) were added by the late 1830s and who remembered their childhood at Halligarth as a time of great joy and delight. In fact, they had quite an extraordinary upbringing, for Laurence and Eliza both took a very liberal attitude to the raising of their many children and a very keen interest in their education, development and happiness, "Although his [Laurence] manner was grave, almost to severity, he loved to see others happy."[4]

Halligarth became Laurence's retreat from the world, into which he poured his energy, creativity and love. He liked nothing better than to stroll around his small domain, checking the progress of his trees and listening to the woodland birds that homed-in on the little copse, like thirsty animals to an oasis. On his walks he was greeted and followed by a menagerie of animals, farm stock, pets, and wild birds raised from eggs or rescued and restored to health, all of whom he fed from his bulging pockets of leftovers from the last meal. He was accompanied by:

> "… the … Skye-terrier … Rough, who had lost one eye … one or two cats … an ox [who] would appeal for a caress … while a pony would be shoving its frowsy brow against its master's shoulder … a splendid gamecock usually stalked dignifiedly by the Naturalist's side … A flock of pigeons would hover over his head, sometimes alighting on any available part of his person. A hooded crow … some ducks … Even gulls and cormorants sometimes helped to swell the throng."[5]

This was the real Laurence, the humble and intelligent man who loved all the creatures of God's world, who would:

"... effect a disappearance by simply stretching himself at full length in a field of grass ... where the corncrake delighted to nest and over which the skylark loved to pour his melody ... [a daughter] would at times invade his solitude, and she always found him gazing straight into the sky, or watching the movements of some insect creeping among the surrounding grasses."[6]

Here at Halligarth, Laurence tried to forget about his financial vulnerability and the regular arguments with his brother and benefactor. Here, he fed his hungry brain, immersing himself in all the branches of natural science and in agriculture; read and collected books on natural history and Norse mythology, amassed specimens of archaeology and geology, taught himself languages, played the violin and kept up with the politics and medical progress of the day. The inside of the house was as crammed with an assemblage of oddments, books and boxes, as the outside with pets and plants, as his brain with knowledge, schemes and plans.

"Over the mantelpiece hung useless flintlock fowling-pieces ... a variety of weapons in use among savage tribes ... bunches of quills; clusters of pony-hair, that were very suggestive of scalp-locks; some queer stones, fossils, and pretty shells. On the mantelpiece itself were books of every description, rising tier on tier, all well thumbed, yet frequently covered with dust ... The sideboard was crowded with medicine bottles and the chemical apparatus of his profession ... Besides that parlour, where he usually sat, the Naturalist possessed what his children called a den. A den it truly was ... There is a tradition in the family that once the piled-up heaps were overturned, and a plough was discovered which had been missing for years. In one corner of this den there hung a skeleton ... one shelf contained medicine bottles out of number, with brown-paper parcels, bones and boxes."[7]

There was also the parcel with a portion of Burke's skin! And the collections did not just fill the parlour and Laurence's den, for:

"... somewhere in the mysterious space in the roof was stored for some years a collection of stuffed animals, the gifts of well-known naturalists. These creatures were periodically put out on the lawn to air; and a queer sensation they produced there."[8]

Such macabre curios gave rise to local gossip earning Laurence a reputation among the credulous for dabbling with the occult.

Such was Laurence's world in which his children were raised. He was a wonderful father, a father who encouraged them to have as many pets as they wished – there were usually two or more dogs of different breeds, an unlimited number of cats, once an otter, twice a seal and numerous kinds of birds including seabirds, starling, crow, merlin, sparrow-hawk, peregrine and even a snowy owl. Laurence took the children out on natural history rambles and found the time to explain to them not just his artefacts, stuffed specimens and the living creatures of his world, but his theories for their existence and particularly their place and meaning in God's great plan. His daughter, Jessie M. E., later said of him that: "The first thing he did when coming down in the morning was to read and meditate over a chapter in the Bible. After that he read a dictionary!"[9] Biot described his father as a student of 'Natural Theology'. Laurence also believed that his children could equally well learn from others. When any visiting scientist or naturalist turned up at their door, as they regularly did, Laurence allowed his children in on the adult discussions. He even took them out to the ships that anchored briefly in Balta Sound, on their journeys to and from the northern unknown. In 1827, when Tom was just two years old, Laurence took him onto a ship to meet Captain (later Sir) Edward Parry who was returning from an unsuccessful attempt to reach the North Pole by sledge boat. Though not fully comprehending, Tom was fascinated by the stories of adventure from the great man and in response to their visit, Parry tore one of his prayers, that he daily gave to his crew, out of a notebook and gave it to them.

As a doctor for the northern islands of Shetland, Laurence spent a great deal of time treating the sick and was rowed or sailed between the islands, often in poor weather and at the height of winter if necessary. On these excursions he would take his fowling-piece so that when he had free time he could go out and bag more birds for identification.

Like his brother Arthur, and his father before him, Laurence was a skilful practitioner and did not always charge his poorer patients. On one occasion an Unst man returned from the Greenland whaling with a badly injured leg. Unfortunately, it became gangrenous and Laurence had to amputate and then oversee the patient's recovery. The man, who had been a tailor, had no money to pay Laurence, so it was arranged that he came to Halligarth and returned the service in kind, making shirts for him and repairing his clothes.[10]

Eliza shared Laurence's deep and committed Christianity, but hers was "... of the most unquestioning kind, – childlike in simplicity ..."[11] On Sunday evenings she gathered the family and the servants into her room for her 'preachment' when she read from and expounded on the Scriptures. And it was from her own Bible, on a desk in her room, that Eliza taught her children to read. A room that was a very special place to the children for that was where she spent most of her time. Eliza had had a 'terrible accident'[12] (the details of which were never recorded), which caused her lameness and necessitated the use of a stick for support. She regularly suffered great pain that may have been associated with her lameness and had a large canopied bed which her children later remembered standing around "time out of number" when her pain was at its most severe. That bed was also a refuge for the children when they were ill. However, despite the pain and illness, Eliza had an impulsive and joyous nature and was so full of energy that her children never saw her room as an invalid's retreat where they ought to feel restrained. Eliza's intellectual energy also led her into exploring the myths and legends of the people she had come to live among and into an involvement with the knitters. She encouraged and instructed the women of Unst in their skills and brought in fine foreign examples of lacework.[13] In the 1830s, Arthur Anderson's presentation to Queen Victoria had created an immediate appetite and flourishing market for such goods among London society.

Coming from the south, near Glasgow, into the very different social structure of a Shetland estate, Eliza had brought with her a fairly inflexible attitude to those outside of her class. Referring to the tenants and their families in her book *Sketches and Tales of the Shetland Islands* (1856), she said:

> "The lower class, again, are confidential with their superiors, polite and perfectly respectful in their demeanour towards them. They never presume on familiarity, or seem betrayed into forgetfulness of the difference in rank. This is a favourable and well known trait."

It was a close and loving family at Halligarth. The children all had pet names as well as their baptismal names. The oldest girl Mary was known as *Nye*, the next Isabella was *Tribby* for tribulation, and later ones were *Wildie* for her stubbornness and independence, and *Lalya*. These pet names, closely suiting their characters, were given to them by Laurence and it was not until they had long passed infancy that they were addressed within the family by their baptismal name. Laurence also gave three of their children the baptismal names of predeceased siblings, decisions that upset Eliza who believed in the continuing existence of her dead infants in heaven.

Prodigy

The first seven years of the life of Laurence and Eliza's eldest child Tom had been at Buness with his mother, his uncle Thomas the laird, his cousin Ursula and Sinclair Bruce and, latterly, his younger brother, Biot. During the first five of those years Tom had seen more of his uncle Thomas than his father, who was studying in Edinburgh. By the time he was only 16 months old, intrigued by the stone monument in the garden of Buness that marks the spot of Biot's experiments, he had learned all the letters of the alphabet from his uncle's words engraved on the stone. His mother, naturally, described him as "singularly attractive and intelligent … naturally modest, sweet, and pliable …"[14] Tom had more than the usual thirst for knowledge and was exuberant and mirthful. He was also extremely active and there was an occasion when being implored by his mother to be quiet, he answered "I was never made for stillness mamma." That was an aspect of his character that would predicate his life. Being the first boy-child born in Buness for so many years and having such an endearing personality, Tom had the full attention of all the family and he was spoiled, even though his mother thought it did not turn his head.

It was a year after Captain Parry had stopped in Balta Sound that Dr Adam Clarke, the evangelist, had preached in Buness to a packed living room. Although the three-year-old Tom had had to be removed as he was so restless, when the singing started he was transfixed. By four years old, Eliza said that he:

"… could read any part of the Bible fluently … [and was] captivated with its quaint but nervous phraseology, its sublime poetry, and its matchless narrative."[15]

By six he was writing by copying out on his slate anything he could get an adult to write down for him.

While Eliza devoted herself to encouraging and guiding Tom in his reading and writing, Laurence imbued him with his own passion for natural history, outdoors in the garden and on the shore, and indoors among the books in his den. Tom's first wildlife interest was in birds and at that time his preference, even above all his easier reading books available, was his father's copy of Bewick's *British Birds*. From this beautiful book he copied the illustrations and learned the plumage of all the common birds. Tom was a child to whom the learning of things in which he was interested was a pleasure, but to whom the more mundane side of education was a boring pursuit. From nine to eleven years he received his formal education from his parents and also from the parish schoolmaster – the Rev. John Ingram, son of the Rev. James Ingram the parish minister – in the evenings. After that, he went to the local parish school along with 50-90 other local children, each day, like all the other children, taking a piece of peat for the large fire in the earth-floored schoolroom. There he studied subjects that his uncle Arthur would have approved of such as Latin, Greek, algebra and mathematics, while at the same time teaching himself grammar, elocution, geography and history from books. Having received a standard education of the day up to this point, however, he was not sent south for his secondary education, as were most children of the wealthy and professional classes. This was nothing to do with his health for he had grown into a robust child, nor because of lack of money, for Thomas would have provided it. Laurence rationalised that he kept him home because he could hardly get a better education elsewhere, both his parents being so well educated and enlightened. Then of course, being so close a family, they could not bear to part with him. In reality, this was all partly true, but the principal reason was probably that Laurence recognised something of himself in Tom. The child had great potential and Laurence thought that, with fatherly guidance, he might achieve in natural history what he, Laurence, had failed to do. From then on he put all his love, energies and ambitions into Tom's development.

At the age of nine, in 1834, a close friend of the family suggested that Tom might turn his insatiable curiosity in natural history to botany and this study Tom took up with such alacrity that his father nicknamed him, 'Linne the Little' (after Linnaeus the great Swedish botanist).

Tom's introduction to botany was in the garden where he quickly learned the names of all the common flowers and shrubs that Laurence and Eliza had planted. Then Laurence took him into the most colourful and diverse plant communities around Halligarth and Buness, the ungrazed Shetland hay meadows that awaited the late summer scythe. Tom was overwhelmed; he waded knee-deep through a kaleidoscope of colours – reds, pinks, blues, yellows, greens, violets and whites – of campions, ragged robin, orchids, forget-me-nots, lady's smock, sedges and grasses, horse-tails, vetches, trefoils, knapweed, parsley angelica, all waving in the wind between ditches brimming with the gold of marsh marigold. Here, where stamens and anthers spilled so profusely out of corollas, Tom began to learn about the structure of plants. Then Laurence took him onto the slopes of Nikka Vord behind Halligarth where the sward was tightly grazed by sheep and ponies and

Rev. John Ingram.

where tiny pyramids of eyebrights and heath orchids, needle-slender flax, prostrate tormentil, cat's foot and meadow rue, were dwarfed by ten centimetre heads of self-heal, St John's wort and scabious. It all seemed so easy at first but then he found that the non-flowering plants – grasses, rushes, sedges and ferns, never mind the mosses and the lichens – were just a little more difficult, but he was not discouraged. He brought them home along with the flowers in his vasculum, examined and identified them with the help of his father's magnifying glass and then pressed them for his collection.

Tom's botanical knowledge also came from his father's many books on natural history, while Laurence's 'flora' of Unst – a list of plants he had made a few years earlier[16] – provided a spur and a challenge for Tom; to improve on his father's achievement. Other sources for his general knowledge and appetite for tales of adventure came from the popular journals of the day – the Tory *Blackwood's Magazine* and the newly established *Chambers' Edinburgh Journal* – that were regularly delivered to Halligarth.

Tom the botanist as a child.

But Tom was not just interested in collecting and learning the names of plants and animals. At a very early age he also studied plant classification, a complex subject, even for an adult, that requires a precise knowledge of the characteristic structures of each of the many plant families. Now, he could correctly classify his new discoveries as he botanised all over Unst. On such a small island, only 20 by 8 km, he became a familiar, odd and amusing little figure to the local people and a curiosity to his relatively uneducated peers. As the son of the doctor, a nephew of the Haa, well spoken and well dressed, Tom stood out from his contemporaries. While they ran around in bare feet playing games when they were not doing chores on the croft or the shore, he, self-absorbed, wandered about collecting his specimens of flowers, grasses, seaweeds and shells, rode his pony or went fishing.

It was not long before Tom could tell at a glance what plants he would find at a new site or spot where he and his father had not been before. In 1837, he spent a few days exploring an area of the slopes of Nikka Vord where there were small patches of almost bare ground among the brown outcrops of serpentine. There, after much searching, he collected two little flowering plants scattered very thinly over a large area: he could identify neither.

Even at this early stage in his botanising, Tom had already accumulated a long list of native plants, much longer than his father's, many of which were new records for Shetland. That year, one of the many travellers who called in at Unst and was hospitably entertained at Buness and

Sir William Jackson Hooker by Maull & Co.

Halligarth, was the young botanist, Dr William Dawson Hooker (1816-1840). Dr Hooker was brother of another, more famous botanist, Sir Joseph Dalton Hooker (1817-1911), and both were sons of the eminent botanist, Sir William Jackson Hooker (1785-1865), then Professor of Botany at the University of Glasgow, later the first Director of Kew, whom Laurence had met through the Wernerian Society in Edinburgh in the early 1820s. Dr W. D. Hooker was returning from an expedition to the North Cape when bad weather had forced his ship into the shelter of Balta Sound in early September, just short of Tom's twelfth birthday.

Dr Hooker, conscious of his appearance and state of his clothing after some time exploring in the far north of Norway, wrote in his journal for that day:

> "We had not entered the bay many minutes, when Mr [Thomas] Edmondston, the proprietor of North Unst, and of several other isles, sent us a pressing invitation to come and have breakfast with him, which we gladly accepted, as soon as we heard that no ladies were to be present. So, shaving ourselves, and putting on the most decent clothing that our wardrobe afforded … we went ashore, and met with the kindest reception … When he found out my name he promised to introduce me to his brother, Dr [Laurence] Edmondston, who, several years before, had been acquainted with our family."[17]

The next day Dr Hooker and his companions were taken by Laurence on Shetland ponies to Herma Ness to see the *bonxies*, via the chromate workings.

"Though not a scientific man himself, he [Thomas] thought it a pity that so beautiful and rare a bird should be exterminated by a mercenary set of people, who sometimes come and shoot them in great numbers, for sale in London. This spirited gentleman, who well deserves the thanks of all Naturalists, built therefore a wall across the point where these birds breed, and employs a man to watch that none of them shall be killed*. I am happy to add that his plan promises to succeed perfectly; at first there were but two pairs of Skua Gulls, and now there are twenty."[18]

*Under the influence of Laurence no doubt.

A day later, on the 3rd September:

"Dr Edmondston brought his two sons on board to see our remaining Reindeer. The eldest [Tom] is a particularly intelligent boy, passionately fond of Natural History; I was shown some of his attempts at drawing, highly characteristic of the objects for which they were intended. Since the first edition of this Journal was printed, that is in the autumn of 1837, my father [Sir William Jackson Hooker] received a very interesting communication from Dr Edmondston."[19]

This communication to Sir W. J. Hooker at Glasgow, from Laurence, contained several of Tom's plant specimens, a "remarkable variety" of the sea pea and:

"…an Arenaria, quite new to Britain, the Arenaria Norvegica [arctic sandwort], discovered by his son in Shetland, together with a catalogue of the phnogamous plants of these most northerly islands, the 'Ultima Thule' of the British group. Of this list Mr Edmondston observes, 'imperfect as it may be, it is the only thing like a commencement of a Flora Shetlandica which we have; and it is the production of a boy of eleven years of age, who never attended Botany till within these few months, and who possessed only two books, and had no other assistance whatever.' Under these circumstances, I have thought the catalogue worth inserting, and I trust it will be a stimulus to this young gentleman's future exertions in the cause of Botany."[20]

So, Tom's flora of Unst, and his find of a new plant species for Britain, was included in Dr Hooker's privately published paper of the results of his expedition – *Notes on Norway* (1839). This is the very first known published list of Shetland's plants and it is remarkable that it is by a child of only eleven years! Little did the Hookers realise where their encouragement would lead Tom.

This introduction of Tom's to the professional study of botany could not have been gained from a more influential, supportive and intellectually gifted family of botanists. The previous year Sir W. J. Hooker had published a *Brief Memoir of the Life of Mr David Douglas* (1836), about the intrepid Scottish botanist and explorer from humble origins at Scone, near Perth. Douglas is best remembered for the North American fir tree named after him, but he despatched, and personally brought back to Britain, an incredible number of new species of shrub and tree, principally for the Horticultural Society that funded his expeditions. Douglas (1799-1834) had been an earlier protégé of Sir W. J. Hooker and almost a son to him and the latter perhaps now recognised a similar potential in the young Tom Edmondston. Tragically, however, Douglas had died, under mysterious circumstances, whilst exploring and botanising on the Pacific island of Honolulu in 1834, at the early age of 36.

Tom was, of course, very fortunate in being the son of enlightened, loving and comparatively well-off parents and having the support and encouragement of his wealthy uncle Thomas, the laird, who continued to act as genial host to visiting travellers and scientists to whom Tom was introduced. His political influences were wholly Tory, from his father and Uncle Thomas, and he never got to know his other uncle in Shetland, Arthur, in Lerwick, which was not really surprising considering Arthur's Whig views and outspokenness. Tom was also very fortunate that early in his life he met and struck up a warm relationship with Sir Edward Forbes (1815-1854), the father of

Edward Forbes by Leonard Charles Wyon.

oceanography and friend of, not only Sir W. J. Hooker, but Charles Darwin. Edward Forbes called on Tom's father in the company of John Goodsir (1814-1867), a brilliant anatomist, contributor to the Wernerian Society and Professor of Anatomy at Edinburgh, on a marine dredging expedition in 1839, when Tom was just 14. Forbes was an all-round naturalist who, like Laurence and his brother Arthur, Hibbert and Darwin, had been taught by Robert Jameson at Edinburgh. Both Sir W. J. Hooker and Forbes gave substantial help and encouragement to Tom's future career. But there was yet one other very happy coincidence for the budding botanist.

Tom's first plant list of the most northerly inhabited island of the British Isles contained one highly unusual species, but what was probably of just as much interest to botanists was what was missing – plants that had simply never reached the islands. Sir W. J. Hooker was interested not just in the location of plants but their distribution, so Tom's list, incomplete as it was, was still of great interest and value to him, particularly in relation to his son's list for the North Cape. The list contained far less species than that for the British mainland, but then, no botanist would have expected anything different. Shetland, after all, was covered in ice up to the end of the last Ice Age only 12,000 years previously, and its relative geographical isolation from Britain and the continent ensured a comparatively limited immigration of plants.

Critically for Tom though, there is a plant community on Unst that is almost unparalleled in the British Isles and quite unusual on a world scale. The location for this community is a moon-like desert on the slopes of a headland just above Thomas' chromate quarry at Hagdale, called the Keen of Hamar, only a kilometre distant from Buness and Halligarth. For the botanist, the exceptional nature of the Keen of Hamar lies in the sparsity of its flora. Whereas the plant cover everywhere else in the British Isles (except high on some Scottish mountains) has utterly changed since the retreat of the glaciers and the subsequent development of a temperate climate, the plant cover on the Keen has remained virtually unchanged. Incredibly, in this tiny enclave on Unst, isolated more than 480 km from their nearest relatives on the mountains of Scotland and Norway, some of the plants of the original sparse arctic-alpine cover of this country have survived close to sea level.

In turn, Jameson, Hibbert, Traill and other scientists whom Thomas had taken to view the chromate quarries on the Keen of Hamar, including his brother Laurence, had taken no notice of its plant life, or rather the lack of it, under their feet. Had Forbes' visit to Unst, in 1839, been just a few years earlier, it might have been he that first recognised the significance of the site and its flora. As it was, no one knew of it until it was discovered by a boy!

It would be simplistic to consider the precocious Tom, not as a child but as a kind of young adult, but a diary he briefly kept in 1835 illustrated his quite natural boyishness mixed with a conservative formality and earnestness:

"On the 20th of this month I completed my tenth year, and I feel grateful to God for preserving me so long and I pray Him that he will in future protect me ... I rose in the morning about eight, washed myself, went down stairs and had breakfast; went to Mary Park. Saw both my aunts [Mary and Janet] and sat awhile with them. Came back and wrote a few lines of an index to Chambers' Journal, which, however, I must give up. Spent some time in keeping the crows away from the chickens – my tame crow attracts the wild ones. After dinner went to Swinnaness with Herman [his Shetland pony], got a heavy shower when coming back; saw a splendid rain-bow. [Thursday] Rose at eight, said my prayers, and went down to breakfast. Went an errand to Buness. Biot, little Mary, and me were bidden to dinner, and afterwards Uncle [Thomas] invited Biot and me to stay all night and have a rubber of whist. I won tolerably, and so did Biot. [Friday] Mamma says that this last which I have written is very ill done, both in respect of writing and blots, and that I must try and do it better. I came from Buness after breakfast; went to Swinnaness for Murphy [another pony], and, after dinner, read Natural History to Papa. The Member of Parliament for Orkney and Shetland [George Traill] has been in Buness for these two days, and I have been there almost the whole time."[21]

On Tom's eleventh birthday, Laurence had given him a common place book in which to record things of interest. In the pages of this book Tom revealed the depth of his intelligence and the potential scientist that was in him, even at such an early age. Entries included a very erudite comment on the midge, quotations from Shakespeare, the letters of Publius Lentullus to the Senate of Rome concerning Jesus Christ, Theories of the Earth, the prayer of Charles XII of Sweden to St Nicholas, an account of the equipment of Linnaeus on his botanical tour of Finland and notes on parrots, seals, storks and curiosities he noted from papers and journals and books![22]

This was the child then, who was to discover no fewer than four extremely rare British arctic-alpine plants on the Keen of Hamar. Tom's first discovery, the arctic (or Norwegian) sandwort (*Arenaria norvegica*) – that was included in Dr Hooker's paper on his expedition to Norway – was actually identified for him in 1837 by Dr Gilbert McNab, a visiting botanist.[23] It is hardly surprising that Tom failed to identify this beautiful little plant with its tiny white flowers, since it was unknown in Britain! In 1838, the discovery was credited to Tom in Sir J. D. Hooker's *British Flora*. Tom's second discovery, also identified by another botanist, was the mountain sandwort (*Minuartia rubella*), another small and white-petalled flower that Tom had sent, unknowingly and unidentified, within a collection of plants, to the Botanical Society of Edinburgh in 1840: the botanist William Beeby (1849-1910), who 'discovered' the mountain sandwort on a visit to the Keen of Hamar in 1886, was probably unaware that Tom had already unwittingly collected it nearly 50 years earlier. Alas, the plant was extremely scarce on the Keen of Hamar and by collecting whole specimens, including the roots, as was the fashion in those days, Beeby probably did much to bring about its eventual extermination. Tom's third discovery was the northern rock-cress (*Cardaminopsis petraea*). Today, the first two plants are known only from a handful of sites in Britain, while the third is entirely confined to its mountains.

Rare as these plants were, his discovery of them was as nothing compared with the discovery of *the* plant with which Tom is most closely associated – the Shetland mouse-ear (then *Cerastium arcticum* var. *Edmondstonii* now *Cerastium nigrescens*). This little plant is closely related to the arctic mouse-ear, a circumpolar species, which in Britain occurs on the top of only a very few mountains in Scotland. Although it is of the chickweed family, it is nothing like the garden weed and, unlike the other arctic-alpines of Shetland, its white flower is relatively large and showy, while its leaves are almost purple. Tom's sister, Jessie M. E., many years later, gave one of the best descriptions of her brother's flower:

Tom's mouse-ear on the Keen of Hamar by Bobby Tulloch.

"It has delicate white flowers, finely veined with faint sea-green. Its delicious perfume is as elusive and bewitching as its tints. It blooms on the most sterile ground exposed to bitter winds and salt spray. It lies low on the gravely earth, opening its fragile coronal with a trust and a courage that appeals to the human soul. When you take it in your hand it looks fragile enough to be blown to bits by a breath."[24]

Tom also found this plant when he was eleven!

In Dr Hooker's paper (1839) he noted that he saw the mouse-ear in June 1837 and the arctic sandwort in the following month. An indication of Tom's botanical knowledge at this early age is that he recognised that his specimens of the mouse-ear were not the same as those described from the mainland of Scotland, remote as he was from herbariums, libraries and other far more experienced botanists. It is quite remarkable therefore, that at his tender age he fully understood the complex descriptive terms for plant structures used by academic botanists and was able to make the necessary comparisons with his own specimens.

Tom's mouse-ear, as well as throwing light on the past distribution of arctic-alpine plants, illustrated one of the characteristics of island floras and faunas: precisely the same characteristics that Darwin found so fascinating in the Galapagos: that isolation allows the evolution of new forms and species. The mouse-ear on the Keen of Hamar was once more closely related to its neighbours that were widely scattered at this latitude at the end of the last Ice Age. Through climate change its distribution became entirely limited to its few remaining habitats on mountains and on the Keen of Hamar where, cut off from the influence of the other populations and over ten thousand years or so, it evolved into a new mouse-ear.

Extensions to Property

With five children by the late 1830s, Halligarth was becoming too small, but Laurence had no money to be able to do anything about their predicament. He turned to Thomas and they discussed what was to be done. In 1839, Thomas informed him that he now had finance available to construct an extension. Thomas' generosity to Laurence in providing an extension to Halligarth, virtually doubling its size, was not all it seemed: it was to salve his conscience. Unknown to Laurence, he was drawing up yet another a new will[25] in which, despite his promise, he was now going to leave the estate in life rent to Ursula and, failing her, it would go to his favourite young nephew, Tom the botanist and failing him, Biot and then his other young nephew and namesake, Yankee Tom. Laurence was cut out completely! Unusual as it was to have an illegitimate daughter living openly in the house, it was unheard of for an estate to be left, even in life rent, to that daughter. No one, except Thomas' solicitor William Sievwright (1791-1870), and perhaps Ursula, knew what he had done; the latter possibly guessing from a remark her father once made to her when she had been sorely slighted by one of the family. Thomas had comforted her with the words: "Never mind, you will be riding when they are still walking."[26]

The money for the extension to Halligarth came from the chromate and particularly from the largest and most successful quarry, the vertical lenticular mass, 20 m wide and 30 m deep, at Hagdale. This was later described as:

"… large enough to warrant the installation of a steam pumping plant and in the stream caused by this pumped water there was a horse-operated crushing and sorting mill … The quarry is believed to have produced

William Sievwright solicitor.

113

about 20,000 tons of ore, or probably more than the total from all the other quarries in the island together. The high grade vein yielded ore of 45% chrome oxide ... A fisherman ... told me that he had seen seven schooners (maybe an exaggeration!), all in the harbour at one time, and all waiting to pick up a cargo of ore ..."[27]

The price of a ton of chromate varied over the years from about £8-9 (£425-475) in the early 1820s to around £3 (£175) when the industry ceased about 1870.[28] At an average of £5 (£300) per ton this meant that Thomas could have earned a gross income from 20,000 tons of chromate over the 50 years of quarrying of upwards of £6 million in today's terms! It was little surprise to Laurence then, that Thomas *found* he had money to extend Halligarth in 1839 and build "... a new manor-house at Buness, and two other dwelling-houses in his vicinity; and at Uyea Sound"[29] while almost tripling the extent of the Buness estate from around 170 acres of arable ground in 1820 to around 453 acres by 1843.[30] Not that all of this land had been purchased from, or excambioned (exchanged) with other proprietors; some had come from simply extending the boundary of the farms onto the *scattald* or directly enclosing part of the *scattald* itself. As Thomas, himself, said in 1840:

"... for more than a century back (and tradition for centuries) it had been the immemorial practice for the proprietors of town lands or enclosed ground to add to these by individually taking from the common or scattold and enlarging, or adding to the said town lands thereby appropriating the pieces of scattold thus enclosed for their own use and constituting it their 'individual property' ... every proprietor (almost without an exception) myself among the number have been in the habit of adding a few acres from the scattold or common to their town lands from time to time ..."

As had become their established practice, in February 1839, Thomas wrote to Laurence when he wanted to discuss the plans for Halligarth. Unfortunately, he was then away from Unst during the actual building work and some confusion arose, because they misjudged the alignment of Halligarth.

"I know of your sentiments is, that a building on the south Gable of the house appeared to you the most eligible, but the kind, extent or description of erection you have never mentioned to me ... The new building will occupy the same position in relation to Halligarth that the old House of Buness does to the new ..."[31]

Thomas went on to say that the building would consist of four apartments and would cost £80 (£5120).

The problem was that Buness and Halligarth were not in the exact same alignment and the latter had a south-west gable but no south gable on which to put a 'T' shaped extension as had been added on the east end of Buness. The builder thought he was to build an extension, not at right angles to the existing house, but of the *same* alignment on the side that appeared to be facing south. What he did therefore, was to construct an entirely new building of the same dimensions as the original and parallel to it, with a gap of less than a metre between them; the two buildings were then linked by a short passageway! Despite the awkwardness and incongruity of the final double-building, the new Halligarth continued to provide a very happy home for Laurence's family and was to be the birthplace of five more children.

Visitors welcome and unwelcome

Visitors of all descriptions continued to arrive at Buness, but not all were welcome. In 1835,[32] Thomas was away from Buness on one of his frequent trips to Edinburgh or London; on this occasion to see his hero, Wellington. In those times, when Ursula was still a teenager, Eliza moved into Buness with the children to look after her and keep her company when Thomas was away. Eliza did not voluntarily go to stay in Buness. She disapproved heartily of the ménage and thought Buness "...*discreditable by having in it Ursula* ..."[33], an opinion she had hardly suppressed during the seven years she had spent there before moving into Halligarth. She had to go because of the obligation she and Laurence owed Thomas and because Sinclair Bruce, Ursula's mother who continued to live at Buness as the housekeeper, was not treated by Thomas as the lady of the house, even although Thomas was raising Ursula as his daughter. Thomas may have been generous to Sinclair in some ways but he did not allow her to forget her position. On occasion, despite the fact that Ursula was her daughter, Sinclair was clearly instructed to treat *her*, not so much as her daughter but as one of the Edmondston family. For when there were guests at Buness and she, as the housekeeper, proffered them a glass of wine, she was required to curtsey and say, "Your health, sir," and when she came to her own daughter she had to curtsey to her and say, "Your health, ma'am."[34]

While Eliza was staying at Buness on this occasion, a piano-tuner and his assistant arrived in Unst, and as Buness had one of only three pianos on the island, they came to the house and offered their services. Unbeknown to Eliza, while the piano-tuner and his assistant were busy tuning the piano in the dining room, a maid came in and unlocked the press to retrieve something, in the process revealing the family silver. Before they left, the piano-tuner quietly unsnibbed a window. Fortunately, Thomas always made sure that his factotum, Peter Sutherland, was also in the house when he was away and when Peter was on duty at Buness, he slept with a gun and ammunition by his bedside: Thomas wanted his property well protected!

That night, Eliza, sleeping in the bedroom above the dining room, heard noises from the room below and ran along to Peter's room and woke him. He snatched his gun and ran downstairs to find the dining room door locked. Being a powerful man he put his shoulder to the door and burst it open. There was nobody there. The piano-tuner and his assistant had heard their footsteps and fled empty-handed. By the morning, before they could be apprehended, they had left Unst on the packet from Uyeasound to Lerwick. The piano-tuner was none other than William Hare, the fellow criminal of William Burke, on whom he had turned King's evidence to gain his freedom. Not long after Hare and his assistant fled Unst, an Inspector of Her Majesty's Prisons, Frederic Hill, confirmed Hare's presence in Lerwick.[35]

Little did Hare know that his latest escapade had taken him within a stone's throw of a piece of his accomplice's skin that lay just across the field in a box at Halligarth!

A more welcome visitor was Edward Forbes who, like the visiting terrestrial naturalists, was keen to both find new species and to throw more light on the geographical distribution of species. Tom, then 13 years of age, was allowed to accompany Forbes and his father on a short tour of the islands around his home.[36] This was the first time he had been in the field with such an accomplished, all-round naturalist and he learned a great deal about marine biology, mountain floras, plant distribution and probably a lot more. For Forbes, although himself only 24 years of age, was probably the greatest living naturalist of the time and shortly to become Professor of Botany at King's College, London. He was also one of only a handful of great men, including Hooker and the geologist Sir Charles Lyell (1797-1875), whom Darwin was then considering as an editor for his seminal work *On the Origin of Species*. Forbes was also an enlightened man of some humour and generosity and, like Hooker and others, was very impressed by Tom and took a strong liking to him. From then on they corresponded regularly.[37]

The following year Tom expressed a desire – and was given permission by his parents – to carry out a mammoth three-week botanical tour of all of Shetland. First he went by the sailing packet to Lerwick, then overland the 50 km to Sumburgh at the southern tip of Mainland from where he wound his way back home via West Mainland and the intervening island of Yell, using family connections for overnight accommodation. His mother later said:

"He was always hospitably received, and entertained as long as he chose to remain at the manses, or residences of the gentry or tacksmen [factors]. Indeed, the wayfaring traveller need never be at a loss for shelter or refreshment, albeit there are no hotels or places of public entertainment."[38]

These years of the 1830s were a time of great development for the young Tom that laid the foundations for his future career. They culminated in his meetings with the great naturalists of the day, the publication of his list of plants and then his first excursion from Shetland to the big city of Edinburgh in 1840. For Laurence, who no longer had the time, nor perhaps the frame of mind, to observe and record the birds of Unst in the way he had when *he* had been a teenager, these were the happiest of years as he coached and encouraged a gifted boy who showed all the signs of one day becoming a great naturalist like Forbes: he and Eliza were the proudest of parents.

CHAPTER TEN

POLITICS ON BOTH SIDES OF THE ATLANTIC

"My dear Sir, How's a' wi' you? And how is it that I have not heard from you for so long? And how is it that you have not been to see your friend the Duke [of Wellington] *this year? He is looking well and hearty.* [Did you know] *that he has become a Free trader now (?) in the same Boat with your most humble Friend and Servant … Sae cam of it shud sae be, itt da Orkna folk an da Shetland folk will hae me for der Parliament man I'll be lippen for a vote fra da Laird o' Buness and a' da friends itt he can get to vote for me."*

Arthur Anderson (1792-1869)

The political views of Thomas, 'A Shetlander' and Zetlandicus

In 1837, Thomas wrote a long letter in response to a letter from his fellow landowner, Sir Arthur Nicolson of Fetlar.[1] In it Thomas revealed that he had previously been managing his land and tenant-fishermen in the manner of most Shetland landowners. In other words, requiring them to sell their produce only to him, but that two years ago, as had some other landowners, he had changed the system, charged higher rents but allowed his tenants to sell to merchants (middlemen) direct.

"I held my lands in the old system for 25 years. At the end of that period the tenants were due <u>in all</u> about £50 [£3100]. *The new system has continued about two years, and the debt now due by tenants to myself is full £500 sterling* [£31,000], *and I have no doubt but the half of that sum is due to their outriggers, alias the curse of this country, middle men. My system was <u>unlimited</u> freedom. In short they had permission to dispose of themselves as they pleased. On paying me their yearly rent, they paid pretty well for 2 or 3 years, but ever since there has been a …falling off. For the last three years I solemnly declare to you, though living on the spot, I have not been able to <u>scrape</u> so much in the way of rents as could pay public burdens and keep tenants houses in a tenantable state. It is true that the last three years have been hard ones* [disastrous harvests and poor fishing], *but what has erroneously been termed the "free system" has demoralised and destroyed the people, and has engendered laziness and extravagance to such a pitch that I fear we of the present generation will be able to do little towards redeeming the blunder of ever letting our tenants out of our <u>own</u> hands … so convinced am I of the utter worthlessness of all <u>systems</u> but the one that gives to the proprietor the <u>ipsa corpora</u> itself or <u>themselves</u>, viz, fish, butter, oil, etc, that I am resolute <u>this ensuing season</u> to revert to the old system, with the modification, that I will keep the lands at their high (nominal) rents, and give the tenants <u>the</u> high price for their produce, and sure am I that the man who long departs from the good old rate will <u>cause</u> his lands to leave him, that is to say if his lands be his only source of revenue."*

Thomas, having tried, had found it impossible to operate his estate outwith the prevailing system (whereby the tenant-fisherman was tied to selling his produce to the landowner) and was now going to return to it. This system would now remain in place on the Buness estate until modified, then abolished, under Thomas' nephew some 40 years later.

Meanwhile, Arthur was up to his old tricks again and the older he got the more irascible he became. The next case against him, following his fracas with Riach at Fort Charlotte, was brought in 1834. It was brought by a Lerwick schoolteacher, George Heddell – of the Lerwick family with whom Arthur had already clashed. The initial dispute in this case was over Arthur's reaction to the account given to him by Heddell for teaching his daughter Mary. As the term was not over Arthur considered the account premature and in a note to Heddell, delivered the next school day by Mary, declined to pay it. According to Arthur, Heddell was then abusive to his child and she returned home in tears.[2] The dispute, as was inevitable with Arthur, got out of hand and came to a conclusion, after words were exchanged between the two, on a Sunday following church, when Heddle alleged that Arthur had struck at him with his umbrella.[3]

> "That on Sunday last the 7th Int, between the hours of one and two o'clock afternoon when the Petitioner [Heddle] was returning from Church, Dr Edmondston assaulted the Petitioner by striking him three times on the left shoulder and arm with an Umbrella in the Public Street of Lerwick, and as on other occasions the said Dr Edmondston has threatened to destroy the Petitioner."[4]

This time the caution was £20 (£1200). Arthur had made many enemies, but he also still had some influential friends who stood by him. In this case it was William Hay who generously stood surety on his good behaviour.

What must have seemed the last straw in Arthur's downfall, from once respected, prominent and wealthy citizen of Lerwick, came about the same year as his conviction for striking at Heddell, when he found himself unable to pay the rent for his apartment at Fort Charlotte and, at the age of nearly 60, was evicted.[5] It was the ultimate humiliation, for Thomas, his brother, had to come to his rescue and proud though Arthur was, he had to accept accommodation that Thomas found and paid for in Irvine's Close, one of the narrow lanes that plunge from the Hillhead in Lerwick to meet the Street just above the shore. Even then, after separating from his housekeeper and children, he was forced in December 1836 to write to William Hay:

> *"Peter Hay, who is the landlord of my daughter and her mother, has been in to-day urgently demanding a half years rent, 35/- [£106]. I happened to be in the room at the time and he mentioned among other things that he had 30/- [£91] to pay to you this day. I said that if I happened to see you the affair might be settled. He rejoined that nothing would be better than an order on you. I replied that I would do no such thing as I could not be sure that such a proceeding would meet your approbation. When he calls on you to settle, if you would return the 30/- you would confer a great favour on me, but I have no right to expect it and I will not let Tait know whether or not I have been disappointed."[6]*

It appears that Arthur was hoping that the benevolent William Hay might pay the rent on his behalf so that he would be in debt to him rather than the landlord. It is the plea of a desperate and proud man.

118

The following year, in 1835, when his young nephew, Tom the botanist, had casually entered in his diary that the Member of Parliament for Orkney and Shetland had been entertained at Buness for two days, he had not appreciated that this was something of an historic event. George Traill was Shetland and Orkney's joint MP following the 1832 Reform Act. Prior to this each island group had its own MP. Unusually, for Thomas, he was entertaining, not a Tory but a Whig (or Liberal).

Thomas, however, had made his true political leanings very clear in the letter to Sir Arthur Nicolson on Fetlar in which he bemoaned the state of British politics, fearing a threat to the established order of things that had kept the aristocrat and property owner in power for so long. Thomas viewed the European revolutionary movements, sparked in Paris in 1789, Catholic Emancipation (1829), the widening of the franchise in Lord Russell's Reform Bill of 1832, the abolition of slavery in 1833 and the rise of the Chartists in 1837, all as signs of a coming revolution in Britain: a fear shared by many in the establishment. The political shift to the left that he astutely recognised was also undermining his trust in the parties of the right.

"I am truly delighted to find that your good sense has prevailed over your former liberalism. When I last had the pleasure of speaking on politics with you, you were no advocate of the Peers, and but for them where would have been the property and titles of England, and since in the present day what security have we for life, property and everything else that is dear and valuable to us, but in the House of Lords. It is certainly not from Melbourne, Russell and Co, and their Popish master that we have any good to expect. ... unless the Lords can stay our downward course till England is itself again we must perish in revolutionary violence ... There is hardly such a being now a days as the pure 'old Whig'. The force of circumstances has made the Tories, Whigs, and the Whigs, Radicals. Therefore neither Whig nor Tory are applicable terms. The proper terms for parties are Conservative and Revolutionists, and may God grant that the former may soon have the ascendancy over the latter. I may also tell you that it is my opinion that the nonsensical franchise that has been such a bugbear has done little good towards the amelioration of our islands, but on the contrary it has infused a spirit of radicalism and dissatisfaction throughout the length and breadth of the land."

In another letter to William Hay[7] Thomas again made clear his attitude to both the Corn Laws – a tax on the imports and exports of wheat, passed in 1815 under the influence of and in the interests of landowners to protect the price in Britain – and the Reform Bill.

"My firm belief is that we ought not to be compelled to depend upon foreign countries for the supply of bread, and that the landed interest [proprietors] at the present time requires protection. We live in strange times. The admirers of the Reform Bill will likely find that many reforms will follow in its train ... I attribute our present condition to the effects of the reform Bill."

The election of the first MP for Shetland and Orkney under the Reform Bill, jointly and not separately, was not universally received as a good thing in Shetland. As it happened, the next to consider standing as an MP was another Orcadian, Thomas Balfour, who was a Tory – although the terms Tory and Liberal did not quite mean the same thing then as they do today. But he had a rival in Lord Dundas (Earl of Zetland) who was also very much a Tory. Arthur Edmondston, despite his Whig leanings, supported Dundas and opposed Balfour, writing to the latter and telling him so in no uncertain terms.[8] Thomas, in Buness, however, was a great supporter of Balfour and he too wrote to him[9], but sycophantically, in *his* usual expansive and tortuous prose:

> "... *you may safely rely that whatever little influence I possess shall be in active operation far and wide throughout the limits of this Country. True Conservative principles prompt me to be at my post, in addition to which I have now sincere personal esteem and friendship to stimulate and urge me to the performance of a duty in which I delight, and my only regret is that my power of doing you a service is not commensurate with my wishes. I hope you know me <u>now</u> sufficiently to require no further protestations of my kind feelings towards you.*"

Shetland and Orkney each had a population of just under 30,000, however, the number of electors (eligible property owners) in Shetland was only about 150 while in Orkney there were more than double that. For Laurence, the voting structure meant that regardless of the political views of Shetlanders they would always be outvoted by Orcadians. He therefore published a pamphlet entitled: *On the Claims of Shetland to a Separate Representation in Parliament* (1836). It was rather long-winded and in the end came down in favour of keeping one MP for both counties. Like his brother Thomas he was a Tory and thought this was the best way to retain a Tory MP. Arthur Anderson, the 'liberal' Shetland entrepreneur, newspaper owner and supporter of the tenant-fishermen, also opposed the principle of a single MP for the two sets of islands and also published a couple of pamphlets, but he proposed a plan whereby the liberals might get the best of both worlds; two Liberal MPs, one for Shetland *and* one for Orkney, as opposed to one Tory MP for Shetland. His scheme required a pledge from enough Shetlanders that they would "... support such candidates only as come forward on Reform and Liberal principles ..."[10] His namesake Arthur – Dr Arthur Edmondston – not at all cowed by his recent bankruptcy and summons for assault, took exception to Anderson's proposal that the electorate should necessarily vote for Liberals. Prior to the Reform Act of 1832 he had written an open letter to Earl Grey, the then Prime Minister, appealing for Shetland to have its own MP.[11] Now, in response to Arthur Anderson's

Arthur Anderson.

120

proposals, despite the fact that he was a Whig and supported a separate MP for Shetland, Arthur expanded this letter into a pamphlet to attack Anderson and his ideas, entitled *To the Electors of Zetland* (1836).

In his pamphlet, addressed as the others, to the people of Shetland, Arthur began by taking issue with the use of the word 'Shetland' in the titles of both Anderson and Laurence's pamphlets, which *he* considered simply a modern fashion introduced by the Dutch and Flemish fishermen. This propensity to become side-tracked was typical of Arthur. He insisted, instead, on the use of the term 'Zetland' for the islands, which had been used, he said, since time immemorial and which, "Sir Walter Scott, in his interesting novel of the 'Pirate', has very lately given this orthography the authority of his immortal name." Thus he entitled his own pamphlet with 'Zetland' and even signed himself 'Zetlandicus'! In fact, Arthur was wrong. The word 'Yetland' had been used until c1650 when the Scots replaced the 'Y' with a 'Z': the use of the term 'Zetland' was not *that* old.

Up to now Arthur had kept some of his deepest prejudices under control, but now, betraying the bitterness of one who had fallen so far from grace and lost his inheritance, he displayed them in an ugly personal attack on Anderson.

"You are well aware of the feudal respect always felt in Zetland for persons of superior rank, and the sneering contempt with which the inhabitants view the affectation of equals who pretend to be considered their superiors. Of Mr A's [Anderson's] character and pretensions, few of you can have any personal knowledge. He left Zetland when young, about twenty-five years ago, when acting as the menial servant of a friend of mine, entered as a volunteer into the navy, became captain's clerk before he quitted the service, and is at present a ship-broker in London. He had seen little of Zetland when he left it, and knew less except from books, and he has not been in the country since. In his ephemeral attempts at composition respecting his native land, he has plagiarized openly from a well-known work [Arthur's *A View of Zetland*], and by garbling and travestying certain passages, he has pawned them upon the public as his own. By sobriety and industry, however, he is supposed to have rendered himself independent in pecuniary matters; but unlike the other members of (Central Reform) Association which he praises so highly, he is devoid of the imposing and truly important attributes of birth, liberal education, blood-connexions in Zetland above the grade of meniality and personal rank in society."[12]

Had Arthur Edmondston known that Arthur Anderson would go on to be the co-founder of P&O and out of his own pocket found Shetland's first secondary school – the Anderson Educational Institute, and the Widows' Homes, both of which grand acts he would have approved, he may not have written what he did.

Thomas, on the fence, sounded out Balfour on all three pamphlets in 1836:

"*My last letter was a long one enclosing a few remarks on Anderson's appeal to Shetlanders to become Radicals, he has made a feeble attempt to answer it, Since then other papers have appeared under the signatures 'Zetlandicus' & 'A Shetlander' the latter in the form of a Pamphlet, the one for and the other against separation of Orkney and Shetland if you have seen them let me know your opinion.*"[13]

Lerwick from Bressay with Anderson High School and Widows Homes by Henry Saxby.

Rev. Thomas Barclay by John Irvine.

Coyly, Thomas did not admit that he knew that the two 'anonymous' pamphlets were written by his brothers! But that was not the end of the matter. An old enemy of Arthur's then took the opportunity of his wild attack on Anderson to wade in with a few blows himself. *A Lauda<u>tory</u> and Congratula<u>tory</u> Epistle to Zetlandicus, The Great Unknown of Thule, Including Short Hints for Roasting a Goose* was published by the Rev. Thomas Barclay, under the pseudonym Claude Halcrow – of Claud Halcro of *The Pirate* fame, aka Arthur himself. It was an hilarious and barbed spoof of Arthur's pamphlet, the very title of which was an entertainment of references to the good doctor.

First 'Halcrow' unmercifully mimicked Arthur's verbose and opinionated style:

"Most Erudite Countryman … I have lately perused, with peculiar delectation, an emanation of thy incomparable genius, in

122

which the vanity, absurdity, illiteracy, radicality, and plebeism, of a certain Zetlandico-exotic-interloper, bearing the Scandinavian, and therefore particularly anti-aristocratic, patronymic of Anderson, are most ably, and in a never-to-be-too-much-lauded manner, objurgated, and held up to Zetlandic opprobrium."

Then he mocked Arthur's stubborn and misplaced loyalty to the term 'Zetland' when everybody else was using 'Shetland' and suggested that Arthur should have gone the whole hog and demanded that anyone not using Zetland should "... have the letter Z branded by a hot iron upon his posterior ..." Then he ridiculed his use of Latin quotes and attacked his prejudices regarding Anderson's class and his high opinion of his own worth and works:

"And so this person [Anderson] has been plagiarizing, from the immortal work of the historian of Thule too. Yes, yes, I know the theft. I recollect, in an 'ephemeral' scribblification of 'the person', he says that the 'main land was sixty miles in length,' a discovery which he never could have made but for that immortal work. But, then, scribblers stick at nothing; I actually know an 'ephemeral' scribbler, my dear Zetlandicus, who wrote an anonymous article in a newspaper, and finding it was not praised to his liking, in fact not praised at all, – he, himself, wrote another anonymous article in the same newspaper in which he bestowed no small praise on his own previous article."

Arthur just had to take it on his well-worn chin.

Ten years later, Arthur Anderson himself successfully stood for Member of Parliament for Shetland and Orkney. He was a generous man and bore no grudges against the Edmondston family with whom he was actually on good terms, evinced by the very friendly letter he wrote to Thomas, partly in dialect and very gently pulling his leg:

A LAUDATORY AND CONGRATULATORY

EPISTLE

TO

ZETLANDICUS,

THE GREAT UNKNOWN OF THULE;

Including Short Hints for Roasting a Goose.

BY

CLAUDE HALCROW, ESQ.

A ZETLAND ELECTOR.

"No. 1.—The real Zetlandic Goose, (*Anser cænosus, Lin. Syst.*)

CAATION TO VEESITORS.

Dis fool has an ill vyndit way o' hissin an' cacklin at folk altho' dey may no be middlin wi' him, an' foreby is no ower particlar in tryin to *fyle* dem, *as muckle as he can.* But whan he does sae, just point your finger an' laugh at him an' he'll be still, for da creter canna bide skimpin."—From the *Catalogue and Directions of the Zetland Zoological Society.*

Dedicated to the Shetland Patriotic Union,

AND SOLD BY ALL BOOKSELLERS, FOR THE BENEFIT OF THE POOR OF THE PARISHES OF LERWICK AND GULBERWICK.

PRICE ONE PENNY.

(Which please put i da brod on Sunday.)

LERWICK:
PRINTED AT THE THULEAN PRESS.

1836.

A Laudatory and Congratulatory Epistle to Zetlandicus *1836, attributed to the Rev. Thomas Barclay.*

"My dear Sir, How's a' wi' you? And how is it that I have not heard from you for so long? And how is it that you have not been to see your friend the Duke [of Wellington] *this year? He is looking well and hearty.* [Did you know] *that he has become a Free trader now (?) in the same Boat with your most humble Friend and Servant … Sae cam of it shud sae be, itt da Orkna folk an da Shetland folk will hae me for der Parliament man I'll be lippen for a vote fra da Laird o' Buness and a' da friends itt he can get to vote for me.* [I may call on you and seek your] *candid opinion and advice on the matter … I was proud to receive some time* [ago] *a copy of the Shetland Flora, the production of my young friend your nephew and which I think does him credit."*[14]

In the short and long term the efforts of Arthur Edmondston and Arthur Anderson and his liberal supporters were unsuccessful in achieving separate MPs for Shetland and Orkney. Today, there is still only one MP for both groups of islands, although each now has a Member at the Scottish Parliament (MSP).

Despite the relentless series of mishaps in his private life, the court cases and fines and the enforced move to Irvine's Close, Arthur was still able to produce yet another pamphlet designed to give the public the benefit of his intellect. This was a return to the safer ground of medicine and to his undoubted expertise in that field. Despite the slings and arrows his enthusiasm was undiminished and the paper's title was longer than any of its many predecessors: *A few observations on the pernicious effects which result from the indiscriminate application of irritating substances to produce excoriation and ulceration on the external surface of the body, with a view to relieve and to cure internal diseases* (1837). In reality, contained within Arthur's usual grandiloquence, was, for once, some very sensible advice against the fiction of the then current belief that, just as ointments may alleviate the symptoms of disease in the joints, so might other external applications alleviate the symptoms of disease of the internal organs: alas it was to be his last conversation with the good citizens of Shetland.

The year after Arthur's last publication, Laurence at Halligarth wrote the last of his papers on natural history, *Observations on the Distinction, History and Hunting of Seals in Shetland* (1838), for the Wernerian Society. Not to be outdone by his brothers by way of publications, Thomas, too, produced his first and only pamphlet in 1839 – the same year as his nephew Tom's plant list appeared in Hooker's *Notes on Norway* – entitled *A letter to the chromate proprietors of the scattalds of Baliasta and Haroldswick*. This was the open letter replying to the accusation that he had sold chromate from the *scattald* and had not reimbursed the other owners with their share. Thomas had persuaded the proprietors that the division of the chromate collected on the *scattald* should be at the entrance to his quarry. This convenience would allow one person, Thomas, to sell that chromate along with that excavated from the quarry and would be much more commercially efficient. The Trust that had been set up with the late William Mouat as trustee, had agreed to this.

In his open letter, Thomas denied that he was selling any chromate not his own and made a counter-claim that others, including the Rev. James Ingram, had been unfairly obtaining returns for chromate gathered on the *scattald*. Thomas then opened up a can of worms by quoting from an accusatory private letter he had received from William Cameron (d1839) – the nephew and heir of William Mouat, and grand-nephew of Thomas Mouat of Garth the old adversary of Thomas Edmondston of Buness, who had died in 1836.

"I am told that you sold from the Scattolds, previous to the chromate becoming an article of generally known value, or of a particular management, a considerable quantity, of which the other heritors have not partaken. This what I am __told__ …"[15]

Things got more heated when the trust appointed Gilbert Spence, then superintendent of the quarry, as a trustee without, in Thomas' mind, properly consulting himself, and Thomas told Spence so. Spence then wrote a long letter to Thomas in response. Intentionally, or not, Spence's letter was libellous, directly accusing Thomas of taking money for chromate that had come from the *scattald* and that did not belong to him. Thomas took Spence to the Court of Session.[16] However, before the case had got very far Spence made a public retraction and abject apology. Thomas was triumphant!

Charles and 'the panic of 1837'

While Thomas had been making a small fortune in Unst in the 1820s, Arthur losing his money and reputation through libel and ultimately, bankruptcy, and Laurence was struggling to make an adequate living with the promised but grudging support of Thomas, Charles was thriving. Despite some depression in the economy he had built his grand new house – now occupied by ten children – and his business, with the help of his eldest son Laurence Augustus (1814-1865), was still expanding and he was beginning to dabble in politics himself, and not just as an independent observer like Arthur.

At the peak of his fortune, in 1835, he wrote his will and, in addition to the legacies to his immediate family in Charleston, he planned to leave a very generous £400 (£24,400) to his brother Laurence, noting in his will that this would be in addition to the £100 (£6100) that he had already lent him. Despite being so many thousand miles away he had kept in touch with the family and was well aware of Arthur's tribulations and touchingly, but not unconditionally, he left an annuity of £10 (£610) to:

"… my unfortunate brother Arthur [but] in trust to my brother Thomas for the use of Arthur at the discretion of Thomas … with my most anxious solicitations that he will reform and be himself again."[17]

Meanwhile, the Nullifiers in Charleston – determined to invalidate Federal laws when they did not suit Carolina – now firmly believed that it was the tariffs imposed by the North that were the cause of economic problems of the Southern States and particularly South Carolina which through agricultural depression had:

"'… lost almost 70,000 people to emigration during the 1820s, and would lose nearly twice that number in the 1830s'. The protective tariffs 'tended to raise the prices of [imported] manufactured goods and, in so far as it discouraged the sale of foreign goods in the United States, reduced the ability of British and French traders to acquire American money with which to buy American cotton. This worsened problems of low cotton prices and exhausted lands'."[18]

Charles, as a leading merchant and trader in cotton, suffered from these tariffs and expected to suffer even more if there was any question of the abolition of slavery in America. So it is more than likely that he was one of those who met with John C. Calhoun (1782-1850) in the house in Church Street in Charleston where many of the Nullifiers' plans were hatched in the 1820s and 1830s.[19] Calhoun was a very able Congressman from South Carolina and a leading Nullifier who became Vice-President to President Andrew Jackson in 1829. In the 1832 legislative elections, the Nullifiers swept to victory in Charleston and across the state and while the northern cities became quite divided on the major issues of tariffs and slavery, Charleston's elite became almost entirely united for slavery and against the tariffs. It was a great shock to them therefore, in 1833, when the British Parliament ended slavery in the West Indies; a reminder to Charles of the differences, not just between the North and the South, but between America and the country of his birth.

The local Charleston economy continued to decline in the 1830s. One of its main newspapers closed in 1832, followed by the Charleston Theatre a year later – a psychological blow to a city that considered itself to be the epitome of the cultured South. Lack of employment then led to impoverished mothers increasingly placing their children in orphanages and to a rise in alcoholism. Charlestonians, in addition to blaming the tariffs for the drop in trade, also blamed the lack of confidence of traders in the health of their port, following outbreaks of cholera there, from 1832-1836, coinciding exactly with the outbreaks in Britain. There were, however, other reasons:

"… what Charleston lacked was rail connections to the West, a harbour deep enough to accommodate large steamships, a broader range of crops and products to export, and a growing pool of free, educated and ambitious workers … For when the city's decision makers at the turn of the century had promoted upland cotton and reopened the slave trade, in the long run they had backed the wrong horses. As it moved West, cotton left behind exhausted soils and crowds of slaves whose labour it was often impossible to employ profitably."[20]

Such problems had an uncanny similarity to the unprofitability of the farm-fishing tenures in Shetland and the problems for all when the crops and fishing failed.

Charles was heavily involved in the cotton trade, but he had also dipped his toes in the slave trade. In addition to his household slaves, between February and May 1824, along with one Robert Brown, he sold nineteen slaves, and between 1833 and 1837, a further 17.[21] He did not, however, appear to be involved in the general slave trade that reopened in Charleston in 1803, until it was officially abolished in 1808 by the US Constitution, during which time tens of thousands of African slaves were imported. But, as a trader, he would not have turned down a business opportunity when it arose and it is quite possible that he was involved in the smuggling of slaves after 1808.[22] This 'illegal' trade was quite common at the time and nobody, who was caught, was ever punished. Quite probably he fitted in slaves in his ships when he had spare cargo space on his regular trade runs to the Caribbean.

In June 1836 the economic situation was such that:

"The last six months have been fraught with events long to be remembered, particularly by the commercial world. At the Commencement, Speculation ran so high, that every article rose above its value. At the last the Bubble burst and great is the explosion. At the North almost every merchant has failed. Here there have been but few, although many met with heavy losses, which have already been noted. Chs. Edmondston is the only large mercantile house that has made a regular assignment, many others have suspended payments for a while."[23]

A few years later similar economic problems would arise in Shetland.

Charles was a shrewd businessman and not blind to the signs of the impending economic crisis, but he had great confidence in his business. In that year of 1836, when his was the only mercantile house paying its way and when all others were reneging on their debts, he went on a commercial trip to the Caribbean on one of his own vessels. On this trip, as was his occasional practice, he took Mary with him and he left the business in the hands of his eldest son, Laurence Augustus, who was now twenty-three and registered as a clerk at 3 East Bay. In his absence, in what was later called 'the panic of 1837', the price of a pound of cotton fell from 18 cents in February to 8 cents in May. Charles would now only get back 40 per cent of the price he had paid for his cotton! He returned to find that his business was virtually worthless, but rather than declare himself bankrupt he liquidated his real estate holdings and other assets, including his beautiful mansion on the Battery, to pay off all his creditors. The sum he owed was estimated at about $125,000 ($2.5 million).[24] He and Mary had enjoyed the house and their wealthy status for less than ten years and it was as severe a blow socially as it was financially. Now Charles had a taste of the misfortunes of his brother Arthur, albeit on a rather larger scale. Charles' connection with the house he built, however, has not been forgotten.

But Charles, like Arthur, was a very determined character and was far from finished. He managed to keep their summer house in North Carolina and moved the family to a smaller house at 8 Legare, a short distance away. This address did not have the status of the house on the Battery but they still lived among the middle class at least. Here, at 55, Charles began the long and painful struggle of salvaging his finances while remaining a commercial merchant at the Central Wharf. Having done the honourable thing in repaying his debts in full, his reputation, unlike Arthur's, was intact and he and the family could hold up their heads in Charleston. Such was his reputation and financial recovery that within ten years, in 1847, he was elected President of the Chamber of Commerce and by 1852 he had become President of the South Carolina Insurance Company; he was financially comfortable again, but he never regained his former wealth.

CHAPTER ELEVEN

FAME IN EDINBURGH, DEATH IN LERWICK

"He showed me all his most beautiful collections, &c., and gave me the new volume of his work for you. You will see yourself quoted all through the book, and in the preface he calls you 'his old and dear friend'..."

Thomas Edmondston (1825-1846)

Shetland in the 1840s

Europe of the 1840s was now at last seeing the beginnings of social and political reform after a lengthy period of war and reaction. In Britain it was a time also of agricultural change that was sweeping from England through the lowlands of Scotland to the Highlands and Islands, where the people were being cleared wholesale to allow the introduction of improved breeds of sheep. In the middle of the decade there was the great potato famine that devastated Ireland and, to a lesser extent, Scotland. Some of these changes had already touched Shetland, but they had yet to have any real impact on the majority of the people, the tenant-fishermen.

In the northernmost isles of Britain, the 1840s opened with the economic collapse of the Shetland Bank and the major Lerwick business of Hay & Ogilvy, which bankrupted the Hay family and had a knock-on effect on the local fishing industry. William Hay was to recover, with financial help from his friends, and with two of his sons set up their own very successful Hay & Company in 1844 and, as the economy grew, many other new Shetland companies became established. The decade was to end, however, in failed harvests and destitution. It was an increasingly tough time for landowners who were finding the land tax and their public obligations, to church, school, prison services and the poor, increasingly burdensome. As Arthur Edmondston had foreseen at the very beginning of the century, there was an urgent need for Shetland landowners to improve their agricultural incomes by enclosing and improving. However, it was often carried out in conjunction with clearing and moving the occupying tenants, just what Arthur had argued against. On the fishing side, severe gales in September 1840 brought about the loss of several herring boats that had the effect of setting back that fishery for 40 years. On the positive side, the *haaf* fishery continued without major catastrophe and there was expansion of line fishing with larger vessels now sailing to the Faroe Bank just west of the Faroe Islands, where large cod could be caught just as fast as the fishermen could pull them in.

In Unst, in 1840, the Rev. James Ingram, who had been the minister for twenty years, now had the support of his son, the Rev. John Ingram, and just as Thomas Mouat had contributed a description of the parish of Unst to *The Old Statistical Account* in 1792, the Rev. Ingram, with the help of his son, now contributed a piece to the *New Statistical Account of the Shetland Islands* (in

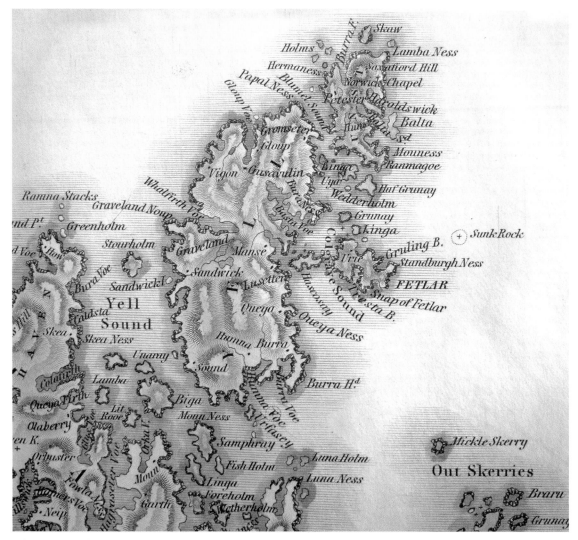

The North Isles 1840 from the New Statistical Account.

the *Statistical Account of Scotland* 1841, Edinburgh) that once again recorded the social and economic conditions of the time.

As in 1792, the *Account* reported that the Mouats of Garth (now Mouat Cameron of Garth and Annsbrae) were still the principal landowners, owning half of the parish, while Thomas Edmondston had substantially increased his share to about a quarter. The population of the island meanwhile had risen by 50 per cent, from around 2000 to an unsustainable 3000, partly as a result of a reduction of the death rate and partly due to the increase in the number of fishing tenures, the latter resulting in a decrease in average farm size. However, the Revs James and John Ingram, who had a glebe of 14 acres compared to the average tenant farm of 6 acres, were at pains to point out that, despite the increasing concern expressed by visitors to Shetland about the alleged "… wretchedness … and oppressed state of the peasantry":

"... there are but few of Her Majesty's subjects, of the same class, who are treated in a more kindly and indulgent manner by their superiors; who enjoy so much liberty; who pass through life with so little labour or care; or who have more reason to be contented with the situation and circumstances a kind Providence has assigned them. They do not live in affluence; but they seldom want the necessities, and they have many of the luxuries of life, with one-half of the toil that people of their class are doomed to undergo, in more genial climes ... Favourable seasons and successful fishings have placed many of them in easy circumstances, and enabled them to indulge in the luxury of tea, formerly little known among them, but now used in the greatest number of families twice every day."

A footnote qualifying this account of such an idyllic existence, however, noted that:

"Since this Account was drawn up, the circumstances of the people have been sadly altered. A general failure of the crops, for five or six years in succession, has reduced them to great poverty, and it must be long, even under the most favourable circumstances, before they can regain their former state."

The problem, as ever, was that the tenants could hardly grow enough food for their own needs and that it only needed a year or two of poor harvests to precipitate them below the breadline into starvation.

Where they wished to and could, the proprietors helped their tenants over these difficult periods. Among their other obligations they also provided the local school, of which there were three in Unst in the 1840s. The Ingrams noted that: "There are no persons in this parish from six to fifteen years of age, who cannot read a little."

In the same publication, Laurence at Halligarth contributed a piece on *General Observations on the County of Shetland*. In his piece he deplored the new merchant-controlled economy and firmly defended the old ways of the patrician landowner who would:

"... vigilantly excite and direct the energies of his tenants, – assist them with capital and counsel, – receive and provide a market for the various produce of their industry, – keep a store containing every necessary article they may require, and careful attend to the many subordinate arrangements of order and discipline which the peculiarity of their position and co-operative industry may demand."

He sincerely believed that while the tenant "... obeys the laws and retains his solvency, no subject of Great Britain can enjoy more unrestrained liberty." The problem as he, and the establishment generally saw it, was that although there was the potential to keep many more animals and grow better crops, because of "bad seasons [and] desultory habits [that] indispose him to regular and vigorous exertion on his farm" the people are frequently brought to the verge of famine. He was a firm believer in rotation, proper weeding and draining of the ground and made many comments on how improvements could be made to agriculture. Some of these arable practices he carried out on his own small acreage at Halligarth but, as Thomas had pointed out, it was not possible to compare the results objectively with the traditional agricultural methods. Laurence gained a reputation as an agricultural improver that was true in theory but hardly justified in practice.

Although Laurence also believed that the Greenland whaling "contaminated the morals of the unsophisticated youth," he was not as harsh in his condemnation of the few forms of enjoyment available to the ordinary farmer-fisherman as the puritanical Ingrams who, he said, condemned dancing.

"Music and dancing have been recently much discouraged, from the most erroneous notion that they lead to vicious excesses. The effect of such a check to an enjoyment in itself innocent, and to the love of home, fostered by pleasurable associations, can be easily imagined."

Laurence then went on to support the popular myth that the greedy and rapacious Scots, following the transfer of power from Denmark in the 15th century, had destroyed the egalitarian society and culture of the descendants of the Vikings. It is hard to believe that he did not know that the Vikings had been far more thorough in their eradication of a people and their culture, the Picts, when *they* had occupied Shetland from the 9th century.

The ancient language was a dialect of the Norse, being similar to what is spoken in the Faroe Islands; but, for more than a century, it has been disused, and is now quite forgotten. From this latter cause, and from the destruction of every ancient record and document that the earls Stewart [Earl Patrick] and their Scottish retainers [Bruce of Muness etc.] could collect, any old ballads or histories which Shetland might have possessed, have been lost. That such did exist can hardly be questioned: for the geographic position, and many excellent harbours of this country, rendered it a favourite resort of the heroic sea-kings; and there are extant in Faroe many sagas and poems (in some of which Shetland is mentioned). Those two groups of islands were for a long period united under one government and bishopric; but Faroe was fortunately not scourged, as was Shetland, by royal favourites and greedy adventurers, taking advantage of the unsuspecting and defenceless Udallers, unprotected as they were by the Government of Scotland, to which they had been conditionally consigned, and ignorant of its language and laws."

This myth, with its attendant revisionist noble and adventurous Viking, later flowered, with the help of Laurence's daughter, Jessie M. E., towards the end of the century.

The young Tyro

Early in 1840, two letters arrived at Halligarth from Edinburgh. The first was to Laurence from his friend Patrick Neill in Canonmills, informing him that the salt beef he had sent from Unst was regularly on his table along with ling and tusk from the islands, and that a *bonxie* brought to him from Ronas Hill in 1816, and therefore at least 24 years old, was still alive and well.[1] The second letter was to Tom and was a reply to one of his, from Edward Forbes, who had visited Unst the previous year. Tom had enthusiastically launched himself into collecting marine specimens for Forbes and had enquired about the possibilities of exchanging pressed Shetland plants for those which could not be found in Shetland: he was keen to broaden his botanical knowledge and to compare his Shetland specimens with those from the mainland of Scotland. He also sought advice from Forbes on what books he should purchase that would help him with his studies. The reply from

Tom the botanist as a boy.

Forbes indicated the breadth of the 14-year-old Tom's natural history studies and the closeness of their friendship.

"My Dear Friend, – Circumstances have so fallen out that I have not been able to answer your most interesting letter before this … I am sadly puzzled what elementary books to select for you. There are much better books in French than in English, and introductions to Botany are more numerous than similar works on Zoology … I enclose you a paper of mine on the star fishes … I should be very glad if you can give me any information on the Medusa's head starfish, said to be called the 'Argus' in Shetland … Mr Campbell tells me that you have sent some notes to the Botanical Society on the botany of the Zetlands. The plants you mention are good and most acceptable to the Society, and you may exchange them for foreign or other British ones … I remain ever very sincerely yours."[2]

The following month Forbes replied to another letter from Tom, thanking him for notes on *"… the 'Piper' and the 'Argus'. At the present moment they are most valuable"*,[3] requesting notes on other marine species and instructing Tom in how to preserve specimens of starfish and molluscs. Then in June 1840, the young tyro made his very first visit south to the Scottish mainland, where he was to stay until September in the company of his mother and his uncle Thomas. One of the reasons for the trip was to give Tom the opportunity to meet the outstanding men of botany in Edinburgh and them the chance to meet the young discoverer of so many rare plants. The trip was also to allow him and his mother to meet up with her many relatives and to enable her to seek treatment for her disability.

They departed Unst on the afternoon of one of those magical Shetland summer evenings, just like the one on which Dr Laurence Edmondston of Lerwick, Tom's grandfather, had written his letter to Mally, his grandmother, all those years before. It was a night when the wind held its breath, when it was so quiet that the smallest sounds were carried across great distances and when the stillness added a spiritual quality to the atmosphere that somehow imbued everything and everybody with calmness and peace. Eliza recorded:

"On one of the last days of June, the voyage commenced in a six-oared boat. It was a most beautiful afternoon and the sea was as still as an inland lake. There came on no darkness. The sun just hid himself in the north west for a short time, leaving a dim, delicious twilight, while the boatmen rowed softly, and now and then a solitary sea-bird skimmed along, as if, with eager wing and cry, it was hastening to its nestlings. Then majestically uprose the god of day again, and still the expanse of ocean slept calmly on. Lerwick was reached before eight in the morning, and the same evening the travellers embarked in the steamer for Leith … [we] first called at Kirkwall, in Orkney, then at Wick, then at Aberdeen, finally reaching Leith on the afternoon of the 3rd July, and throughout those two days and nights the weather continued perfectly fine."[4]

No doubt, Eliza wished that such plain sailing could be the future pattern of her precocious son's life.

The trip south by sea from Lerwick was a new experience for Tom. He had never travelled overnight in a large boat, although he had made many short trips in small boats among Shetland's many islands. The passage was on the wooden paddle steamer *Sovereign* that ran between Shetland and the mainland in the summer months when the weather was reasonably dependable. In the winter, when the weather was frequently stormy, the journey was still made by the tried and trusted method of sail.

It might be thought that Leith would have had an extraordinary impact on young Tom. Although both Balta Sound and Lerwick were busy places at the height of the fishing season in the early 19th century – with dozens of Dutch and Scottish fishing boats anchored just offshore or tied up alongside the wooden jetties, the foreshores cluttered with wooden buildings and bustling with people: fishermen, gutters, coopers, carters and other tradesmen and women – they could not compare with Leith. Here, Tom was confronted by the great stone harbour packed with towering sailing ships and the most modern screw-driven steamships, the quaysides piled high with crates and burlap-wrapped exotic cargoes, its shipyards, warehouses and cobbled streets jammed with jostling crowds and huge horses pulling laden drays. His uncle Thomas organised a hansom to take them through the port and they made their way up the broad mall of Leith Walk, to the home of

David MacBrair (1806-1893), Eliza's brother in Edinburgh. The great metropolis, by then contiguous with Leith, contained further new experiences for Tom, from the unsavoury narrowness of Old Edinburgh and the grandeur of the rising New Town, to the towering Castle, the North Bridge over Waverley Station and the awesome sight of his first railway engine.

However, impressive as it all was, it did not capture his interest. What he was really looking forward to were the opportunities to meet with the great names of botany, with whom he had been in correspondence for several years, and to botanise in new environments, far richer in their diversity than Shetland. Far from attracting his attention, the port and city were not of importance or interest. It was: "*Oh, for*

Leith Harbour from the Pier.

the woods, – oh, just to get to the plants of Arthur's Seat."[5] It was the flora of the volcanic rocks of the great park by Holyrood Palace at the foot of the Royal Mile and of woodlands, quite absent in Shetland, that he burned to see. A few days later, under a broad canopy of trees near Glasgow, for the first time he held in reverential hands the pale and delicate twinflower (*Linnaea borealis*), bearer of the name of his hero, Linnaeus, after whom he had been nicknamed as a young child by his father. Just four days after he arrived in Edinburgh, Tom wrote a letter to him in Unst, so brimming with enthusiasm that it must have painfully reawakened Laurence's own youthful ambitions and the memories of his friends and teachers of 20 years previously.

> "*My dear Papa, – The chief thing I have to tell is that I am acknowledged the sole discoverer of Arenaria Norvegica and Lathyrus Maritimus [sea pea]. I drank tea last night with Dr Graham [surgeon and Professor of Botany and Conservator of the Botanical Garden], and took some of my specimens with me. He received me very kindly, and shewed me many specimens, and as I wished it, we looked over them all, comparing them with mine … Dr [Sir W.J.] Hooker has published a new edition of his Flora, and therein mentions these two plants as found by me … Dr Graham bids me always apply for any plants I wish for from the Botanic Gardens. He is extremely urgent for me to come with him and a party of students for a week on a botanical excursion to Clova [Glen Clova in Angus], by far the richest place in Great Britain, for variety and rarity of [mountain] plants … I got an order from Dr Balfour to see the Museum of the Royal College of Surgeons. It is a magnificent place. I saw Mr MacGillivray there; he was remarkably kind – shewed me all over the Museum, and invited me to dine with him today. He desired me to give you his very best thanks for the notes you sent him. I then went to the College [Edinburgh University] and gave your letter to Mr Small [librarian]. He took me all over the library, and told me to come whenever I wanted books. I met Professor Jameson as he was going to his class-room; he was also extremely kind. He was in a hurry then, but told me to come back, and he would give me an order to be in the Museum every day …*"[6]

Tom was in his element, lionised by professors and old friends of his father. He had even won over Jameson. Dr John Balfour, whom he met, was one of the founding members of the Botanical Society of Edinburgh in 1836, later becoming the Professor of Botany at Glasgow, before returning as Professor to Edinburgh and Keeper of the Botanic Gardens. Balfour was much impressed by Tom and took him on his botanising class to Roslin Glen just outside the city. He made such a great impression on Tom that he later dedicated his *Flora of Shetland* to Balfour.

The following day Tom reported back to his father on his dinner the previous evening with MacGillivray, Laurence's old friend from his own Edinburgh days.

> "*He showed me all his most beautiful collections, &c., and gave me the new volume of his work for you. You will see yourself quoted all through the book, and in the preface he calls you 'his old and dear friend' …*"[7]

The 'volume' that Tom spoke of was Volume III of MacGillivray's five volume work, *The History of British Birds*. Sadly, this major work of MacGillivray's was not in a style that was pleasing to either the interested birdwatcher or collector. There were no full plates of the beautiful watercolour portraits of the birds that he had recently produced; he simply could not afford to have these included. These volumes were heavily criticised and did not sell well, losing MacGillivray much of the money he had invested in them, money he could ill-afford to lose.

In fact, MacGillivray had said much more about Laurence in the Preface to Volume III than Tom had given in his letter:

> "From the sea-girt rocks of Zetland, the voice of an old friend has come to assure me of his sympathy and esteem. That friend, DR LAURENCE EDMOND-STON, well known as any enthusiastic observer of birds, who had added much to our knowledge of those of his native country, has supplied me with several important articles, and will enrich the remaining volumes with the results of his investigations respecting the habits of the feathered denizens of his semi-Scandinavian Isles."

Dr John Balfour.

Later, in Volume V, published in 1852, MacGillivray acknowledged a "short account of the Birds of Shetland" sent to him by Laurence. This was a development of the list that Laurence had previously written for the Wernerian Society. He also quoted long descriptions by Laurence of several species of gull including the skuas. Laurence's account was probably the most comprehensive account of Shetland's birds to date, but alas it disappeared, not to be replaced until he had gained an enthusiastic ornithologist for a son-in-law.

In Shetland, Tom had met and greatly impressed both Dr. W. D. Hooker and Forbes and now, in Edinburgh, in just one day, the young lad had become acquainted with four more illustrious names in natural history. He told his father that Dr Robert Graham (1786-1845) – who oversaw the move of the Royal Botanic Gardens in Edinburgh to its present site from its old site in Leith Walk – had actually introduced him to his class "*... as the discoverer of those two plants.*"[8] At 14, he was a celebrity. The effect of all the praise and attention, the meetings, interviews, conversations, dinners and outings with such important figures on the young and impressionable Tom, was to turn a sense of pride into one of cockiness. Tom was flattered by the attention, but began to take it as his due. Such familiarity with the great academics of the universities, at such a young age, would later make life difficult for him when he became a student.

In the meantime, he simply soaked it all up and whenever the opportunity arose went out botanising. He visited his father's other old friend, Patrick Neill, and reported back on his printing house and on his collection of animals. *"His old skua is failing fast, I fear. He has some gannets, shags, penelopes, parrots, tortoises, and splendid golden eagle, and king vulture."*[9] He and his mother visited relatives, travelling by canal for his mother's comfort, to Glasgow, where they called on the head of the other branch of the family, Sir William Edmondstone of Duntreath (1810-1888), and to the University where Tom became acquainted with Dr W. D. Hooker's father, Sir W. J. Hooker, Professor of Botany. Back in Jameson's Museum in Edinburgh he told his father that he had found "*... the well known face and figure of Strix Nyctea* [snowy owl]" that Laurence had shot and sold to Bullock. Jameson invited him to attend his final lecture of the year of which Tom said "*It was on volcanoes and other branches of meteorology. He is rather a dry lecturer, and hesitates a good deal, but is clear and most instructive nevertheless.*"[10] Tom found the Museum fascinating and divided his free time, after the University closed for the summer, between it and the Botanic Gardens. His appetite for knowledge was voracious. If he was not at one natural history institution, he was at another, or out botanising, or pumping some expert for information. He reported home enthusiastically:

> "*I am employing every moment of leisure in drawing. Mr Small is remarkably kind to me, he is indeed a worthy soul. I have nothing to do but go to the College Library and ask him for any book I wish to see. Then there is a little room off the outer hall with writing desk &c., which he calls mine, where I go and sit as long as I like. I have been engaged for two days on Donovan's 'British Shells', in copying the figures. It is a capital work – and I am studying it very hard; also other works on various subjects, especially Mathematics, and different branches of Natural History, but Botany continues ...... to be my favourite.*"[11]

In August, he reported to his father that he had met up with yet another previous acquaintance of his.

> "*I called for John Edmondstone the bird-stuffer to day. He is a fine good natured old chap, and I had a long talk with him about Waterton and Demerara. He is a good practical ornithologist, and remembered you immediately. I saw all his birds – they are beautifully preserved. He uses no wire. He told me his method which he learnt from Waterton, and which is quite easy.*"[12]

Tom was an assiduous letter writer and in another to his father he told him how he was collecting information on tree planting for him:

> "*All those I have happened to fall in with are gardeners, florists, horticulturists or nursery-men, agriculturist, botanists ... and I have got as much instruction as possible on every available point. I do hope it will be productive of some beneficial results on our little experiment with trees at Halligarth.*"[13]

The letters indicate the seriousness with which Tom took his studies that so impressed his seniors. But he was still a young lad and could write to his younger brother Biot, then 13 years old, who had just been to the Faroe Islands with their father:

"Are you attending to our garden? … I think I told you I have got some capital arrows …...I have also got some slate pencils of a capital sort, also a good stock of black lead ones, and pens and a knife for you."[14]

Tom occasionally touched on the condition of his mother in his letters home. In August he wrote: *"Mamma though not strong, and unable to walk, is pretty well."*[15] The treatment she had received for her lameness seemed to have helped her and the following month they returned to Shetland, Tom brimming over with new knowledge, with a deeper understanding of both the natural world and the world of academia, and with a whole new set of eminent contacts. He arrived home in the autumn with a very different perspective from that with which he departed in the spring. Unst suddenly seemed a rather small world. Wonderfully familiar though it was, it could no longer provide sufficient challenge to hold him. On the other hand, having grown up in that small island, whose seashore boundaries were so visible and physical, where every feature and every person was linked so personally, the leaving of it with little chance of returning regularly was not going to be easy for him.

Through the winter of 1840-1841 Tom remained at Buness, corresponding with Sir W. J. Hooker and Graham, and in February 1841 began a correspondence with Charles Babington (1808-1895), Professor of Botany at Cambridge and an expert taxonomist, who was preparing his own Flora of Britain: later he would support Tom in his efforts to have his mouse-ear recognised as a full species.

For six months or so they carried out a regular correspondence. Tom provided information on the flora of Shetland and Babington provided him with advice while seeking specimens of plants that Tom was more than happy to provide from his herbarium of carefully dried and pressed plants. One of the pieces of information on Shetland's flora that Babington was interested to learn from Tom was that:

"The highest land in Shetland (Rona's Hill) having an elevation of from 1500-2000 feet [2400 m-3200 m], has very much the same vegetation on its summit as at its base … 2nd. The very few Alpine plants which we do have, are chiefly met on the lower ground …"[16]

Shetland is far enough to the north of the Scottish mainland that the climate at sea level is equivalent to that of the mainland hills. So, the plants to which Tom referred, including his own finds on the serpentine of Unst, are to be found at decreasing altitude the further north one travels, there are also many fewer species than on the Scottish mainland.

"The many very fine plants which abound on the mountains of Scotland (bear in mind that we Shetlanders do not consider ourselves as belonging to that ancient country) are, with few exceptions, unknown here."[17]

Tom was not the only one at Halligarth receiving requests for information on Shetland's natural history at that particular time. It was a fine tribute to his acknowledged expertise in the field

137

Storm petrel by William MacGillivray.

of ornithology that MacGillivray sent Laurence the manuscript of his *British Land Birds* asking him for an opinion. He also sought guidance on the nomenclature of the Iceland gull and another little known northern species: "*I wish you had given me a poetical and particular account of Mother Carey's* [Mary, mother of Christ] *Chickens, instead of the four lines you sent me …*"[18] MacGillivray was referring to the tiny storm petrel that breeds in rock crevices in some of the uninhabited little islands and within the walls of Shetland's famous 2000-year-old Broch of Mousa. The storm petrel, barely as large as a swallow, patters on the surface of the ocean to feed on plankton and it was sailors, watching small flocks of them feeding in the wake of their ships, who gave it its biblical nickname.

Arthur's Demise

That winter of 1841, in which Tom spent his time corresponding with the eminent botanists, studying textbooks and working on his herbarium, and Eliza gave birth to her fourth daughter, Arthur Edmondston's health deteriorated.

It was Arthur's final year that brought him his most serious legal trial. He had been prosecuted in 1832 for an assault on Marion Fraser and in 1834 for striking at George Heddell with his umbrella and found guilty on both occasions. In 1840 he was at it again. He was now 65 and a life, latterly, of overindulgence in drink and of impoverished circumstances had broken his health. He now lived alone in a small, damp flat, paid for by Thomas, in Irvine's Close, a lane just off the seaward side of the Street.[19] Although he was penniless and near starving, Arthur remained an immensely proud, though curmudgeonly old man. A kindly neighbour, seeing his condition and his weary struggle up to his flat one day, sent her maidservant to his door with a tray of hot food. She placed the tray at the top of the steps that led up to the door and knocked. When Arthur opened it he asked her what this was all about and when she told him there was some food for him he bade her 'be gone' and threw the tray after her down the steps![20]

While the Street itself was constricted, barely the span of a man's arms in places, the steep lanes that led off it, up to the Hillhead and down to the shore, could be even narrower. One summer evening in 1840, when Arthur was returning home and had entered the close, he was confronted by Robert Brown (1796-1874), a blacksmith who also lived in the close, and a group of children at the bottom of the steps leading up to his door, who shouted obscenities and taunted him about the legitimacy of his daughters. In his mind's eye he saw his girls cowering in tears. Without a second thought he drove his way through the melee, cursing them and waving his stick, knocking some aside as he fought his way to the door. There, he turned to confront them as they scattered laughing and shouting; one of them, the eight-year-old John Brown, was holding his head and being led away by his father.

Arthur was charged:

"That on Monday evening the 13th day of July last 1840 … Dr Arthur Edmondston … On the lower side of the main Street of Lerwick did … wickedly and feloniously assault, beat and bruise John Brown, a child of eight years of age … to the effusion of his blood, by striking the said John Brown a severe blow upon his head with a walking Stick or Staff which laid bare a part of the Skull and occasioned the said John Brown much injury."[21]

The case was brought in December by his old protagonist, the Procurator Fiscal, James Greig. Because of his previous convictions for physical violence there was every chance that he would receive a custodial sentence in the Lerwick Tolbooth. If this happened there was little doubt that he would not survive it. Luckily, when Thomas at Buness heard of the incident, he put up the £10 (£640) bail for him. Arthur's defence against the charges was that children, as well as Robert Brown, John's father, had been rioting outside his house and insulting his children. He did not specify the nature of the insults, perhaps not wanting to bring any more humiliation on his children. On that day, he told the court, he had had to elbow his way past the children to reach his door and he may have accidentally touched John Brown.

In the event, the court sympathised with him and he got off, but he was now an exhausted old man and within two months, on the 27th February, 1841, he died. At his side was Charles Ogilvy (1802-1844) of Seafield, the son of the man whom he had beaten into second place when he became the first Chief Magistrate of Lerwick back in 1818. His last words to Ogilvy reflected his professional curiosity and devotion to lost causes to the very end: "Will you look if there be any change in my face?"[22]

On his death the Sheriff Clerk had his repositories sealed and a roup was held of his belongings to pay off creditors. After the expenses of the Clerk and the Selling Agent, Arthur – doctor, past magistrate, past owner of several properties in and around Lerwick, and the Haa and land which he had inherited from generations of Edmondstons on Hascosay – left a grand total of a £13.8s.8d (£858). The most expensive item sold was a spyglass that was bought for £1.15s (£110) by Joseph Leask of Bankfield, for whom Arthur had planted the trees fifteen years earlier. His brother Thomas paid the funeral costs of £8.9.10d (£545).[23]

Arthur died a lonely man and a figure of fun, having alienated his family and many of the good people of Lerwick. But, in his lifetime, he had contributed a great deal to Shetland through *A View of the Ancient and Present State of the Zetland Islands* (1809) and the many privately published papers that shed light on subjects as diverse as ophthalmia, natural history, the local fisheries and agriculture improvement. He had been instrumental in the establishment of the Lerwick Library and improvement societies and had been responsible for demonstrating the further possibilities for tree planting around Lerwick. He had fought valiantly for several good causes, even if his strategy had been wildly wrong. He had never failed to impress knowledgeable visitors, even though they found him somewhat stubborn and prejudiced. And, he had revealed, on his beloved sister's death, that he could be sensitive and sentimental. His intentions had always been good but his character had been fatally flawed.

The last words on Arthur were written by his nephew (Thomas Edmondston 1825-1874) who, touchingly, in 1868, erected a tombstone on his grave in Lerwick, on which he had, perhaps humorously, inscribed in recognition of Arthur's tenacious adherence to his own rectitude:

"SACRED
TO THE MEMORY
OF
ARTHUR EDMONDSTON, M.D.
THE HISTORIAN
OF ZETLAND
HIS NATIVE COUNTRY"

So, just as the beginning of the 1830s had brought the death of Henry in Newcastle, reducing the five brothers to four, so the death of Arthur in Lerwick in the early 1840s, reduced them to three; Thomas, Charles and Laurence. In the year an impoverished Arthur died, leaving two illegitimate children, Charles, on the other side of the Atlantic, had re-established a modest livelihood to support his family that had grown to eleven. It now looked as if they had survived their financial downfall, at least as long as the growing political rift between the North and the South did not entirely destabilise their situation.

Altogether, it was a year of very mixed emotions for the Edmondston family for, in the early summer, Charles returned from America for his one and only visit to his homeland and his two remaining brothers whom he had not seen for over 40 years. He was ten years too late to see Henry but just months too late to see Arthur. In recognition of his many achievements in Charleston and despite his recent financial problems, his home town of Lerwick made him an honorary Burgess.

A happier summer

In that summer of 1841, having been away most of the winter, Tom and Biot were together again, spending their time in their favourite pursuits of sailing, fishing and shooting. One memorable day,[24] their uncle Thomas took them, along with their father and their visiting uncle Charles on the *Haaf-fish,* out to the seabird colonies at Burra Firth. They were accompanied by Thomas' man, Peter Sutherland, and a young friend of Biot's, each taking a turn at the rowing. There was no wind but a low swell gently raised and lowered the boat as they pulled towards the mouth of the voe. After taking the boat into the entrance of one of their favourite caves where they could see, but could not reach, the light of an exit over 30 metres away, the older boys demanded to have some sport.

They rowed on until they came under vertical cliffs whose narrow ledges above them were lined with bickering and jostling guillemots and plastered here and there with the nests of kittiwakes that circled above their heads calling excitedly. Unbeknown to Tom, however, the three elder Edmondston brothers decided to have a little amusement at his expense. Biot's friend was first to try with the gun. The target of guillemots was static but the rise and fall of the boat made it necessary to choose one's moment carefully. At the report of the first shot the kittiwakes screamed and fled their nests and a crowd of guillemots spilled off the ledges into the water around them, leaving only a small proportion still on the ledges unwilling to leave their young in the face of an unknown enemy. With every shot a few more left but in their confusion always a few more returned. Biot, his friend and Peter shot several birds off the cliffs, but all Tom's efforts, much to his chagrin and embarrassment, brought down nothing. After many suggestions as to what he might be doing wrong and much sympathy for his failures from his elders, it was revealed that Peter had been loading the light fowling piece with powder, but not with shot! Tom took their trick at his expense with good grace and perhaps the guillemots were grateful too!

That summer rolled past all too quickly and the time came for decisions regarding Tom's future as he approached his sixteenth birthday. Advice was sought from the great men who knew Tom, including Sir W. J. Hooker who had now moved on from Glasgow to become the first Director of the new Gardens at Kew in London. At the same time the Regius Chair of Civil and Natural History at Marischal College in Aberdeen became vacant. To his surprise and delight, up against stiff opposition, MacGillivray won the Chair and became the Professor at the college in 1841, moving his family of nine back to his home city of Aberdeen.

Opinion was, that gifted as he was in natural history, there were precious few openings to make a living in that field and that Tom needed a profession. It was decided that he should therefore study medicine at Edinburgh, which curricula, as it happened, had a large element of botany. So, in September 1841, he and Biot set off for the home of Eliza's brother, their uncle David in Edinburgh, Tom to attend university and Biot to go back to school.

Hols Hellier, Burra Firth by Henry Saxby.

CHAPTER TWELVE

HUBRIS

"All Well. God be praised … I am now sitting with my loved boy here – he is well but has gone through dreadful expense and fatigue – we flew into each others arms and wept tears of gratitude to God who has so providentially conducted me to his relief."

Dr Laurence Edmondston (1795-1879)

Tom's stumble

Tom's return south was almost as spectacular in the academic botanical world of Edinburgh as it had been the previous year. Just prior to entering the University he read a paper to the Botanical Society of Edinburgh *On the native dyes of the Shetland Islands*. Then, days after his sixteenth birthday, he was elected Assistant Secretary to the Society and on that day read a second paper, entitled *The Botany of Shetland*, which was the first time anybody had described the flora of the northernmost islands of Britain. An excited Tom wrote home after the second lecture describing how "… *I could hardly get on sometimes for the cheering*".[1] It was a triumph.

Tom matriculated at Edinburgh in November 1841 at the age of 16, and began his studies for a medical degree just like his father, uncles, grandfather and great-grand-uncle before him. This was not a particularly young age to begin university; Darwin had matriculated at 14 and MacGillivray at 12! Tom's professor in natural history was the same man who had lectured his father, Hibbert, Fleming, Forbes and Darwin; Robert Jameson. Tom accepted the need to study medicine and take up a medical profession even though the study of botany was the subject most dear to him. His sister, Jessie M. E., later wrote of him that "…his wonderful memory made education easy for him. He scarcely required to take notes of the lectures."[2] That is not to say that he did not work hard – "*I am continuing the same round of occupation – classes during the day, and studying for them at night, occasionally relieved by a little botany, or Blackwood's Magazine, or 'Charles O' Malley'*."[3] He attended the Theatre Royal one night to watch a Sheridan comedy, but thought "… *going to theatres a very useless way of spending my time and money*." Study and botany were everything to him and he had little time for anything else, but such devotion could not have endeared him to his fellow students.

Edinburgh University.

Curiously perhaps, many of Tom's letters home were not to his father and mother but to his uncle Thomas. Their relationship had always been close. Tom loved his parents dearly but, whereas his father was increasingly an austere man of high moral rectitude, his uncle was a man who liked to enjoy life and with whom the growing Tom could occasionally have some fun and excitement, just as Laurence had had in *his* younger days. Just as consequential was the fact that it was Thomas who was funding Tom's studies, which his father was unable to. In his letters to his uncle, Tom revealed Thomas' 'conservative' influence on his own politics.

Thomas Edmondston (1779-1858) as an older man

> *"Every shop window is filled with portraits of 'the Duke of Wellington in the House of Lords', 'Sir Robert Peel, first Lord of the Treasury', &c., &c. I have seen a lot of H. B.'s caricatures on the downfall of the Whigs. I shall send you one or two. One represents the Duke putting an extinguisher on a candle almost burnt out, called 'Whiggery'; its grease, running down the sides of the candlestick, is formed into capital likeness of *Lord Melbourne and Lord J. Russell."*[4]

*Lord Melbourne was a supporter, and Lord John Russell a champion, of the Reform Laws which were an anathema to Thomas.

In another letter, Tom described his youthful reaction to the call for the repeal of the protectionist corn-laws, knowing how it would amuse his uncle:

> *"There is an anti-corn law agitation going on here. Petitions for signatures are at the corner of every street. Another promising youth and myself have had some amusement pretending to sign our names to these precious documents, but, in fact, writing nonsense instead, such as, 'You be low'd', 'Corn Law for ever', 'Down with agitation'."*[5]

Such jocularity, however, was dampened in November 1841 when Tom's much-loved seven-year-old sister, Jessie Helen, died in an accident. For the boys in Edinburgh, Tom at university and Biot at school, it was an event that emphasised their remoteness from the family. In the spring of the following year, Tom was steeling himself to another six months away from home and wrote to his uncle Thomas in Buness of his plans to follow up his lecture on the plants of Shetland with a Flora, but first he told him about his plans for the summer:

> "*It has been proposed to me that I should attend Graham* [Professor of Botany] *in summer, so as to make out the year, to count in the medical curriculum. I think that there is little doubt he will give me a ticket – in fact he has as good as offered me one, at all events, strongly recommended my staying and competing for his gold medal, which he says, 'I should be sure to take.' It is offered as a prize for the best herbarium composed of the plants within a ten mile circuit of Edinburgh.*"[6]

The competition Tom had entered into required the collection of as many species of plants as possible between 20th July, 1841 and 20th July, 1842. In early May he told his uncle Thomas that he was already a fortnight behind his competitors and needed to get on with his fieldwork. He also mentioned that he had his own botanical pupils and that he was having some problems with associates at the Botanical Society.

> "*I am in grand repute among them all – one of my successful pupils made me a present of a very handsome snuff box – made from a walnut at Virgil's grave which he had cut himself … I begin to find like most other people that I have enemies, and a number of the underlings of the Society have linked themselves against me by misrepresentation and calumny and endeavour as much as they can to annoy me.*"[7]

Dr Robert Graham.

Tom was looked up to by his own young pupils but his substantial achievements in the field, appointment as Secretary to the Botanical Society, his intimacy with the great men of the day, the preferential treatment he received from senior academics and just a little hubris, was making him rather unpopular with his peers; not that he felt he was getting any more recognition than he deserved. It affected him badly though and he told his uncle he could not sleep for worrying about it. Tom was also not getting on well with his other uncle, his mother's brother David, with whom he was staying, falling out with him over payment for his lodgings. Thomas was so generous with the allowance he gave Tom that the young man took the ready supply of funds for granted and did not seem to be aware just how privileged he was.

In June that summer, despite her chronic disability, Eliza was delivered of her ninth child, Jessie Margaret (Jessie M. E.), who was named after her deceased sister, Jessie Helen, who had died the previous year. That same month, Thomas, on one of his regular trips to Edinburgh, met up with Tom and was impressed with the herbarium of Edinburgh plants he had put together for the competition. On 27th July Tom wrote to his mother, proudly telling her that he was studying with Babington who had come to Edinburgh to work on foreign plants and that: "*I have made some discoveries in the Flora of this district ... The prizes are to be decided on the 1st. I have no fear of the result.*" He went on to tell her that he had presented his herbarium of "*... between seven and eight hundred species, nearly twenty of which were not formerly noticed in the circuit specified.*"[8] This was a little disingenuous as the 20 new plants were not actually all full species.

The prizes were to be presented on the last day of classes on the 2nd of August, but the day before, Professor Graham announced to the class, from which Thomas happened to be absent, that some plant specimens of one herbarium presented for the prize required immediate verification. Professor Graham was referring to Tom's herbarium and by 'verification' he meant that he required fresh specimens. If those were presented to him the following day, Graham informed the class, then that herbarium would be entitled to the prize. Indirectly, Tom became aware of this condition, but 24 hours did not leave him nearly sufficient time to procure fresh specimens of all 20 or so new records. The next day he approached the Professor to plead his case but the prize was awarded to another. Eliza, later hinted that there might have been petty jealousies that had poisoned Graham's mind against Tom, and Laurence, through his own investigations, discovered that Graham, the acknowledged expert on the local flora, had been somewhat startled to find that his young pupil had come up with so many records he himself had overlooked.

A few days later Tom wrote despondently to his uncle Thomas.

"*My dear Uncle ... I have been able to do very little of late ... it is vexatious to find hopes disappointed, and petty envy and jealousy occupying the place of the kindly feeling one had anticipated. The temper is (for the time) soured, and a general disgust and morbid misanthropy will creep over one. However, I am learning to bear these things with more Christian resignation, and the lesson will be useful to me in after life ... The day of awarding the prize came, and a student with not half the number of plants that I had got the prize ... In my own self-defence I have drawn up a list of the new plants found by me this summer for the purpose of publishing them in the Phytologist.*"[9]

The result of the competition was a disaster for Tom: a serious setback in his spectacular progress to date and a catalyst for a change in the priorities of his life. In effect, Tom was accused of cheating by his Professor and Vice-President of the Botanical Society and, he thought, his friend and supporter! Tom had already been assured by Graham that he would win and had been supremely confident: he was, after all, the outstanding student of his day. There seemed no rational reason why Graham queried Tom's new plant records, nor gave him a more reasonable amount of time to have them confirmed. To have given this remarkable student only 24 hours to present confirmation, without even informing him directly, was a strange decision. Tom had a reputation for diligence and application, was a model son and student. There was no reason for Graham to have believed for one moment that Tom might have done something at such variance to all that he knew about him? Why then, did he question the integrity of his most outstanding student and protégé of his illustrious colleagues, Sir W. J. Hooker and Professor Edward Forbes, without the most careful consideration of the evidence? There are several possible explanations, none convincing and some unthinkable. Whatever the truth, the sixteen-year-old Tom, prince among Scotland's young botanists, was shattered.

In a second letter home a few days after the event, he spoke of working on his Flora and laid out his plans for the coming term for family approval. It seemed, in the face of a dreadful disappointment and humiliation, that he had bravely surmounted the crisis. But a couple of weeks later, under the pressure of facing his fellow students and those who had slandered him, and before there was time to receive loving and supportive letters from home in commiseration, he cracked. The family received a "short incoherent note, saying he was off to London, where he intended to take any situation he could get, giving no address ..."[10] On reception of this communication, Laurence and Eliza were overwhelmed with concern for their precious and talented child. What on earth was his state of mind, what might he do, what harm might he come to?

That cursory note, like his previous letters, took over a week to reach Unst. Within hours Laurence had packed a case. He made a midnight journey by boat to Lerwick, caught the packet to Aberdeen and from there journeyed on to Edinburgh where he met up with Eliza's brother David to find out what had happened. He found that Tom's uncle David did not see his son in quite the same light as his parents. Laurence wrote home on the 29th September from Edinburgh, *not* to his Eliza, his wife and mother of Tom, but to Thomas his brother, who was funding Laurence's pursuit of Tom. He asked Thomas to pass on the news to Eliza and to inform her that he had not time to write to her! Even after 17 years of marriage his psychological dependence on his brother had not changed. The letter revealed as much about Laurence's agitated state of mind as about the news of Tom.

> "*He* [David MacBrair] *has got his* [Tom's] *address in London and all necessary information ... I* [will] *see poor Tom himself – all that his Uncle David tells me of him seems referable to inexperience and thoughtlessness – presumption of youth and a combination of adverse circumstances – but he must be instantly brought back to his duty with paternal kindness and firmness ... David judges him still harshly – making us allowances for anything ... I of course will not at present fly in his face with argument ... I shall be off tomorrow ... God forgive the infatuated boy for his misconceptions of all our views – God forgive him ... I feel able for this journey – it is a righteous one and God prosper you who gave me the means. I feel strong in the support of a merciful providence ... There is no fear of my* [not] *catching him in London – it does not seem as if any foreign situation was in his view.*"[11]

From Edinburgh, Laurence told Thomas, he took the coach the following day for Darlington. What he wrote next revealed an upset, weak and nervous character:

> "[I] *was taken ill ... near Edinburgh from mental anxiety and bodily debility and for the first time in my life fainted. I thought I was to finish there my pilgrimage – at last could stammer out the word to the guard* [for] *a glass of brandy – a house was luckily near.*"[12]

From Darlington Laurence went on to London by train "*... sometimes travelling at 50 miles an hour ...*"[13] arriving in London late in the evening two days after leaving Edinburgh. Early the following morning it was an exhausted and worried father who eventually found Tom, still abed, reading. They flung themselves into each others' arms and wept in relief. For Tom, responsibilities were now on someone else's shoulders and for Laurence, he had found his prodigal son. There, sitting beside him on the bed, Laurence heard how Tom, unable to face his accusers and receiving little sympathy from his uncle David, had taken the steamer from Leith to London to get as far away from everyone as possible. Providentially, with no plans as to exactly what he should do, just when he was disembarking at Blackwell, he had met a gentleman whom he had known at college. This gentleman had taken Tom to his own house. As a loving father, Laurence gave Tom the benefit of any doubt about his alleged transgressions. Together they prayed that Tom might find the strength to face the world again with Christian fortitude.

> "_All Well. God be praised … I am now sitting with my loved boy here – he is well but has gone through dreadful expense and fatigue – we flew into each others arms and wept tears of gratitude to God who has so providentially conducted me to his relief._"[14]

In this letter, again to Thomas, but with lines for Eliza, Laurence blamed disappointments, misapprehensions, bad health, fears of displeasure from his parents, sleepless nights and poor counsel for Tom's flight from Edinburgh.

Two days later, on 4th October, 1842, both father and son wrote to Thomas; Tom writing under instruction from his father, who reminded him how much they were both beholden to Thomas. Tom repeated the reasons his father had given his uncle for his precipitate and ill-judged decision to leave Edinburgh. In this letter Tom asked his uncle to give his "… _best love to my dear Mama_"[15]: neither wrote immediately to Eliza. The following night they took the train back to Leith to await the packet for Lerwick and there Tom wrote to his mother.

Whatever the fears and concerns Laurence suffered before he caught up with Tom, they were nothing to those of Eliza, back on Unst, unaware of Tom's state of mind or health and desperately awaiting news via Thomas. It was, therefore, an immense relief to her to know that they would shortly be at Leith and boarding the packet for home. Her hopes, however, were dashed by autumn gales. First, the packet, after ten days at sea, was forced to turn back to Leith. Then, as the dreadful weather continued

Eliza Edmondston (MacBrair).

147

unabated, it and its frustrated passengers had to wait for a further two months before they were able to return to Shetland: an interminable delay to Eliza. Eventually, father and chastened son arrived back in Unst just before Christmas, nearly four months after Tom's despairing adieu.[16]

That winter, the family rallied around Tom and he found comfort and solace among them, especially from his doting mother. His younger brother Biot, now 15, was still at school in Edinburgh and now bound for the ministry, but Halligarth was still full of children and childish laughter. There was David (5), his sisters Mary (10), Isabella (3), Margaret (1) and the infant Jessie M. E. and, of course, all the family pets. In this atmosphere of love and support Tom quickly recovered his equanimity and was soon once more absorbed in his favourite pursuits. Meanwhile, Laurence wrote to his old friend MacGillivray at Aberdeen, seeking advice as to what to do with Tom. In his reply, MacGillivray suggested that Tom continue with medicine from which he could make a living, rather than changing to natural history, but that in the meantime he study Shetland's Crustacea and Mollusca. It was a field he was moving into himself and he knew that Tom already had some experience from collecting for Forbes. MacGillivray also revealed that he had parental problems of his own: not surprising since he had nine children and very little money.

> "*I attend to what you say respecting your son, and will be happy to do what I can on his behalf … It is a great pity that young men cannot divest themselves of the prejudices and follies so apt to beset them, and take a prospective view of life … they are especially preposterous from about fourteen to twenty … If yours, with the abilities which he has, would just go on steadily, and modestly, who knows but he may be yet the most distinguished of our naturalists. I really wish that he and John [his son] may share the glory and the profit between them.*"[17]

MacGillivray's choice of words concerning Tom, "*steadily, and modestly*", confirmed both the youth's habit of throwing himself into things with great abandon and that his head had been somewhat turned by all the attention he had received from the great and the good. By a curious coincidence, the footsteps of MacGillivray's son John, who was also such a problem to him, and who also became a naturalist, followed those of Tom a few years later.

After the New Year, Tom sent a draft of a paper on his mouse-ear to Babington for comment, requesting Babington to send him a specimen of another species of mouse-ear for comparison.[18] Tom wanted to prove that his mouse-ear from the serpentine of Unst was a full species and not just a variant on the species that was found on one or two of Scotland's mountains. Time was on his hands and he thought he might as well earn some money, so in the early summer of 1843, he wrote to his uncle Arthur's old enemy in Lerwick, the Rev. Thomas Barclay. Thomas and Laurence had remained on good terms with him and Tom wrote seeking advice on the idea of giving a series of botanical lectures in Lerwick.[19]

The Rev. Barclay reacted favourably and Tom spent a successful summer in Lerwick, earning some money and lecturing to a surprisingly large audience. Every week he wrote to his uncle Thomas, giving him all the news and gossip, telling him how impressed he was with the Rev. Barclay and his sermons.

> "*260 whales have been killed at Ura Firth. Large shoals of them have been seen on the west side. I wish some would come your way. A Greenland brig has arrived with 4100 seals. They have a live one on board, and I went to see it. It is different from any I have seen … I have*

heard one of the finest possible sermons from Mr Barclay yesterday. He preaches his farewell next Sunday [to become Principal of Glasgow University]*; he merely mentioned the fact of leaving, and there were one hundred pocket handkerchiefs up.*"[20]

Disruption in Unst and Quiescence in Aberdeen

In that summer of 1843, just before Tom came to Lerwick, there occurred a great schism in the Scottish Church in Edinburgh whose repercussions rocked Unst just as they rocked the whole of Scotland. The Patronage Act of 1712 had established the right of patrons, in Shetland's case the Earl of Zetland, Lord Dundas, to appoint the minister of the parish, regardless of the opinion of the local congregation, while it was the responsibility of the local heritors, such as Thomas Edmondston, to provide his stipend. The established Church of Scotland had initially accepted this civil interference in the running of the Church. However, opposition to the principle grew over the years, culminating in the 'Disruption'. At the Church of Scotland General Assembly in Edinburgh on 18th May, 1843, 190 ministers walked out of the meeting on George Street in the New Town to Canonmills, Patrick Neill's village that was rapidly being swallowed up by the city. There they set up the Free Church, under whose rules the congregation would be permitted to choose their own minister without the landowner's interference. This event was another step in the growth of evangelism and down the road of Victorian social reform. The downside for the third of the ministers who left the established Church was that in pushing the state and the laird aside they had to give up their churches, manses, glebes and stipends and would now have to depend on the very limited largesse of each member of the congregation, however poor.

Such was the strength of the Established Church in Shetland that Unst was one of only four Shetland parishes where a majority of the population supported their 'disrupting' ministers, the Rev. James Ingram and his son the Rev. John Ingram. In fact, such was the commanding strength and presence of the 67-year-old puritanical patriarch and stern disciplinarian, that 80 per cent of the people of Unst followed him into the Free Church. The old man had one advantage in taking the courageous step away from the Established Church that many ministers could not; he owned his own home and its grounds. So the brave new Free Church in Unst was initially a tent in the Ingrams' garden. Shortly after, with financial support from a sponsor in England, two Free Churches were built in Unst: one at Hillside by the Ingram's manse and one at Uyeasound at the south end of the island.

The Ingrams and Thomas Edmondston had never got on, partly due to the existence and the presence of the illegitimate Ursula at Buness. Thomas, an unapologetic man of the Established Church and laird, tried everything to prevent the Disruption occurring in Unst. He even went as far as to seek an interdict from the Sheriff of Lerwick to prevent a meeting of the secessionists in the Established Church building itself.[21] He was successful in this, but providence, in the form of a gale, prevented it reaching Unst and being served in time and so the meeting and the split went ahead. That only three parishes in Shetland followed the Ingrams' lead into secession, was partly due to the efforts of Thomas' friend and namesake, the Rev. Thomas Barclay in Lerwick, who was also a fierce opponent of the Free Church.[22]

These events did not touch Tom to any degree, so involved was he in his teaching, writing and botanising. In that year, at the age of 17, the busy young man published five papers in the *Phytologist*, the *Zoologist* and the *Annals and Magazine of Natural History* on Shetland's flora and fauna.

First was a popular article in the *Zoologist* about the incredible feat that year of a local man called Josie (Joseph) Matthewson. Josie was cragsman who had captured a sea eagle on its nest with his bare hands, 150 metres above the sea on the cliffs of Herma Ness.

Another of Tom's papers, *Notes on the Northern Diver*, in September 1843, concerned the mysterious birds that both his father and uncle had written on – the great northern diver and the *immer-gös*.

"A few weeks ago my uncle Mr [Thomas] Edmondston of Buness, shot a young bird of this species (*Columbus immer* of the older writers [including his uncle Arthur]), which was evidently a bird of the year, the quills being almost unformed, and, in short, being scarcely fledged. This proves that the Northern Diver breeds in Shetland, a fact I have long suspected. The specimen alluded to was killed from the company of five individuals, two of which were old birds and three similar to the one procured."[23]

Tom, at 17, was perhaps exaggerating just a little, that he had "long suspected" that the species bred. Nevertheless, how could a "scarcely fledged" bird have flown from its nearest breeding grounds in Iceland?

A third paper was specifically on his Shetland mouse-ear in which he made the case for its recognition as a new species – this was the one he had sent in draft to Babington for comment. When Tom had first discovered his mouse-ear, there were two recognised species of this arctic-alpine plant, a *Cerastium latifolium*

Rev. James Ingram.

occurring only on one or two mountains in Britain, and *Cerastium alpinum* in Scandinavia and the Arctic. Tom compared his mouse-ear with both by examining herbarium specimens. He came to the conclusion that he could not separate the two recognised species and claimed that his was the only true *C. latifolium* in Britain.

This paper appeared in the *Phytologist* and was entitled *Notice of a New British Cerastium*. It was accompanied by drawings and the statement:

"Having for some years entertained the opinion that the plant above figured, although generally referred to Cerastium latifolium, was distinct from the plant called by that name in Britain, I have paid considerable attention to our alpine Cerastia, and am disposed to conclude that my plant is truly distinct from the C. latifolium of Smith and Hooker."[24]

Although Tom's mouse-ear had been included in Hooker's *British Flora* in 1838, his paper of 1843 established Tom as the finder of the new plant and a botanist to be reckoned with. Today, the Shetland and Scottish mouse-ears are recognised as two sub-species of a circumpolar species *Cerastium nigrescens*. Tom's Shetland mouse-ear, *C. n. nigrescens*, nevertheless, with its densely tufted, fleshy, hairy and purple leaves, remains a very distinct plant from its Scottish cousin. In botanical circles and in Shetland it is affectionately known as Edmondston's chickweed. Whether it remains a full species or not, Tom's plant occurs almost entirely on the small area of the Keen of Hamar, and nowhere else in the world.

It was now more apparent than ever where Tom's true interest lay, and it was not in continuing his medical studies that MacGillivray had originally suggested for him. Laurence and Eliza, and particularly his uncle Thomas, eventually agreed, along with the support of Tom's other scientific mentors, that he should now devote his studies full time to natural history. In the autumn of 1843, after misadventure in Edinburgh and the recovery of his confidence, it was a more focused and responsible Tom who matriculated at the University of Aberdeen to study under MacGillivray, now Professor of Natural History at Marischal College, who would also keep a fatherly eye on him.

Besides his many studies, Tom continued his regular corresponding with the great botanists of the day, and writing papers. In the summer of 1844, after his first winter at Aberdeen, he did not return to Unst but stayed on to arrange for the publication of his *Flora*. There, he wrote to Professor Balfour in Glasgow, asking and receiving permission for it to be dedicated to him. He also had a technical correspondence with Babington concerning the value and correctness of the various schools of plant nomenclature and with Sir W. J. Hooker who was seeking Shetland plants for Kew.[25] In his letter to the latter, Tom mentioned that seeds of the arctic sandwort that he had sent to a

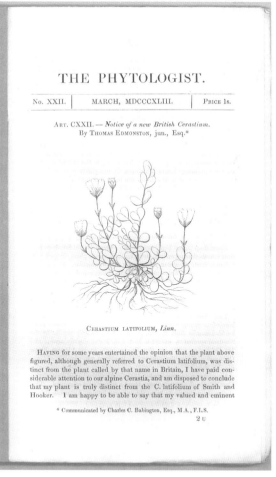

Notice of a new British Cerastium, by Thomas Edmondston 1843.

151

grower had germinated but that the plants were "*strikingly different*" from their parents.[26] It was to be another hundred years before this difference was explained, coincidentally by another botanist with Unst connections.

Through the summer of 1844, Tom continued his botanical and zoological lecturing in the county of Moray in North East Scotland, and corresponded regularly with his uncle Thomas. He also went botanising to some of the most famous plant sites in the Cairngorms, covering prodigious distances over very rugged and mountainous ground, inspired by his mentor and Professor, MacGillivray, who himself, in his younger days, had also walked and botanised all over the Grampians, often sleeping rough in the open air. In July Tom wrote:

> "*My dear Uncle, – I am just starting for Clova, and have but little time for writing, but I must drop a line to tell you how I got on. I wrote last from Banchory. I reached Kincardine O'Neil that night, walked to Aboyne next morning to breakfast and reached Castleton (34 miles) by half-past four P.M. I have never been off my feet since. Glen Castleton, Ben Avon, Ben-na-Buich, Ben Mac Dhui, and Loch-na-Garr have all been visited. I was at Camlachie yesterday, which is part of Clova. As to discoveries they have been very numerous, especially mosses and lichens. Of the latter I have found an entirely new genus, a most singular plant. I got the two rarest plants British plants in Camlachie –Gentiana nivalis and Sonchur alpinus, in a new station.*"[27]

In a letter to him in June 1844, Balfour neatly summed up the busy and restless Tom, "*You are a sort of peripatetic Encyclopaedia of Natural History.*"[28] And so the encyclopaedist returned home to Unst via Orkney at the end of the summer with a notebook full of lists of plants and pen and ink sketches. While there, wasting no time, he carried out some more dredging for marine species before setting off once again in October for Aberdeen, the University, and further courses with MacGillivray. When he arrived he wrote to his uncle about his lengthy journey, his plans for the *Flora* and the need to get subscribers and some financial return.

> "… [it was] *a tedious disgusting passage from Lerwick of five days – becalmed … then a heavy gale of SW wind in their teeth … Mr Duncan has got more than 20 or 30 subscribers in Lerwick and thinks he is to get as many more – so I hope we may perhaps make a <u>bob</u> or two by the <u>spec.</u>* [speculation] *if so there will be the better encouragement for them to go on with further works.*"[29]

He also sent his thanks for his uncle's support and love to all at Halligarth and to Ursula, asking to be remembered kindly to Sinclair and Peter.[30] In another letter the following month an excited Tom told his uncle that the *Flora* had gone to press! The letter also made it plain that he and his father's old friend had struck up a warm relationship. Tom referred kindly and familiarly to '*Mac*' and his daily walk along the shore with him.[31] Proudly, he went on to tell his uncle that MacGillivray had asked him to speak to the class about his ideas on classification, something that he had been developing for several years. For all his faults in his relationships with his peers, MacGillivray was an inspiring teacher, regularly taking his students out into the field and was much loved by them.

In a letter to his uncle in early November 1844, from Aberdeen, which mightily impressed but rather strained the now 65-year-old Thomas' brain, Tom explained his thoughts. The passage illustrated both Tom's intellectual precocity and his strong Christian and conservative beliefs he had assumed under the influence of both him and his father.

> "*I think that the best and most authoritative form of publishing a full explanation of my views, together with a history of previous and contemporaneous systems, and the exposition of the metaphysical principles on which I conceive the arrangements of natural objects may and ought to be conducted, will be, as 'Philosophy of Botany' reducing, not only the mere classification, but also, the structural and physiological principles on which that should be founded, to order and system … I believe that all the works of God are perfect, and it would be contrary to all analogy, drawn from the consideration of physical laws and phenomena, to conceive that animal and vegetable structure, fitted for certain functions, is not also a subject to certain immutable laws.*"[32]

In yet another letter to his uncle,[33] Tom related that when he gave MacGillivray the money from him for his entrance to his course the Professor stared at the notes and said "*It's really disgraceful to take money from you – but I'm terribly hard pressed just now and really a guinea is a vast sum to me.*" Actually, MacGillivray, with his large family, negative return from his books and a poor university salary, was always struggling financially. In the same letter, Tom went on to say that his lodgings were six shillings (£20) a week and that he was "*… out of the weary needful,*" having got through £20 (£1320) in the month! Tom had no idea what it was like to struggle to survive on a low income. The letter ended with a cryptic remark about a natural history position that was becoming vacant but that he was bound to secrecy. His plans had been to complete the course at Aberdeen, but as with the way of things in Tom's life, events overtook him.

CHAPTER THIRTEEN

THE VOYAGE OF THE *HERALD*

"[Eliza] awoke from sleep with a dream of her boy. She saw the ship on the placid Pacific Sea, and a boat, and the Captain with letters in his hand …"

Jessie M. E. Saxby (1842-1940)

Professorship

In the 18th century, Scottish universities were 'open' establishments, in marked contrast to the more famous duo of Oxford and Cambridge in England: neither religion nor class was a barrier to entrance. This tradition of liberality, combined with the intellectual fervour of the Scottish Renaissance that continued into the 19th century, and the reputation of its natural history and medical schools, was what attracted people like the Frenchman Biot, Hibbert, Forbes and Darwin to Edinburgh. Like St Andrews and Edinburgh, there was only one university in Glasgow at that time. Its Professor of Moral Philosophy, from 1760 until his death in 1796, John Anderson (1726-1796), had exemplified and expanded the Scottish liberal attitude by making a practice of giving a series of popular lectures, quite outwith the University, to anyone interested. On his death, Professor Anderson's legacy, as he had requested, was put towards the founding of a new college. This became known as the Andersonian University of Glasgow, later to become the University of Strathclyde. In late 1844, the Chair of Botany at the Andersonian became vacant and a friend of Tom's brought the advertisement of the post to his attention. On the 17th December, Tom hastily wrote to his uncle from Aberdeen.

> "*The first thing of importance I have to tell you, is about a speculation I have embarked in, with a good deal of hesitation, as it was impossible to get advice from you or papa in time … The professorship of Botany in the Andersonian University of Glasgow is vacant … I immediately wrote to Dr Balfour* [Professor of Botany at Glasgow University] *to know about it … It appears that there is no salary attached, but the fees must constitute the professor's income; but he said, "an active energetic person like you, would make something good of it." I consulted with MacGillivray … He strongly advised me to become a candidate, and offered testimonials, and all assistance in his power … The election takes place on the 15th January* [1845], *so you will see that no time was to be lost.*"[1]

It is indicative of Tom's self-confidence, that after studying for only one year (1841-42) at Edinburgh and less than two years (1843-44) at Aberdeen, he felt prepared enough to apply for the post. Tom obtained references from a formidable group of his eminent supporters, including Babington, Balfour, Forbes and MacGillivray, and also from Sir W. J. Hooker at Kew. With backing such as this how could he fail! Sir W. J. Hooker wrote:

"Mr Thos. Edmondston has been long known to me personally and by correspondence. From his earliest years he evinced the most uncommon zeal in the cause of Natural History, and has never ceased to improve himself in the various branches of it, especially in Botany. With this knowledge is combined a liberal education and an ardent desire to devote his life to the cause of science. I consider him well qualified to lecture upon Natural History in general, and to fulfil the duties of a Professor in any Academy or University."[2]

On 16th January, 1845, in a ferment, Tom wrote again to his uncle Thomas who, as his financial supporter, was less than enthusiastic with Tom's plans, seeing how little he had made out of his previous public lectures. Tom swept his concerns aside and wrote to reassure him that this was an opportunity that he could not turn down.

"This state of suspense is tantalizing … I set off for Glasgow [from Aberdeen] *a fortnight ago; got to Edinburgh that evening, and went to Glasgow same night. I called on all the Directors* [Andersonian], *leaving copies of my testimonials with them. Uncle D.* [David MacBrair] *happened to be in Glasgow, and staid a day, going among all his friends who had any influence in the matter. I returned to Edinburgh on Friday at midnight; staid with Uncle D. Next day went to Currie to see the Barclays* [Rev. Thomas], *and next morning at five started for Aberdeen, which I reached at six P.M., most unenviably knocked up. I had a great ado and expense seeing the Directors."*[3]

On 25th January, Tom wrote to his mother asking her to assure his father that he was still alive and informing her with great joy that he had been accepted for the post of *"… Professor of Botanical Science in the Andersonian Metropolis of western Glasgow"*![4] He went on to say that he would have to see out the lectures at Aberdeen until March and commiserated that she had again been unwell. On the same day he wrote to his uncle, informing him too that he was *"Professor of Natural History and ex officio Conservator of the Museum."*[5] Tom also asked Thomas to tell the Rev. John Ingram, the Free Church minister and his former teacher in Unst, how prophetic *"… his constant 'professoring' of me has turned out."*[6] It may not have been uncommon for a sixteen-year-old to attend university, but for one to go on to become a professor at the age of 19 was quite extraordinary.

Later that month, MacGillivray wrote Laurence some reassuring lines about his son.

"His conduct has all along been most exemplary, and he has gone fairly to work as a student, regularly keeping up with the business of the class, and although infinitely superior to the rest, submitting like them to examination. I often walk with him on the shore, and fishing station, for molluscs, zoophytes, and the like. He is now about as fond of zoology as of botany, and is also anxious to have a general knowledge of geology, on which subject we may enter in a few days."[7]

Adding fondly,

"I wish you would get him to go to bed regularly at some particular hour every night, otherwise he will greatly injure his health, which is not very firm at present … I never go to bed myself till 2 and am up at 8."

At last came the point of departure from Aberdeen and from the kind and fatherly MacGillivray, whom he never saw again. On 8th March, Tom wrote to tell his uncle about his last few days at the University and the farewell dinner in his honour which reflected an improvement in his relations with his peers. Tom left the really important news until the end. The dinner was attended by 30 students,

"medical lecturers, two or three M.D.s, and several advocates and solicitors. The chairman made a splendid speech in proposing my health, and I did my best in returning thanks. You see I am coming out rather ... Well! My book is published at last. A copy goes by this post."[8]

Tom's *A Flora of Shetland* (1845) was one of the first county floras to be published in Scotland and the very first published account of the plants of Shetland, with a list of flowering plants, grasses, sedges, rushes, mosses, liverworts, lichens and seaweeds. The review in the *Phytologist*, by his botanical acquaintance Hewitt Watson, pointed out the particular value of Tom's work to botanists but it was probably not as enthusiastic as Tom might have wished.

"... from the position of the Shetland Isles, like a connecting step between Great Britain and the more arctic islands ... [the] list of their plants will possess more geographical interest than usually attaches to a local flora ... And on the whole, though not free from some of the defects of haste and youthful inexperience ... is a creditable evidence to the author's ability and industry of research."[9]

The *Flora* was not without its faults, mainly due to Tom's relative youth and impetuousness, his isolation from experts and the centres of learning and the difficulty, in a time of few roads, to cover the ground. Nevertheless, whatever the criticism, the result was sufficiently substantial to stand for nearly 150 years before a new one appeared! Tom was right to be proud of his achievement.

Tom then moved to Glasgow where he settled down to long hours in preparation for his lectures in botany and geology. On the way he stopped in Edinburgh again to see the Rev. Barclay and his family and called on Robert Chambers (1802-1871), through the latter's childhood acquaintance with his mother, who invited him to dinner to meet a number of scientific people.[10] Robert Chambers and his brother William had established the *Chambers' Edinburgh Journal* in 1832, a very popular and instructive weekly magazine to which Tom's mother Eliza, brother Biot, and sister, Jessie M. E., were all to contribute. Chambers had anonymously published a hugely controversial book entitled *Vestiges of the Natural History of Creation* in 1844. This was an all-encompassing description and explanation of the world that, in some ways, was a precursor to Darwin's *On the Origin of Species*. In fact, Darwin later admitted that it had paved the way for his book and even felt that it had quite taken the wind out of the sails of his own theory of evolution. Life, according to the author, developed spontaneously, was still evolving by transmutation from the effect of external circumstances (Lamarckism), from one generation to the next, and did not require God's intervention except as the original creator of the Universe. The book caused a sensation in both secular and religious circles and was an instant best-seller. It was translated into several languages and by 1860 had gone though 20 editions in Britain and America. An added piquancy to the book and its contents was that Robert Chambers successfully hid his identity as the author for ten years, though there had been suggestions that he might be responsible, but then, there were also rumours that it might be Darwin, Lyell or even the royal consort, Prince Albert! Having the opportunity to discuss the cultural, scientific and political topics of the day, with someone as radical as Robert Chambers and his circle of scientific friends, gave Tom a very different perspective on the world than he had yet encountered in his family or among the university academics he had come to know.

Just before he settled in Glasgow, Tom received a final letter from MacGillivray reminding him of the negligent side of his character: "… *I have been told a number of things about you which vexed me …However, it is all over.*"[11] He warned Tom that these things can be carried into adulthood. The following day, Tom wrote to his uncle Thomas to apologise for some unpaid bills that had been sent to him directly. Although creditors had threatened to prosecute Tom, there had been nothing criminal in Tom's behaviour and his remiss in paying the bills was simply due to a young man's thoughtlessness; one who had been bankrolled by a loving and indulgent uncle.[12]

In Glasgow, Tom became as popular as he had been in Aberdeen. A Glasgow newspaper of the time that commented on his appointment to the Andersonian gave a brief description of Tom at 19:

Robert Chambers.

"He was slightly, but symmetrically formed, his height scarcely attaining to middle size. Yet the shapely head, with its close brown curls, the high intellectual brow, and the quick beaming eye, added to the lines which study had imprinted on his noble countenance, gave him the look of being older than he was – only twenty. His carriage and manners were refined and gentlemanly, but although he dressed well and in good taste the sombre colours and loose fit, and somewhat careless adjustment of his clothes, announced the student rather than the young man of society and of the world."[13]

Tom the botanist circa 1845.

Shortly after this, Tom sent home a daguerreotype of himself. The process of fixing an image on silver-plated bronze plates had been invented by the Frenchman Jacques Daguerre just five years previously and had become all the rage. This portrait makes him appear slightly older than his years, confirming the description in the paper.

Tom proposed to charge one and half guineas (£100) for the series of Botany lectures for the summer session, with an excursion on Saturdays thrown in. Not all his applicants were strictly students and one who wrote to Tom fairly fulfilled Anderson's wish for his institution to be a 'college for the people' in the best tradition of Scottish education.

> "*Sir. – I wish to enter your classes on botany, mineralogy, and geology, but as I am only a journey-man bootmaker, if you would take work from me instead of money I could give you material and workmanship not inferior to what you would get in the best shops of the city, and at a cheaper rate.*"[14]

Regrettably, the bootmaker's offer could not be taken up, for just as Tom was settling down to prepare for his first lecture he received a letter, on the 29th April, 1845, from his mentor and friend, Edward Forbes in London, now Professor of Botany at King's College and a Fellow of the Royal Society.

Out of the Blue

The opening lines of this letter stunned Tom. He had to read them several times over before he believed what his eyes were telling him. In just two sentences the world became his!

"*Dear Edmondston. – Before stating what I write about, I must request an <u>immediate</u> answer by return of post to this. An expedition is going out to the Pacific and California. It <u>sails in a fortnight</u>. This morning I have been sent for to the admiralty to say whether I could recommend a naturalist at a moment's notice, as Prince Albert had desired that a naturalist should be appointed to accompany the expedition. The salary will be between £250 and £300 [£16,500-19,800] a year, finding mess out of it. This I consider good pay. Now it seems to me that this* *would be an admirable opportunity for you, both to pursue your scientific aims, and to lay the basis of a distinguished reputation. It is very short notice, but I went to the Oregon on a shorter notice, having got all ready in a week. It may lead to much better things than your Andersonian appointment could possibly do. Now, if you write at once, saying that you would like to go (there is no time to consult friends at a distance), I will do everything in my power to get your appointment. Should it be so, you will have to come to London at once to prepare. There will be no time to get any replies to any letters of yours to Shetland, but I feel sure both your father and uncle could desire no better prospect for you. Write at once, as everything depends upon promptitude. In haste. – Ever yours."*[15]

What had happened was that a German physician, naturalist and geologist, Ernst Dieffenbach (1811-1855), who had already been on a previous expedition to New Zealand had been offered the post but had turned it down at the last minute.[16] The admiralty and Forbes were therefore desperately seeking a replacement and Forbes' thoughts lighted on Tom. Naturally, Tom leapt at such an opportunity, especially as the alternative, as he now saw it from his new perspective, was of spending his valuable energies trying to din classification into *"the dull skulls of obtuse Glasgow burghers."*[17]

Forbes knew that Tom's uncle Thomas was the boy's sponsor and it was to him, not to his parents that Tom immediately wrote, even though this potential step was not just about money but would involve a long absence from home and possible danger. The expedition might also be the platform to launch Tom to botanical stardom, just as Forbes' to Oregon had done for him and Darwin's on the *Beagle* just ten years previously had done for him.

"My dear Uncle. – ... This appointment is of all others the most desirable I can conceive ... everything combines to make it the most eligible thing that could happen. I would be certain of a good appointment when I came home again, if God spares me. One thing clouds the prospect. You may easily guess how distressed I will be to leave the country without seeing you all ... I fear much that this news will, for the first at least, distress mamma in her present weak state, therefore I do not write to her. You will also tell papa, and consult together on the subject."[18]

Tom went on to tell his uncle that he was accepting the position, but that of course, should Thomas or his parents veto the proposal, there would still be time for him to receive a letter in London. Then, graciously, he wrote to tell MacGillivray the great news. He thanked him for his wonderful lectures, the subjects of which would now prove invaluable and he promised to bring him back *"a large stock of birds and shells"*.[19] By return of post he received letters from each of his parents, both approving his plans but already anticipating his absence. His father's agonised but proud:

"My dearest Thomas. – Your letter to your uncle of the 1st inst. [May] has agitated me a good deal from the idea of your being so far from us ... The salary is good. It is under the wing of government ... Above all, it will compel your too fervid intellect and brain to necessary repose, and tend to mature and consolidate your constitution ... So far so well ... You will become what

I so early vaticinated, 'Lin. The Little' ... May God preserve you; – use the means of safety, leave the result to His Providence ... My dearest son, in one sense this is a joyous epoch for you, in another it is solemn. The scene is untried, and you can hardly expect that all those whose hearts beat so warm and true to you, will be alive to welcome your return; but God will ever be with you to protect and console you ... If you should never again hear from your father, take this as his last earnest counsel, to view as the substantial paramount business of your life to prepare for a glorious future in the world to come. Again, my dearest Thomas; farewell. – Your ever tenderly affectionate father."[20]

And from his mother:

"My dearest Tom. – The short notice, and surprise of your letter, almost takes from me the ability to say a word to you, but yet I must say that my reason tells me the appointment is what we ought to have wished for you ... may God, of His mercy, turn it out for your good. With His blessing all will go well with you, and, oh! I pray you seek it fervently and constantly, and be sure of your mother's prayers many times when you are sleeping. The bairns are all well, I will not let them cease to talk of you ... May heaven's blessings be ever with you my dearest boy."[21]

Tom now had to inform the Andersonian that he would not even deliver his first lecture before departing; a confrontation that he was, quite rightly, not looking forward to. After having sought the support of so many influential people in obtaining the post, on the eve of his first lecture, he now had to tell them that he was not taking it up! On the 7th May, the day he left Glasgow, he wrote once again to his uncle to keep him up to date with all the news.

"I start for Liverpool today ...The expedition is to be for three years or more ...connected with the survey of the Californias and Columbia, probably on to Texas ... I ought you know to have delivered my Introductory Lecture yesterday – and the Directors and Trustees together with the professors were waiting en masse ... The Directors were much vexed at my departure, but all agreed that it would be madness in me to lose such a golden opportunity ... Balfour ... swears he would have given up <u>his</u> Professorship for such a berth ... if we do not meet again on earth, in the mercies of an all merciful creator we will meet in a better place. I trust I shall ever bear myself so as to bring no discredit on the family which you have so unsparingly bestowed on me ... to you my gratitude ever will be, as it deserves to be, boundless ..."[22]

Tom took the train from Glasgow to Greenock, left there by steamer at 5pm and arrived in Liverpool by 10am the following morning. That afternoon he took the train from Liverpool and arrived in London late that evening.[23]

Meanwhile, back home in Unst, a brief correspondence between Laurence and Thomas, at just the time when they were both so proud of the achievements of their son and nephew, revealed that their relationship, particularly regarding the annuity, had become rather fraught. Thomas wrote formally to Laurence at Halligarth, from a few hundred metres away at Buness, *"It is now time to square up our annual affair ... You have so far delayed giving me any receipt for six years."*[24] The following day Laurence replied, acknowledging that he had received £440 (£28,600) for that period.[25] The rather extraordinary arrangement that they had long ago agreed to – whereby Laurence returned to practice medicine in Unst and look after his brother in return for the annuity and promise of the inheritance of the estate – was turning sourer every year that passed. This was perhaps inevitable as the two were very different in character and one could not live his entire life financially dependent on the other without friction. The businessman in Thomas disapproved of the manner in which Laurence ran his affairs, particularly in regard to the expense of his agricultural experiments. In addition, Thomas, whose health was slowly deteriorating, was now becoming a chronic invalid. Those two things combined, gradually hardened his feelings against his brother to whom he had once been like a father. For Laurence, it was a kind of exquisite agony to watch the spectacular progress he had envisaged from an early age for his gifted son and to know it depended entirely on the generosity of his brother; especially when he received so much of Tom's news, second-hand through Thomas. Eliza, knowledgeable of the arrangement and well aware of the strained feelings between the brothers lived with Laurence's torment daily, but Tom and the other children surely knew nothing of it.

So, a fortnight after his first letter to his uncle Thomas, Tom was in London and at last able to tell his parents and his uncle some of the detail of the plans for the expedition. The first thing he did was to call on Forbes who took him to the Admiralty to meet Captain Beaufort (1774-1857),[26] Hydrographer to the Government and deviser of the international 0-12 wind speed scale. If he had met some eminent people in Edinburgh, it was nothing to the great and the good he was to meet in London.

By a quirk of fate, that would cause ripples at Balta Sound not many years later, another British expedition was planning to leave the shores of England at that same time: this one to the Arctic. Under the command of Sir John Franklin (1786-1847), the *Terror* and the *Erebus* were heading for the North West Passage. Tom dined aboard the *Erebus* and met that expedition's Assistant Surgeon and Naturalist, Harry Goodsir (d1845), brother of John Goodsir, the Edinburgh University anatomist whom Tom had met in Shetland when he had accompanied Forbes on his visit there six years previously.

Next, Tom had to get down to the exciting task of amassing all the clothes and equipment he would need for several years voyaging.

"There is such an immensity of apparatus for the collection and preservation of quadrupeds, birds, reptiles, fishes, insects, plants, shells, rocks and fossils required, that I have done nothing but run from Regent Street to Bishopsgate ever since I came. And then there are dinners and soirees, and parties, and breakfasts, and society meetings where I must go and meet this naturalist and that, to get directions, and hints and advices … The Admiralty supply me with certain things, such as, paper for drying plants, alcohol and glass bottles for spirituous preparations … Books also … clothes … shoes … bedding … mess furniture, table cloths, towels, candles, even down to soap …"[27]

In two separate letters to his uncle and his parents, Tom then described the expedition under the command of Captain Kellet (b1806), hinting at a political as well as an expeditionary purpose.[28] The alleged political element was associated with the ownership, or lack of it, of large parts of the western coast of North America. At that point, early in 1845, Texas had not yet been annexed by the

United States, while the latter's claim to Oregon was not to be recognised by Britain until the following year, and it would be another three years before Mexico ceded California to the United States. In early 1845, therefore, there was still a British interest in the whole Pacific coast of North America, not that California could have been held by the British had it been claimed and Mexico ceded it.[29]

With great delight, Tom sat at his desk to describe for his family the ships of the expedition, spell out the names of the exotic places he was to visit and hint at the voyage's alleged political purposes:

"[The Expedition] *consists of two vessels, a large 26 gun frigate the "Herald" … one of the old "Jackass" frigates mounting no guns on the main deck but larger than the new six and thirtys … and a brig the "Pandora" to act as leader … we go first to Madeira and Teneriffe … then to Rio de Janeiro and around Cape Horn to Valparaiso … calling at Panama, Lima … our principal object is to survey the coasts of California and the Galapagos Islands … if Franklin makes the north west passage he is to join us, and if he does not make his appearance earlier we are to go as far north as the entrance to the Bering Straits to meet him. We return home by the Falklands and Society Islands … this is expected to take from 3-5 years … I believe the project for meeting him* [Franklin] *to be all of a* <u>blind</u> *to cover the real political objects of the survey. Britain is expected to get California from Mexico and our real business is to survey the coasts of that country … however, that may or may not be.*

All the Naturalists here are on tiptop expectation regarding the good things I am to bring home. The British Museum folk are half mad about it, as scarcely anything is known from the west coasts. There will certainly be a splendid coast to be examined, if God grant me life and health for that purpose."[30]

Every naturalist with whom he came into contact made requests of him and gave him advice. His head reeled with the catalogue of demands and suggestions.

"[Sir W. J.] *Hooker directs* [me] *to the highest mountains; to Cryptogramia and sea weeds; wishes for seeds and live plants in hermetically sealed glass, and refers* [me] *to the most erudite foreign books as* [my] *study. Edward Forbes wants every thing from the sea depths. Another begs for bats; another for butterflies; a third for fossils, and a fourth for beetles.*"[31]

Through Forbes, Charles Darwin instructed Tom on equipment and requested information on the southern extent of glaciers on the Pacific side of the North American continent, inviting Tom to contact him when he knew the route the *Herald* would follow.

"[Take] *a good stock of small steel rat-traps, with which he can easily take many rodents … I can think of one special point of geological interest on the NW & Californian coast viz to ascertain in what latitude southward great angular erratic boulders have been transported by floating ice over plains and across wide valleys.*"[32]

In his letter to his parents, Tom added that the expedition was also to survey the coast of New Albion (Oregon territory) and that:

162

HMS Herald *in Feejee by T. Glen Wilson.*

"Wyld, the Queen's geographer, however, not only does not think they [Franklin's expedition] *will make the passage, but does not believe they will ever be seen again. They themselves are much more sanguine, and the officers are taking out dancing shoes for a grand ball we are all to have at Valparaiso when we meet."*[33]

Tom then morbidly recalled the fate of *"yet others … Douglas sometimes rise unpleasantly before me"*[34] – Sir W. J. Hooker's protégé David Douglas, the great botanical explorer from Scone in Perthshire, Scotland, who died on an expedition in Hawaii in 1834 – and looked forward to when he might be back home again in Unst.

Finally, Tom told them of his meeting with a galaxy of Britain's geologists at the Geological Society at Somerset House. There, he was introduced to William Buckland (1784-1856) – the geologist who was the first to describe and name a dinosaur; Sir Henry de la Beche (1796-1855) who had just established the Geological Survey of Great Britain; Adam Sedgewick (1785-1873) – a brilliant Cambridge geologist, liberal Anglican priest and holder of one of the greatest geological collections; and perhaps the greatest of them all, Sir Charles Lyell – the geologist who championed the theory of the immense geological history of the Earth and provided such vital support for Darwin.[35]

Impressed as Tom was with all these great men, and involved as he was with all the scientific equipment he had to take with him, the youth in him was still excited by those things he had enjoyed with his uncle and his brother Biot and that reminded him of home. To his uncle he wrote:

> *"I wish you saw the beautiful gun case I have got, £75 [£5025] it cost. Damascus barrels … rifles … everything complete.* I tried it at Battersea Road … [fired] the ball within a 9 inch target every time at 150 yards … the gun is made by the finest maker … I got carte blanche to get it."*[36]

*Apparently, this was presented to him by Prince Albert, although Tom never mentions it.

He went on to say how much he looked forward to using it at Burra Firth on the *Haaf-Fish* with Thomas and Peter Sutherland. Meanwhile, he was able to reassure everybody at home about his shipmates and his accommodation on the *Herald*.

North Unst, perhaps Herma Ness, by Henry Saxby.

> *"I like my messmates very much, they are very pleasant fellows, and the captain is an exceedingly agreeable man … The other officers are also very pleasant fellows … I have got a good library of books, and we have a large chart room under the poop, where I have shelves and a table for my study, which is very convenient, as of course neither in the gun room, nor in my little crib of a cabin, can study be carried on to advantage."*[37]

After all the pressure from Forbes to hurry south, and a mad couple of weeks cramming in all the people he had to see and all the things he had to do, it was not until 25th June that Tom wrote home for the last time from England, on the eve of departure. Not yet 20, Tom, the country lad of good family from the most northerly island in Britain, a little over three years from commencing university, was now on the very south coast of Britain on the verge of a momentous voyage of discovery. That evening he wrote home with such a lump in his throat.

"My heart is very full and I can say but little … I am just on the eve of leaving – The old rocks of Shetland, and the beloved household faces rise pre-eminent among the objects left behind … God ever bless you all … Should I never see you again, dearest Mamma, my last breath will be a prayer for your happiness … The Captain has come aboard, and there's the pipe. All hands make sail! Signal ditto to our Consort the Pandora. Hoist away main royals. Adieu, adieu, God bless you."[38]

On Thursday, 26th June, 1845, Tom left Plymouth Sound aboard H.M.S. *Herald* under the command of Captain Henry Kellet, C.B., accompanied by the sloop *Pandora* under Lieutenant Commander James Wood. The expedition consisted of 350 men, plus twelve midshipmen, marines and scientists. As Tom stood on the deck of the *Herald* as she moved out of the Sound under full sail, he must have recalled and compared his present situation with his meetings with Sir W. J. Hooker's son aboard *his* ship in Balta Sound, only eight years previously. Dr W. D. Hooker had been returning from what had seemed to him then to be the remote country of Scandinavia. And here he was now, setting out on a much more ambitious scientific enquiry, literally in the steps of Darwin whose journal of his voyage on *The Beagle* had been published just six years earlier.

Voyaging

After a rough trip through the Bay of Biscay, the *Herald* reached Santa Cruz in Tenerife on 13th July, when Tom reported to his family that he was learning Spanish when he could find the time. Then it was across the Atlantic to the most eastward projection of Brazil by 9th August, then down the coast of South America and across the equator. On board the *Herald* life was good, for Captain Kellet was a liberal and relaxed officer and the *Herald* was a happy ship. Tom was even subjected along with others to the traditional baptism for those crossing the line for the first time.

"I was second on the list, and on my name being called by Neptune's secretary, two 'constables' bandaged my eyes, and led me on deck. As soon as I got on the quarterdeck, I was half smothered with buckets of salt water poured over me, and the engine playing right over my face. I was then seated on a plank placed over the main hatchway, and under which, on the maindeck, was a large sail filled with water, with two or three sailors swimming in it. Neptune (represented by an old captain of the foretop), with his wife and child, was seated on a gun carriage. A number of questions were asked me, to which I answered nothing, keeping my mouth firmly shut. My face was then lathered with a villainous composition of tar and grease thickened with oatmeal, and Neptune's private physician, opining that I must be faint, thrust up my nose a cork, with half-a-dozen needles stuck in it by way of scent bottle, thereupon the plank was withdrawn from beneath me, and I tumbled headlong into the sail full of water below; the sailors who were in it seized me as soon as I fell, ducking me under water; at last, half drowned, I managed to scramble out, and doubling up a middy, who was preparing a bucket of water for me as I emerged, I gained the quarterdeck, and was soon assisting, in serving the others the same way. The ship was a queer spectacle during the whole affair;

discipline was for the time suspended, and the captain and officers were enjoying the fun, and got as well soused as any."[39]

On 19th August, barely two months out, they arrived at Rio de Janeiro and Tom was bowled over by his first experience of tropical vegetation.

"How shall I describe my feelings on my first 'wanderings in the wilds' of a Brazilian forest … No country in the world is to be compared to Brazil in the variety of its natural productions, consequently, there is no place which is so properly the Elysium of the naturalist."[40]

A month later, they were offshore from the River Plate in hurricanes and temperatures below freezing making for the Falklands, which they reached on the 23rd September. Tom picked up a chill from the change in seasons but was full of the joys of his new life and wrote long letters home to parents, uncle and brother Biot, describing the new sights, the people, their culture and all his activities from shooting and skinning birds, drying flowers, writing notes and packing up specimens to be sent home via Rio. Sometimes, he told them, the Falklands reminded him so much of the voes and islands of Shetland, but not for long.

"I am continually finding a 'Basta voe,' or a 'Durie voe,' among the retired inlets, and was much delighted the other day at finding a perfect little 'Hoonie'*. Every now and then, however, a flock of penguins, a huge albatross, or an ugly vulture, hovering over my head, destroys the illusion, and I am forced to awaken from my dream of home, with a sigh, to confess that I am nearly at its antipodes."[41]

*Huney, a little island just south of Balta Sound.

Dreary and cold as the weather had been in the Falklands, it was nothing to what they faced at Cape Horn in October. Tom was a good sailor, seasoned by the many trips he had made from Shetland to the mainland and home again, but this was a new experience. Nonetheless, he wrote home as if this was just another bit of awkwardness to be borne with calm fortitude.

"We were all mighty glad to get away, though it was 'out of the frying pan into the fire,' with a vengeance. We had about a day of fair wind, but since then, oh such weather! gale succeeding gale, and always in our teeth, driving the poor ship to the southward and eastward … Of a truth, this same Cape Horn amply deserves the not very amiable character it has received; last night, however, it out-did itself, and blew not a storm but a regular hurricane. We could shew no sail but a main trysail, and mizen staysail, and she was making six knots of leeway. The captain, first lieutenant, and master, were on deck all night, and many a time none on board thought the vessel would get off her beam ends again. Luckily we had a good moon, and by its light the scene was most awful and sublime. We carried away gangway boards, and other light affairs, but the old ship stood it bravely on the whole, and, thank God, we found ourselves still above water in the morning. Notwithstanding that the hatches were battened down we shipped two seas, which smashed the sashes of the gun-room windows, and quite flooded us below. The weather is intensely cold, and the appearance of enormous icebergs visibly explains that we are in an inhospitable region of the earth, or rather, sea …"[42]

In late October, the *Herald* and *Pandora* safely rounded the Cape and entered the benign waters of the Pacific. There, they passed Mosquita Point, where Captain Robert Fitz Roy (1805-1865) of the *Beagle* helped in the rescue of the crew of the wrecked British man-of-war HMS *Challenger* exactly ten years earlier, in 1835. Then, on 16th November, they arrived at Valparaiso in Chile. There Tom hired three horses and a guide and started inland, desperate to get into the Andes. The reports of his adventures deeply unsettled his parents but his brothers, especially Biot, would have been envious of his adventures.

"A puma had been committing great ravages among the cattle at the foot of the Cordillera, and I was just calculating whether I could spare a day to go and find him, when we overtook four men, one of whom carried El leon, as they call him, dead of course, across his saddle. They had killed him that morning, having hunted him with dogs into a tree, lasso'd, and dispatched him with their knives. The puma measured 6 feet 9 inches. The four fellows bivouacked with us that night, to my considerable uneasiness, and the exquisite terror of my guide, for these mountaineers are more than half banditti, call themselves guardos del camino (guards of the road), and levy black mail, if not with the courage, at least with the perseverance of Rob Roy. They talked big at first, but my double-barrelled gun and rifle, and the 'accidental' removal of my poncho shewing a brace of pistols at my belt, and treating their hints for money with quiet nonchalance, speedily silenced these fellows, for they are at least as great cowards as bullies. The guide and I judged it right, however, to watch turn about during the night, and I was very glad when we started at daybreak for Quillota."[43]

Nearly forty years later, one of Tom's little sister, Jessie M. E., would write of similar adventures, but hers would be fictional.

On 30th November, Tom wrote his mother from Valparaiso telling her of his natural history pursuits, both marine and terrestrial, and of the number of specimens he had collected. In about a fortnight he hoped to get to Lima and then on to the Galapagos:

"… an uninhabited volcanic archipelago, perhaps the most singular and anomalous group of islands in the world. Every plant and animal in them is peculiar, and found no where else, while it seems the last spot on earth where certain creatures yet linger, now only found fossils elsewhere … I anticipate much pleasure in spending a few days there."[44]

Tom, like nearly all British naturalists, would have read the *Voyage of the Beagle* and he looked forward to visiting the Galapagos which he thought would be the highlight of his adventures.

Just before Christmas, on 20th December, Tom visited the ancient city of Lima where he watched a bullfight and attended a mass, both of which made an enormous impression on him. Then, on Christmas Eve, they left for the Galapagos, passing a *"dull broiling Christmas-day"*[45] at sea in ninety degrees of heat. After the Galapagos the plan was to go on to Panama where Tom eagerly looked forward to getting his first letters from home after seven months. After that, Captain Kellet informed him and the rest of the crew, they were off to spend the summer on the Columbia River and then to winter about San Francisco.

The expedition reached the Galapagos on 6th January, 1846, landing at Charles Island (Santa Maria). Then on to Chatham Island (San Cristobal) on the 12th, James Island (San Salvador) on the 15th, before setting off back to the mainland of South America on the 16th. Unfortunately for Tom, they were only there four days instead of the month that Tom had hoped for. However, he made what he called "*a noble collection, well nigh everything being new here*."[46] That he *did* make a '*noble collection*' on such a brief visit, after the islands had been combed by the likes of Darwin, David Douglas and several other naturalists, is an indication of his botanical expertise and boundless energy. The next few days at sea were even busier, writing up his notes and meticulously preparing and pressing all his specimens.

"*On the 22nd we were off Cape San Francisco, standing round Galera Point*"[47] (then in Peru, now Ecuador). That afternoon they anchored off the River Sua in the Bay of Atacamas, and on 24th January a party went ashore to collect wood. Tom eagerly went ashore with them to do more exploring and collecting and to compare the flora and fauna with the Galapagos. The midshipman, John Anderson, described the scene and their day ashore.

"Sua Bay is distinguished by two cliffs, or bluff promontories, enclosing a sandy beach … [that] stretches far into the land, which is covered by an almost impenetrable forest and under-wood … a boat landed Mr Thomas Edmondston, the naturalist, accompanied by Mr Whiffin, captain's clerk, Mr W. Billings, assistant-surgeon, and myself, with several others. Mr Edmondston carried a silver-mounted rifle, presented to him by Prince Albert, while I carried for him a large tin case for specimens and a butterfly net … We then struck into the wood, and soon lost our way, and continued wandering till about four o'clock … We then obtained a guide, who took us by a small track to the beach, where we found the two boats waiting. One of the men took the guns and specimens, &c., off to the boat, and laid them in the stern-sheets, and as the water was shallow, and the surf rising, the men tucked up their trousers, and came to carry us off. Mr Whiffin was first, and Mr Edmondston was carried on the back of Thomas Stocker, coxswain of the whaler; myself and Mr Hutchinson, midshipman, following."[48]

The ship's log for that day recorded the following event succinctly and coldly:

"24.1.46 (afternoon)
'Working party on shore … … a small Whale Boat for officers.
6 (pm)   Heavy swell from the Westwards.
6.10   The Whale Boat returned with the body of Mr T. Edmondston Naturalist. In the act of getting into the Boat a rifle left in the Boat, accidentally went off, the Ball (first wounding Mr Whiffin in the arm) passed through his head & he died instantly.
6.30   Cutter returned with wood.
8   Carpenter employed making a coffin
25.1.46 (afternoon)
1(pm)   Launch Boats & party to inter the remains of Mr T. Edmondston deceased.
6   … …up Boats
26.1.46
4   Weighed & made sail."[49]

Lieutenant Trollope's account of the final events onshore that fateful day was more detailed.

"It was getting late; we were tired and heartily glad to go on board. The surf ran high, but being pretty damp it did not give us any concern. Several were already in the boat, and I was getting in, with the naturalist close behind me, when the leg of my trousers lifted the cock of a rifle. The piece went off, sending its charge through the arm of Mr Whiffin, and making a perfect furrow through the skull of the unfortunate Edmondston. He uttered a slight exclamation, and fell into the water. A man immediately raised him to the surface, but life was gone. So suddenly had the accident taken place, that nobody in the boat knew what had happened, Mr Whiffin not even being aware of his wound. When the melancholy news became known on shore, everyone, by tacit consent, discharged his gun, and each report operated upon me like an electric shock; I almost fancied I beheld another death."[50]

Thousands of miles away, at the precise time of his death, Jessie M. E. later recorded that Tom's mother, Eliza, in Halligarth:

"… awoke from sleep with a dream of her boy. She saw the ship on the placid Pacific Sea, and a boat, and the Captain with letters in his hand, and he was speaking of "poor young Edmondston," She was made aware that the letters were about her son's death … Profoundly moved, the mother rose up, and after tearful prayers, she recorded in her note-book the whole incident."[51]

Laurence and Eliza then waited for a communication in dreadful anticipation.

Tom, the bright and intelligent young lad so full of innocence, confidence and adventure, had become a well-liked fellow on the ship. Life in close quarters among men on whom his life depended, and away from his peers whom he felt beneath him and from superiors whom he felt he had had to impress, had changed and matured the young naturalist. His sudden death was a tragic and melancholic event.

The first to hear of the event in England were J. D. Hooker and Edward Forbes. For all those who had recognised his early promise and great potential, it was as if the starburst of the rocket that had been ignited in the unlikely setting of Baltasound in Shetland, had shone far too briefly in the sky, and it was a painful reminder to Sir W. J. Hooker of the loss of his previous protégé Douglas, whom he had also launched into Pacific orbit. For MacGillivray, it was a sad blow to lose a student and young friend of such promise.

Even accounting for the distance, there must have been a delay in the passage of letters home, for it was six long months before Eliza and Laurence received the terrible news for which she, at least, was half-prepared. On 13th June, 1846, J. D. Hooker wrote to Laurence "*It is with the most unfeigned sorrow I have received from the Admiralty the intelligence of the death of your talented son by an accident in the Pacific.*"[52] It was as if their flower had been cut down before it had even blossomed. What recriminations there were in Laurence's soul for allowing Tom to have left on such a dangerous expedition, and yet he knew that neither could he have held him back. From that moment on, Laurence never used his own gun again.

In *his* personal papers, Forbes recorded the loss and the true worth of Tom:

"... Mr Thomas Edmondston, who, but a youth, had already given good earnest of his powers, and love for science. We remember well the zeal and delight with which this young genius – for such he assuredly was – entered upon a mission so suitable to his talents and taste, and so likely to prove prolific in discovery. Alas! all these hopes and anticipations were fated to be destroyed."[53]

There are only three lasting mementos of Tom's last botanical expedition and resting place, for, alas, as his mother recorded "... the voluminous correspondence of young Edmondston with his beloved and valued friend Forbes, was some years ago unfortunately destroyed, and with it, it is believed, his journal and sketches ..."[54] Berthold Seemann (1825-1871), who became the expedition's naturalist in 1847 recorded the first:

"The piece of oak which was placed at the head of his grave will in future be searched for in vain; but his brother naturalists will meet on the shores of the ocean on which their talented colleague died, an evergreen shrub with dark red panicles. It is the Edmonstonia pacifica (Seemann)*, a monument erected to his memory by an ardent admirer of his talents. This plant is figured in plate xviii of the 'Botany of H. M. S. Herald,' and is so different from all known genera, that it will probably become the type of a new natural order."[55]

*The plant was subsequently renamed *Tetrathylacium macrophyllum*.

The second is his contribution to our knowledge of the flora and fauna of the Galapagos, compared with the American mainland, as recorded in correspondence between Darwin and J. D. Hooker, and in a scientific paper by the latter in 1851. The pair were particularly keen to know – in relation to theories of the evolution of species – which species had made it to the Galapagos from the American mainland, which species from island to island within the archipelago, and had subspecies or separate but similar species evolved on the Galapagos? In this regard, accurate recording was critical.

In July 1846, Darwin, more interested in Tom's botanical records than his death, wrote to J. D. Hooker when he heard the news. "*I was very sorry to hear about your poor Edmondston. The Galapagos seems a perennial source of new things: I hope you know which islands he visited.*" In September, J. D. Hooker replied: "*I have done all of Edmonstones Galapagos plants that have been received ... As it is, they modify the results drawn from the examination of previous collections markedly.*"[56]

In fact, according to J. D. Hooker,[57] Tom's Galapagos collection, of all those that had previously been made, was second only to that of Darwin himself, despite a visit limited to only four days, and included several unrecorded species: an astonishing achievement. Darwin, though, raised a question mark about the list when he responded to J. D. Hooker. "*... Many have referred to your curious geographical results on this archipelago. – I suppose you feel sure that the Edmondston's Collections from the mainland* [South America] *have not been mingled with those of Galapagos.*" J. D. Hooker swiftly dismissed his worries, however. "*I have excluded all of Edmondston's plants than can have been from the Coast.*"[58]

The third memento is a small and naïve painting of Tom's grave. The existence of this painting, by the midshipman John Anderson of Glasgow, who was a witness to Tom's death, was unknown to the Edmondstons at the time, but, by happenstance, it was spotted nearly twenty years after Tom's death by a brother of the future husband of Tom's sister, Mary (1832-1898).

> "*It was a bright summer's day in 1863, in the city of Glasgow, that* [Symington] *happened to be looking into a print-seller's shop window, and observed a water-colour drawing which was entitled 'The Lonely Grave'. It represented a tropical scene on the banks of a beautiful bay. A British frigate lay at anchor on an unruffled sea, and some stately palms over-shadowed a mound on a slight eminence. At the head of the mound was rude cross, and on looking closer the gentleman read the name engraven on the head-stone. It was one familiar to him ...*"[59]

The name of course was Edmondston. The picture then passed to a descendant of Tom's other sister, Jessie M. E., and down through the family.

For those on board H.M.S. *Herald* their expedition was not finished. There were several more years of exploration, firstly three fruitless trips north in search of Franklin's expedition. On one, in 1848, they were joined on the Atlantic side by Sir James Clerk Ross (1800-1862) with the *Enterprise* and the *Investigator*: the latter being the vessel on which Biot had come to Balta Sound 30 years previously. But, as Wyld had predicted to Tom in London in 1845, the officers of the *Erebus* and the *Terror* never danced in Valparaiso. Sir John Franklin and his men never returned and

'The Lonely Grave' by John R. Anderson.

were last seen by whalers in Baffin Bay in July 1845, around the time Tom and the *Herald* were crossing the equator. Three years later, Lady Franklin (1794-1875) arrived in Unst. Unable to go to the Arctic in search of her husband herself, she journeyed as far north as she could in the British Isles to be as near to him as possible. But it was to be five more years before the Orcadian explorer, John Rae (1813-1893), revealed the tragic and unspeakable fate of Franklin's expedition and was vilified by Lady Franklin for his trouble.

The *Herald* then went on from 1852-1861 to explore Australia and the South West Pacific. Seemann left the expedition in 1851 to write his account of the voyage and by chance his successor was the naturalist John MacGillivray (1821-1867), the son of William MacGillivray of Aberdeen, who had been on a previous survey in the Pacific with the great Thomas Huxley aboard H.M.S. *Fly* and *Rattlesnake*. Sadly, John was dismissed from the expedition in Australia, where he then settled, allegedly for writing and selling material relating to the expedition without authority.

What would Tom have achieved had that tragic accident not befallen him short of his twenty-first birthday? Would he have gone on exploring like David Douglas before him, after writing up a great account of his voyage, or would he have returned to an academic life in Scotland or England, to a university, or perhaps to Kew to take on Hooker's great works there? Might he have developed an association with Darwin having returned with more data for his theory of the evolution of species? Or might he have returned to Buness in Unst to become the laird and a gentleman naturalist? He had a few weaknesses – Eliza felt sometimes that he was not always methodical in his approach to his work and there were times when he was less than accurate and occasionally evidenced a lack of commitment – or was it simply that with all his talent too many things attracted him and that new opportunities arose too quickly? But then, he was hardly yet a man when he died and, sadly, just at the time when maturity was showing signs of ironing out these few wrinkles in his character. There is no doubt, however, that Tom had had the potential to become one of the foremost naturalists in Britain of his day. And, had he lived, there would now be a well-trodden and hallowed track to his home at Halligarth and to the site of the compact, little arctic-alpine with the large and fragile white petals, his Edmondston's mouse-ear, on the serpentinite of the island of Unst, within view of his place of birth.

CHAPTER FOURTEEN

THE FARTHEST NORTH AND THE FURTHEST WEST

"Farewell to you my dear parents, may the blessings of the Almighty always descend upon you, & may he guide you safely through life until you reach the goal of heavenly bliss – I, your son, am about to part from you; to seek my fortune, & work out my destiny in a foreign land, and amongst an uncivilized people: fear not …"

Thomas Edmondston (1825-1874)

Loans and Charity

With the death of Tom in early 1846, the heart was torn right out of Halligarth. All the promise that Laurence and Eliza had so looked forward to was no more. For Eliza, the pain of losing her best and firstborn was almost intolerable. For Laurence, it was the end of the dream that his son might fulfil the potential in natural history that he himself had failed to do. He believed that it might have been his own scientific ambitions that had led him to push Tom towards his early death. It was a culpability he carried with him to the end of his life. In a letter to Darwin some time later, Laurence explained that Tom's death had also been the death of his own interest in natural history: after it he wrote very little more on the subject. Just four days after the first anniversary of Tom's death, Eliza was delivered of her eleventh and last child, a fourth son, whom they christened Thomas (1847-1923), in Tom's memory. Over 50 years later, in a letter to the naturalist A. H. Evans (1855-1943), *he* noted of his father, Laurence:

"He had given his very best to Science, so he used to say, and his love of it seemed to be buried in the grave of the son who died in its service."[1]

For the old and ailing Thomas the laird, the loss of his nephew, whom he had come to regard almost as a son, was a savage blow. He had his Ursula, but he had no male heir, like Laurence and Eliza, to replace Tom. He was now 67, almost an invalid, and no longer had the strength to replace his love and hope in another. Biot, now 19 and training for the ministry, became the oldest son and endeavoured to take on his brother's mantle of seniority; a brother with whom he, more than his younger brothers and sisters, had had a very special relationship. The natural gaiety and innocence of the remaining five children still at home, who had seen so little of Tom over the previous five years – the youngest of whom hardly knew him – was a comfort and help in their parent's recovery. They were Mary, now fourteen, David nine, Isabella six, Jessie M. E. four, Ellen just one and the infant, Thomas.

On the other side of the Atlantic that year, Charles and Mary celebrated the wedding of their third son, Patrick (1819-1871), who married Catherine Ann Devereux (1823-1871), whose diary of

Ursula Edmondston (1819-1898) as a young woman.

the Civil War was later published as the *Journal of a Secesh Lady*. In the same year, their oldest daughter, Jessie Mary (1821-1886), who had married Dr Amory Coffin (1813-1884), gave birth to *their* third child. Their first child, Amory (1841-1916) after his father, was now five and would later feature in his aunt's *Journal* as the only Edmondston to leave a record of his active role as a Confederate soldier. Meanwhile, Charles and Mary's fourth son, Thomas (1825-1874), born the same month as his now deceased cousin Tom the botanist, was having difficulty settling to a job.

It was during this period that his uncle, old Thomas, who had recently become a Magistrate, was approached by William Hay for a loan. The latter was recovering from the bankruptcy of Hay & Ogilvy that had forced him to sell all his property, including his home, Hayfield, in Lerwick, and the family home his father had purchased many years ago at Laxfirth, a few kilometres to the north. In response to his letter, Thomas wrote, in July 1845, that the fishing was not good and that "*Age and poor health have deprived me of any relish I once had for the extension of property*." Nevertheless, with Christian virtue, he spoke of "*… doing as I would be done to …*"[2] to help Hay. In a second letter a week later, in response to a further communication from Hay, Thomas made an offer, "*I could advance you say £1000 or £100 or £200 more* [£67,000 or £6700 or £13,400 more] *… this is the utmost I can go to you or any other friend*."[3] Hay accepted the proffered loan and Thomas replied in August that he was pleased at the price Hay had paid for some land he was purchasing on the outskirts of Lerwick, and in a generous mood of friendship offered a firm £1500 (£100,500), adding that "*I do not wish this transaction to be known by anyone but Mr Cheyne and Mr Sievwright*."[4] The Cheyne to whom he was referring was Henry Cheyne (1804-1868), William Hay's factor and son-in-law. William Sievwright, a noted and trusted figure in Shetland, was Thomas' solicitor in Lerwick. With some of this capital, a grateful William Hay was able to regain his home at Hayfield and begin rebuilding his business. Thomas' loan was a commercial transaction of course, and was on the security of the Hay property. The following April, in a business letter he wrote to William Hay, who had and continued to have a close relationship with the family for many years, Thomas added:

"I perceive from the 'Advertiser' that lands … are again in the market, together with Laxfirth – It must be very distressing to you not to possess your father's favourite residence on which he lavished so much mind and money … could a <u>very few</u> hundreds aid you in acquisition of the place – as I should be most pleased to help you as far as I was able, this of course to yourself, and if you may have no intention in the way I suppose – just let my observations keep."[5]

In the event, William Hay, did not recover Laxfirth, but the scale of Thomas' loan to him over this period, in helping him regain his private property, was an indication of the wealth he had acquired through his chromate quarry and of their close personal ties. The next generation of Edmondstons, Ursula and Biot, also became friends with William's sons, Arthur (1835-1896) and George Hay (1828-1890), so carrying on a friendship with that family started in their great-grandfather's generation. It is clear that Thomas had spare money to loan when there was a good business opportunity or when his family needed it, except that is, in the case of Arthur's bankruptcy, when there was only a limited display of brotherly love.

The year of Tom's death was a depressing time all round in Shetland with little brightness on the horizon. The previous year there had been a poor harvest, particularly of the potato, and a poor return from the fishing. Shetland had had many bad harvests in the past and would in the future, but this time it was particularly bad for the poor harvest was not just for a single year but continued up to 1849. Conditions were particularly harsh in the early spring when the winter supply was exhausted, reducing the population to near starvation. The famine occurred not only in Shetland but on the Scottish mainland, in Ireland, northern Europe and even in Canada. Luckily, Shetland, because of the fishing, was not as dependent on the potato as Ireland and the disaster was not on the scale that it was there or in the West of Scotland. Nevertheless, the Inspector (for relief and destitution), Captain Robert Craigie R. N. (b1799) stated "I do not believe that Ireland itself can produce instances of greater want and penury than I have witnessed in some parts of Shetland and especially in Yell."[6]

Although there were the beginnings of improvement for the social welfare of the citizens of the British Isles at this time, for example the Poor Law Amendment Act of 1845 that brought schools under the control of the state, there was no state structure that took care of the starving and unemployed, bar the workhouse. Not even the Victorian 'Liberals' believed in interfering in the social situation except to minimal degree. In 1846, the authorities in Lerwick, the Commissioners of Supply, successfully pleaded for assistance from the government. In the past, notably in 1837, the grain, or meal, that had been supplied, had been given as charity. However, it was now thought that this was no longer good for the morals of the people and it was arranged through the Board for the Relief of Highland Destitution that meal – one and a half pounds per day to adult males, three quarters to adult females and a half pound to children under 12 – should be given only in return for work for the public good. In Shetland this was mainly the construction of roads; hence the term 'Meal Road'.[7] Prior to 1847 there were only two roads on Mainland, both of which led out of Lerwick – one to Scalloway and one to Laxfirth – but during the famine approximately 190 km of road network was added to these. The meal that was distributed was not a generous handout but merely subsistence to ensure that such remuneration did not compete with other employment. The authorities tried to persuade the proprietors to contribute towards the costs, and most did. However, on the basis that there were no roads planned for Unst and Fetlar, Thomas and his friend, the landowner of Fetlar Sir Arthur Nicholson, refused to contribute. But there was more to it than that. Thomas claimed that the Unst, Fetlar and Yell men, being *"fishermen and farmers cannot leave their homes with any advantage to themselves to work on "trunk roads leading from Lerwick to Mossbank"* [the point on Shetland's north mainland adjacent to Yell]."[8] This was of course true, but he failed to not point out that these tenants were required to fish to him as part of their rental, so there was no '*advantage*' to him either if they worked on the roads. In fact, if they did, he would lose out too! On the other hand, in 1847, Thomas did employ a number of men on a short piece of road in the early part of the year, before they could fish or work the land, and paid them meal out of his own reserves.[9] This amounted to the equivalent of about 2½ pence (75 pence) daily, and in 1849 he had spent £100 (£7000) employing his tenants to build a stone wall of 1300 fathoms (2.6 km).

Andrew Smith, who had toured the northern parishes of Shetland, including Unst, Yell and Fetlar, in a report to the Board, cast poor light on old Thomas' attitude to his tenants in 1848.

"While Gifford of Busta by every means in his power induces a feeling of Independence among his tenantry not only in his transactions with them but in allowing them to dispose of their labour in the best markets; the latter, Edmondstone [Thomas of Buness], evinces quite a contrary view by endeavouring in every way he can devise to shift the responsibility of providing for the poor on is estate from his own shoulder to those of the Board, at the same time advocating the cause of his tenantry for almost eleemosynary aid during the voar [spring] and peat season, and this in one of the islands best adapted for agricultural purposes."[10]

Confirmation of Thomas' reluctance to part with his own money to support his tenants in this time of distress was revealed in a letter he wrote a year later to Captain Craigie. In it he pleaded that the high level of support, expected by the Board from landowners in Shetland, unfairly compared *"the slender resources of this country … in this remote and destitute corner of the Empire"*[11] with the large Highland estates with their much greater rental income. In this *cri de coeur* he omitted to mention that he received a substantial additional annual income from the export of chromate, above and beyond his rental. Nor did he mention the generous financial support he had been able to give to William Hay just a few years earlier.

It was at this time that the poor relationship between Laurence and his brother, exacerbated by the latter's declining health, deteriorated markedly. It all began in January when they fell out over Laurence's persistent claims that his agricultural practices at Halligarth were a success – practices that were now being carried

Buness from Halligarth, pre-1870, origin unknown.

176

out successfully elsewhere in Shetland – and his suggestion that they be extended over what Thomas considered the best ground at Buness.[12] In Buness, nursing his irritation with Laurence, he scribbled a letter on a board across his knees. On the other side of the yard, where labourers were digging drains in the fields at Halligarth, Laurence could sit at his desk in his den and gaze back across the same fields to the tall grey walls of Buness. But when *he* took up the pen his resolve weakened. He insisted that he was just trying to give Thomas his opinion and advice, that he did not want to upset him and that he wished to remain his *"sincere friend and affectionate brother."*[13]

In another letter, Laurence regretted human failings that had caused the rift between them. He wanted to talk to Thomas face to face but his brother insisted that their discussions must be by letter.[14] Perhaps he did not have the strength to carry on a heated argument. On the other hand, it allowed him to be expansive, if not long-winded, and he did not have to pause in full flow to listen to a counter-argument. So, what might have been settled verbally was stretched out over a whole year, each missive simply deepening the division. The exchanges eventually resulted in Eliza joining in and herself writing a barbed letter to Thomas, concerning her injured propriety when she had had to live in the same house at Buness as his illegitimate daughter, prior to moving into Halligarth. The spat culminated in September 1847 with an extraordinary letter from Thomas of 36 foolscap pages (!), in which he cruelly pointed out what Laurence's other brothers had thought of him and yet, what he had done for Laurence over the years.

> *"Your conduct towards me on Friday last compels me to try a last effort to* reclaim *you and to restore your apparently total loss of confidence in my actions, veracity, principle and everything that is dear to me … your elder brother* [Charles] *or rather his conduct towards you needs no comment. Your brother Henry seemed to give you none of his confidence … your brother* [Arthur] *you seem to think has not treated you well, been jealous of you, and bunked as far as he could your literary fame, neglected answering your letters and in place of confidence and affection displayed cold indifference – your fourth and last brother is myself."*[15]

And, Thomas added, turning the blade, for 30 years the ungrateful Laurence had lived under *his* roof.

In the heat of the argument, of course, both distorted the truth. Thomas knew well that Laurence had not lived 30 years under his roof. What he meant, and succeeded in doing, was to remind Laurence that he was, and always had been, entirely dependent on him; as a student and medical apprentice in Edinburgh, as a salesman for his chromate and, the cruellest jibe of all, that he only lived in Halligarth by Thomas' favour for the last 15 years. Not for the first time did Thomas omit to mention their original contract which he had never put to paper. On the other hand, he had good reason to be a little bitter over Eliza's behaviour. However, what most upset Thomas was the lack of recognition of his financial generosity to all the family over a long period of years, though this was entirely of his own making as he was so secretive in his financial dealings.

In his Day Book,[16] however, Thomas recorded those payments: the £60 (£3600) annuity he gave Laurence; regular payments to his nephew, the deceased Tom, including a munificent £110 (£7260) in 1844 when he was lecturing and botanising away from Shetland; annual payments of around £20 (£1400) to Biot between 1848 and 1854 when he was studying for the ministry; lump sum payments to his brothers Charles totalling £520 (£26,000), Arthur £250 (£12,500) and Henry

£550 (£27,500); and other smaller payments to other members of the family. In one of the last references in his Day Book to these many payments to the family, Thomas wrote one sentence that he hoped would redeem his reputation for posterity:

"Father, Mother, Sisters during a period of more than 50 years more than £2000 [£100,000], these sums have been entered in a memorandum to show that my earnings have not <u>all</u> been [kept] to myself."

In his long letter to Laurence, Thomas admitted that he might have said *harsh and bitter things in the heat of the discussion*[17], but that he had never tried to hurt Laurence in cold blood, he had even given him regular financial assistance without Laurence having to ask, forgetting that he had always demanded receipts and that he had promised it anyway. He also conveniently forgot that once his younger brother had committed himself to their arrangement there was no turning back: Laurence was in an invidious position. Unfortunately, the arrangement they had made, or at least the fact that Laurence was financially dependent on Thomas, became public. Laurence believed it was Thomas who had revealed the situation. Laurence then had to explain his position to Biot who, bitterly, if a little ungratefully considering the financial help *he* had received, confronted his uncle. Thomas' reaction was to sit down and pen his response to Laurence:

"*… you heard how readily he* [Biot] *joined as far as he was able in my condemnation … he denounced me as an unprincipled villain …*"

Later in the letter, Thomas acquitted Biot, but then he turned on Eliza:

"*It is more than 20 years since she came to my house, and remained in it till she was the mother of, I think three children, if she thought my house discreditable by having in it Ursula my child, I did not force her to enter it, I had another house provided for her …* [I treated] *her as a lady and a sister … because she was your wife.*"[18]

Once again, Thomas was a little disingenuous as Eliza had had no choice in where she first lived as Laurence's wife, for he was away at university and they depended utterly on Thomas for financial support.

Thomas was so angry, even mortified, by the antagonistic feelings towards himself and Ursula that had emanated from the family at Halligarth that, when once more, unbeknown to Laurence, he sat down in 1847 and rewrote his will to remove the name of his favourite and deceased nephew Tom, he now placed his American nephew, Yankee Tom, ahead of Biot and once again left Laurence out of it:

"Primo, to and in favour of Ursula Edmondston my daughter procreated between me and Sinclair Bruce and residing with me in life rent and to the heirs of her body … whom failing to Thomas Edmondston son of my brother Charles Edmondston of Charleston and to his heirs whom failing to Biot Edmondston son of my youngest brother Laurence Edmondston whom all failing to my own nearest heirs …"[19]

Old Thomas, now 68, assumed that Ursula, though 30 and unattached, might still marry and have children. If she did, her eldest son would inherit Buness. Failing that, Thomas spurned Laurence and turned instead to his other brother's family in Charleston, deciding that Thomas (1825-1874), his namesake, would be next in line, but, as previously, he told no one.

In a letter to his friend, Dr Basil Spence, in the cold, bitter days of Shetland in February 1848, it is apparent that the deterioration of the relationship between old Thomas and his brother Laurence, had reached the point when the former now sought medical advice for his condition elsewhere:

> *"Believe me your presence would have been a high treat to us, as the winter and <u>Yule</u> have been very dreary and gloomy, but thank God I have been able to keep upon my legs, and been no worse than my usual <u>weakly way</u>, which has been a great blessing to me. I have found your 'Rhubarb Pills' to suit me most admirably, and they are just about a finish, and I would much like to have another Bag of them, by the post, if I am not <u>very soon</u> to have the pleasure of seeing yourself, but as we now have a thaw again, I hope you will soon be here for at least 'twa or tree nights'. We have a good deal to chat about."*[20]

Two years later, in 1850, as if he had had some inkling of his brother's intentions, Laurence tried desperately to make things up with old Thomas. In a letter – which Thomas had demanded – acknowledging the payment of the £60 annuity, Laurence thanked his brother for his generosity and apologised for his ungrateful manner. It was an anguished letter that a son might have written to a father whose love he had lost and it revealed the terrible grief that both suffered with Tom's death.

> *"I never was, am not – never can be conscious of a feeling different from that of boyhood – manhood – age – warm brotherly affection – peculiar and specific – and perfect friendship – such as no other participates ... We shall not longer hence – God willing join <u>him</u> [Tom] whom I hourly commune with, and the saviour will gently conduct us through the dark portal where he will be waiting to receive us. My heart is often ready to gush out then I think of that sweet incomparable boy – but we shall assuredly meet him again."*[21]

The Redoubtable Lady Franklin

Meantime, social life, at least on the surface, went on and new visitors continued to arrive from afar at Baltasound, some, like Eliza, disapproving of the Buness household. One observer who commented, to her diary, about the shocking situation of the open presence of Ursula, was Sophia Cracroft. She was the niece and companion to Lady Franklin who visited Shetland in 1849 to travel as far north as she could to seek out news from the Greenland whalers of her husband, Sir John Franklin, who had left England four years previously in 1845, just before young Tom, and of whom nothing had been heard since, despite much searching. They landed at Uyeasound at the south end of Unst along with Eliza's brother David MacBrair, having travelled up from Leith with him and Captain Robert Craigie, the Inspector of (Famine) Relief, and from there went on overland to Buness. There, Lady Franklin met Laurence and Eliza and shared commiserations for two souls who had never made a rendezvous in the Pacific. Miss Cracroft recorded:

Lady Jane Franklin by Amelie Romilly.

North by Henry Saxby.

"We went into the dining room which was very hot and not very sweet. We found there a young woman who he [Thomas] introduced to us as his daughter. We had heard before that she was illegitimate. She seemed very shy."[22]

Then she, along with Lady Franklin and accompanied by Eliza, Biot, his sister Mary and David MacBrair, set off in two traps on the 5 km track to Burra Firth. There they inspected the schoolhouse built by Thomas and the *haaf* station at Fiska Wick, where the boats were kept and the fish cured on a steeply sloping bank covered in slabs of rock. Standing on the highest point of The Ness at Fiska Wick they looked northwards, between Herma Ness on their left and the towering height of Saxa Vord on their right, towards the mouth of the narrow, almost cliff bound firth, 4 km ahead of them. Lady Franklin enquired if the furthest point she could see was the most northerly point of Britain. On being told that there were stacks and skerries a further kilometre beyond the entrance to Burra Firth she asked if she might be taken there. A 'request' was made for a boat to the fishermen by Eliza, and, coming from the laird's sister-in-law, was speedily acceded to. They could not guarantee that they could take the party as far as the stacks, the sea was calm enough within the Firth, there was no wind to speak of and the tide would be slack, but there might still be a bit of a swell in the open sea. Lady Franklin, however, was determined to make a pilgrimage to the nearest point of Britain to the Arctic and her husband and she was not a lady to be crossed. In a small open boat, rowed by four of the estate's tenant-fishermen, they set off from Fiska Wick. It would have taken them half an hour to row the length of Herma Ness, its precipitous slopes and cliffs and the sea through which they moved speckled by puffins and guillemots.

Lady Franklin might have picked any other day of the year and been disappointed, but that day it was as calm as it ever could be. A fisherman pointed to the nearest sharply rising group of stacks in front of which hundreds of large white seabirds with black wingtips were soaring and plunging into the sea: the skerries of Muckle Flugga. But Lady Franklin saw another black rock rising out of the sea beyond and shook her head. They pressed on for Utsta, the Out Stack, at 60° 51 minutes north, the most northerly point of the British Isles. As they drew close she could see it was just a shapeless, black lump of steep sided rock, inhabited temporarily by a couple of gulls and one fat and lazy Atlantic seal that slid reluctantly into the sea as they approached. The men stopped rowing as they drew near but Lady Franklin demanded to be landed. This time the fishermen shook their heads, if the boat hit the rocks and stove in a plank that could be the end of them all; even in the summer months they would not survive long in the cold sea. For a few minutes they stood off carefully studying what little swell there was. Then, with Lady Franklin perched in the furthest extremity, they inched in towards the Out Stack. For one moment they held the boat at arm's length from sharp and dangerous rocks and, as Lady Franklin recorded in her diary: "… Utsta, said to be the most [northerly] rock or isle in the whole Dominion [and I] went close enough"[23] to touch the seaweed skirting its base. Satisfied, she allowed them to take her back to Fiska Wick from where they returned to Buness for a supper of halibut, fowl, plum pudding and champagne!

Lady Franklin was a formidable and well-travelled lady to whom this outing, in a small open boat among the wild and lonely stacks and skerries off the north coast of Unst, was only a small adventure. It was she who was perhaps the most responsible for getting her husband the position as leader of the famous, if not infamous, expedition in search of the North West Passage.[24] She had even volunteered to take part in the expedition herself, an incredible suggestion for the 1840s. At the very time that Lady Franklin arrived in Shetland, a small overland party searching for her husband and led by the famous Orcadian arctic explorer, John Rae (1813-1893) – that by coincidence included the 24-year-old Shetlander, Halcrow Humphrey (1825-1916), who went on to become a noted explorer in Canada in his own right – was being driven ashore by ice at Cape Krusenstern on the arctic coast of Canada in the most terrible of conditions.

By a strange set of coincidences there were other 'connections' between the Edmondstons and John Rae. He had first qualified as a doctor from Edinburgh, matriculating just as Laurence was graduating, and Sir Walter Scott – on the same Lighthouse voyage in 1814 when he met with Arthur in Lerwick – had called on the Raes in Orkney, lifting from Rae's sisters the characters of Minna and Brenda for *The Pirate*, just as he had lifted Claud Halcro from Arthur. Many years later, Jessie M. E., who was seven at the time of Lady Franklin's visit, wrote a poem to Rae's memory entitled *The last of the Argonauts*. By then, she was an exponent of Shetland's Norse heritage and attributed Rae's feats to his Viking blood, erroneously, as his parents were not Orcadian.

The Amazing Adventures of Yankee Tom

In 1846, Charles and Mary's third son, Patrick, who had married Catherine Devereux, briefly attended the military college of West Point. The experience he gained there was to result, nearly 25 years later, in him being given the authority to raise and train local militias in the Civil War. Catherine was the daughter of a very wealthy plantation owner and, as part of the marriage settlement of $10,000 ($200,000), she and Patrick were given two plantations amounting to 1894 acres and 88 slaves.[25] The first was called Looking Glass and the second they named Hascosea, after the Shetland island that had been so many years in the hands of the Edmondston family.

Charles Edmondston and his sons (Patrick front left [?] and Yankee Tom, back right [?]).

At this time, Charles Edmondston and Mary still lived in Legare Street in Charleston, but regularly spent time in Aiken, some 225 km away up the Savannah River. When Charles had returned home to Shetland for his visit in 1841, he had struck up a friendship with his illegitimate niece, the 21-year-old Ursula. From 1846 onwards, he and his wife regularly corresponded with her and gradually Mary and Ursula became drawn together through their letters, to the point of exchanging confidences; even Charles wrote kind, solicitous and philosophical letters to her. In 1848, Ursula sent a shawl to Mary[26] and in November 1849, Mary wrote to Ursula to tell her that her boys, James (1831-1896), then 18 and Thomas, or Yankee Tom as he came to be called, then 24, had emigrated to California, though the latter had not yet arrived. Mary was particularly fond of her Tom, adding in her letter with reference to his cousin from Halligarth who had died in Peru: "*May God, avert that another Tom, may perish in this unfortunate region.*"[27] She had good maternal reasons for being worried for the boys, for, although California may be on the same continent as Charleston, it was almost 4000 km away.

Yankee Tom had briefly attended West Point like his elder brother Patrick, but in 1846, when he was 21, went to New Orleans to try and establish himself as a merchant, along with his younger brother James. In 1849, he was persuaded that there was much money to be made in business in San Francisco where the gold rush was creating great opportunities for entrepreneurs. In his head he saw himself repeating the success of his father when he had arrived as a young man 50 years ago in Charleston. The idea of the journey across America as much as the wealth waiting at the end of it also spurred him on, but before he departed he left a highly emotional and rather self-conscious farewell for his parents. A

Hascosea.

farewell – echoing the sentiments his deceased cousin and namesake expressed in his farewell letters only four years previously, though with a little more hyperbole – that may not have been as reassuring to his parents as he had intended! It was signed by him and dated "Monday morning before daylight – 5th Feby. 1849."

> *"Farewell to you my dear parents, may the blessings of the Almighty always descend upon you, & may he guide you safely through life until you reach the goal of heavenly bliss – I, your son, am about to part from you; to seek my fortune, & work out my destiny in a foreign land, and amongst an uncivilized people: fear not because such is the place of my destination that I will find it more difficult to get along through life; but be assured that the mind is the most powerful weapon a man can use, & when wielded properly it will present opposition to every assailant & overcome every difficulty … Hard! Hard!! Indeed it is to part, but one and all farewell, brothers and sisters, Father & Mother think & pray for your devoted though absent son."*[28]

When Yankee Tom made this momentous decision he must have been quite unaware that his uncle Thomas at Buness had made him his heir after his cousin Ursula, or he might have made a journey in quite the other direction. The boys' destination was California and they were joining around 40,000 other 'forty niners' who took either the Santa Fé trail in the south, or the old Lewis and Clark, Oregon Trail, in the north, travelling westward in their covered wagons around 19-24 km a day across the dusty dry lands and over the mountainous Sierras.

Yankee Tom's story survived because he told it to his aunt Eliza in the early 1850s and she then made it into a piece for *Chambers' Journal* where it appeared over five weekly issues in December 1855. This was Eliza's first published piece of writing and she made an excellent tale out of it.[29]

While Yankee Tom set off from New Orleans on the 8th April, 1849, with three like-minded friends aboard the steam-boat *La Belle Creole* for St Louis on the Mississippi, intent on following the northern route, his brother James set off on the Santa Fé trail through Mexico for San Diego. The boat was packed with emigrants and they were not long out of New Orleans before cholera, which was rife in the city they had just left, began to fell the passengers, babies, husbands, wives, sons and daughters alike. The corpses were either dumped into the river or the boat stopped for just enough time to allow a burial party to go shore. Happily, Yankee Tom and his friends survived this part of the journey and arrived in St Louis six days later and over 1200 km up the river.

At St Louis they added six to their party, now made up of: one who had travelled much in Mexico; a gentleman of New York travelling for the pleasure of the journey; a South Carolinian merchant; a doctor from Charleston; an Irishman; a German; Yankee Tom and three others. None had made such a journey before so they were in ignorance as to what equipment, food and clothing they required. Nevertheless, they pooled their resources and bought what provisions they considered the necessary.

> "Liberal provision was in the first instance made for creature comforts, vulgarly called meat and drink, consisting chiefly of flour, bacon, coffee and whisky, with tin drinking-flasks and two or three cooking utensils … [other purchases included] two tents and a coil of strong hempen rope. Each man was provided with a pair of blankets, a buffalo-robe, several pair of waterproof boots, reaching above the knee, besides the ordinary changes of clothing and linen … Each one … had a good rifle and bowie-knife, and a Colt's revolver, which is a pistol

183

capable of firing six shots in succession from one loading ... ample supply of powder and lead ... a few trinkets, looking glasses, and some red cloth for the purpose of trade with the Indians, should anything of the kind be found necessary or desirable."

Amassing provisions took ten days and on 25th April they embarked on another boat up the Missouri for Independence (near Kansas City), about another 700 km. Four days later they landed at Wayne City and the next day walked to Independence. There, among the milling crowds of men and families also planning to make their fortunes in California, they eventually were able to purchase twelve mules as "wild as untamed deer, and probably even more refractory"! With the help of some Mexicans this innocent party managed to hitch the mules to their hired wagon,

"... and in this fashion the animals set off at their full speed, dragging men and wagon after them. Thus our travellers careered through the streets of Independence, and were dubbed by the bystanders amidst shouts of laughter and applause, 'The Crescent City [New Orleans] Menagerie Company'."

Despite losing the Irishman to cholera, they set off with their 'teams' of mules and two wagons, plus an Indian pony or Mexican mustang each, on the 1st May "in good spirits." The first day of their overland journey was not encouraging: they made only 16 km! The following morning, Yankee Tom found that *he* had now caught cholera. However, after three days rest he miraculously recovered and they set off again, only to find that their doctor companion had the measles! After a further twelve days and 190 km they found themselves on the banks of the Kansas River in the state of Kansas. The route they had followed was: "well defined, from the hordes of emigrants that had preceded them, parties of whom they frequently overtook." Here the party fell out with each other and eventually agreed to split with the original four – Yankee Tom and his three friends – taking one wagon and half the mules.

The reduced party crossed the Kansas River in two trips on a ferry-boat and made camp on the far bank.

"It was a singular and cheerful sight – the extensive camp [of many emigrants], the open savannah, the smiling river, and the numerous watch-fires, the deep-blue heavens and the evening-star."

Although some 20,000 took this route westward that year there were many days when they saw no one "except ... when a mounted Indian would cross the path, sweeping by like a whirlwind." This was a relatively easy part of their journey and each night they were able to camp near to a wood and water with some pasture for the animals. In the morning they would enjoy their coffee and bacon before setting off again. The savannah proved to be rather devoid of food and game, except for turkeys that they occasionally shot, and they eventually passed out of the territory of the Pottawattimie and into the territory of what were considered the far less trustworthy Pawnee. More problematical, however, was the lack of grazing for their animals as the animals of the preceding emigrants had passed across the grasslands like locusts leaving very little for those behind.

Eventually they reached Fort Kearney, not far from what was then called the Nebraska River, now the Platte River.

"Fort Kearney is the first military station in the Indian territories. Here are about 100 troops, mostly mounted, and such is the moral force of the government, that this handful of men keep in thorough check many thousand savages … The appearance of the fort, as our travellers drew nigh, was most picturesque. From 1500 to 2000 emigrants were encamped on the plain, their tents and wagons clustering around the fort."

Just prior to their arrival, a party of Pawnee had stolen some oxen from other emigrants and Yankee Tom, attracted by the adventure, volunteered to join the party in their pursuit. The posse, led by a soldier, found the Pawnee after two days' hard riding and successfully bartered for skins, moccasins and buffalo-robes in return for the missing oxen. The four then rested up for a few days before setting out to cross the Nebraska River. Although the scenery through which they passed might be uplifting there were many reminders of the cost to others of the journey.

"All along the route they met with graves, marked by a small slab of wood, on which was rudely carved, by some pious hand, name, a date, "and died of cholera" – sad and frail memorials of the dead, no doubt watered with survivors' tears. Not unfrequently these resting-places of mortality had been torn up and violated by the prairie-wolves, which, gorged by, or perhaps scared from their prey, had often left a human hand or leg, or, more generally, only the soiled and torn clothing in which the body had been no doubt hastily interned."

For over 300 km they followed the Nebraska River westward, enjoying buffalo hunts but wearing out themselves and their horses, and weakening the mules through the delay and lack of pasture. Eventually, if they were to make their way north-westward on the trail, they had to cross the river that was one and half kilometres wide, albeit shallow. This they accomplished without loss and pushed on through some hills and woodland that ended with a steep descent onto an arid plain. The first and weakest of the mules died at this point. After several days with virtually no pasture they reached Fort Laramie in Wyoming. This was the country of the Sioux, whom Yankee Tom found handsome and independent. They arrived exhausted with their animals in poor condition. But luckily, Yankee Tom:

"… met with a great and unexpected pleasure in finding in the fort at Laramie a young officer who had been his class-mate at West Point Academy. This circumstance made the time pass most agreeably, and facilitated greatly the refitting of the travellers' stores and appointments."

About the middle of July, some three and half months after setting out from New Orleans, including 75 days and over 1000 km of overland travel from Independence, they set off from Fort Laramie. For ten days the travelling was

Old Fort Laramie by William Hen Jackson.

monotonous, rugged and arid as they approached some foothills and for the first time in their journey they were forced to dig for water. They struggled on to a more pleasant country on the Green River and there met up with a village of Snake Indians where they were fed and entertained and swapped some tobacco for venison. This was also the time and place where trappers and traders met to swap stories, but Yankee Tom had learned that there was no romance in this way of life, even though the gathering:

"… was not unlike an English fair. The traders were six or seven in number; the trappers ten times as numerous. Some of these latter had Indian wives and children with them. The trapper, living entirely in the wilds and among the Indians, generally forms a domestic relation with some young squaw, and as long as she pleases to follow him they remain together, When she thinks fit to leave him – which, however, she seldom does – she goes back to her tribe with her children, and he takes another wife … [Yankee Tom] could perceive no good, but evil, in this mode of life, whatever wild charm genius may have thrown around a 'Hawkeye'."

From this point on the Green River the party chose to go directly through the mountains to California via the South Pass, following the trail of the celebrated Kit Carson. After several days of rugged climbing they reached the Pass at 1000 metres and it was very cold.

"In general, the ground was very spongy, quite like an Irish quaking-bog; and they were in the utmost consternation many times, for fear of the wagon sinking into it. Three weeks they foundered through this cold and hilly region … but the animals grew weaker … [until Yankee Tom's was] the only one remaining [apart from the two pulling the wagon], which he and his friends rode alternately."

They finally had to abandon the wagon which they realised they never should have bothered with in the first place! But then there were many other things they might have done, or not done, in hindsight. So they now packed only the essentials on the remaining three mules.

"Trunks, and almost all their clothing, the greater part of their provisions, and the tent – indeed, every superfluity, and many things hitherto considered essential, and some to which memories and associations clung yet more tenaciously – were all, not without a severe struggle, left on the mountain, perhaps to be useful to some succeeding traveller … Each put on his strongest suit; but boots were all worn out, and they were reduced to Indian moccasins. They slept, wrapped in a blanket, on the earth, and with the sky their only canopy."

Their way forward was now through very rugged rocky country of pine trees and gorges and canyons. They passed other emigrants still pushing forward against the utmost difficulties with their wagons and were glad that they had abandoned theirs. Now they faced the real mountains, the Sierra Nevada, and what appeared at first an arduous ascent.

"It proved, however, more gradual than was expected, and tolerably smooth at first; but when at the computed height of 6000 feet [2000 m], they experienced inconvenience from the rarity of the atmosphere and increasing cold, neither men nor beasts could advance otherwise than slowly, becoming breathless on the slightest exertion. This of course increased as they got higher, till, when at about 10,000 feet [3300 m] in altitude, they were obliged to pause to rest every fifty yards. On the summit, there was snow falling, and lying thick on the ground; as they descended on the other side, it became sleet, and then rain, accompanied with thunder and lightning, the effect of which in that region was terrific."

They lost another mule and were now down to two and travelling among giant pines that entirely lacked grass for the animals or game for the men and their provisions were reduced to coffee and pollenta (a meal porridge): they were in a serious way. They still came across other emigrants but they were no better off and anyhow, attitudes had hardened to selfishness to ensure survival. At one point they went a fortnight without any meat until they managed to shoot a fine buck. By now they looked like tramps.

"They were nearly barefoot. For a month they had only had one shirt apiece; their hats were crownless; their outer garments ragged and soiled; and, above all, hunger almost constantly depressed their energies."

And then!

"… on issuing from a thicket, they were cheered with the sight of a tent with a sign-board, bearing the interesting legend 'Wiskey for sail'."

They were in California, only 60 km from Sacramento!

That night they rested in some sort of peace for the first time in months but still kept a lookout at night for Indians or robbers. In the middle of his watch, Yankee Tom heard footsteps approaching and cocked his rifle, calling out a challenge to the shadowy stranger:

"… who with the utmost *sang-froid* walked towards him, presenting his own piece, and saying: 'Darn it, old fellow, two can play at that game'!"

He was a gold prospector searching in the dark for a new digging which he wished to keep secret!

On the way down to Sacramento they passed many gold prospectors at their diggings at Weaver Town. There they looked for food only to find prices so exorbitant they were forced to sell the penultimate mule for $40 ($800) that gave them a meal of "beef-steaks, wheaten cakes and excellent coffee," plus $20 ($40) left over, part of which they used to buy some food for the last mule! At Sacramento they lost no tears and sold it at auction for $100 ($2000), splitting the money between them.

At this point, after four months of epic travel together, they went their separate ways. One of the four settled in Sacramento and the three others, including Yankee Tom, went on to San Francisco. There the latter became very ill, partly through fevers, but mainly due to the intense hardships he had suffered on the protracted journey from New Orleans. In fact the rigours to which he had subjected his body, including the effects of the cholera, would be with him for the rest of his days, leaving him physically handicapped and bedridden at times, particularly towards the end of his life.

In San Francisco, by incredible chance, Yankee Tom met up with his brother James, who had also made the journey safely by the southern 'Spanish' route. But neither San Francisco, nor its autumn climate, inspired Yankee Tom and because of his poor health also, he decided that he would not stay. Instead, after all that effort, he decided to go home! First, he booked a passage by sea to Panama, on the appropriately named *Panama*, where he arrived after 24 days. Then, after six days there, he crossed the Isthmus of Darien and boarded *The Empire City*, a 2000-ton passenger ship, for New York via Jamaica. From New York he took another steamer back home to Charleston, completing a 12,000 km voyage from San Francisco in 40 days. In total he had travelled almost 20,000 km: his next voyage would be somewhat shorter and in another direction.

In August 1850, after Yankee Tom had safely returned from California, Mary wrote again to Ursula to say that Charles had no funds to assist him in his career, only enough to keep the family, but that Yankee Tom would surely do well if he had the funds. Mary added to her letter, "*I have been led to say what I have done by the deep interest you have always expressed in Tom's welfare.*"[30] In the light of later events it is tempting to read something more into these remarks. Was Mary trying to interest Ursula in Yankee Tom? Did she, as his mother, have thoughts about a potential future for him with Ursula? Did she and Charles, in fact, now secretly know that Ursula was the heir to Buness and that their son was next in line? Or perhaps they knew the former but not the latter? Charles was now President of the South Carolina Insurance Company – an indication of the esteem in which he

Charles Edmondston, daguerreotype in 1855.

Mary Edmondston, daguerreotype in 1855.

was still held by the commercial community despite his business having failed a decade earlier – but he still had several of the family at home to support, including Yankee Tom. Shortly thereafter, Charles was back on the wharves as an agent again, at the ripe old age of 73!

Three years later, on 21st April, 1853, Charles wrote Ursula a letter, the news it contained actually preceding the arrival of the letter itself: "*I am ... sorry that my dear Brother* [Thomas] *for whom you are obliged to act as amanuensis is so incapacitated from writing.*"[31] Then, on the 25th, he added "*This ought to have gone by our dear Tom who left us on the 23rd Sunday in the ship* Huron *for Liverpool, to go on from there immediately to Buness.*" A momentous decision had been made, and Yankee Tom actually arrived in Unst ahead of the letter, in the early summer of 1853: an event that threw all at Baltasound into an exquisite turmoil.

For Laurence and Eliza, Yankee Tom must have been a most painful reminder of their brilliant son Tom, for the former was the same age as their son would have been, had he lived. He was also a rival for Thomas' affections, or why was he here? For Ursula, whose thoughts had often strayed to the young cousin she had never met, but whose praises had been regularly and not very subtly sung by his mother, his arrival brought hope, at least of an ally and perhaps more. On the surface, however, she was just happy to meet someone else from the Charleston family whom she had come to regard with warm affection. For old Thomas it was a very special meeting, also a little awkward and potentially embarrassing. He had provided the money for the young man's fare from America and he was hoping that his nephew would turn out to be a suitable person to manage the estate, perhaps even inherit, failing any heirs of Ursula. But the last thing he would have wanted was any revelation of the contents of his will.

In that same year that Yankee Tom arrived at Buness, his Aunt Mary, sister to Thomas, Charles and Laurence – for whom Thomas had built the house of Marypark at Baltasound – died unmarried. Her loss was a blow for old Thomas who had been very fond of her. The following year, in 1854, in a cordial letter from the lawyer Sievwright to Ursula,[32] he mentioned that he was delighted to hear that old Thomas had managed to get to the drawing room: indicative of the deteriorating state of the old man's health. Later that year, Ursula had a letter from Charles who was also unwell: not surprising considering that he was still trying to earn a living to support a large family at such an advanced age. He told her that he and Mary had been living with their son Patrick, Catherine and family, for eight months at Hascosea, in North Carolina, and that and a spell of two months at the Springs in the Appalachian mountains with Bessie (his daughter Elizabeth 1822-1907), had restored his health.[33]

Earlier that year of 1854, old Thomas was pleased to hear of some unexpected interest in the very northern part of the Buness estate. In the month of March, David Stevenson (1815-1886), grandson of Robert, the founding member of the great Stevenson family of lighthouse builders, and uncle of Robert Louis Stevenson, arrived in Unst and made two attempts to land on Muckle Flugga – the sharp-ridged precipitous rocks just north of Herma Ness – but the weather was so appalling that it proved impossible.[34] David was there to survey a site for a lighthouse, required because of Britain and France's war with Russia in the Crimea (1853-1856). The British Government had decided that a naval fleet should blockade the Russian White Sea ports of Archangel and Murmansk, which would involve a dangerous sea voyage from the north of Scotland around Norway. A lighthouse on Unst was required to guide shipping, particularly on their return from there and from the Baltic, through the treacherous water around the north of Shetland. The Admiralty wanted the lighthouse built on the most northerly piece of rock possible, Muckle Flugga, just where tides and winds swirling round the northern end of Unst regularly kick up the most terrible seas. It is an area where the Unst fishermen caught *saithe* and where Thomas took his *Haaf-Fish* to shoot seals and his nephews to shoot birds on the cliffs, and also where Lady Franklin had come to be near her husband. Unfortunately for David, when the Elder Brethren from Trinity House in England happened to arrive, it was the one day in the year, as it had been for Lady Franklin, when the sea was flat calm and they saw none of the problems foreseen by David Stevenson and instructed him to press ahead with the construction of a lighthouse.

The first attempt at building the lighthouse involved housing the men in temporary accommodation on the Flugga itself. This was difficult enough in the best of weathers because it was virtually impossible to lie alongside the rocks of the Flugga in the almost continuous swell, and every item going ashore had to be lifted out of the flit boat by a hoist strung above it, while the boat itself sat moored between the stacks like a rolling egg between two stones. During several storms in the first winter the sea broke over the top of Muckle Flugga, 66 metres above sea-level, and almost washed the men and their huts away! David was therefore forced to revise his original plans and to build permanent accommodation on the stack. There was also a need for a base for the lighthouse staff somewhere on the north coast of Unst. The most obvious place for the shore base was Fiska Wick in Burra Firth, owned by old Thomas. So, in 1856, he sold it to the lighthouse authorities who completed the lighthouse the following year.

Muckle Flugga 1858 by Frederick Schenck.

CHAPTER FIFTEEN

THE NEW GENERATION

"… he could obtain a situation if he returned home for he is very beloved in his native city and therefore he would not be without employment … he is of a very retiring disposition and would rather suffer than ask for many things … So dear, Ursula be kind and do all in your power to make his stay with you, all pleasant and agreeable."

Mary Edmondston (1789-1872)

Loss and re-acquaintance

Just before Yankee Tom arrived in Unst, Laurence lost his good friend Patrick Neill, who died in Canonmills in 1851. Then a year later, he lost perhaps his closest friend and colleague in natural history, William MacGillivray, who died in 1852 at the age of 56. The fifth and last volume of his *History of British Birds* was published posthumously after a life of some hardship, physical excesses in the botanising days of his youth, financial struggle and disciplined and loving devotion to his work and to his family and students. At the time, only a few appreciated his greatness. Audubon said of his natural history illustrations: "… I think them decidedly the best representations of birds I have ever seen …"![1] MacGillivray was sorely missed by Laurence who had appreciated the guidance and support that MacGillivray had given to his, sometimes wayward, son, Tom the botanist.

The following year, Edinburgh lost one of its most influential professors at the University and the inspiration for so many naturalists in the Edmondston story. After teaching the great and the good for 50 years, the redoubtable Robert Jameson died. The Chair of Natural History therefore became vacant. The filling of Jameson's Chair had been Edward Forbes' greatest ambition and there was little doubt in anyone's mind that he, above all, was the man to fill it. Almost ten years earlier he had sent Tom off on the *Herald* and had then made a second research visit to Shetland. Since then he had kept in touch with Laurence – in 1851 he had sent a friend with a letter of introduction[2] and in 1852 had written to advise Laurence on his meteorological recording and in passing mentioned that he had been unwell.[3] Tragically, Forbes had no sooner been awarded and taken up Jameson's old post when he too died, at the early age of 39, after a very short illness. In many ways, through his expeditions and the breadth and depth of his knowledge, Forbes had been the model for Tom and an indication of the path Tom might have followed had he survived his voyage. It was a sad coincidence that Forbes, too, didn't live to fulfil his own promise. For Laurence, the loss of so many fellow naturalists that he had corresponded, debated and met with over the last 30 years, in such a short time, must have been a heavy blow and must have further eroded his interest in natural history.

The most remarkable among the many remarkable pupils of Robert Jameson, who *did* fulfil his potential, although no one remarked on him at the time, was of course Charles Darwin. Laurence

Charles Darwin.

had been continuing his medical studies at the Royal College of Surgeons when Darwin was briefly studying medicine at Edinburgh University and their paths crossed through their mutual friend MacGillivray and at the Wernerian Society meetings. After that, they did not communicate with each other for many years, not until the spring of 1856 when a letter from Darwin must have reawakened Laurence's appetite for the subject and perhaps old wounds. That letter, unfortunately, has been lost, but a fragment of Laurence's reply has survived:

> "… *Still they may not be decisive for as you may know – the vaunted conjugal fidelity of the* [Noah's] *ark bird has like most general rules had its exceptions. I have no idea that the wild pigeons feed far from their breeding place, but believe that they remain … in the vicinity of their caves & as to crossing to the Mainland of Scotland that is a feat of navigation I should never give them credit for – They have always been very numerous in these islands & always present the usual uniform colour of the Rock dove – I am delighted to hear you are occupied in the effort to throw light on the interesting & difficult subject of Varieties of Species – & I beg you will freely command me when you suppose I may be of use in your researches – Your query as to drifted Trees I can answer you in the affirmative – but instances of them are less frequent now than formerly …"*[4]

Darwin's inquiries about "*drifted Trees*" were in relation to his interest in how islands become colonised, for example by blown seeds or living, sea-carried animals on driftwood, and he filed Laurence's letter under "*the means of geographical dispersal of plants and animals*". At the time Darwin was trying to persuade, even his supporters, that there was no need to postulate that islands like the Galapagos had once had land-bridges to allow their colonisation. The accepted view at the time was that the strange biotas of these islands could be explained by the fact that they were the remnant of a flora and fauna that was once more widespread, but that the collapse of land-bridges had isolated them and while the rest of the world had changed they had remained unchanged. Darwin had been trying to demonstrate that the immigrants arrived by air and sea and then evolved to fill the vacant niches. Darwin travelled down many routes in search of evidence for the key to the evolution of species. One area of study he pursued was the creation of the variety of show pigeons through breeding, such as tumblers and fan-tails. Darwin bred pigeons himself but he needed to compare these with the wild originals: rock doves.

Darwin replied to Laurence, on the 3rd May, 1856,[5] thanking him for information on the interbreeding of the rock dove and the domesticated pigeon and asked for two skeletons of the rock dove for comparison in his researches on variations within domestic animals, using his sketches of the skeletons in his book on the subject and acknowledging the source:

"As I so often refer to the size of the C. livia, or rock pigeon, it may be convenient to give the mean between the two measurements of two wild birds, kindly sent to me by Dr Edmondstone from the Shetland Islands."[6]

Later, in the same book, in reference to domesticating rock pigeons Darwin quotes in the same work from Laurence's old friend MacGillivray:

"Dr Lawrence Edmondstone informs me that a wild rock pigeon came and settled in his dovecot in Balta Sound in the Shetland Islands, and bred with his pigeons; he has also given me other instances of the wild rock pigeons having been taken young and breeding in captivity."

Darwin was an inveterate letter writer and collector of information relevant to his various studies and even the relatively small amount of data he got from Shetland – from others as well as Laurence – was carefully analysed and more was demanded.

"*I thank you for the information in regard to drifted trees, it adds one more archipelago to my list. – If any fact should ever occur to you in regard even to any very slight variation or differences in Habits in regard to any of the domesticated animals in the Shetland Islands I should be most grateful.*"[7]

He went on to ask Laurence if any large quadrupeds had been dug up in the peat, in other words – had there been a land-bridge from Scotland to Shetland at the end of the Ice Age? Later that year, Darwin wrote again to Laurence to thank him for the pigeons, at the same time expressing his sympathy for the irreplaceable loss of his son, Tom.

Rock dove by William MacGillivray.

"I was not aware until I received your letter two months ago, that you were the father of the Naturalist, whose fate, I assure you, I most sincerely deplored at the time. – I can well believe, for I am a father, how this loss must have damped all your zeal for Natural History."[8]

In the following year of 1857, Darwin wrote twice more to Laurence,[9] requesting information on the variation in rabbits and ponies on the islands and seeking a skeleton of the former. Once more, he included the furnished skeleton in his book on variation in domestic animals: all part of his great study on evolution. Two years later, in 1859, Darwin published his classic work, whose full title was *On the origin of species by means of natural selection, or the preservation of favoured races in the struggle for life*, that swept all memory of Chambers' *Vestiges* into the bin of history.

New Blood

The year after the arrival of Yankee Tom at Buness, a visitor arrived at Halligarth who, in his own way, would also bring great changes to the family. In the summer of 1854, two young brothers touring Scotland on their holidays took the steamer to Shetland and made their way up to Unst. The elder was Stephen Saxby (1831-1886), who was studying for an M.A., and the younger was his brother, Henry (1836-1859), who was 18 and had not yet begun his university studies, although he was to take up medicine three years later. Their main interest was ornithology and this is what brought them to Shetland. Henry was born in London, but his boyhood and early youth were spent in the Isle of Wight and North Wales as his father moved jobs. The boys' father, Stephen Martin Saxby (1804-1883), like Laurence, was no ordinary man, although ostensibly a naval engineering instructor, particularly in steam, on which subject he published *The Study of Steam and the Marine Engine* (1862). He was also an early proponent of using magnetic anomalies to test ferrous metals for faults. The beauty of using magnetism was that it was non-destructive. However, as well as being a very practical man with metals and engines, he was an inventor and visionary in other nautical-related fields. One of his inventions was the spherograph, which was designed as an aid to navigation.

The spherograph was simply two circular pieces of paper, one overlying the other and of no more than five inches radius, the upper of which was transparent. On each piece of paper lines were inscribed representing lines of latitude and longitude according to stereographic projection. The centre was held by a pin so that the transparent upper paper could be revolved over the lower. What the spherograph did was to indicate the course, distance and differences of latitude and longitude in Great Circle sailing. Great Circles on the globe are the shortest distances between two points – the equator and all the lines of longitude are Great Circles. The elegance of the spherograph in its day was that it only had to be set with the correct starting and finishing points, no calculations had to be made that might result in errors.

S. M. Saxby's other area of expertise – that was briefly to make him an international celebrity – was his claim to be able to predict the weather based on the phases of the moon. In 1868, in the *London Standard*, he published a prediction of 'impending atmospheric disturbance', spring tides and an equinoctial gale at 5am local time on the 5th October; only he gave no location. On that date the moon would be new and at the nearest point in its orbit to the earth, in other words it would exert its maximum gravitational pull on tides. The not unusual combination of very high tides and an onshore wind resulting in weather damage, somewhere in the world, was therefore quite high. The following year a local meteorological afficionado in Nova Scotia came across the prediction and embroidered it a little for local consumption. Spectacularly, and right on cue, but nothing whatever to do with the phase of the moon, on the morning of the 5th October, 1869, a tropical cyclone arrived from the Gulf of Maine in the Bay of Fundy in Nova Scotia – a bay notorious for some of the world's highest tides. The result was winds of over 160 km per hour, a lifting of the tide two metres above the usual high spring, devastation and death. The storm became known as the Saxby Gale, or the Saxby Flood, and naturally, because it had been 'predicted', it hit the headlines and made S. M. Saxby famous.[10]

With such a father, the boys had some acquaintance with meteorology and this, with the combination of their interest in birds and Henry's thoughts of studying medicine, made it unsurprising that, when in Unst, they should meet up with Laurence at Halligarth that summer of 1854. At that time, most of Laurence and Eliza's large family of seven were still at home, although Biot (27) was now a minister in Scotland and David (17) was also away. Henry delighted in their company, especially the little mischievous, wild and intelligent 12-year-old Jessie M. E. But what he was most absorbed by were all the northern birds on their nesting sites, birds he had only seen on passage on the shores of his home country; birds such as the elegant whimbrel with its lilting call, that Laurence's brother Arthur had first recorded on Hascosay all those years ago. Then there were the northern seabirds such as the rare *bonxie* that Laurence and old Thomas had protected on Herma Ness, and its cousin, the dimorphic arctic skua, and so many others, such as the *rain-gös* and the *immer-gös*. Then there was Laurence's almost encyclopaedic knowledge of them all and of the many rare migrants that passed through in the autumn and the spring. On his side, Laurence was charmed by the young man's enthusiasm and his obvious devotion to his favourite subject and he would have found him a rare antidote to his newly arrived American nephew. Henry had stumbled upon a world that seemed to offer him everything. The combination of the birds, of Laurence's way of life, his family, his medical practice and the attraction of the remote island

Jessie M. E. as a girl,

Dr Henry Saxby circa 1860s.

landscape set an idea in Henry's mind that would not be dislodged. In 1857, he matriculated at Edinburgh to study medicine and, four years after his first visit, in 1858, he returned to Halligarth for the summer and then again in 1859.[11] Henry always kept a detailed diary, mainly on birds, but the diary for this period had few ornithological entries, his mind being elsewhere – he was wooing the young Jessie M. E., perhaps entranced by her lively character.

Jessie M. E., after Tom the botanist, was the most gifted of the children. She had not had the advantages of further education of her elder brothers. Hers was mainly gained from her parents, extensive reading from a large and eclectic library and listening to the conversations of the many interesting and sometimes famous visitors to Halligarth and Buness. In addition to the many scientific luminaries already mentioned should be added: John Lucas Tupper (1824-1879), a poet and sculptor, friend of Rossetti and early member of the Pre-Raphaelites; Sir George Webbe Dasent (1817-1896), a Scandinavian scholar, author and some time editor of the *Times* who, after visiting Halligarth in 1860, sent copies of his books to the family; and Sir Henry Dryden (1818-1899), architect and artist who was touring Shetland's medieval churches for his forthcoming book *Ruined Churches* (1874): all of whom made a mighty impression on Jessie M. E. and her siblings.[12] One of the most exotic visitors, however, was a Frenchman and close relation of the now deceased foe of old Thomas' hero, the Duke of Wellington: he was Prince Louis-Lucien Bonaparte (1813-1891), nephew of Napoleon!

Prince Lucien was actually born in England. He had private means and devoted his life to the study of languages and particularly the English dialects. In September 1858, he visited Shetland to seek out any remaining examples of the *Norn*, the old Scandinavian-Shetland language that was spoken before Scots became the accepted tongue. Among several Shetland amateur scholars he sought out Laurence, who had a reputation as a linguist and Scandinavian scholar. Jessie M. E. later recalled this visit and the freedom that the Edmondston children were given when even such a grand personage as the Prince arrived at Halligarth.

"I can recall the amazement with which I heard that the French Emperor's near relative was coming to visit our father … It was our father's habit to allow any of us who cared to be present to remain in the room when he was entertaining savants; and, as the conversation was generally confined to those scientific and literary subjects upon which his guests were at home we, bairns, thus had the opportunity of receiving instructions at the very fountain head. Neither book, nor lecture, could fire young souls with love for science as the words of a Master could, and so we listened and learned. No exception was made in the case of Prince Lucien."[13]

Laurence and Eliza later sent Prince Lucien a collection of vernacular Shetland words, a study that Yankee Tom was later to take up. Laurence also wrote out the *Parable of the Sower* (Matthew XIII) in the dialect for Prince Lucien, which was subsequently published privately by him.

Old Thomas, now 79, also wanted to meet the Prince, though he was by then quite infirm and in his dotage. Laurence took Prince Lucien over to Buness and at the meeting was somewhat embarrassed by his brother's behaviour. As Jessie M. E. later recalled:

"The old man [Thomas] cherished a doting hero-worship for the Iron Duke, who had frequently shown him marked kindness and corresponded with him until his death. Wellington's portraits, at various stages of his career, presented by himself, adorned the dining room at Buness; and the Laird was fond of exhibiting them to his visitors, relating, at the same time, anecdotes of his Hero. Imagine my father's feeling when, having escorted Prince Lucien to Buness, the old gentleman began to enlarge upon his cherished theme, even alluding to Waterloo! Fortunately the Laird's articulation was very indistinct, his condition of mind and body far from what it had been; and Napoleon's nephew was generous enough to look upon the incident from its right point of view."[14]

Jessie M. E., then, had a rich education and a unique and happy childhood in Halligarth in a large family with a great deal of freedom. Laurence and Eliza had encouraged her to participate in their intellectual discussions and as their generation, including her uncle Arthur, had not only discussed their interests but written about them too, it was almost inevitable that Jessie M. E. would herself want to put pen to paper. She may not have been as precocious a child as her late brother, but there is no doubt that she was a bright and determined little girl. At the age of 10 she showed the first signs of her proclivity in literature when she wrote of herself delightfully:

> "My face is white, my hair is brown,
> I should not like to live in town;'
> They say my tongue is far too long,
> I should much like to write a song;
> I like to ride and climb the rocks
> And in this way get many knocks,
> For I'm as wild as wild can be,
> There is no taming can tame me,
> And I go by the name of Wildie."[15]

When she was at the tender and impressionable age, coming on 13, her mother was putting together the stories and descriptions of Shetland she was to publish as *Sketches and Tales of the Shetland Islands* (1856) and this encouraged Jessie M. E. to take up the pen. She may have published a poem at 13,[16] but one of the earliest pieces of prose writing that survives is a little essay she wrote a year later entitled *The English, Scotch and Irish Character*. It was a naïve and patriotic piece with many good things to say of the history of the English, but she had a poor opinion of Ireland and especially its lower classes.[17] She sent the piece to Robert Chambers the following year, hoping to have it published in the hugely popular *Chambers' Edinburgh Journal*. He was favourably impressed and encouraging, being an old friend of her mother's, but did not publish it.[18] The first published works attributed to her were a short story in the *Family Herald* and a poem about the Vikings in a Scottish venture, *The Scottish Annual* (1859), when she was 17. The latter came about through the visit to Unst of another rather remarkable young man.

One of the contributors to this anthology was Jessie M. E.'s mother, Eliza. Hers was a short tale of Shetland called *Menie Henderich*, which was a romance – very loosely based on her husband's struggles – about the youngest in a family of the ancient Henderson lineage of his mother. Another contributor was an Andrew James Symington (1825-1898), whom the editor of the anthology particularly thanked for his help. Andrew Symington was an up-and-coming merchant in Paisley. He was also a poet, an artist and something of a naturalist, who had already published several books on nature. Three years later he was to publish *Pen and Pencil sketches of Faroe and Iceland* (1862), an account of a trip he made from Leith to those North Atlantic islands. He also met Laurence and was so favourably impressed that he put a very fulsome dedication in his book:

> "To Laurence Edmondston, Esq., M.D. of Shetland, corresponding member of the Royal Physical and Wernerian Societies, Edinburgh. Honorary Member of the Yorkshire Philosophical and Manchester Natural History Societies etc – This volume is affectionately inscribed by his son-in-law A.J.S. – May 1862."

The dedication may just have had something to do with the fact that he had married Jessie M. E.'s older sister Mary in 1860, after which they moved to Paisley. It was Andrew Symington's brother who had accidentally discovered the painting of Tom the botanist's grave in South America.

In addition to the account of his travels in Faroe and Iceland, and in the United States in the 1870s, Andrew Symington published many poems and, as author of Blackie and Sons' series of *Men of Light and Leading* (1880), he wrote two volumes of *William Wordsworth: a Biographical Sketch*. The combination of his interest and talents in the arts and nature, his love of travel, and the fact that he came from the same Scottish locality and had a similar background to Eliza, made him irresistible to the family.

The American Cousin

Family tradition has it that Yankee Tom came to Buness, or was perhaps even sent, to marry Ursula, now 34 years old and six years older than he, and so secure the Buness estate under the Edmondston family name. It is true that old Thomas paid his fare, but he had already made the young man second in line to inherit after Ursula anyway. Perhaps he thought that his young American nephew might be better material than anything in Unst, Laurence's sons included, and that he might therefore be a suitable suitor for Ursula. If so, he was to be disappointed.

On his side, Yankee Tom left America and the hot climate of Charleston for the cool, damp climate of Shetland because he had not succeeded in establishing himself, his father could not support him, and perhaps he had been made aware of the contents of his uncle Thomas' latest will. He came because he saw an opportunity, but he did not like what he saw. Almost immediately, he became aware of the now almost bitter relationship between his uncles, Laurence and Thomas. He would have felt his uncle Laurence's suspicions of his presence and found that the virtually bedridden old Thomas was now almost senile. Like Eliza, so many years before, he found Shetland society and culture and the Buness household mores limited and rather boring. He hesitated before coming to a decision and behaved rather badly in the interim, threatening to leave for home at least once.

Ursula's situation was becoming increasingly intolerable. She had been well brought up as the daughter of the laird, had been educated in Lerwick while under chaperone and was well regarded by many of her father's influential friends. But she was now getting past marriageable and childbearing age. Most importantly, her illegitimacy probably precluded marriage, for

Yankee Tom as a young man.

who in Shetland 'society' would marry her? And if there was some man, not of 'society', whom she wished to marry, there was no way her father would have approved or allowed it. Ursula was well aware of Eliza's and Laurence's thoughts about her; the former disapproving and the latter perhaps a little jealous and afraid of her potential threat to his promised inheritance. On the positive side, she had struck up a warm friendship with her uncle Charles on his visit that had subsequently included her aunt Mary and other members of their family in South Carolina, and she had come to rely on their distant correspondence for moral and spiritual support. Mary had also talked up her son and continued to do so. Ursula now saw that her American cousin could be where her future support might lie and, despite his weaknesses, she found that she was becoming rather fond of him. Whatever, she needed his help, because for the last four years of old Thomas' life her father was virtually helpless, suffering repeated attacks of paralysis and coming more and more reliant on Ursula and his American nephew.

It was a period of unrest and some controversy in the family, as Yankee Tom's behaviour and Ursula's frequent correspondence with South Carolina revealed. In a letter to Ursula from Aiken in April 1855, Charles referred to the news that his son wished to leave Buness. He urged Ursula to persuade him to stay; for his own good and because he wanted his brother Thomas' "… *remaining years to glide as placidly as possible.*"[19] In May, Mary wrote to sympathise with Ursula, expressing their love for the "*great invalid*", adding "*our means now are so circumscribed that we could not afford to cross the Atlantic.*" She evinced her understanding of Ursula's predicament and, quoting Wordsworth, admired her love and strength, "*The prayers I make will then be sweet indeed – And sound thy praises everlastingly.*" Her letter was a reply to Ursula – who had expressed her concerns for Yankee Tom – and, despite her previous fears of the difficulty of finding a good position in Charleston for her son, Mary told Ursula that, before he left Charleston, her son's salary:

> "*was very handsome* [and that] … *he could obtain a situation if he returned home for he is very beloved in his native city and therefore he would not be without employment … he is of a very retiring disposition and would rather suffer than ask for many things … So dear, Ursula be kind and do all in your power to make his stay with you, all pleasant and agreeable.*"[20]

Mary did not expect her son's stay in Unst to be a permanent one.

The following year, in March 1856, the "*retiring*" Yankee Tom fathered an illegitimate child that, unlike his uncles, he did not acknowledge and care for. That year, Charles wrote a very supportive and loving letter to a very troubled Ursula concerning the growing suspicion and ill-feeling between Laurence, Biot and old Thomas at Buness.

> "*If any of the members of the Halligarth family, young or old should so far forget themselves, as to show the least disrespect, incur an unkindness or even a coolness to their worthy brother and Uncle, I shall find it difficult in my heart to forgive them.*"[21]

Charles' letter to Ursula went on to urge her to encourage Yankee Tom to stay. However, leave he did for the Scottish mainland under the cloud of his illegitimate child, only returning under the entreaties of his father and Ursula. Charles wrote again to Ursula three months later, in June 1856.

> "*I cannot express to you the satisfaction …at the information of Tom's return to Shetland … I am no less happy at his return on your account* [which will] *no doubt relieve you from a load of responsibility … I am particularly gratified at your account of the reconciliation between your Uncle* [Laurence] *and yourself – and you must try my dear Ursula to bear and forbear a Christian like feeling with much that may appear offensive at the moment, and I know you have had trials enough with one and another, out of your Father's House to fight against.*"[22]

While Laurence feared for his inheritance, Yankee Tom, through the growing helplessness of the rapidly deteriorating physical and mental health of old Thomas, was becoming a vital support for Ursula. Later that year in September, Mary wrote to Ursula from her son Patrick's house at Hascosea, unaware of Yankee Tom's misdemeanours, asking after her "*cherished child*". As in many of her letters she ended by asking a service, for Ursula was a very good knitter. "*Now dearest Ursula, I am going to ask you a great favour and that is that you would knit for me two pairs of open sleeves, with Frills, to them with edging to the frills, to resemble lace.*" Mary wanted to give them to friends to whom she was under "*great obligation.*"[23] The following year she got the sleeves and thought them exquisite. This exchange of presents, sometimes in the form of foodstuffs, was a regular occurrence. In one letter to Ursula, Charles spoke of receiving salt fish,[24] in another of smoked meat and sometimes there were 'live' presents, and sometimes presents flowed in the other direction. In March 1857, he told her that:

"The [Shetland] *ponies, as you say did arrive, but that was all as to the little one, he got here half dead. I doubt very much whether he will recover – the others look very well … A supply of rice and flour is also on the way."*[25]

Sir Faithboy

Old Thomas had been laird of Buness now for more than half a century. From a sound base he had greatly extended the acreage of the estate, not just in Unst but on the adjacent island of Yell and on the Shetland mainland, and even bought substantial property in Lerwick. He had been a canny businessman, exploiting the chromate find early and to its fullest. His letters to his friends and sometime competitors, Sir Arthur Nicolson, William Hay and Thomas Mouat of Garth, revealed a friendly wiliness that took financial advantage of these connections when it could. In politics he was extremely conservative and he was a strict churchgoer, by this time a Ruling Elder of his Church to the General Assembly.[26] On the surface, he appeared generous to his young brother Laurence, but in reality he made life very difficult for him. Like his late brother Arthur, at least as far as his personal morality was concerned, he was a hypocrite, in having an illegitimate child and not marrying the mother to legitimise her. In this instance, of course, he followed a long tradition among the powerful in society. Although he had briefly tried the system, pioneered by others, of freeing his tenants to sell their produce to whomever they wished, when he found it unprofitable he had reverted to insisting they sold it to him. To his tenants, whatever they thought of him, he was God. They depended upon him entirely for their homes and their livelihoods and to an extent, in that he sponsored the teacher and the minister, for their education and religious care. The majority therefore were afraid of him and probably disliked him.

Considering his position and wealth, it is not surprising therefore that sometime in the late 1850s a book appeared in Unst entitled *Historical remarks on a Refugee Nobleman in Unst*, whose authors' were anonymous.[27] This was a scurrilous and very thinly disguised attack on old Thomas and those around him: an attempt at a grand Rabelaisian tale and a lampoon of their lives. On its appearance, Thomas bought up as many copies as he could and had them burned, and when a second edition appeared he bought all the copies and disposed of them too. The authors were two men from Norwick in Unst; one the son of a former teacher and the other purportedly a licensee who had been crossed by Thomas. Barring open antagonism, which would have been fatal as far as their living was concerned, this attack was one of the very few ways Thomas' tenants and enemies could get back at him. In the spoof, Thomas was called Sir Faithboy, from his habitual use of the expression 'Faith, sir …' Sinclair Bruce was Lady Faithboy, Ursula was Fabula, Yankee Tom was Artemeous, and Peter Sutherland, Petro. But it was not only the family and the inner circle that were mocked, the story was full of many other colourful and well-known contemporary Unst characters, also thinly disguised, such as Frederick Stickle, a fiddler, Madge Coutts, reputedly a witch, and several relatives of Ursula.

The gist of the tale, as all good lampoons, had an element of truth to it that was developed into a fantasy and although the characters were pilloried for the readers' amusement it is arguable whether or not there was anything libellous in it. For example, in reference to old Thomas' relationship with his housekeeper Sinclair Bruce, and the reaction of the local Church, the story tells how:

"Notwithstanding all the good things, and reputed great wealth at the Castle [Buness], a sad gloom pervaded the countenance of Lady Faithboy [Sinclair]; care had made premature furrows, which marred her otherwise finely developed 'human face divine'. Her grief became very great, for the news went abroad that no marriage ring adorned her finger.
And the rulers, and chief elders, and deacons did bring Sir Faithboy into judgement concerning this grave offence; but Sir Faithboy having great power in the land, was not excommunicated, but received back to the Church, where he remained an <u>honourable</u> member all the days of his natural life."

Aspersions were also cast in Yankee Tom's direction, who was reputed to like his dram, whom the story tells, had written a parody of the 31st Chapter of proverbs:

> "Whene'er my fainting spirits sink,
> Give unto me the strongest drink;
> Nought can ease my troubled soul,
> Like care-beguiling alcohol.
> Alcohol, sweet alcohol,
> All enlivening alcohol;
> When care and love disturb my soul,
> Bring unto me sweet alcohol."

All good knock-about stuff!

Fun was also made of old Thomas' collection of guns and swords and his propensity to exaggerate his adventures and tales of prowess, particularly his story of the shooting of the whale in Balta Sound.

"Above the marble mantle-piece [at Buness] hangs trophies of many a hard-fought battle, among which are to be seen a richly-enamelled sword taken from General Saladin at the storming of Askelon, and a battle-axe, bearing a curious device found among the ruins of Gaza. An old blunderbuss belonging to the Spanish Armada, seemed to be Sir Faithboy's favourite trophy. Petro [Sutherland] the secretary kept it in good order for his special use; and truly it was a formidable weapon, for on one never-to-be-forgotten occasion, Sir Faithboy shot a monstrous whale with it, which measured in length sixty and four cubits."

But, besides the humour, there were other, unamusing barbs that betrayed the authors', and clearly the locals' feelings and fears about their landlord.

"As Sir Faithboy waxed in wealth, he increased in tyranny. Patches of ground which the hardy Shetlanders had reclaimed from the marshy waters, were mercilessly wrested from him and given to others, from whom extravagant rents were extorted. Cottages were levelled with the ground. The same land that formerly cost the tenant £4.10s [£225] annually, realised at a later date £24 [£1200] annually. This additional rent was exacted to defray increased taxation, was it? Who brought about the poor-rates in Unst, and who pays those increased taxes? Not the landowners, but the people!"

Accusatory as this was, the only possible litigious suggestion about old Thomas was that he might have had an affair with a certain 'Katherine' of an island called Papa Stour – on the west side of Shetland – where he sojourned on one of his seal-shooting trips. The authors though, were careful not to make this suggestion directly in black and white.

The danger for Thomas lay in the temptation to take the perpetrators to court and having the distinction between fact and fantasy questioned on a public stage: a trap into which he did not fall. It says something about the Unst folks' attitudes to Laurence and his family that they did not appear in the book. There was one intriguing vignette in the story that sheds a little light on the relationship between Yankee Tom and Ursula. It suggested that although Artemous (Yankee Tom) may have seen Fabula (Ursula) as a way out of his penury, the pair actually fell in love and it was the implacable opposition of Sir Faithboy (old Thomas) to a marriage between his daughter and a penniless relation that almost drove Yankee Tom away. The authors did not know of course, that old Thomas had already put Yankee Tom in his will. The revelation of Thomas' 'apparent' opinion of Yankee Tom might also explain why they did not get married in his lifetime.

In destroying as many copies as possible, Thomas did the only thing he could. Nevertheless, the book gave a great deal of amusement to the Unst folk and probably also to a few of Thomas' competitors and acquaintances.

In the autumn of 1858, when Yankee Tom was again away from Shetland for a time and old Thomas, now bed-ridden and semi-conscious for much of the time, was requiring constant nursing, the kindly and caring Charles wrote as usual to Ursula with a few words of comfort and support.[28] Both he and Mary frequently quoted appropriate passages from the Bible in their letters, drawing on its words to reassure Ursula of the righteousness of her sacrifice and the eternal love of a Father. In one letter, Charles told Ursula of the comfort he himself gained from the scriptures. "*It is the blessed Sabbath morning and my reading on this day, is that excellent book 'Family Worship' which I first saw in Buness in 1841.*"[29] But the comfort was too late, for by the time that letter arrived in November, old Thomas the laird, was dead.

PART III

BROKEN PROMISE, LOST FORTUNE AND REFORMATION

CHAPTER SIXTEEN

CIVIL WAR ON BOTH SIDES OF THE ATLANTIC

"… the said Thomas Edmondston promised and engaged that in the event of the pursuer going to reside and settle in Unst in Shetland, as a medical practitioner, and as the medical attendant of the deceased, he, the said deceased Thomas Edmondston, would make him generally his heir and executor."

Dr Laurence Edmondston (1795-1879)

The Will

It was, in some ways, a great weight off Laurence's shoulders, although he would have castigated himself for such thoughts. For more years than he cared to remember he had been under a heavy obligation to his brother. Not only had he personally been dependent on his annuity, but Thomas' money had also paid for his sons' education. Thomas even owned the very roof he lived under. Perhaps now he would be free of all these burdens. With the death of Thomas in November 1858, Laurence, at 63, was now the last of his generation living in Shetland, having already lost his brothers Henry and Arthur and his three sisters. The remaining family members of his generation – his brother Charles and his wife Mary – were alive and relatively well and would very soon celebrate their golden wedding. Of Laurence and Eliza's children, the eldest son, Biot (31), was shortly to be appointed minister at Menteith near Stirling. Then there was Mary (27); David (22); Jessie M. E. (17); Isabella (20); Ellen (14); and finally, Thomas (12), of which only the last three were still at home.

Laurence was expecting that Thomas' will, as he had promised some 40 years ago, would leave him the Buness estate, something that he had thought about so frequently, particularly in his worst moments of depression. The last few years of Thomas' illness, as his mind had deteriorated, had been very trying for Laurence, for there was always the chance that he might forget their deal altogether. Worse still, he might be influenced by those close to him. It was a very nervous and apprehensive Laurence who awaited the reading of the will and when it appeared it was not William Sievwright, the family lawyer in Lerwick, nor even Ursula who produced it, but Sinclair Bruce, in whose care Thomas had left it: an indication perhaps of just how close their trust had remained all those years.

Strange and foreboding as this was to Laurence, it was as nothing to the shock of the will's contents.

"I do hereby of new Dispone and Convey to and in favour of … Ursula … and to the heir of her body … whom failing to the persons [Yankee Tom] … all my heritable property and Estate … as if she had been my lawful heir …"[1]

Only now did he discover that his brother Thomas had left the entire estate in life rent to Ursula and the heirs of her body, failing heirs, to Yankee Tom and his heirs and failing Yankee Tom, to Biot and his heirs, then his younger brother David and so on. Laurence was stunned and embittered by the betrayal. As the illegitimate Ursula was not married and had no children, and as long as that remained the case, the estate would eventually go to Yankee Tom. But if Ursula did marry and have children, even at the late age of 40, the estate would go to them and not only out of his hands but out of the Edmondston family name.

At Thomas' death his estate was substantial, consisting of 450 merks of land, not counting the *scattald*; he had an annual income of £1200 (£67,200) that included a much reduced income from chromate; there were bonds in the bank – including £2300 (£128,800) from William Hay[2] – worth from £11,000-£13,000 (£616,000-£728,800); there were the Lerwick properties from 'the Street' to the Hillhead and other large sums in the bank under Ursula's name. Thomas had left[3] an annuity of £20 (£1120) and free life rent in Buness to Sinclair Bruce, and lump sums of £200 (£11,200) to Charles; £350 (£19,600) to Yankee Tom; £350 (£19,600) to Biot; £100 (£5600) to young Thomas and £50 (£2800) to each of the other five of Laurence's children. He had also left an annuity of £10 (£560) and free life rent of Beachpark, a building next to Buness, to Peter Sutherland who had been living there for at least 15 years and where he had christened a son Thomas Edmondston Sutherland (b1849) after the laird.

To Laurence, who had expected the whole estate, Thomas had left only Halligarth and its lands in life rent, not even the title deeds, and an annuity of £80 (£4480). There was no indication of an earlier will in Laurence's favour as Thomas had promised. He was devastated. Having spent the best part of his life fulfilling their agreement at great personal cost and having looked after Thomas, as agreed, throughout his illnesses, he had very little to show for it. There was only one course of action he could follow and that was to challenge the will and take Ursula to the High Court in Edinburgh. This he did, seeking £15,000 (£840,000) in loss or damage. His case was that there must have been a disposition of Thomas in 1819:

"… in favour of the pursuer [Laurence] … the said Thomas Edmondston promised and engaged that in the event of the pursuer going to reside and settle in Unst in Shetland, as a medical practitioner, and as the medical attendant of the deceased, he, the said deceased Thomas Edmondston, would make him generally his heir and executor."[4]

Ursula's and Sievwright's response was that there was no will in Laurence's favour drawn up in 1819. Laurence could not believe it. Then, less than a year after the death of old Thomas, came a second unexpected blow. In 1859, Yankee Tom and Ursula married: the former was 34 and the latter now 40. Effectively, the control of the estate was in Yankee Tom's hands, for it was not until another 20 years that the Married Women's Property Act (1882) granted married women the full rights of separate ownership of property.[5] However, when he thought about it calmly, Laurence realised that this cloud actually had a silver lining, for surely it was highly unlikely that they would have heirs and therefore Buness must eventually fall, not to him, but at least to his eldest surviving son, Biot.

The next thing that happened that year was that Jessie M. E. and the young medical student who had been staying with them, Henry Saxby, declared their love and wish to marry. Laurence and

Eliza, however, did not approve of their early marriage as Jessie M. E. was only 17. *Wildie*, however, lived up to her name and the pair eloped to Edinburgh and married there in December 1859. They returned to Unst and Halligarth as man and wife in the spring of 1860 – in time for the wedding of Jessie M. E.'s elder sister Mary to Andrew Symington and their departure for mainland Scotland – when they were accepted back with open arms. Like her mother and grandmother, Jessie M. E. fell pregnant almost immediately, producing her first child, Henry junior, in October 1860, within ten months of the wedding. During part of this time Henry served as an assistant to Laurence and then for two years he was back in Edinburgh and St Andrews, completing his medical studies from 1862.

Mary's wedding to Andrew Symington had taken place just before Laurence presented his case to the High Court and, combined with the return of his lively and errant daughter and her husband, it briefly lifted Laurence's spirits. He was also heartened by the support of his eldest son, the Rev. Biot, who had written from his ministry near Stirling to his uncle's old friend, Sir Arthur Nicolson of Fetlar.

Dr Laurence Edmondston (1795-1879) in late middle age.

"*I hope you will excuse the liberty I take in writing to you. You may perhaps have heard that my father feeling himself deeply wronged by my late Uncle of Buness's settlement of his estate on his natural daughter, has most reluctantly and after the intervention of friends … resorted to an action in the Court of Session having received legal advice that he will be successful … In or about the year 1819 my uncle made my Father aware of the terms of a deed executed by him at that time in my Father's favour but containing a provision for his daughter and stated that he had nominated you and my father as Trustees for him.*"[6]

Biot continued:

"*I think it most probable, considering the early intimacy and confidence subsisting between you & my Uncle that he may have spoken to you something about his feelings and intentions towards my father and consulted with you – perhaps even mentioned generally what he had done or intended to do …*"

Then he asked Sir Arthur if he remembered anything of that occasion that might have a bearing on his father's case, going on to reveal the prejudice that had always been there, just under the surface.

"That an ancient property should be diverted from its legitimate succession & an old respectable family disinherited and expatriated cannot surely be right."

The letter went to Sir Arthur's Fetlar address and since he was not there, followed him to London where, three weeks after it was posted, he replied.[7] It was probably a month therefore before Biot received his response and it was not the one he and his father had hoped for. Sir Arthur recalled that Thomas had asked him, and Laurence, in 1819 to be trustees should anything happen to him, and it did contain the provision of an annuity for Ursula, but it had concerned her care and education only and had said nothing about the inheritance of the estate. He added that Thomas had frequently visited him at his home at Brough on Fetlar but had never raised the issue again.

Laurence's case came up in Edinburgh in June 1860, but judgement was not arrived at until January 1861[8], two and half years after Thomas' death. In the meantime, Biot's younger brother David, who had returned to Unst after a brief spell away from home, and was in business at Baltasound as a fishcurer and merchant, was made the tacksman or leaseholder of the Buness estate by Ursula and Yankee Tom. The estate had been leased latterly to a Mr Hunter from Lerwick, but the couple, unable, through lack of management experience, to run it themselves, now took the opportunity to mend some family fences. David then moved into Marypark near the shores of Balta Sound, the house that had been built by old Thomas for David's aunt Mary.

The judgement of the High Court went against Laurence and he finally had to face the reality of his brother's actions. His only compensation was that at least one of his sons was the estate manager and another, Biot, might, in time, inherit it. In the meantime he nursed his bitterness.

Coinciding with the winter of Thomas' death was the inauguration of an all-year-round paddle steamer from Lerwick to the Scottish mainland, itself replaced by the first screw-driven ship two years later. This immediately improved communications with the south, providing a quicker, more comfortable and more reliable service. At the same time, the population of Shetland, through the creation of many more small farms and the improvements to health, reached its maximum in 1861 at around 31,000, including about 2000 men at the Faroe cod fishing, Greenland whaling and the merchant navy. From now on there would be increasing emigration. The new service also brought north to Shetland a figure who was to become as notorious in these islands as the recently deceased Patrick Sellar (1780-1851) had become in Sutherland. His name was John Walker and soon he would be in Unst as factor for the Garth estate, clearing tenants to replace them with sheep – now more easily transported south to market – and advising the proprietors and managers, such as David, to do the same; he would also soon be defrauding the chromate proprietors.

The final event of those momentous few years that was to influence all their lives in ways they could not have imagined, had, unknown to them, occurred in October 1859, several thousand kilometres away at Harper's Ferry in (now West) Virginia. There, the passionate abolitionist John Brown (1800-1859), and a small party of zealots, including several of his sons, seized a US arsenal hoping to ignite an insurrection that would prompt an uprising and bring freedom to the black slaves of America.

America and War

On that side of the Atlantic, Catherine Devereux, the wife of Charles' third son Patrick, was recording in her diary – *The Journal of a Secesh Lady* (1979) – what she imagined must be the diet of her brother-in-law Yankee Tom and Ursula in Shetland:

"Made some Brandy and Peaches & put up some in their own juice to send to Ursula & Tom. Poor Shetlanders. They never taste any thing of that sort from their native land. A greasy pudding with currants in it, & that fried, is their greatest native luxury. I ought to beware! The taste of these Peaches may give Tom nostalgia … Ursula will not thank me for awakening association of home & native land in Tom's bosom."

The following year, Charles and Mary moved from Legare Street in Charleston to Aiken, where they planned to celebrate their golden wedding anniversary on Christmas day 1860, when Charles would be 78 years old. Catherine Devereux recorded her preparations in early December for that very special event and the cornucopia of foods that was then available to her. From New York she had sent to her: "... mushrooms, catsup, essence of lemon, jars of lime, bleached Jamaica ginger, East India ginger, and vanilla beans." From those ingredients she made a very special cake to take from their plantation at Looking Glass for Patrick's parents.

"Pure white – on the top Papa's and Mama's Monogram – 'C. M. E.' – surrounded with the words '25 Dec 1810- 25 Dec 1860' done in pure white comfits. Then beading of white sugar plums, festoons, etc., on the side of the first tier. The second is divided by sugar plums into eleven medallions, each medallion containing the Initials of one of their children beginning with Laurence & ending with Henry. I have succeeded in keeping the icing smooth & white & am more proud of my chef d'oevre than was ever Eude or Soyer*."

*Famous French chefs of the time.

Catherine Ann Devereux.

211

From the plantation it took them and the cake four days to reach Aiken, and in her diary she recorded all the family who were able to be present at the golden wedding celebrations of Charles and Mary and, coincidentally, the 24th wedding anniversary of their son Laurence and his wife Sarah, and the 23rd anniversary of the wedding of their daughter Jessie Mary and her husband, Amory Coffin:

"Lawrence, Sarah and their son Willis; Charles [junior 1816-1874]; Patrick and myself; Jessie [known also as Mary], her husband and children; Bessie [Elizabeth]; Isabella [b1829] – and her two children; James and Henry. Poor Carrie [Caroline 1824-1902] was prevented by her situation from taking the journey, indeed we afterwards heard that her daughter was born on the 24th. She was the only member of the family on this continent who was absent – Tom [Yankee Tom] in Shetland, Rob at sea completes the circle."

It was a poignant celebration with glittering reminders of Charles and Mary's past wealth and status within, and outside the distant sounds of the chariots of war.

Charles Edmondston.

"The children had provided the supper … We sorted out all the relics of Mama's former grandeur, the elegant buff china, the glass, and the table fairly groaned with her silver … Papa entered in a suit … woven for this very occasion in his own native land, of his own Shetland wool … leading Mama, elegantly dressed in a rich brocaded black silk dress and lace cap, collar and sleeves to match."

There were 25 in all at the table and later:

"Papa [Charles] danced a Highland Fling with Isabella to the tune of the Fisher's hornpipe. He had a Scotch bonnet on his head & he took the steps as well as a man of thirty could have done, throwing out his legs from the knees as the true Horn Pipe ought to be danced but rarely is, & snapping his fingers at the right moment in unison with the music, as not one man in fifty could do now."

Even though Charles and Mary were no longer as wealthy as they once had been, their children, or at least some of them, were. Their anniversary presents included, a drawing room carpet, armchairs from New York, a silver egg stand, salt cellars, butter dishes, vases and china ornaments. Mary received new "toilet appurtenances such as Mama delights in", caps, embroidered handkerchiefs, lace collars and sleeves and stockings. Catherine recorded that "At last, worn out with happiness, the dear old lady and gentleman retired, Papa repeating that it was 'the happiest day of his life'."

It was hardly more than a year previous to that happy Edmondston gathering at Aiken, on 2nd December, 1859, that John Brown was tried and hung for treason after his failed insurrection at Harper's Ferry in the state adjacent to the Carolinas. Many of the pro-Federal Republicans and Unionists of the North had tacitly sympathised with his cause and his actions. This drove the Southern Democrats and secessionists to believe that the North intended a bloody suppression and so militias were raised. Patrick, because of his previous experience at West Point, became a captain with the Scotland Neck Mounted Riflemen – Scotland Neck was a great bend in the Roanoke River in Carolina that had been settled by Scottish Highlanders in the early 1720s.

Following the election of the anti-slavery Republican, Abraham Lincoln, as President,

"... the South Carolina legislature, which has assembled to choose the state's electors, set a special election for December 6 [1860] to choose delegates to a convention. In Charleston on December 20, 1860 [five days before the Edmondston celebrations], the convention unanimously voted an Ordinance of Secession, declaring the state's ratification of the Constitution repealed and the union with other states dissolved ... By February 1, 1861, six more states had declared themselves out of the Union. On February 4, a convention of those seven states met in Montgomery, Alabama, and on February 7 it adopted a provisional constitution for the Confederate States of America. Two days later the delegates elected Jefferson Davis its president."

The Ordinance was passed in the St Andrew's Society Hall, with which Charles had had a long association, both as a member of the Society and as its president. At this point in the dispute, the South – what was to become the Confederacy – believed they would win any war with the North. And so did British politicians of all persuasions and many of the British public. In fact, most supported the South, for many industrial cities in Britain depended upon a continuing importation of cheap cotton.

Under the surface of the anniversary celebrations at Aiken that Christmas there lay subdued tensions. The young men were confident that whatever happened between the North and the South they would protect their homes, family and way of life, and while Charles and Mary feared for the future of all their extended family, the young women feared for the lives of their husbands and children. But the fear was vague, no one could really imagine how a war might affect their lives and property or that black slavery, on which they had entirely come to depend, might possibly be abolished.

The divisions between the North and the South were not clear cut. There were Northerners who supported slavery and there were Southerners who supported the Union. One of the latter was Major Robert Anderson (1805-1871), a Unionist from Kentucky. He was based at Charleston's Fort

Moultrie. Despite a gentleman's agreement between the North and the South, the day after Christmas and the Edmondstons' celebrations in 1860, he spiked the guns at Fort Moultrie, destroyed the stores and moved his force onto the island of Fort Sumter that commands the entrance to Charleston's harbour. The Southern Democrats and secessionists demanded that Major Anderson withdraw, but the Northern Republican administration ordered him to stay.

One of the Edmondston family at the anniversary party at Aiken was Amory Coffin junior, the son of Charles and Mary's daughter, Jessie Mary. Amory was 19 and in patriotic fervour had enrolled as a cadet at The Citadel – the South Carolina Military Academy at Charleston. Entirely unaware of it, he had placed himself right at the centre of the events that would spark off the Civil War real and proper.

"Anticipating attempts to reinforce and provision the fort [Sumter] from the sea the State authorities ordered the construction of a two-gun battery on Morris Island commanding the entrance to the harbour, and Major P. F. Stevens, with a detachment of cadets from the Citadel, went down to lay out and build it. Two 24-p'dr guns were put in place with embankments and traverses of sand and a bomb-proof magazine for the ammunition … at 2 o'c on the morning of the 7th January … a telegram announced that the [Union} steamer 'Star of the West' with supplies for the fort had sailed from New York and would attempt to pass in … I [Amory] was on duty that night at the Citadel … and [as] ordered a field-piece [was] run out in front of the sally-port to fire the signal of alarm … [that] quickly spread around the city … Early in the morning of January 9th 1861 the … 'Star of the West' was seen coming up the channel, a course that took her directly in front of the guns of [our] battery [on Morris Island]."[9]

Amory went on to describe the confrontation:

"A solid shot sent skipping across her bows called her to a halt, but, paying no attention to this command she came bravely on until a second and a third shot directly in front and over her bows caused her officers to realise the situation and, after a brief hesitation, halt and retire from an action for which they were wholly unprepared."

This was an act of provocation that the North chose, for the moment, to ignore. The South then reinforced their threat to Fort Sumter.

"Under the masterly engineering skill of Gen'l. Beauregard, batteries of mortars and siege guns were planted on James, Sullivan and Morris Islands, and a circle, that grew stronger every day, was drawn around the fort [Sumter]."

All this was done in the gentlemanly way of the times, at least until the war got truly under way:

"During the winter the garrison of Fort Sumter was permitted to send daily a boat to Charleston for market supplies of fresh food, and their mail was also delivered to them."

Three months later, on April 4th, Abraham Lincoln ordered another attempt at the re-supply of the garrison on Fort Sumter that also failed. A few days later,

214

"... Gen'l. Beauregard felt that his preparations were sufficiently near completion to warrant a summons to the fort to surrender, and several notes, under cover of flags of truce, passed between the opposing parties ... Although he was greatly out-numbered, and there was no prospect of relief by his Government, Major Anderson refused to consider the conditions of surrender, and declined to yield his position, except under the application of force ... As a result of these negotiations he was notified that fire would be opened upon his defences on the morning of Saturday, April 12th, 1861."

And so it was that, at 4.30am that morning, Amory was awakened by the first aggressive shot of the Civil War. He watched the engagement all that day from the shore while his Confederate Commander, General Pierre G. T. Beauregard (1818-1893), also watched it, standing on the piazza of the mansion at 21 East Battery, that Amory's grandfather had built at the height of his prosperity, almost 40 years previously.

Amory's unit was sent out on that Saturday night to Sullivan Island and there he was recognised by the commanding officer, a Colonel John L. Branch, who brought him up to his observation post as a temporary aide-de-camp. From there, with the aid of the Colonel's field glasses, in great excitement, he watched the entire bombardment of Fort Sumter.

"The firing during Saturday had been with solid shot and shell, but on Sunday morning the use of red-hot solid shot was begun from Fort Moultrie. The shot were heated in a small furnace built for the purpose on the terreplein, and were fired from a specially prepared mortar that placed them with much accuracy directly upon the wooden barracks of the fort ... The effect of this was soon evident in the dense clouds of smoke that were seen to ascend from Sumter. The barracks were on fire. The resulting distress to the garrison was quite evident for they were seen throwing barrels and boxes over the parapet and through the embrasures to the rip-rap or beach of broken stone at the base of the wall. Much of their ammunition was jettisoned in this way and they were forced to recognise that their position was no longer tenable. About 12 o'c, in response to a summons from Gen'l. Beauregard, the flag went slowly down, and a white flag, a signal of surrender, took its place ... not a man on either side of the combat had received the slightest injury."

The Civil War had begun!

Robert (1832-1861), Charles' sixth son, now 29, also took an active and short-lived role in the Civil War. He was second mate on the Privateer *Sumter* at the time of the golden wedding celebrations, but died in Charleston of a fever on the 5th June, 1861. His ageing father, who had been a vigorous man and a pillar of strength to all the family throughout his life, had himself suddenly fallen ill and the shock of Robert's death was a fatal blow to him. He died just ten days later, on the 15th June, five days short of his seventy-ninth birthday, surrounded by the rest of his family, leaving his brother Laurence at Halligarth as the last survivor of the five brothers.

Charles had died within two months of the commencement of the War and his passing was important enough in Charleston for the local *Charleston Mercury* to record, on the 15th June, 1861, that he had been, not only a prominent merchant in the city, but "... one of these of whom our community has a right to be proud ... his unchangeable probity as a merchant, made him an exemplar among his brethren." The Charleston Port Society for Promoting the Gospel Among

'Charlestonians viewing the bombardment of Fort Sumter' from in front of 21 East Battery by Frank Vizetelly.

Seamen, to which he had belonged for much of his life in Charleston and of which he became president in 1851, eulogised him as an "… honest, upright and intelligent merchant, a warm friend, a useful citizen and sincere Christian …." Catherine, his daughter-in-law, added her own last comment on him, "… we have lost our stay, our support … the one to whom we could always turn for aid and counsel." Charles' paternal generosity and love was not just for his family. Catherine goes on to say, "He was the centre and heart of the Scotchmen in Charleston and the widows and daughters of many of his deceased countrymen looked to him as their protector and nearest friend."

Of the five brothers, Charles had been the most successful financially, even though he had lost much of his fortune. If he had been a ruthless man his trading business might well have survived the crisis of 1837, at the expense of others. The fact that he chose to pay off all his debts, even at the painful expense of selling off most of his personal and family assets, was an indication of his integrity. Nevertheless, like so many other Southerners he somehow managed to reconcile his sincere Episcopalian beliefs with slavery. There is no doubt that he accepted the established position of the Church on slavery; that the Bible legitimised it and that bringing slaves to Christ brought them civilisation and salvation.

With the 'official' start of the War, others in the family now took up posts with the Confederate Army. Catherine's brother, John Devereux, was appointed Major and Chief Quartermaster for North Carolina, a position he held until the end of the War and James Edmondston – Charles' fifth son, who had returned from California – became a captain of Ordinance. Catherine's husband, Patrick, tried several times to get an active post in the army but was unsuccessful, partly because he was excused due to the large number of slaves he owned and partly due to poor health. Finally, in 1863, the youngest brother, Henry, was also conscripted. The day-to-day necessities of life then became more and more difficult to obtain. Catherine recorded towards the end of 1861 that, because of the blockade of Charleston and the other southern ports:

> "The price of Salt, of Leather, & in consequence shoes now became alarming. Coffee, Sugar
> & luxuries of various kinds had long been enormously high; but provisions being plenty, there

had been no suffering. But now with salt at 10, 15 and in some instances $28 [$470] a sack, negro shoes – brogans – at 4, 5 and $6 [70, 85 and $100] per pair, things began to look serious."

At Looking Glass, in February 1862, Catherine noted down Patrick's instructions to the slaves should he be absent, and in the telling, revealed their fears and her attitude towards them.

"Mr E. was off this morning. Before he left he had the negroes summoned & told them of the enemy below & gave them orders that when the Plantation Bell should be rung & the Horn blow at the same time, every one of them should assemble in the lot and accompany me to Hascosea. The team is to be driven out & all the wheels on the plantation, lest they [the North] should be able to haul supplies to their boats. The work of moving the Cotton, Meat, etc. is to go steadily on & he charged them in his absence to remember their duty to me and to give me no trouble. They were much affected and poor things in much fright, for they know that they are the objects sought after by these miscalled Philanthropist[s]. They entreated me not to leave them & I have promised to remain at home & take what care I can of them."

In January 1863, after two years of war, the 21-year-old Amory, who had now graduated from the South Carolina Military Academy, was appointed Assistant Professor of Drawing at the Academy with the rank of 2nd Lieutenant. In June he wrote to his Uncle Tom (Yankee Tom), in Buness on Unst.

"*I have nothing new about the war, to communicate. Vicksburg still holds out and our hope and belief is that it will continue to do so and that we will be ultimately victorious there. I enclose you a drawing of our new permanent Confederate Flag which will give you some idea of how it would look in bunting. The Union of this flag is the old flag of Gen Beauregard consecrated by many a splendid victory in our southern cause.*"[10]

Vicksburg, in fact, surrendered to the Unionists after a very short siege and the North then began its final subjugation of the South. Patrick then became a captain with instructions to organise 90 men of the Home Guard to obstruct roads in the face of the Northern advance. The following month of August saw the commencement of the Northern bombardment of Charleston. Catherine thought the end was very near.

"We expect it [our houses to be burned] constantly that I keep our clothes all packed up & the trunks standing by the windows, so that if necessary I can, myself, throw them out & thus have something to wear … All of our negroes have left."

For the whole of the following year of 1864 the War raged around them with threats to Savannah, then Charleston and Wilmington, coming ever closer. In December 1864, Amory and his younger brother Charles, were fighting with the Cadets at a place called Tulafinny Bridge near Pocotaligo on the South Carolina-Georgia border, defending Southern communications between Charleston and Savannah. His mother, Jessie Mary, wrote to Catherine and Patrick and gave them the full account of what ensued.

Amory Coffin.

"One of them [the Cadets from the Military Academy] ... was shot in the knee and dropped instantly. Amo [Amory] and one of the Cadets immediately rushed forward to pick him up, when [another] fell shot in the cheek. Amo snatched [his] gun took deliberate aim & saw the Yankee who had shot [the second cadet] drop. He then carried [the first] to the rear & turning his head to pass an order (he acting as adjutant to the corps) received this ball, it striking him in a slanting direction in the forehead & glancing over the left temple. He fell without knowing anything more. Charles E. [his younger brother at 16] was just in the act of firing his gun, when one of the Cadets called out 'Lieut Coffin's killed! Shot in the head!' Charlie says he felt as tho <u>he</u> was shot & his eyes blinded & he knows he missed his aim. He did not look in the direction in which his brother was until someone called out 'Coffin go pick up your brother,' when he ran to him and found one of the cadets assisting him to rise ... Charlie carried him to the rear where the wound was examined and dressed."[11]

Amory wrote a second letter to his uncle in 1866 to tell him about this adventure, modestly omitting his heroics.

"*... I daresay Mother or Aunt Kate have told you of the brilliant little fight of the Cadets* [at the Military Academy of South Carolina] *at Pocotaligo where I was shot in the head with a rifle ball and came very nearly to death – from the wound ... I only recovered in time to march through the State before Sherman's army ... we were withdrawn to the mountains to check the passage of raiding parties from East Tennessee. Here we remained ... until the news of Lee's and Johnson's surrender reached us – when we were disbanded and left to find our own ways home as best we could.*"[12]

Letters from Carolina to Yankee Tom in Unst during the Civil War were censored and approved by General Beauregard's staff. They told of a difficult time for a family once wealthy and served by many slaves, now seeing the approach of poverty and starvation due to the blockade, lack of opportunity to earn any money and the absence of their men folk. Writing to a friend in December 1863, Yankee Tom in Edinburgh, told him that he had recently received news from his family.

"I have lately recd. Letters from my darling old Mother (God bless her). My youngest brother Henry poor fellow – had been drawn in the conscription – and marched off to Lee's army in Virginia. Leaving, poor dear lad, a young wife and child destitute, or rather a burthern on my poor Mother and friends – and they alas barely able to feed the numerous hungry mouths crying for bread."[13]

Yankee Tom, safe, thousands of kilometres away in another country, suffered torments for his mother, brothers and sisters. Every letter that escaped the blockade brought increasingly worse news of their situation as the very society in which he had been raised crumbled under the Northern onslaught. Fate, though, had given to him the opportunity to be able to help them in a way he had never imagined when he had lived under his father's roof. Through the munificence of his deceased uncle Thomas, and his marriage, he and Ursula were able to provide them with very substantial financial and material support. Several letters through 1864 and 1865 illustrated their predicament and his help. In January 1864, his mother wrote to him from Aiken, where she was with Henry's family too.

"I feel it is a privilege to be your Almoner in contributions to the comfort of many … For your munificent present … The Widows, the Orphans, the poor Soldiers Wives and Children … $100 [$1700] into savings Bank for housekeeping; to Carrie [Caroline] $100 [$1700] and Belle [Isabella] $25 [$425] … Our troubles are too great but I will not enumerate them for it would grieve you – I wear homespun instead of flannel and am thankful that I am able to procure it … I have never felt so severe winter, as this for many years past. The poor soldiers are suffering terribly. Many, very many, of the elite, of our land, are without shoes, stockings and blankets, all of our Females, from the highest to the lowest, from the Oldest to the Youngest, are employed in knitting, for the soldiers as well as for themselves – yarn, both woollen and even cotton, is very difficult to obtain … I am so cold that I can hardly write."[14]

Isabella then took her mother to her home in Augusta in Georgia. In May, Mary wrote again to Yankee Tom, that she was trying to feed 15 souls, both black and white, but *"now my funds are nearly exhausted."*[15] She went on to tell him that his brother Laurence was still at his home trying to do business, but effectively living off the money he had made before the war.

The next letter, sent in August 1864 to Yankee Tom, was from his sister Jessie Mary, mother of Amory, thanking him for £100 (£5800), telling him of the siege of Charleston and that their mother was quite ill, but that:

"She bids me tell you that the 'Bale' of goods which you sent her, was burned up in the Elizabeth … she was very sorry to lose it – but quite rejoiced that it did not fall into the enemy's hands or benefit any Yankee … I have an abiding confidence, that our righteousness and hallowed cause will be benignly favoured by an all-merciful and all-just God: and that the cradle of secession will emerge from the blood and horrors of the conflict which is now upon her with her brow crowned with triumph and ever glorious Palmetto be more honoured than ever as an emblem of victory."[16]

219

The *Elizabeth* belonged to John Fraser & Company, one of the most successful blockade running firms in the Civil War, which had an office in Liverpool that was basically a front for the Confederate government in Europe. Unfortunately for the Charleston Edmondstons, she had gone aground off Cape Fear with their 'bale' in the autumn of 1863. Jessie Mary's confidence in her "*all-just God*" was sadly misplaced, for on 18th April, 1865, shortly after General Robert E. Lee had sought sanctuary at 21 East Battery when fires raged in Charleston – the same Lee who had led the US Cavalry against John Brown at Harper's Ferry – the last Confederate troops surrendered to Sherman at Durham in North Carolina.

Just before that, Catherine wrote a last few bitter entries in her diary:

"On April 14, 1865, the War Department staged a massive victory celebration at Fort Sumter on the fourth anniversary of its fall. At noon Major Anderson ran up the flag he had lowered previously, while gaily decorated ships and all the forts in the harbour sounded a salute."

Union officers now occupied Charles' grand old property at 21 East Battery and, almost four years to the day since General Beauregard had stood on exactly the same spot, it was now *their* turn to enjoy the scenes of victory from the piazza!

Catherine's world, now shattered, was turned upside down:

"April 16th 1865. How can I write? How find words to tell what has befallen us? *Gen Lee has surrendered*! Surrendered the remnant of his noble Army to an overwhelming horde of mercenary Yankee knaves & foreigners.

April 23rd 1865. We sift the news … Lincoln's death seems the only certain item & that is affirmed … 'Exult not over thine Adversary,' but if Booth intended to turn assassin why, O why, did he delay it for so long?"

In October 1865, Catherine recorded that they had just heard of the death of her brother-in-law, Laurence, the eldest son of Charles and Mary. It had taken six weeks for the news to reach them from Aiken, a journey that had taken them only a few days before the War. Mary took her son's death very badly and in despairing mood resolved to go to Shetland to live with Yankee Tom. She requested that Patrick meet her in Philadelphia so they could take their leave of each other. However, when he arrived, he found her with his sister Carrie and so exhausted from the journey from Savannah that she had changed her mind. He took her back to live with him and Catherine.

The end of the war was the end of the old Southern regime, with several letters from Carolina in early 1866 deploring the changes. The first letter was from Mary to Yankee Tom, from Carrie's home.

"*Bessie is without a Servant* [black slave]*, all have left her – this is what I anticipated. Mr Agnew paid their wages and made handsome offers, which they all refused … The 'Freedmen', as they are called are more favoured than the White Men.*"[17]

The second was from her daughter, Jessie Mary, who told Yankee Tom that her husband (Dr Amory Coffin) had lost his plantation and slaves and that it had been occupied by the Yankees.[18]

The third letter was from Jessie Mary's son, Amory junior, who, after serving in the war, struggled to find employment. He told his uncle that he "... *drove a wagon backwards and forwards on the hack line between Augusta and Columbia for some time at five dollars* [$80] *a month and my rations*."[19] Shortly after, he started a school in Aiken and later went on to make a very successful career in engineering.

At the end of 1865, Patrick's ex-slaves had been share-cropping and were paid a proportion of the harvest, but by January 1866, the last entry in Catherine's diary, she recorded that Patrick had made contracts with them: they were freemen and would in future work only for wages like everybody else: something the tenant-fishermen of Shetland could only dream of. Patrick died only five years later in 1871 and his mother, Mary, the following year in 1872. Catherine died in 1875.

CHAPTER SEVENTEEN

AN END TO OLD WAYS

"By the way, while I think it, I may as well mention that Uncle Laurence has at last called at Buness – had an interview – of a very affectionate kind and has accepted the annuity left him by uncle Thomas – Wonders will never cease from off the face of the Earth."

Thomas Edmondston (1825-1874)

The cost of management

While dramatic events were happening in America in the 1860s that would forever change the society of its Southern States, things were also changing, albeit less spectacularly, for the people of Shetland. Practices of landowners over their tenant fishermen, accepted as tradition and right through long use, were increasingly being called into question, mainly due to political, social and agricultural reforms emanating from the mainland and partly because of disastrous local natural events that would result in two investigative government commissions and culminate in the crofting reforms at the end of the century. These changes marked the beginning of the end of the old subservient relationship between tenant and landlord. For the owners and managers of the Buness estate it was, on the whole, a difficult retreat fought on the backfoot with the weapons of rationalisation and justification. But it was not only a time of social and financial changes for the Edmondston families at Buness, Halligarth and Marypark, for the next decade there was to be a plethora of births, marriages and deaths.

At the turn of 1863, at the height of the American Civil War, when Yankee Tom and Ursula were master and mistress of Buness, the newly qualified Dr Henry Saxby, a heavily pregnant Jessie M. E. and their two-year old Henry junior, returned from Edinburgh to Halligarth where Henry became Laurence's permanent assistant and successor. To the joy and delight of them all, in February, in Jessie M, E.'s mother's room:

"… on our father's [Laurence] birthday, our mother gave welcome to their first granddaughter who bore their joint names [Elizabeth Laura]. They had not named any son or daughter after themselves, and it pleased them well that their 'Oy' [granddaughter] should be so named."[1]

Their pet name for Laura was *Lalla* and she was to be a very special child in the family because of all the concatenations of her birth – delivered by her grandmother, named after her grandparents, born on her grandfather's birthday, and in the exact spot where her own mother had been born. She was also to be Jessie M. E.'s only daughter, who, when she learned to speak, informed her mother that she was her *"one wee lassie."*

222

The other members of the crowded household at Halligarth were Jessie M. E.'s older sister Isabella (26), her younger sister Ellen (19) and brother Thomas (17). The other brothers and sisters had flown the nest. David (26) had married Margaret Hamilton (1838-1871), the daughter of the Rev. Zachary Hamilton (1805-1876), minister of Bressay, in 1862, and they lived in Marypark within sight of Halligarth and Buness. The same year *Lalla* was born, Margaret gave birth to Anne (1863-1918), the first of her three daughters. At the same time there were ominous signs that David's constitution was not strong. In a letter from Yankee Tom to his deceased uncle's old friend, Dr Basil Spence of Lerwick, in September 1863, Tom noted:

> "... *he himself* [David] *poor fellow is looking wretchedly ill – he has been overworking and exposing himself entirely too much between Balta Sound and Uyea. He is now in Lerwick for a little change and in order to an enforced relaxation from business. Poor lad I earnestly hope he may recover for the sake of his wife and little ones – I believe he has had the worst of it among them from the first to last. I have given him a renewal of his lease for three year – for I believe if he was suddenly pulled up now that it would be an awkward matter for him.*"[2]

But things were not going so well for Yankee Tom either. In a series of letters to friends and family he revealed *his* poor state of health. First, from Albany Street in Edinburgh, where he stayed in rented accommodation for half the year through much of the 1860s and until his death, he wrote to Dr Spence – who was becoming his confidant just as he had been his late uncle's – that he was accompanied by Ursula and her close friend Miss Sievwright and that they were whiling away the time with "*Concerts, Soirees and Cricket Matches ...*" He went on to tell Spence that his family in Charleston were surviving as well as could be expected in that "... *cruel, bloody and unnatural war ...*" He opened his letter, however, with the news that "... [I have] *now entirely recovered the use of my hands ...I am sure you will be pleased to learn that my Doctor has given me permission (should I continue to improve) to spend the summer in Shetland.*"[3] In another letter, in 1864, he noted: "... *with assistance I'm managing to drag my weary legs two or three times up and down the room ... It is very tiresome to be always tied to my armchair.*"[4]

Similarly, in a letter from his sister Jessie Mary to him in Unst in 1863, when he was not yet 40, clearly in reply to one from him, she commiserates with him on his comment that he "*is a cripple for life.*"[5] A year later, Yankee Tom wrote to a Dr Copeland that he was learning to walk with a crutch under his arm and the support of a man, "*My spine has recovered strength, but my joints from want to use are very weak and my feet turned inwards and my toes downwards from the same cause.*"[6] In October of that year, in relation to medical treatment, Yankee Tom also informed his cousin Laurence that "*All my hopes and thoughts are fixed on 9 Albany Street* [Edinburgh] *and I shall feel uneasy and unsettled until safely housed there – I hope you will drop me a line now and then.*"[7] The following year he had his portrait painted there, for £14.14s (£850), by a Mrs Knox.[8] Further, in Amory junior's letter of 1866, telling his uncle about his action in the Civil War, there is a hope expressed that his uncle is "*recovering*"[9] and in a letter of Yankee Tom's to Prince Louis-Lucien Bonaparte in 1866, there was yet another mention of his illness.

The physical weakness that Yankee Tom had picked up, possibly from the hardships he had suffered on his trek to California more than a decade previously, had returned with a vengeance and effectively made an invalid of him. There were also suggestions that Yankee Tom's physical

Yankee Tom in middle age.

handicap was exacerbated by gout, too much of the good life and lack of exercise. However, his incapacity did not prevent him from retaining a full involvement in all the issues of the day. In 1863, he was pursuing an idea that the Shetland proprietors and merchants should take shares out on a steamer to trade with the mainland. Then, in August of that year, 45 whales were driven ashore at Harold's Wick, just to the north of Balta Sound, and Yankee Tom, just as his late uncle would have done, pressed for his share as a proprietor. In this case his land did not extend to the shore so he did not get it.[10] In October, he wrote to the authorities in Edinburgh, requesting that they increase the salary of the teacher at the Burrafirth school, that his uncle Thomas had built and presented to the Church some years earlier.[11] Up until then, he and his late uncle Thomas, as proprietors, were responsible for the salary of the schoolmaster, but now grants had become available for school expenses although the State was not to take over the schools entirely for another eight years.

Yankee Tom also dabbled briefly in archaeology and quite unintentionally found himself entertaining some quite unsavoury company. In 1863 he sent some human remains he had dug up, at what was thought to be an ancient burial site on the hill behind Buness, to the Anthropological Society of London that had just been established.[12] That year, the honorary secretary of the Society came all the way north to Shetland and Buness to investigate the discoveries. He was so impressed by the number of anthropological sites on the island that the following year the founder and first president of the Society, James Hunt (1863-1869), came to carry out more intensive investigations. Unfortunately, he found that most of the sites had already been opened and his visit was therefore rather unproductive. While in Unst, Hunt stayed with Yankee Tom who, due to his poor health, was not able to accompany him in the field.[13]

Ostensibly, Yankee Tom appeared to be following in the steps of his uncle Laurence in his acquaintanceship and involvement with the men of stature in science of the day: both Hunt and Darwin were members of the Ethnological Society of London. However, Hunt and his fellow members of the Anthropological Society were not ethnographers, but racists, and he a misogynist. Hunt had established his Society in opposition to the Ethnological Society when the latter admitted women to its ranks! After his death, the Society disintegrated in confusion without his leadership.

The weather at the time of Hunt's visit, the year Jessie M. E. and family returned to Shetland, and the summer of the following year, was dreadful in Shetland. Yankee Tom, in a letter to Dr

Spence in July 1864, expressed sympathy for his tenants who had nothing to fall back on in such bad years. These years, he too, as landowner, saw a drop in *his* income from rent and fishing; losses that would fan the embers of change in land management.

> *"The Crops are very backward, and the fishing as yet a failure. If the men do not make a good fishing this year, it will be a serious matter – as last year they were poor – and the past winter was a very ruinous one – The snow lay upon the ground for six consecutive weeks – and many of our Tenants lost their whole Stooks* [of Corn] *– At Buness we lost* <u>thirteen</u> *(13) Ponies old and young – and when we suffered so heavily, you can imagine how it must have fared with our Tenantry."*[14]

In 1864 there was a great reduction in the estate income. In addition to poorer returns from the tenants' fishing there was a drop in the price of chromate and, as Yankee Tom went on to inform Dr Spence, *"… there is every appearance that the mineral is failing. We expect to work the Hagdale quarry out this winter – and as yet no other quarry has been discovered."* There had also been a continuous draw down by Yankee Tom and Ursula of the capital they had been left by old Thomas, due to the hugely generous support they were giving to their relatives in Carolina during the Civil War. In a letter to his uncle Laurence, possibly in response to a request for money, Yankee Tom spelled out his income in 1864, and *"by what I am obliged by law and the necessities of my relatives to pay out of it."*[15] The annual rental from the land, bank interest and dividend from the chromate now amounted, he said, to only £735 (£42,630), half what it had been only five years previously. Out of that income he was obliged by law to pay £65 (£3770) towards the minister's stipend and the schoolmaster's salary, and by the terms of his uncle's will an annuity of £80 (£4640) to his uncle Laurence. Then he had to pay £139 (£8060) in sales tax and £60 (£3480) in income tax and was paying out £100 (£5800) to support his mother in America, and an additional cheque for £750 (£43,500) to keep *"a house over her head."* Finally, he was paying out £2.2s (£122) a week to keep the rooms in Albany Street, which they occupied in the winter, and the same price to have a *"private Phaeton"* permanently on hire. This was a letter designed to get his uncle off his back. However, it is clear that Yankee Tom and Ursula were living well above their income, which was probably why they sold the large property in Lerwick, from the Street to the Hillhead, to the Union Bank in 1866, for £1500 (£87,000).[16]

A year later, Yankee Tom was making very little profit at all out of the chromate. When William Chambers, the owner of *Chambers' Journal* and the brother of Robert the editor, called at Buness while touring Scotland on the *Pharos* as a Lighthouse Commissioner, Yankee Tom complained of the problems of selling chromate of iron due to the competition from foreign countries as, *"… at present some thousands of tons remain unsaleable at remunerating prices."*[17] In fact, another year later, Yankee Tom and Ursula were forced to sell her father's bonds to Equitable Life for £2600 (£150,800) and then a further £350 (£20,300) in 1869. They were spending their inherited capital just as fast as they could cash it in!

The lack of warmth between Yankee Tom and Ursula at Buness, and their uncle Laurence at Halligarth, that had become a feud on the opening of old Thomas' will and their marriage, still simmered. Laurence, cutting off his nose to spite his face, had even refused to accept the annuity his brother had left him even though he could hardly survive without it. However, in September 1863, Yankee Tom recorded, almost incidentally, in one of his many letters to Dr Spence.

"By the way, while I think it, I may as well mention that Uncle Laurence has at last called at Buness – had an interview – of a very affectionate kind and has accepted the annuity left him by Uncle Thomas – Wonders will never cease from off the face of the Earth – Seriously however I am very happy to think that he has at last ceased from strife. For I never could (nor indeed wished), forget that he was my dear Father's Brother, and as such alone entitled to my affectionate respect – And I had all along determined, and acted up to the determination that in no event would I have allowed my feelings to get the upper hand of what was my duty – that I would never even attempt to visit on him his mistaken course of conduct towards my wife and myself – I do not think that the Buness & Halligarth families will ever be on terms of very close intimacy nor indeed have I any desire that such should be the case – but still as near relatives, we can and should keep up the decorous interchange of the courtesies of life which when neglected are of necessity a public Scandal – The red men and the whites have buried the hatchet, and it is to be hoped, that it will never again be exhumed."[18]

The following year, despite their deteriorating financial position, Yankee Tom and Ursula gifted Laurence the deeds of Halligarth and the 18 acres of arable land that went with it. Since it was rent free and there was no way they could possibly realise its capital value, it was a gesture, but for all that, a thoughtful one, very much appreciated by Laurence. All the labour and love he had put into establishing his little acre of diverse woodland and garden against all the odds of climate and soil were now worthwhile.

In 1864, Jessie M. E. and Henry moved into the cottage of Ernesdaal, just five minutes walk from her parents. For Laurence and Eliza it was the best of times again for they now had two of their children's families about them, ownership of Halligarth and a guaranteed annuity. Then there was the pleasure of Laurence's shared interest in ornithology with his son-in-law Henry, who began to produce a superfluity of notes on Shetland's breeding birds and migrants for the *Zoologist*. Between 1859 when he married Jessie M. E. and 1871 when they left Shetland, Henry added around 60 new birds to the Shetland list and contributed 67 papers to the *Zoologist*! Like his father-in-law, Henry was excellent in field identification, a meticulous recorder and dissected his specimens to establish their sex and feeding habits.[19] He was also particularly interested in Shetland's rarer breeding birds and was in danger of becoming a soft touch for Shetlanders returning from the whaling who were looking for a few shillings reward for eggs of northern species they had collected in Greenland, presenting them to him as having been found 'under da broo o' da bank', a vague Shetland phrase that could mean anywhere! And there was another side to Henry; he was a very competent amateur artist who, in his leisure time, filled his sketchbook in the 1860s with watercolours of the coast of Unst.

Clett Stack, Fetlar by Henry Saxby.

While Yankee Tom and Ursula were under a financial squeeze in the 1860s, mostly of their own making, Shetland's most successful entrepreneur was also giving away *his* money for good causes. In 1862, Arthur Anderson – chairman of P&O, the shipping company that he had co-founded and the old foe of Dr Arthur Edmondston in Lerwick – built the first secondary school in Shetland. At first he sought financial help from the Shetland establishment but they would not support him in the substantial costs of construction because Anderson wanted the school to be available to everyone, which meant free to the poor; whereas the landowners, merchants and others wanted it to be fee-paying and therefore selective. So Anderson, not put off by their lack of support, went ahead entirely on his own with the building of what is now known as the Anderson High School. Four years later, again with his own money, he established the Widows' Homes in Lerwick for "the indigent widows of fishermen and sailors who had perished at sea."[20] Although he did not contribute, Yankee Tom wrote to congratulate him on his efforts.

Books and Plans, Ends and New Beginnings

In 1866, Jessie M. E. and Henry's third child, Stephen, was born in Ernesdaal, while a few hundred yards up the road at Halligarth, Eliza was putting together her reminiscences of her first son, Tom the botanist. At the same time, a few hundred yards down the road from Ernesdaal at Marypark, David, tacksman of the Buness estate and responsible for collecting the rents from the tenants and managing the home farm, was composing a long letter to his cousin Yankee Tom, proposing a radical change of estate management. This was necessary to counteract a reduction in estate income due to the falling off of rental income and exacerbated by the final exhaustion of the chromate quarry at Hagdale after 40 years operation.

Since David was running the estate, and as he was not very active, Yankee Tom looked around for something to do to while away the time. He had met and been impressed by Prince Louis-Lucien Bonaparte on his visit in 1858, and was well aware of the minor efforts of both Laurence and Eliza in the field of Shetland dialect. He was also conscious of the literary and scientific achievements of Laurence and his brother Arthur. Encouraged by Ursula, who, of all the Edmondstons, was best versed in her native dialect, Yankee Tom began collecting words and phrases of the old tongue with which he was entirely unfamiliar. By 1866 he had amassed a sufficiently reasonable collection to be able to write to Prince Lucien for support. He told the Prince about his work, requesting that he might be permitted to dedicate the book to him and, by the by, thus gain some repute by association.

"I have been engaged during a long and painful illness in gathering words and phrases peculiar to the Orkney and Shetlands Islands, more especially the latter, & have succeeded in collecting some four thousand of these fully Six to Seven Eighths of which have never appeared in print in collected form, & the great bulk of them entirely unknown out of the Island. My collection may prove of value to the Philologist, and I propose issuing an edition of some two hundred and fifty copies."[21]

The book was published as *An Etymological Glossary of the Shetland & Orkney Dialect* (1866). There was no reference in it to Prince Lucien, but the work was supported by the Philological Society after parts of it were presented at two Society meetings. The following year, Yankee Tom sent a copy with an accompanying letter to his distant relative, Sir Arthur Edmondstone of Duntreath, revealing that he had rapidly assumed the politics of his deceased uncle. Sir Arthur replied:

> *"I am very glad to find our political views agree. I never heard anyone of our name being a radical. I, like you, am of the old Tory school, and as such am not much pleased with the course our Conservative Government is taking regards Reform. Explain it as they may, it is a downward democratic movement ... Gladstone is a dangerous man."*[22]

The Reform that Sir Arthur was referring to was the Second Reform Act (1867). At that time five out of six adult males had no vote and the Act extended the electoral franchise in Britain to include about one million urban workers. Like the first Reform Act, it was seen by the aristocratic and wealthy as a dangerous step.

In the book preface, Yankee Tom acknowledged the help of the Rev. Thomas Barclay, now the Principal of Glasgow University, the same Rev. Thomas Barclay of Lerwick who was attacked in print by Yankee Tom's uncle Arthur, more than 30 years before, and the same who had also helped his late cousin, Tom the botanist. Yankee Tom also acknowledged that some 400 items came from Jamieson's *Scottish Dictionary* and that "A large number of words, which had escaped the author's research, were found among Mr Grant's papers ..."[23]

William Grant (1828-1865) was a rather tragic Shetland figure who had been a thorn in the side of the establishment. His health deteriorated into mental instability probably through alcoholism and he had to leave Shetland for Glasgow where he died of tuberculosis in 1865. Grant had also met Prince Lucien at Buness several years before, on his Shetland visit. Prince Lucien had been much impressed by Grant's collection and had given him encouragement and advice. Grant died, however, before anything was done with his collection and it was this that Yankee Tom included, with acknowledgment, in his own work. Grant's work, that was subsequently lost, contained more than 2000 items and it is likely that Yankee Tom's publication was heavily indebted to it.[24] What Yankee Tom had collected, as he pronounced in the title of his book, was principally 'dialect' words and phrases that were spoken in Shetland in the 19th century. The majority of these items were of Scots derivation, for the old 'language' of Shetland, the Norn, that had evolved from the Scandinavian of the Norse, had died from lack of use in the centuries following the ceding of Shetland to Scotland in 1469, though some of its vocabulary had lingered on in places into the 19th century.

That summer of 1866, when Yankee Tom was home at Buness and seeing through the final preparations for the publication of his book, there occurred one of those unexpected summer storms that had last occurred some 34 years previously, in 1832, when it was so well described by Edward Charlton. This one particularly involved the *haaf* fishermen from Norwick on the north coast of Unst, taking away several fathers, husbands and sons. Yankee Tom collected money in aid of the widows and families of his tenant-fishermen who were lost in this tragedy, including thirty guineas from an Edinburgh citizen. One of those lost was Peter Anderson (b1829), the father of the then five-year-old Basil Ramsay Anderson; a boy who would grow up to become Shetland's greatest dialect poet and whom Jessie M. E. would later admire and befriend.

While Yankee Tom was putting his etymological dictionary together his aunt Eliza was working on her own very personal tribute to his cousin and namesake, her son Tom, who had died so tragically in South America 20 years earlier: her first and best. Like Yankee Tom she wrote it at a time of poor health. Her memorial to her dear son took the form of a book that she published in 1868 as *The Young Shetlander or Shadows over Sunshine*. In putting it together, Eliza contacted many of those academics who had known Tom, including W. D. Hooker's brother, Sir J. D. Hooker,[25] who had just taken over as Director of Kew on the death of their father, Sir W. J. Hooker. She also contacted Professor Charles Babington at Cambridge seeking addresses of others she might contact in piecing together Tom's brief and tragic career. In her letter, she touched on the very painful subject of Tom's 'disgrace' at Edinburgh University in 1842, when he had been virtually accused of cheating when competing for Professor Graham's medal. Babington's warm reply to that letter at last shed some light on Tom's rejected collection of plants.

> "*Several of the plants in the list enclosed are not recognised as species and half even as varieties at the present time. Several also of them are not noticed in Balfour's Flora of Edinburgh (1803). It is probable that he found only a single specimen of the Festuca ovina vivipara* [Viviparous fescue], *for no other botanist records it as growing on the Pentland Hill* [just outside Edinburgh], *nor do I think it is a likely place for it to inhabit, as it is a native variety caused by the high elevation of the spots upon which it grows.*"[26]

Tom's inclusion of sub-species and varieties to boost his list had not been very clever and must have irritated Graham. Clearly, Babington had implicit trust in Tom's claim to have found a specimen of the viviparous fescue, even though it had not previously been recorded. Now this fescue is one with which Tom would have been familiar as it is common in Shetland. It is a distinctive fescue as the neat seed head of other fescues is replaced by a shaggy head of young plants – hence its viviparous appellation – so surely Tom could not have been mistaken? All in all, Babington's letter suggested strongly that although Tom may have over-egged the pudding, he was sure he had not cheated, a great comfort to Eliza and Laurence.

Radical Plans

David had now been running the Buness estate, rent free, for six years while continuing to make a living as a merchant and fishcurer at Baltasound, handling most, if not all, the fish caught by his cousin's tenants. In the summer of 1866, when Yankee Tom was back at Buness, much recovered from his illness, and David's second three-year lease was coming to an end, he was presented by the latter with a proposal for a new estate plan along the lines of what was already happening elsewhere in Shetland. David's problem was that he could not make enough out of the rental to make a living. In his evidence to the Napier Commission – a Royal Commission set up to look into the condition of small tenanted farms in 1883 – David later described what he had proposed and carried out in 1867.

> "Up to 1867, the crofts on the Buness estate were mostly runrig*; and in that season the whole property was carefully gone over and divided out in separate lots, so each tenant got his farm by itself. Up to this time the scattalds or hill ground were pastured by the people in common, and it often happened that the principal stocks belonged to tenants of other proprietors, shopkeepers and squatters. Those not on the Buness estate were requested to remove their

animals. A certain proportion of the scattalds were enclosed and let out in sheep farms, but in nearly every case a portion next to the town lands was reserved for the crofters."[27]

*Runrig was a system where each tenant farmer had small individual arable strips of land scattered throughout the arable ground of the township.

David proposed to rationalise the tenant system by re-dividing the arable land and consolidating individual shares into more efficient units. He also, like other landowners, intended to 'rationalise' the *scattald* or hill grazings, on which the tenant crofters thought they had an ancient right to put their domestic stock and on which they depended.

This all sounds very reasonable, except that there is no reason, having removed those who should not have had animals on the hill, to enclose "a certain proportion", unless the motive was to remove some *scattald* from the tenants. When questioned by the Commission in 1883 regarding the effect of this on the tenant, David's view of landowner and tenant rights over the *scattald* became clearer.

Yankee Tom's response to David's plans, on the 18th August, 1866, was ambiguous:

"My dear Cousin I have read over your communication relative to the future management of the Buness property. I think your views judicious, and have no doubts they will work well when put into practice … The remuneration you ask I think reasonable, and I have no doubt … we can come to a mutually satisfactory and beneficial decision – It is needless for me to enter more into detail just now … Suffice it to say just now that I like this plan … & I have no doubt whatever that our plans, founded as they are and carried out as they will be on principles of rectitude and fair dealing between ourselves and with a sincere desire and determination to bring enlightened views to bear on the impingement of the Tenantry – I doubt not … that we will succeed in improving them (Tenantry) both the people and the property – I would never wish to lose sight of the one in dealing with the other. I have honestly at heart the well being of the Tenantry and I am persuaded that a change for the better must very soon take place, if the present proprietors are to retain possession of the lands: and if the people only knew if a change of proprietor would be exploitation for them – In their ignorance they will not perhaps see this; but we will in time … convince them that in endeavouring to better our own fortunes we have no intention of injuring their real interests."[28]

Yankee Tom's words may be taken at face value, that he genuinely cared for his tenants; or that he was rationalising for his conscience's sake; or, cynically, that he was covering himself in case of later recrimination. Part of the problem of the indebtedness of tenants and of poor rental return from them, was self-inflicted by the landowner. When the fishing provided good returns, lairds, including old Thomas, had encouraged more fishing tenants to settle, but when the fishing was poor these people could not support themselves from the produce of the land. In the case of the northern end of the Buness estate at Burrafirth, the extra people old Thomas had brought in came from the adjacent island of Yell.

Yankee Tom then followed up this communication with a letter to all his tenants explaining the new regime:

"To the Tenants of the Buness Estate. I have resolved to take the management of the Property into my own hands, and to give the Tenants the most ample freedom consistent with a due

regard to the interests of all concerned. That is to say – You shall be released from any obligation to fish to me or to anyone else and shall be at full liberty to fish and to sell your produce of whatever kind to any one with whom you may yourselves bargain – All that I require of you will be prompt payment of your rents at term of Martinmas each year. To facilitate the carrying out of this change of management I have appointed Mr David Edmondston my Factor, and he will take charge under the new system from and after Martinmas first … He will … make out new Leases and verbally let to you your farms … I ask nothing from you but prompt payment of rents, and I shall be rejoiced to learn that you are getting good returns for your produce and are prospering."[29]

Yankee Tom had taken David's advice. He terminated his lease in 1867 and changed his position from tacksman to factor; from making what profit he could from the estate to being paid a salary. David now gave up fishcuring, took full charge of the estate and the farm of Ordale, on the south side of Balta Sound opposite Buness. In 1861, there had been 21 cottages with 98 small farmers in the Ordale area. By the time David had completed his rationalisation of the arable land there, ten years later, there were only the houses of the ploughman, a few workers, two brothers who were moved within the estate to the small farm of Greenside with 70 acres, and the new sheep farm; the others having departed Shetland voluntarily.[30]

Yankee Tom, as he had indicated in his letter to the tenants, then took the same progressive step as had many other Shetland lairds, by releasing his tenants from having to sell their fish to him – a step his uncle Thomas had once taken himself only to retreat from it. In some cases this was a nominal freedom, particularly in the more remote areas of Shetland, as there was no one else to whom the fishermen could sell their fish. The consolidation by David of the Buness estate for his cousin Yankee Tom, however, was not to end in just the movement of tenants and rationalisation of holdings within the estate, it was to be followed in a year or two by the clearance of some tenants altogether.

Arrivals and Departures

The following two years brought new visitors to Buness. In May of 1867, the artist John T. Reid – author of *Art Rambles in Shetland* (1869) – turned up, "It was my good fortune while there [Unst] to share, as so many had done before, the hospitable entertainment afforded by Thomas Edmondston, Esq., the generous laird of Buness." Reid also met Jessie M. E. and provided sketches for her very first foray into stories for boys, nine years later.

The years 1868 and 1869 brought two boys into the world at Baltasound who were to be the forefathers of the 21st century inheritors of Buness and Halligarth. First was another Laurence (1868-1915), born to David and Margaret, in July 1868. Second was another Thomas (1869-1952), born to Jessie M. E. and Henry Saxby at Ernesdaal, in March 1869. It was a time of some joy and of heart-breaking emotions that brought no catharsis or conclusion for the hapless onlookers, but heralded only further and greater upheavals in the family over the following five years, that split and scattered them.

First, however, in 1868, Jessie M. E. began her writing career in earnest by publishing a collection of her poems, *Lichens from the Old Rock*: the 'old rock' being the affectionate name by which Shetlanders call their island home. In that same year her mother, Eliza, was completing the manuscript of her account of the life of her eldest, Tom the botanist, *The Young Shetlander*, from the confines of her bed. She was dying and she knew it, but she was determined to finish Tom's story if it was the last thing that she did. In *The Home of a Naturalist* (1882), Jessie M. E. retold the events of Eliza's passing in February 1869, but first she described the tragic events of April 1868.

"When the MS, was nearly completed the storm burst once more. The little 'Oy' [Lalla] was quickly called Home, and the grandmother's heart was broken. I went 'to tell mamma,' but being cautioned on the stair to try and control myself, as she was very ill, and feeling the child's death acutely, I for the first time realised that our positions were reversed in part. So I was quiet, and going into our mother's room – where my one wee lassie had come to me five years before – I just said, 'My bairn has gone to your bairns, mamma.' … Poor mother! I think I felt more sorry for her than for myself as she wailed, 'O bairn! bairn!' … Before many months she had followed the child, and our mother's room for ever lost that which had made it the dearest, happiest place on earth."

Lalla by Dr Henry Saxby.

Fittingly, Eliza was the first of the family to be buried at Halligarth, in the little cemetery that was created just on the north side of the copse of trees that Laurence had planted thirty years before. She was later to be joined there by most of her family. Laurence was almost destroyed by Eliza's death. She had been his steadfast support through a life of vicissitudes. Fortunately, he still had his daughters, Isabella (30) and Ellen (24), at home and his favourite, the dependable and talented Jessie M. E. close by, whose husband Henry now took over the practice. With their help he came to terms with his grief and was able to ensure that Eliza's account of his first son, Tom, was published the following year.

Besides her highly influential role as wife and mother, Eliza had played an important role in several aspects of Shetland life. At a time when neither was fashionable outwith the islands, she encouraged both Fair Isle knitting and lace making. She was one of those who had collected locally made articles of clothing that went to London under the auspices of Arthur Anderson in the late 1830s and she brought in foreign lacework to inspire the Unst lacemakers *and* she was no mean knitter herself. She is best remembered, however, for her two books, *Sketches and Tales of the Shetland Islands* (1856) and her memorial to her first son Tom, *The Young Shetlander* (1868).

Jessie M. E. had certainly inherited her parents' writing genes and, like her mother, several years later she, too, wrote a remembrance of her own lost child, entitling it *The One Wee Lassie* (1875). Strangely, like her mother, she also had prescience of the death of her own child, but in her case it came years in advance of the event itself. In her account of *Lalla's* all too short life she painted a picture of a child almost too evanescent to live. In the garden at Halligarth, five years before Laura was born and just two weeks before she met and fell in love with Henry Saxby, when she was just 16, she recalled later that:

Eliza Edmondston (MacBrair), in middle age with her knitted two-sided tapestry rug.

"In a snug corner of that old garden, a girl [Jessie M. E. herself] was busy with her pencil and paper, for there had crept over her spirit that strange indefinable foreshadowing of something which often troubled her. She never could grasp it close enough to analyse its nature; but there it was, and under its influence she wrote some verses:

> She came like a sunbeam,
>   And lighting our sky,
> Before her bright beauty
>   The cloudlets did fly.
> …
> But ah! As a sunbeam
>   Whose mission is done,
> On swift wings uprising,
>   Returns to the sun,
> So she left us to sorrow
>   In darkness alone …"[31]

A number of years later, Jessie M. E. admitted to having a gift for second-sight and was on the point of volunteering her services to the Psychical Society when a close friend, Dr Joseph Bell, dissuaded her.[32] *The One Wee Lassie* is too maudlin for today's tastes, like the black-draped Victorian hearse, but its sentiments were genuine enough. Jessie M. E. dedicated it to Cecil, the child of Dr Bell who was to become her close friend in Edinburgh in the early 1870s.

For Jessie M. E., the loss of *Lalla* and her mother, almost within a year of each other was a severe blow, but she was a strong woman and with the birth of her third son, just three weeks after her mother's death, she was back on her feet. In a tribute to her long lost brother and to her mother's love of her first born, Jessie M. E. had christened him Thomas Edmondston Saxby. By a strange quirk of fate, or was it prescience again, he, of her five sons, would be the one who would return to Unst to continue the family tradition in medicine and ornithology.

The inheritance once more

At Buness, the recent deaths within the family, even though he was only 44 and Ursula only 50, raised the question of the inheritance of the Buness estate in Yankee Tom's mind. In April 1869 he wrote to the family solicitor, William Sievwright, in Lerwick. The question was – since he and Ursula had no offspring – could someone on *his* side of the family inherit Buness? Strictly speaking, if the inheritance was to follow primogeniture, it was not Biot who was next in line. Since Arthur and Thomas had had no legitimate children and Henry had no children at all, the heir should be the eldest son of Charles and only after that line was exhausted should any son of his younger brother Laurence come into the equation. This was all a rationalisation of course. The truth was that neither Ursula nor Yankee Tom wanted Biot or any of his brothers to inherit.

"I am desirous of consulting you with respect to a matter of much interest and importance as to the future of the Buness property and Tenantry – I know that you are well acquainted with my late Uncle's Deposition and Deed of Settlement, and as there is no probability that we will

Buness with Yankee Tom's extension by Henry Saxby.

have any children to succeed us, I am anxious to do what I can to assure myself that the property and the Tenantry will be cared for when in the course of Providence we are removed – I have read my Uncle's will … I should think that my nephew [William b1846] my late eldest Brother's Son, is the next heir, failing heirs of my body to my wife and myself and so on until my natural heirs are exhausted – <u>before Biot Edmondston & his descendants can come into the Succession</u> – If this is the case I must consider if it will not be both prudent & necessary, to bring over the youth, now some sixteen years of age in order to bring him up and educate him for his prospective position. His education and associations have been so totally different from the Constitution of society here, that it will become a duty to guide and educate him into the ways of our peculiar system in Shetland – My question then is 'Who in your opinion will be succeeding to the Estate failing my wife and myself' – I shall hope to hear from you at your earliest convenience as I consider the matter to be of considerable importance for the people whose future I am in every way bound to make provision for, so far humanly as lies in my power – I think the wording of the nomination of heirs is to Ursula Edmondston and <u>heirs of her body</u> and then to <u>me</u> and <u>my heirs</u>, without specifying who these may be – If I am right, all my brothers and sisters and their offspring are successively to succeed before Biot and his heirs can come in – I shall await Your reply with some anxiety as I am anxious to take some action."[33]

The nephew to whom Yankee Tom was referring was William James Edmondston (b1846) of America, the son of his eldest brother – and Charles' eldest son – Laurence Augustus, who had died in 1865.

Yankee Tom was right in some respects. The 1847 will of old Thomas, corroborated in 1850, stated: "… the heirs of her [Ursula] body … whom failing to Thomas Edmondston … and his heirs whom failing to Biot."[34] But he was not right in law as Sievwright no doubt pointed out. He had no heirs and therefore Biot was the legal heir. If Ursula's wishes had been any different from Yankee Tom's it would not have changed the result, for effectively on her marriage, her property had become her husband's. The outcome of this debate, however, was a joint settlement of Yankee Tom and Ursula in 1874[35] that tacitly recognised that, now that Ursula was 53, there would be no heirs of her body. Firstly, the joint settlement stated that on the death of either Ursula or Yankee Tom, the survivor was to have life rent of Buness and full control over the estate which was to be feed to David Edmondston. On the death of the survivor the estate would then go to David and his survivors, no longer first to his elder brother Biot. Family tradition has it that Biot had ruled himself out of the succession since he was a minister and therefore unsuitable and also since he was not married at that time and therefore had no heirs. If this was true then this aspect of the settlement, at least, must have been discussed with Laurence before it was drawn up. On the other hand, David might have seemed the obvious choice. He was resident on Unst and had been running the estate for several years now, whereas Biot had no experience of estate management and was living on the Scottish mainland.

CHAPTER EIGHTEEN

WEDDINGS AND FUNERALS

"There is not much in any bank, as our expenses in building the house, his delicate health, and helping our American friends has kept our funds very low."

Ursula Edmondston (1819-1898)

David's Inheritance

The great diaspora of small farming tenants from the Highlands and Islands of Scotland to all the corners of the world, known as the 'clearances', took place mainly in late 18th and the first half of the 19th centuries. Primarily it was an action by the proprietors to increase the income from their land by the introduction of the new breeds of sheep, such as the Cheviots and the blackface along with their shepherds, although a certain number of tenants left voluntarily. As far as the proprietors were concerned, by clearing the tenants they were able to obtain higher rents from sheep farmers, if they did not carry out sheep farming themselves. As with all agricultural 'improvements' in Scotland these began in the lowlands and slowly and remorselessly moved northwards. In Shetland, the earliest such clearances of tenants for sheep took place later; from the 1820s on the island of Fetlar, carried out by Sir Arthur Nicolson. These were followed by further clearances in the 1850s and 1860s after the introduction of the all-year-round steamer service that allowed large numbers of sheep to be easily and rapidly exported to the mainland of Scotland. It also coincided with an increasingly attractive price for wool and mutton. And, just as Dr Arthur Edmondston had predicted in 1809, it was partly the inefficient structure of land and fishing management that led to the serious economic problems, which in turn encouraged the putting down of the land to sheep resulting in extensive depopulation. It was this downturn in rental that had led David to propose the new plan for the estate to Yankee Tom in 1866.

The promoter of sheep farms in Shetland was the Aberdonian, John Walker, who came to Shetland in 1860 and who famously, or infamously, said of the *scattald* on which the small farming tenants grazed their sheep, cattle and ponies and gathered their peat and other useful materials for their thatching, "I saw ... that the commons were of no use to the people, and were doing them harm. I at once resolved to take the commons away from them."[1] Walker had come to Shetland via Australia. He was cold, silver-tongued, hard-working and ultimately, a fraudster, who had a sharp eye for the main chance. At the time he came to Shetland, proprietors like Yankee Tom were desperately seeking ways of improving their rental income, as he had mentioned in his reply to his cousin David's plans for the estate. The fact was that Walker arrived in Shetland with a viable answer to the proprietors' financial problems and they grabbed it with both hands. Walker became the factor for the Garth estate, now in the hands of Major Thomas Mouat Cameron (1819-1892), who had succeeded to the estate after his brother William Cameron's death in 1839 – and used his influence to clear large areas of this estate in Yell and on mainland Shetland to create new viable units. Of course, it was not only the *scattalds* that went under sheep but what had been arable land too: land that often had been worked and improved by the tenants for many generations. In some cases, for example as on Buness to date, tenants were moved only from one part of the estate to another to allow the creation of larger and more efficient arable units, with or without the introduction of sheep. Yankee Tom, moving back and forward between Unst and Edinburgh, was aware of the events taking place and watched them with some interest, but it was David, his cousin and factor of the estate, who recognised the substantial

John Walker and wife.

financial possibilities. By 1870, whatever his attitude to his tenants, David had become a successful farmer and had already created a model farm out of the old small tenancies at Ordale. That year he was awarded a silver medal by the Highlands and Agricultural Society for his Cheviot ewes, and a few years later, in 1874, in an account of agriculture in Shetland, it was said:

> "Mr (David) Edmondston … farms about 2000 acres, including 200 acres of cultivated pasture and arable at Ordale … where he feeds about 100 Cheviot ewes with half-breed lambs, together with 300 one and two year wedders … There is a good steading at Ordale where 40 cattle are generally housed."[2]

In the case of the *scattald* at Baliasta, two kilometres west of Buness, there were no tenants and the land, previously divided among the proprietors after the discovery of chromate, was made into three sheep farms. David later told the Napier Commission: "He could not say how many people had been removed but he did not think that there would be more than 15."[3] There were, however, two cases of the clearance of whole townships and their inhabitants entirely from the Buness estate. These were just west of Balta Sound at Rue, in 1872,[4] which had 99 acres of arable and 695 acres of pasture,[5] and the other was at Burrafirth and Cliff, where it was described, in 1874, that David:

> "… keeps about 400 blackfaced ewes, besides lambs to keep up the stock, and a few wedders … at the north of Unst … including some fine heather at Hermaness … on the Burrafirth farm. There are about 1500 acres including the town land, Burrafirth having been a fishing station."[6]

Before clearance, in 1861, the township of Burrafirth, beside Herma Ness, had some 62 inhabitants, comprising 16-17 families. Ten years later there remained only a few relatives of Sinclair Bruce, the fish factor at Fiska Wick and a shepherd who had been brought in from

Caithness.[7] Arthur Laurenson (1832-1890), a hosiery merchant in Lerwick and a noted old-Norse scholar, visited Cliff in 1894 and wrote of it:

"I went on … to the old 'toon' of Cliff, all silent and deserted, no human habitation for miles, the bright green of the old arable land alone witnessing to what was for long centuries the dwellings of our race."[8]

Others too, tried to express the emotions that spilled out at having to leave townships that had been their homes for generations. One was William Hughson, who was sent by David Edmondston, in 1871, to erect wire fences on the cliffs of Herma Ness, the old *scattald* for the Burrafirth township. These fences were required to prevent the more valuable blackface sheep from the mainland of Scotland, unfamiliar with the dangers of precipices, from falling over. At the end of that day Hughson penned a set of verses and published it privately in 1875, and in the *Orkney Herald*. Two verses here will suffice to illustrate his strong feelings.

"O' Hermaness, if thou wer't free
From "Clearance" bane, I'd sing of thee
Bold Promontory mid the sea
Defence from North'rn wave.
But arbitrary will doth make
Man suffer for the Black-face sake
And thou art bound by wire and stake
A coward tyrant's slave.
…
The strong young men, our island pride
The lovely maid at eventide
Are seen no more – they now must hide
Far, far beyond the Main.
Each fire is quenched, each house laid low
Friend sighs for friend – tears often flow
But 'Clearance' heeds not human woe
Nor cares for human pain."[9]

In nearly all cases of eviction in Shetland, although no one wanted to leave their homes, the people passively accepted their orders. However, there are two local stories in Unst illustrating what might happen to those who refused. David Johnson, West o' Burn at Burrafirth, who had come from Yell, was one of those. He came home one day to find the roof of his house on fire. Another was Sarah Fordyce of Rue, who refused to leave her cottage. She was said to have been offered payment by the laird to take a message for him to Uyeasound, some four miles away. It was an offer she could not refuse, but when she returned the walls of her cottage were being torn town and the stone moved to build the dyke of the new enclosure.[10]

It has been estimated that between the various landowners about one third of the area of Unst was put down to sheep.[11] This was a sad time throughout Shetland. The population of the islands fell from 31,670 to 29,705 between 1861 and 1881. Many left from Unst through removals and clearances in the 1860s and others voluntarily in the mid-1870s, encouraged by agents from New Zealand. Many also went to Canada or to join the growing expatriate population in Leith. Members of one family from Unst worked on the construction of the Forth Railway Bridge.

On the other hand, David Edmondston argued that not all who emigrated were poor and that some who left from the Buness estate for New Zealand, "… carried with them a clear sum of £30-£100 [£1740-5800]."[12]

Not all the establishment of Shetland supported the creation of the sheep farms, even within David's own family. His sister, Jessie M. E., in reply to a query from a friend on the Unst evictions, many years later wrote:

> "The only evictions I remember were those carried out through the evil influence of John Walker of hated memory. That would be …about 1862-65. The Unst people evicted about that time were North Unst folk chiefly. They were some of our best people. Many tenants hearing what was threatened went off to the colonies before the notices to quit were issued. The consequences to this Isle were awful. Few were left besides the old and weak and those who had no means to help them to emigrate. The late Mr Alex Sandison was largely helpful in bringing the herring fishery to the Isle, and that restored a measure of prosperity. But years of poverty and depression brought the people 'very low' as some who came to Edinburgh (and found me) said. I think the evictions went on for a good many years more than from 1862 to 1865."[13]

Painful and destructive of families and communities as they were, the clearances from the Buness estate were not of the order of harshness of the clearances that had been carried out earlier on the mainland of Scotland. In nearly all cases the tenants were offered alternative accommodation. Nevertheless, they left a sense of bitterness that, although leavened by the years, will always remain. Because of his actions, David subsequently became known as 'Black Davie' and that epithet remained in common parlance for over 100 years.

These reforms of estate management on Buness carried out by David Edmondston and other landowners in Unst in the mid 1860s, however, were not considered sufficient to deal with the economic problems of the estates. In 1867, David along with most of the others formed a company, Spence & Co., with the intention of amalgamating all their interests and taking over the leases of all the Garth estate land in Unst. The plan was that certain members would run the shops, others the fishing boats and curing and yet others the sheep and other stock. Perhaps with foresight, David withdrew from the proposed monopoly, for only six years later the company dissolved in debts.[14] Yankee Tom told his friend Dr Spence about David's proposed involvement in the company in a letter in early 1867, going on to tell a little anecdote that illustrated both his antipathy to John Walker – of whom all the Unst landowners, barring Major Thomas Mouat Cameron, were very suspicious and of whose leases Yankee Tom thought inoperable – and the strong feelings of the small tenant farmers to the man they identified as the prime mover in the clearances.

> "Walker was in North Yell last week intending to measure a 'Town' there, but alas for human intentions, he was met on the outskirts of the 'Town' by two young men but lately returned from the south and apparently imbued with liberal principles. These lads informed Mr W. that they

did not intend to have their farms measured just then, and hinted very unmistakeably that if Mr Walker dared to enter their premises he would require to be <u>carried</u> thence as he would most certainly never leave on his own feet."[15]

Although the Edmondstons and other lairds of Unst were successful in confining Walker's activities to the Garth estate in Unst, they did allow him to take control of the chromate activities in his position as factor for the Mouat family that had held the trusteeship for the chromate on the *scattalds*. Shortly afterwards they had to take Walker to Court to recover £2500 (£145,000) of profit he had managed to siphon off in under-the-table deals he had made with the company to which the chromate was shipped, just before he slipped out of Shetland for good.[16]

In the same letter, Yankee Tom revealed his own view of the declining financial position of himself and other lairds, and the justification for land management reform.

"One thing is certain <u>something</u> must be done to meet increased and increasing <u>burthens</u>. The poor rates are something awful, and are yearly increasing. It should not be so, for the tenants are paying the same rents their fathers paid thirty years ago, although produce of all kinds has doubled and trebled in value to them. I can only account for the poverty of the people by the extravagance in dress and living – It would be fair that they should enjoy increased comforts with additional means, but unhappily their wants always keep <u>ahead</u> of their means, and I firmly believe that nine tenths of the tenants in Unst are hopelessly insolvent at the moment. The evil will only become more and more exaggerated unless some remedy is adopted even should it first cauterize the feelings of the patients to be benefited or interfere with their habits. Time will show at any rate one cannot stand still when the world around us is in motion, and <u>go a headitiveness</u> is the order of the day. If we do not attempt to keep up with our neighbours strangers will occupy the land, and do the business for us."[17]

This was from someone who had inherited his position, who was living beyond his means and rapidly depleting the fortune created by his uncle.

The Truck Commission

In some industries on the mainland of Britain, such as coal mining, 'truck' was an advance against wages that were paid only every month or so. The advance was not cash, but a line that allowed employees to purchase items from the company shop. It meant that employees had no choice as to where they 'purchased' their necessities, tying them into the company and leading to debt bondage. It was a vicious circle; the employee never had enough cash to pay off his account at the shop, so had to keep working to try and catch up on the debt. It was a practice incompatible with prevailing ideas on free trade and was therefore investigated by Parliament. In Shetland, the truck system was pervasive, involving the knitter as much as the fisherman, the merchant-cum-fishcurer on a remote island such as Unst, as much as the large landowner who might dictate to whom the fishermen sold their fish.

There was widespread concern about the system among liberal-minded people and, in February 1870, Yankee Tom found himself responding, from Albany Street, to letters from a Reverend in Halifax who was demanding an explanation for the system. Yankee Tom first explained that:

"My tenants are free in every sense of the word, not only as regards disposal of their produce … but … I invited them to accept leases."[18]

Then he set out his position regarding the fisherman-farmer problem.

"I agree most thoroughly with you that the double occupation of farming and fishing is a folly – Between the two the Tenant must be a loser – He is at sea when he should be attending his farm, and ashore when he should be prosecuting his fishing – I have endeavoured to impress this upon the people, but have met with little encouragement."

What Yankee Tom did not say, was that fishing, in many cases, had been a condition of tenure and that many of the farms were too small to sustain a livelihood from the land alone. Neither did he mention that in many cases the 'freedom' to sell produce to merchant-fishcurer rather than the laird was actually an 'arrangement' between the three, with the laird acting as a 'confidential agent' between the tenant and the merchant. This arrangement would be made clear a year later.

In a second letter six months later, Yankee Tom responded to a suggestion that some of the rent should be returned to the tenant to help him out of the financial straits that the system had brought upon him. He also described the actions he had taken selflessly that benefited the tenant and the financial burdens on the laird.

"As regards refunding rents [we must take into account] *the poverty of the landlord as well as the people, of the enormous poor rate & other public burdens … it is simply impossible for them to make such ruinous sacrifices, and from my knowledge of the people I am persuaded it would be productive of positive injury – They would ever after demand as a right what was conceded as a favour and charity … – In our island we have done a great deal for the people – We have been quarrying a great deal of chromate, and at one time the quarries were many hundreds in debt to us – We have expended some twelve or fourteen hundred pounds* [£69,600 or £81,200] *in road making, and some thousands of sovereigns of money dyke building and land improvement – … the last three years over £1300* [£75,400] *have been laid out in building, and I am about to rebuild a part of my house at Buness at an expense of over £600* [£34,800] *– All the monies have been and are being expended in the Island and the workmen are almost all islanders … Several parishes are overwhelmed by the building of Churches, manses, Schoolhouses, the properties of many of them* [lairds] *are mortgaged to meet these demands … Year before last I paid seven shillings & one penny in the pound poor rate – and when* <u>all</u> *my taxes were paid I had but five shillings in the pound to live upon."*[19]

The "rebuilding" that Yankee Tom referred to was a large 'T' extension to Buness, which the visiting Dr R. C. Cowie described as " … a very elegant mansion, surrounded by well laid out gardens and lawns …"

Yankee Tom, however, did have a point about the burdens on the laird, for:

"Among the assessments which had to be paid out of the rental were teinds (tithes), land tax, rogue and prison money, building and repairing parish schools, schoolmasters' salaries,

Yankee Tom in front of his new extension at Buness.

assessments for the poor, building and repairing tenants' houses. In 1851 it was calculated that out of a total rental income of £14,000 [£980,000] for Shetland as a whole, assessments amounted to £7500 [£525,000] or 53½ pence in the £1. Pressures for agricultural improvements and evictions are thus from an economic point of view to some extent under-standable, especially in areas remote from the fishing with good land."[20]

The truck system had become such an integral part of the economic structure that the British Government set up the Commission to look into it across the whole country. However, several Shetland men of influence, including Yankee Tom, Arthur Hay and the infamous John Walker, went to the Commission in Edinburgh to persuade it to set up a separate enquiry into the situation in Shetland. There, in January 1871, Yankee Tom gave his evidence to the Truck Commission when he once again condemned the truck system, pointing out that neither he nor David, his factor, were involved in the fish trade – a trade that had once been an important part of the Buness estate income and that David had ceased his involvement in it only five years or so earlier.[21]

Yankee Tom also explained how he had offered leases to his tenants but that few had accepted. He was asked why this was the case:

"Commission: 'Is it their indifference, or is it their fear?'
Yankee Tom: 'They seem to have been heretofore under such a stringent rule as between landlord or middlemen and tenant, that they are doubtful as to what a lease may imply. They are afraid that it will bind them, without binding the landlord."

He went on:

"My property is managed by a relative, Mr David Edmondston, and he thoroughly understands the people, and I believe has their interests at heart. He has no business connection with them, nor have I. They may fish to whom they like."

A year later, in January 1872, the government appointed W. Guthrie a Commissioner and sent him north to Shetland. David gave evidence to the Commission at Baltasound.[22] When he was questioned about the relationship between the landowner, fishcurer and tenant, it became clear that both his and Yankee Tom's assertions to the Commission, and the latter's reassurance to the Reverend in Halifax and in 1867 to his own tenants, that – the tenants "may fish to whom they like" – was not quite true.

"C: 'Is it usual for the proprietor to enter into any arrangement with the fish-curer for the payment of his [tenants'] rents?'

D: 'We do that on the Buness estate, and I should like to explain the reason of it. The tenants have all been told that they are at perfect liberty to fish to whom they like; but after they have engaged to fish to a certain curer, we wish them to bring a guarantee from their curer or curers for the rent of the year on which they have entered, and during which they are to fish.'"

In other words, the tenants' freedom of choice meant freedom to choose a merchant who was approved of by the landowner and could assure him his rent. David then went on to justify this system, which remained a 'truck' system, except now between the tenant and the merchant-fishcurer, rather than the estate directly.

"'One reason for that [guarantee] – in fact the only reason – is that the men do not get money payments, and therefore a great number of them will be induced to run a heavy account at the shop, and when we collect the rents at Martinmas we would have nothing to get.'

C: 'Then, in fact, that arrangement is made in order to limit the credit which the fish-merchant gives to his men?'

D: 'Yes.'"

Further questioning confirmed that when David himself was the merchant-fishcurer he took the entire risk of the tenants' rents. It is understandable, therefore, why he ceased trading: it relieved him of the risk and passed it to another, allowing him and Yankee Tom to deplore the truck system while implying they had no involvement in it:

"As the system at present stands … The people as a rule do not finger in money one fiftieth of their earnings … and three fourths or thereabouts of them never see money as payment for their produce. Such a state of matters is utterly demoralising …"

The Commission took evidence from all segments of society in Shetland and the system was condemned by all. However, things did not change overnight and it was not until more cash flowed through the economy, particularly through the development of the herring industry, that truck eventually disappeared late in the 19th century.

Weddings, Funerals and Ill-health

Intermarriage between the families of lairds, and between them and other members of the upper echelons of society, such as ministers, was common. David Edmondston had married Margaret Hamilton (1838-1871) in 1862, the second daughter of the Rev. Zachary Hamilton, the minister of Bressay. The Rev. Hamilton lost his first wife in 1840 and had been left with four young children. He married for a second time in 1845 to Elizabeth Mouat Cameron (1813-1898) and had three more children, the eldest of whom was William Cameron Hamilton (1847-1933). The Rev. Hamilton's new wife was the sister of Major Thomas Mouat Cameron of Garth (1819-1892), the grand-nephew of old Thomas' neighbour and competitor Thomas Mouat of Garth. The Edmondstons, Mouat Camerons and Hamiltons all knew each other well, meeting regularly on

William Cameron Hamilton as a young man.

social and business occasions. It was no surprise therefore when David's younger sister, Ellen Edmondston, became engaged to her brother-in-law, David's wife's brother, William Cameron Hamilton, in 1871. During their courtship it was natural that their parents and siblings met more often and no one took much notice that Laurence, the 76-year-old recently widowed and now retired doctor, was often in the company of the 32-year-old Penelope Hamilton (1839-1888), Rev. Zachary Hamilton's daughter from his first marriage (sister of Margaret and step-sister of William). What *was* a monumental and not a particularly agreeable surprise to them all was their announcement of marriage, just two years after Eliza's death. Laurence was not only the father of David and Ellen Edmondston, but he was now to become their brother-in-law!

The two weddings took place in September 1871 and Ellen Edmondston (now Mrs Ellen Hamilton) settled with her husband William at Houlland, not far from her home at Baltasound. But the events were not entirely joyful as Laurence's son and daughter were so disapproving of their father's actions that they refused to speak to him for some time. Two months later, on 9th November, 1871, David's wife Margaret gave birth to their sixth child, Zachary, after her father. The infant did not survive the day and Margaret, already unwell herself, died one month later at their home at Marypark, leaving David with five children from one to eight years old: a not uncommon event in the 19th century.

David's sister, Jessie M. E., now 29 and still at Ernesdaal, had four boys aged from less than one to eleven. She was therefore hardly in a position to help her brother, but even if she had considered it she had problems of her own, for her husband, Dr Henry Saxby, who had taken over the practice from Laurence, had fallen ill. It seems that he may have been suffering from tuberculosis and it was decided that, although he did not need hospital treatment at this point, it would be better for him to be on the mainland where he could get better care. So that same year of the weddings, Jessie M. E., Henry and their children left Unst for Edinburgh.

This was a tragedy on several counts. Laurence was losing Jessie M. E., his brightest and closest child, and he was losing also an ornithological soul mate in Henry. For Jessie M. E., it was a terrible wrench away from her beloved father and from Halligarth and Shetland, where she had spent virtually all her life so far. She knew in her bones that it might be a long time before she returned, but what she did not know was that the move, in the end, would be the making of her. Henry, also, was desperately sad to leave. Not that he was close to the family, except perhaps for his father-in-law with whom he had so much in common, and Jessie M. E.'s younger brother Thomas (1847-1923), who had often accompanied him on his 'birding' outings. No, what he had to leave behind was unfinished business. What had so attracted him on his very first visit were the birds of Shetland and for the few years he had been resident he had diligently amassed a great deal of information. He had foreseen many years of study and observation ahead and perhaps a work to stand alongside those of Laurence, Arthur and his long-deceased brother-in-law, Tom the botanist. And now he had to leave it uncompleted with little prospect, because of his health, of beginning such a study again elsewhere. The year after they left, Henry was well enough to take up a medical practice in Inveraray, the seat of the Duke of Argyll. Like Henry, the Duke was a keen ornithologist and they soon became acquainted.

Alas, Henry's health now deteriorated rather rapidly. Jessie M. E. gathered all her strength to nurse him in his final days, but she

Dr Henry Saxby, self portrait.

herself, besides caring for her four boys, was coming to full term with their fifth and last child. It was a test of her emotional and physical strength as never before, but like her mother Eliza, and her paternal grandmother Mally, she was a redoubtable character. She was also fortunate to find reassuring support and warm friendship from an unexpected quarter: the medical specialist who attended Henry, a well known and respected and very handsome Edinburgh doctor named Joseph Bell (1837-1911). Much, much later, Jessie M. E., in a tribute she wrote to this man,[23] recalled the time when it was decided that Henry must know the fatal truth of his illness and how the telling of it was symptomatic of this great doctor's "heart behind his head".

> "One morning instead of walking straight into the bedroom as usual, he [Joseph Bell] turned into Dr Saxby's study, and he said [to me], 'Look here, child, he must be told the nature of his attacks … You *must* tell him.' The poor, sensitive invalid, nervous, broken! I shrank from such a task, and I cried out, 'Oh, I can't do it. I can't tell him. It will break his heart.'

'Very well, all right,' Joe answered, with a careless toss of his head. 'If *you* won't, *I* must. It's my line. All in the doctor's day's work, you know,' and he smiled.

I thought, 'How callous.'

Presently he said, 'Well, I must get to work. Let's go and see him.' But when we reached the bedroom door he laid his hand on my shoulder, and said, 'Sit where I can't see your face when I am talking to him.'

Behind the curtain I listened and marvelled at the tact, the gentleness, the knowledge of his patient's character, the hopefulness displayed. The bitter truth was suggested so slowly and carefully that before long my husband himself remarked, quite composedly, 'I suppose it is something of that sort that has me.'

From that day ... till his death, I knew the kind soul of Joe Bell, and I carried to him my many griefs and anxieties, sure of ready sympathy. 'Father-Confessor' became his pet name ..."

On the 2nd August, 1873, Jessie gave birth to Charlie Fletcher Argyll Saxby, their fifth boy. Henry held his last son in his arms only once, for two days later, on the 4th August, he died. Just like her brother David, two years previously, Jessie M. E. was now left alone with five young children to raise. Sometime later she wrote a poem with one stanza for each child. Entitled *My Sons* it brims with maternal love and pride for those five boys – Henry (12) (b1860), Stephen (7) (1866-1941), Thomas (4) (1869-1952), Horace (2) (1871-1959) and the infant Charlie (1873-1959) – the first and last stanzas of which are:

"The eldest – grave and silent,
   Who laid his boyhood down
And took Life's mighty burden
   Instead of playtime's crown:
Who quietly and bravely,
   Though still a child in years
Assumed the place beside me
   To stay my widow's tears
...
My boys! – they are not perfect,
   I am not mother-blind;
They sometimes cost me suffering,
   They're often "on my mind."
I dream about their future,
   I dwell upon their Past;
I work for them believing
   Reward will come at last."[24]

Jessie M. E. as a young woman.

Jessie M. E. had no job or qualification with which to support herself and her boys, and she was now many miles away from those of the family who might have been able to help her. She was crushed by Henry's death, but her response was to move to Edinburgh and throw herself into writing. It was an indication of the strength of her character that in her grief and with all her responsibilities, the following year, she managed to produce *Glamour from Argyleshire* (1874), her second book of poems, and another year later *The One Wee Lassie* (1875), the little book in memory of her only daughter Laura (Lalla), who had died in 1868.

Edinburgh was now a very different city from the time of her father, or even when her late brother Tom had briefly attended university there. The New Town was long completed and virtually all the open space between the City, Leith and the old fishing villages of Granton and Newhaven, was now built upon, while on the south side the suburbs were rapidly expanding towards the Pentland Hills, where Tom had collected many of his plants for Professor Graham's competition. As far as its cultural life was concerned though, it was still as vibrant as ever with a very active literary circle, many popular journals and several publishers.

Jessie M. E. had inherited all of Henry's notes that he had made on the birds of Shetland, but she was no ornithologist and could not do anything with them herself. Henry's brother Stephen (1831-1886), the elder brother who had accompanied him on their bird collecting trip to Shetland in 1854, and now a vicar at Clevedon in Somerset, came to her rescue. He took up Henry's comprehensive notes and sat down to edit them, assisted by the Duke of Argyll. Such had been Henry's friendship with, and support from, the Duke that when *The Birds of Shetland* (1874) was published, it was dedicated to him. Henry's posthumous book was the very first devoted entirely to the birds of Shetland and was a notable addition to the already substantial collection of natural history publications from this remarkable family.

More than 60 years previously, Dr Arthur Edmondston had begun the family tradition with the publication of his book *A View of the Ancient and Present State of the Zetland Islands* (1809), and a series of papers on some of the birds of Shetland. In *his* book Henry acknowledged Arthur's contributions to our knowledge of Shetland's birds and particularly the *immer-gös*.

"Dr Edmondston was perhaps the first in Shetland to discard the erroneous and absurd idea which prevailed with regard to this species, and his example was immediately followed by other writers. [Arthur said, it] *can* fly, but that it uses its wings only at particular seasons of the year."

Henry, just as Jessie M. E.'s brother, father and uncle, had become fascinated by this strange and remarkable bird. One particular aspect of its behaviour intrigued him; the way it dived under the water. It did not seem to propel itself under like the shag or the cormorant, nor did it flop with its wings like the auks and some ducks, it just seemed to vanish without apparent effort.

"The mode in which this bird dives cannot easily be explained in words. I have watched it most carefully, but always with an unsatisfactory result; it merely gives a slight *start*, if my meaning may be so expressed, and disappears in an instant."

Although Laurence's eldest son, Tom the botanist, had written a paper describing the shooting and examination of a "scarcely fledged" great northern diver in 1843, which he said confirmed his

Thomas Edmondston (1847-1923) the stockbroker as a young man.

suspicion that the species bred in Shetland, and Henry Saxby had described eggs that had been given him 'allegedly' from a site in the islands, there is no definitive proof that this bird has ever bred in Shetland. A hundred years later, however, there is always one somewhere in the sheltered voes and sounds in the summer and many more in the winter. It is one of the eeriest of Shetland experiences, on a quiet spring day overlooking the sea, to hear the weird cry of this mysterious and solitary bird from somewhere out there among the waves and, perhaps, to catch a brief glimpse of it before it gives "a slight start" and slips beneath the surface.

A couple of years before Henry's death, in 1871, the youngest of Laurence's children, Thomas, now 24, who had been his companion on many birding adventures in Unst, took a trip out to South Carolina to meet his cousins there. One of the families with whom he stayed was Yankee Tom's older sister, Jessie Mary, who had married Dr Amory Coffin and whose son, Amory junior, had so modestly described his role in the Civil War just a few years previously.

There were seven cousins in the Coffin family for Thomas to get to know and when he met Amory's sister, Mary (1852-1924), who was just 19, they fell in love. However, the families in Carolina and Shetland were making other plans for Mary. She was to travel to Shetland and marry Thomas' elder brother, David at Marypark, with his five motherless children: a cousin, now 34, whom she had never met! The Coffins had not yet recovered from the financial disaster of the Civil War and a marriage of their daughter to David seemed a good step for her. Mary, however, preferred the dashing young bachelor to the older, unknown, father and widower. Thomas requested Mary's hand from her father, but he, and Yankee Tom when he heard about the proposal, were both strongly against the marriage. Certainly the, as yet, unestablished career of Thomas did not compare favourably with the secure financial prospects of David. In 1871, Yankee Tom wrote to Thomas in Carolina in October, and in November to London, where Thomas had returned to begin his career as a stockbroker. He accused Thomas of being deceitful, inferring that Thomas had known of the family's plans for Mary before he had even travelled to Carolina: "*Dr Coffin decidedly opposed to a marriage between yourself and Mary – and I must add that I approve of this verdict.*"[25] Thomas was then coerced into promising *not* to continue the affair.

Back in Unst, David was desperately and unsuccessfully trying to raise his young family of three girls and two boys single-handedly, and waiting to see if the young Mary Coffin would arrive from Carolina. Eventually, it became apparent to him that he must look for another wife and mother for his children and he turned to his immediate family for help. Without delay, his elder brother, the

Rev. Biot, found a suitable candidate in Elizabeth Turner (b1831), the daughter of the neighbouring minister for Menteith near Stirling and married them on 21st July, 1874. A couple of weeks later Biot himself tied the knot, with Adela Gray (b1850) from Liverpool. When David's new wife arrived in Unst and met the five children, then aged from four to eleven, including the eldest boy and heir Laurence, she found the children running around undisciplined, bare-footed and wild, with lice in their hair![26] Unfazed, she got stuck into bringing them under control. Her approach, however, was a little too demanding for the younger children and Thomas (4), Laurence (6) and Elizabeth (7) were packed off to Bressay to be looked after by their mother's parents, the 69-year-old Rev. Zachary Hamilton and his wife.

At almost exactly the same time, and before he had been able to do something to stop the impending marriage of Thomas the stockbroker and his cousin Mary Coffin in London in October, Yankee Tom died at Buness on 1st August, just before his fiftieth birthday.

Yankee Tom's character is one of the most difficult to fathom and it may never be known

David Edmondston (1837-1884) the widower with his young family.

for certain if his 'return' to Shetland from Carolina was entirely innocent or not. The little evidence that there is, from the scurrilous and anonymous book that was published about his uncle, old Thomas, suggests that he and Ursula *were* in love. Of one result of their marriage there is no uncertainty; between their generosity to their beleaguered Southern States relatives and their extravagant lifestyle, they managed to dispose of the fortune that old Thomas had made from the chromate and his other commercial ventures.

As far as Yankee Tom's contribution to the Edmondston family tradition of the study and conservation of Shetland's birds is concerned it was rather more limited than his uncles or cousins. He did continue the protection of the *bonxie* on Herma Ness. After reading an accusation in the paper that Shetland proprietors were not protecting the rare skua, he wrote to his cousin David, the estate factor:

> "… *neglecting to protect such a noble bird as the Skua … I think we may manage to preserve the two or three pairs that still frequent the place* [Herma Ness] … *Say to the shepherd that if he faithfully looks after this bird I will … reward him.*"[27]

But that was it.

Soon after Yankee Tom's death, Ursula wrote to father's old friend Sievwright, the family solicitor, revealing that, on their marriage, she and Yankee Tom had made some very specific arrangements regarding the estate. *"There is no property in my late husband's name* [he] *was so very particular these very things should be in my name."*[28] Nonetheless, the cash in the bank, which had been made over to him, was mostly gone, including several large bonds made when old Thomas had loaned William Hay and others substantial sums of money. *"There is not much in any bank, as our expenses in building the house, his delicate health, and helping our American friends has kept our funds very low."* There is no record of the total amount of funds sent to America to help Yankee Tom's family during and after the Civil War, but there is no doubt that it was substantial. The other expenses that Ursula alluded to were the cost of a large extension they had built onto Buness and the costs of keeping the permanent lodgings in Albany Street in Edinburgh where they had spent a great deal of time.

Until now, Ursula had always been in the shadow of either her father or her husband. Now it became clear that she was a strong character in her own right and quite *au fait* with the estate accounts and was not someone who could be taken advantage of. This was confirmed in another letter to Sievwright a year later, concerning continued small scale workings of the chromate and her relationships with her uncle Laurence and cousin David, who, while still managing the estate, was her heir.

Ursula Edmondston (1819-1898) in middle age.

"My Uncle Laurence [was here] *today to speak about Chromate matters, and claiming Chromate rights for Halligarth, he asked me if we should speak to David about it. I told him David had nothing to do with it, he said he meant as my advisor. I told him that I advised myself as far as possible, and asked David's advice on as few things as possible ..."*[29]

The long-running rancour between Ursula, the illegitimate heir at Buness, and Laurence's family had never healed and as far as Laurence was concerned it never would. On 7th March, 1879, he died at the age of 84, and so passed the youngest and last of the five Edmondston brothers – Arthur, Thomas, Henry, Charles and Laurence. Typical of Laurence, he requested to be buried at a lonely spot on Herma Ness, the cliff-bound, sea-girt, seabird headland where he had encouraged his brother Thomas to protect the great skua.[30] In the event, his family disregarded his wish and he was buried next to his first wife Eliza, in the family burial ground at his beloved Halligarth where, from rough fields, he had created the woodland that still stands today, 170 years after it was planted. This was where all his beloved children had roamed so freely with their many pets of so many hues and feathers, and where he had entertained so many interesting people. It was where, most especially, he had watched and nurtured the interests of his first son, the prodigy Tom, and where he and Eliza had received the terrible news of his death.

But what of Laurence himself? What was his legacy compared to that of his wife Eliza, his brother Arthur, his son Tom, or his son-in-law Henry Saxby? He was a man of many intellectual interests and of much talent. Apart from the publications on parliamentary representation, proposed changes to the medical course at Edinburgh University, some pieces on the local dialect, and the observations in the 1841 Statistical Account, his outstanding contribution to his native islands lay in natural history and principally, in ornithology. In the two years of 1822 and 1823 he had produced seven papers on various Shetland birds including one of the first lists of species for the islands. His daughter, Jessie M. E., said that following Tom's tragic shooting in South America Laurence had vowed that he would not use a gun again, and without that essential tool of bird identification in the 19th century he could no longer carry out his ornithological studies. In fact, he had already ceased such studies, or at least writing up any observations, by the time he had returned to settle in Unst in 1830, 16 years before Tom's death. For all his undoubted abilities he did not pursue his natural bent and it can only be surmised that it was his fragile character and his financial and emotional dependence on his brother Thomas that prevented him fulfilling his early promise. He did, however, contribute indirectly to the success of others, notably to *A History of British Birds* (1837-1852), the major work of his life-long friend William MacGillivray and perhaps, in a minor way, to the great works of Charles Darwin.

CHAPTER NINETEEN

THE LAST REFORMS

"The public conscience has been strongly moved by the operation of the Crofters Act, a measure infinitely more damaging to the moral reputation of this country than the worst of all Mr Gladstone's Irish Land Acts. I ..."

Thomas Edmondston (1847-1923)

Literary beginnings in Edinburgh

Of all the Edmondston family and their spouses with enduring talent in this story – Arthur, Laurence, Tom, Henry Saxby – Jessie M. E. is the only one who fulfilled her potential. Arthur abandoned his to pursue phantoms; Laurence became estranged from his through its sublimation in his son, Tom; while the latter, and Jessie M. E.'s husband Henry, died long before they could realise theirs. It was no easy road for Jessie M. E. though, and she had to work hard to achieve her success. She was the only one of the family at the time in sympathy with the many political and social reforms that were taking place; by and large the others opposed them.

Jessie M. E. was educated by her parents and had unfettered access to many fascinating, well-travelled and widely-read scientists, artists and writers of international repute, who regularly passed through Buness and Halligarth. Among the last was Sir George Webbe Dasent. Although she had a keen interest in natural history, it was stories, such as *The Saga of Burnt Njal*, translated by Dasent and read to her by her father, and the influence of her nurse who was a storehouse of Shetland myth and lore and the old Norse ballads, that turned her attention firmly to the legacy of the Vikings.

She was fortunate also that she grew up in the golden age of children's literature. Due to the relatively sudden access to hitherto untapped wealth created by the Empire, Britain's expanding world trade and the explosion of Victorian industry, there was, for the first time, a middle class, whose literate children had time on their hands. Although there had been earlier classics for children, such as *Robinson Crusoe* (1719), *Gulliver's Travels* (1726) and the *Swiss Family Robinson* (1812), it was in the 1850s and 1860s, when Jessie M. E. was an impressionable young girl that a flood of great children's literature appeared. Stories such as *Uncle Tom's Cabin* (1857), *Tom Brown's Schooldays* (1857), *Coral Island* (1858), *The Water Babies* (1862) and *Alice's Adventures in Wonderland* (1865), captured the imagination of that generation of children. Having five boys of her own, an education and upbringing steeped in adventure literature, it was perhaps not surprising that she now turned her creative hand from poetry to writing stories for her boys.

Jessie M. E.'s first general book of prose, *Daala Mist or Stories from Shetland* (1876), was a set of contemporary Shetland cameos. At this stage in her writing she had no idea if she would be successful or whether or not she was wasting her time and she should be out earning a living for her children. It was not all plain sailing. In a talk she gave in the late 1880s, on her struggles to write and publish, she recalled:

"Anyone who has tried to do so (especially a woman!) without influence or experience knows what a heartbreaking thing it is to set one's hopes upon 'living by literature.' I remember … the postman had politely presented me with some packets of MS – 'returned unsuitable, with the editor's compliments'. I had been unreasonably depressed by receipt of [these] missives. But when you expect to buy a peerie bairn's claes with the price of a sensation story, and you get the tale sent back, 'declined with thanks,' you don't feel ready to commend the trade of literateur."[1]

But Jessie M. E. had had a stroke of wonderful luck in meeting Dr Joseph Bell, who became her trusted supporter, literary mentor[2] and very close friend. Dr Bell was no ordinary doctor, but Consulting Surgeon to the Edinburgh Royal Infirmary, the Royal Hospital for Sick Children and the Hospital for Incurables (of which he was one of the founders), President of the Royal College of Surgeons, editor (1873-1896) of the *Edinburgh Medical Journal* and a Professor at the University. Just as in her own family, there was a long tradition of medicine in his. His father, grandfather and great-grandfather had all been surgeons. In her later book in his memory, Jessie M. E. recalled:

"He [Dr Bell] was interested in my literary efforts, and knew that I had no access to books for help. There came [unexpectedly] to me from Messrs Douglas and Foulis' Library a year's ticket, and a polite request to know what books they should send. I thought there was some mistake, and went to the library to enquire, but all the satisfaction that I got was to be told that the subscription had been paid in my name, and they could (or would) give no further explanation … years later he [Dr Bell] admitted that the gift was his."[3]

Possibly more significantly, Dr Bell, or Joe as she called him, also gave Jessie M. E. very objective and, sometimes it seemed to her, painful, even harsh, advice on her literary efforts.

"His interests in my attempts at authorship led him to offer to correct 'proof' or revise MSS. and I was often greatly indebted to his keen literary instinct for help in that way. He would scribble 'gush' over

Dr Joseph Bell from An appreciation *by J. M. E. Saxby.*

passages which I had considered affecting. 'Not clearly stated, say it over again,' would stare at me from a page I had laboured to make effective. High falutin' was his verdict on what I thought fine, picturesque composition!"

On the other hand, he would also lavish praise where he thought she deserved it. Without his criticism and advice, Jessie M. E. knew that it would have taken her a great deal longer to achieve publication.

When he had first met Jessie M. E. it had been a fatherly desire to help her in her tragic situation that had at first moved Bell's heart, and then it was her determination, strength and talent that drew him into a long-term friendship, but it may have been her second sight that cemented his devotion to her. She had not known him and his family more than a year when she came to publish her memoriam to her only daughter Laura – *The One Wee Lassie* – in 1875. This little book was dedicated to Bell's daughter Cecil Bell, whose childish innocence reminded her of her own lost daughter and touched her heart. This dedication touched Bell, but he was astonished when he read the little poem at the end of the book. Jessie M. E. had found this poem, as she said: "… in a volume called *The Shadow of the Rock* … published anonymously." By an uncanny, almost supernatural coincidence, the poem's author was Bell himself! He had written the poem in reaction to the tragic and accidental death of his wife's sister. It was a touching piece of Victoriana, with echoes of Jessie M. E.'s Uncle Arthur's poem on the death of his sister, Ursula, more than 60 years earlier.

> "Weep not for her, for she hath crossed the river,
>   We almost saw HIM meet her at the shore,
> And lead her through the golden gates where never
>   Sorrow or death can touch her any more.
> …
> But weep for those round whom the fight is thronging,
>   Who still must buckle heavy armour on,
> Who dare not pray for rest, tho' sore their longing,
>   Till all the weary working day be done.
> …
> And pray for them, that they, tho' sad and lonely,
>   May still, with patience, bear the cross He sends,
> And learn that tears, and wounds, and losses only
>   Make peace the sweeter when the warfare ends."

Although she professed to second sight, Jessie M. E. was a staunch Christian and she had chosen the poem as it so closely paralleled her own feelings of loss, both for *Lalla* and Henry, and her determination to soldier on through ceaseless literary and political activity, which she did, magnificently.

Jessie M. E. had settled in St Leonard's Bank – on the then south-eastern outskirts of Edinburgh – in a fine quiet cobbled street of terraced houses in an open situation directly overlooking Salisbury Crags, Arthur's Seat and the green pastures of Holyrood Park.[4] There, she spent an increasing amount of time sitting at a table by the window, scribbling away as fast as she could, occasionally lifting her head to look out on a rustic scene and a distant view of the North Sea.

This would be the nearest thing she would find to stimulate the visual memories of her childhood home for a number of years to come, recollections she would lovingly weave into her stories.

One of the ways she found her way into Edinburgh literary society was through *Chambers' Journal*, the journal to which her mother had been a contributor on several occasions and to which she herself had sent her first piece when still a teenager. The Edmondston family had known the Chambers brothers, William and Robert, for many years and Jessie M. E. had met William on his visit to Unst and Buness in 1867 with the Lighthouse Commissioners. Robert's son and namesake was now the editor of the journal and an introduction to him was therefore a mere formality. Through him, Jessie. M E. became acquainted with other writers and publishers in the city. She also met many new friends by joining many of her expatriates in the Edinburgh Orkney and Shetland Society, and through the Church. It was to be the latter connection that was to provide outlets for many of her poems, articles and short stories, most of which were of a moral nature. The publishers and journals that accepted her pieces included the influential Religious Tract Society; the Society for the Propagation of Christian Knowledge; the American Sunday School Union; the magazine of the Scottish Presbyterian Church – *Life & Work* – and many others such as *Sunday at Home* and the *Methodist Monthly*. Other outlets included the plethora of women's and family journals such as the *Family Herald Supplement*, *Leisure Hour*, *People's Journal*, *Mother's Companion*, *Home Messenger* and national newspapers such the *Scotsman* and the *Herald*. Then, of course, there were Shetland's own papers – the *Shetland News* and *The Shetland Times* – to which she contributed throughout her life. Her major fictional pieces for children were serialised in *Chambers' Journal*, sometimes in the *Dundee Weekly News* and also in new children's papers such as *Chatterbox*, first published in 1866, and in the leading publication of the children's adventure genre of the late 19th century and early 20th century, the *Boy's Own Paper* (*BOP*) and the *Girl's Own Paper*, both first published in 1879.

Jessie M. E.'s output, considering she had her five young boys to look after, was prodigious and she rapidly learned to recycle her pieces to get the maximum financial return, publishing the same piece in more than one journal and serialising chapters before publishing the complete story as a book. She became that rare thing in the 19th century, an independent woman who was also a professional writer, or as she described herself to Bell, a tradeswoman: she never thought she was a *great* writer. In the early 1880s she was publishing four separate serialised stories and other articles a year. For example, in 1882, she began a series in *Chambers' Journal* entitled *The Home of a Naturalist* (1889) that was eventually to grow into a book with contributions from her elder brother Biot. By the end of the 1880s the number of pieces published annually had risen to 20. Once she had found her voice her pen never ran dry. *Daala Mist* was swiftly followed in 1877 by a series of books for boys – *Rock Bound – A Story from the Shetland Isles* (1879), *Geordie Roye* (1879), *Breakers Ahead* (1882) and two books in 1884, *Ben Hanson* and *Preston Tower*. Of course, in addition to valuable comments from Bell, she had a ready and critical audience for the drafts of her stories in her boys – especially her youngest, Charlie, who was just entering his teens – who would devour the chapters as quickly as they were written.

Like every author, Jessie M. E. got great satisfaction from seeing her work in print, especially the books. Her vanity was also tickled by seeing her stories, and her name, alongside some of the great literary figures of the 19th century in *Chamber's Journal* and in the *BOP*. In 1880 her article, *Folk-lore from Unst*, appeared in the former next to a story by no less than Jules Verne. In 1886,

Lads of Lunda – published as a book 11 years later – also appeared in the latter. In one issue of the *BOP*, Jessie M. E.'s story was given the cover with an accompanying illustration, relegating a story by R. M. Ballantyne to the inside pages! Another regular contributor to the *BOP* alongside Jessie M. E. was the greatest writer and children's author of his time, Robert Louis Stevenson. To see her own name alongside such masters of the genre gave her an incredible lift of confidence. Coincidentally, she then found herself associated with another unique author of the time who would become a benchmark for crime stories.

In the spring of 1880, Greenland whalers, as remained their custom until the early part of the 20th century, still dropped anchor in Bressay Sound to pick up provisions and the additional crew of Shetland men for the annual summer expedition to the Davis Straits. Theirs was a dangerous trade and they usually carried a doctor, or at least a medical student. This particular year, it was an adventurous twenty-year-old Edinburgh youth of Irish parents who was studying medicine at the University under Jessie M. E.'s friend, Dr Joseph Bell. The name of this student was Arthur Conan Doyle (1859-1930) and besides his ambition to be a doctor he had a flair, like Jessie M. E., for writing. One of his first stories, published after he graduated and moved to England, appeared in *Chambers' Journal* in 1879, around the same time as Jessie M. E.'s, and his first novel, *A Study in Scarlet*, appeared in 1887, introducing to the public his master of deductive logic, the redoubtable

'She capsized at once' and 'Cries of welcome rang from shore to shore' by W. H. Overend for 'Running Free' by Jessie M. E. for Boy's Own Paper *1886.*

sleuth, Sherlock Holmes. Unfortunately for Bell, Doyle let it be known that it was no less than *he* who was the prototype for Holmes. Jessie M. E., in her *Appreciation* of Bell noted:

> "… Dr Bell did not feel flattered by what he called his 'nickname' [Sherlock Holmes]. As late as 1901 he wrote: – 'Why bother yourself about the cataract of drivel for which Conan Doyle is responsible? I am sure he never imagined that such a heap of rubbish would fall on my devoted head in consequence of his stories.'"

As a student of Bell's, Doyle had been very impressed by his almost intuitive ability to pick out non-medical, as well as medical, details about his patients which other observers missed. With the growing public audience for the Sherlock Holmes stories, the newspapers of the day demanded from Doyle examples of Bell's innate detecting abilities, adding embellishment when they got them. Jessie M. E. quoted:

> "The *Strand Magazine* reporting 'A day with Dr Conan Doyle' said (quoting the romancer's words): 'I was a clerk in Dr Bell's ward. A clerk's duties are to note down all the patients to be seen, and muster them together. Often I would have seventy or eighty.
> 'When everything was ready I would show them in to Mr Bell, who would have the students gathered round him. His intuitive powers were marvellous.
> 'Case No 1 would step up. "I see," said Mr Bell, "you're suffering from drink. You even carry a flask in the inside pocket."
> 'Another case would come forward, "Cobbler, I see." Then he would turn to the students and point out to them that the inside of the knee of the man's trousers was worn, that was where the man had rested the lapstone – a peculiarity only found in cobblers … That and one or two similar instances excited Doyle's keenest interest, and set him experimenting himself in the same direction which, of course, was just what I [Bell] wanted, with him and with all other scholars.'"

Doyle, of course, took Bell's attention to apparently irrelevant detail, much, much further, turning him into his fictional detective, with whose shadow poor Bell had to live for the rest of his life.

The Crofters Acts

The latter decades of the 19th century saw great changes in Shetland that finally heralded the end of the old landlord-merchant-tenant regime that had dominated the islands for two centuries. The predominant changes were in the modernisation of fishing, such as the development of trawling and the ascension of 'king herring', as opposed to a past dependence on line-fishing for cod and ling. But there were significant land tenure changes too, the commencement of regular steamer services throughout the islands and the introduction of modern conveniences, such as the telegraph, so vital in commerce.

In 1880 the herring industry hit Shetland just like Yankee Tom and the gold-rush hit California in 1849, with fishing boats from Scotland, England and Holland arriving in great numbers. In their wake came the seasonal army of support; including boat crews, coopers, gutters, packers and net menders. As it happened, Balta Sound, one of the most sheltered harbours in the north of Shetland,

Herring Fleet in Balta Sound circa 1905.

was the nearest to the herring grounds and it also had plenty of flat shore suitable for basing all the necessary support and accommodation. Ursula, who had seen the heyday of line-fishing from Balta Sound, now watched in amazement – and pleasure, since there were financial gains for the estate – from the windows of Buness, as wooden jetties and curing yards virtually rose up in front of her eyes and rapidly spread right around the Sound. In Lerwick it was the same, and in the season Bressay Sound became jam-packed with fishing boats while the streets thronged with the voices and costumes of half-a-dozen European nationalities.

In the face of this development the *haaf* fishing was losing its profitable edge and many of its fishermen now moved from the country into the old capital of Scalloway and into Lerwick to join new and larger fishing boats, or the merchant navy, or the rising tide of emigrants. The *haaf*, however, did not disappear without the cost of further human life. In 1881, a sudden July gale caught the boats from Gloup, a deep voe on the north coast of Yell, on the fishing grounds. Ten of the boats were swamped and 58 men were drowned: a terrible loss to the small communities in the area. This loss, and the fact that several modern decked boats caught in the same gale rode it out safely, was the last nail in the *sixareen* coffin. The *haaf* fishing with hand lines from open boats, that had lasted over 150 years, finally came to an end with just a few boats continuing on into the 20th century. The overall effect of these changes in fishing and the modernisation of the Shetland economy was that, for the first time in their history, the Shetland men and women began to have choices of employment that paid them in cash.

The mid-1880s also saw the final chapter in the modernisation of land tenure in Shetland and Scotland. For a number of years concerned intellectuals and liberals had been petitioning the British government to do something about the conditions of the small tenant farmers of Scotland. The Truck Commission had investigated and outlawed the practice of tying employees to their employers through payment by goods rather than cash. Now attention was focusing on the tenants' lack of security of tenure. In the absence of any regulation, tenants were charged whatever rent the landlord wished and turned off their land with the minimum of notice.

In response to growing pressure, the Liberal government of William Gladstone set up a Royal Commission under Lord Napier to look into the situation in the north of Scotland. Although the Napier Commission was imbalanced by the omission of any tenant and the inclusion of two heavyweight Scottish landowners, Napier himself, turned out to be very sympathetic to the tenants' complaints. Napier and the Commission arrived in Shetland in the summer of 1883 and over relatively few days they posed almost 4400 questions to some 60 Shetlanders,[5] among them those that David answered revealing his perspective of *scattald* rights.[6]

"Commission: 'We have heard a good deal today of the withdrawal of the hill pasture from tenants, and the consolidation of them into sheep farms; has that been the practice upon Buness Estate?'

David: 'Yes.'

C: 'Has that been prejudicial to the condition of the small tenants?'

D: 'I don't think so at all.'

C: 'In the case of the withdrawal of the hill pasture, has there been any proportionate reduction of rent?'

D: 'No, because in all the cases where we enclosed hill pasture it was very extensive, and far more than our tenants could occupy. It was occupied by the tenants of other proprietors all over the island, and we, in almost every case, left some scathold for the tenants.'

C: 'Almost in every case?'

D: 'Almost in every case.'

C: 'And when none at all was left, in this exceptional case was a reduction of rent made?'

D: 'No … the rents were equalised … in many cases reduced, and in other cases increased.'

C: 'The principal complaint we have had today seems to be the loss of the scathold. Do you think there is good ground for that?'

D: 'There may be in some cases, where the tenant has no scathold at all.'

C: 'But, on the Buness property, you think they have [sufficient] scathold, generally speaking?'

D: 'They have all, with two exceptions, sufficient for their arable land; of course, not to keep 200 or 300 sheep, as they used to do, but sufficient to run out young ponies and cattle, and a few sheep.'

C: 'But if they used to keep 200 or 300 sheep, won't they feel it to be a hardship to have lost that power.'

D: 'They do.'"

When questioned why the removed tenant on his reassigned land was not able to keep and benefit from the new and larger sheep breeds, such as the blackface ewes and Leicester rams, that the sheep farmer, including himself, was now able to do, David prevaricated:

"D: 'Because with the scathold left him he has no arable land [to keep the ewes and cross lambs], whilst the large farmer has.'

C: 'Then where does the large farmer get this arable land?'

D: 'It is included in the scathold; it is attached to the scathold.'

C: 'That would show that the larger farmer got the best of the scathold, because he got this town land [previously arable] with it?'

D: 'The town land was not scathold.'

C: 'What was it then?'

D: 'That is where the emigration took place from when the tenants left.'

C: 'But he [larger farmer] got the vacant crofts?'

D: 'Yes, and he keeps the cross sheep on these places.'"

The 'rationalisation' of the tenancies of the estate was not always being done for the benefit of the tenant but was often intended to improve estate income by allowing the development of far more profitable sheep farms. It is clear from David's response to the Commission that the tenants very much got the short end of the stick. Those who remained, with reduced hill-grazing rights, could only watch as their previously hard-worked arable land was put down to the new sheep breeds.

One of the tenants whom the Commission questioned was Robert Robertson of Unst, who told him he was one of those evicted by David from Rue. Another was George Sinclair, a fishcurer and merchant, who succinctly, with a little help from the Commission, explained the importance of the *scattald* to the small tenant farmer.

> "Sinclair: '[F]rom time immemorial the people have had the use of it, and it has been an understood thing that they were to have the scathold with the croft, because the crofts could not keep their families without the scathold.'
> C: 'Do they consider they have a firmer right to this scathold than to the arable portion of their land?'
> Sinclair: 'Yes, they do, it appears that its name would imply that – a commonty for the common people.'"[7]

What the Shetland small tenant farmer had always believed was that the *scattald*, and a number of rights attached to it, was part and parcel of their arable and meadowland, though of course, landowners disagreed. Jessie M. E., nearly 20 years later, as a stalwart defender of the rights of the people, said that Shetlanders paid scat (a tax) "… for the use of the commons [scattald] – the daals and fields and saiters where their animals fed and from whence they got their fuel."[8] There were high hopes among the tenants that the Napier Commission might restore some of their lost rights.

Before anything happened on the political front however, David Edmondston, factor and heir to Buness, died at his farm at Ordale in 1884, at the young age of 47, never having become the laird. David left the family – the youngest of whom was 14 and the elder son and heir, Laurence (1868-1915), 16 – in the care of his second wife, Elizabeth. At this time Laurence and his sister Elizabeth had moved from Bressay to live at Halligarth with their grand-aunt Penelope – their grandfather Laurence's second wife, who died four years later in 1888.

Ever since the Buness estate had come into the Edmondston family its inheritance had proved to be a difficult matter on the death of the incumbent laird, regularly causing family disputes and this time was no different. Ursula, in Buness, now 65, had life rent of the estate and on her death the estate was to go to David or his heirs. But, when Biot had allegedly relinquished his title in favour of his younger brother David, he had never thought he might be alive after his brother's death. So, with the death of David and with his eldest, Laurence, being so young, Biot and his younger brother, Thomas the stockbroker in London, felt that they had still some rights as far as the estate was concerned. On behalf of Laurence, but with their own interests also in mind, a trust was set up to manage the estate until Laurence was deemed competent to take over. The trustees were Biot, Thomas the stockbroker in London and David's son, Laurence. With Laurence being so inexperienced, and with Biot in Stirling and Thomas in London, it was arranged by them, as trustees, that in the meantime the management of the estate should be carried out by Laurence's uncle, the husband of Ellen (Edmondston), William Cameron Hamilton, at Houlland, while Laurence, overseen by him, was let the farm of Mailland and the Home Farm.[9]

Laurence was intensely frustrated with this arrangement which left him as heir, with no control over the estate or direct access to its income. Ten years later, in 1894,[10] when he was 26, he sought to 'disentail', that is, to break the deed of settlement of the Buness estate that gave the trustees

Biot Edmondston (1827-1906) in middle age.

Laurence Edmondston (1868-1915) as a young man.

control over it.[11] In this he was supported by his younger brother and two of his sisters, but by this action he made himself liable to a financial settlement to them of £2000 (£134,000)! His intentions became clearer in 1896 when his uncles, Biot and Thomas, petitioned the courts to prevent him from selling it![12] Laurence had decided that he might be better off realising the capital of the estate than trying to take on the management under his interfering uncles. In the event, he could not sell the estate and settled on waiting for Ursula's death. However, there was a further burden; Biot and Thomas took out a summons against him for various sums of money due them from his father's will.[13]

Meanwhile, following the report of the Napier Commission, Gladstone's 1886 Crofters Holdings (Scotland) Act, did not restore the *scattald* rights to the tenants, but it did, for the very first time, give them security of tenure on their farms and, in 1889 a system of 'fair rents'. Thomas the stockbroker in London, though proud of his Shetland ties and believing he still had a finger on its political pulse, was now somewhat divorced from the Scottish and Shetland scene and showed in his response to the Act just how difficult it must have been for young Laurence to deal with him. In a letter to the landowner, John Bruce (1837-1907) of Sumburgh, in the tradition of his deceased namesakes, his cousin Yankee Tom and his uncle Thomas the laird, he excoriated the Act:

261

"The public conscience has been strongly moved by the operation of the Crofters Act, a measure infinitely more damaging to the moral reputation of this country than the worst of all Mr Gladstone's Irish Land Acts. I ...doubt whether the Statute Book of any country pretending to possess the belief of ...contains a law so inequitable in its inception so one-sided in its terms and so [?] in its operation."[14]

Thomas wrote this letter in support of the pursuer in what came to be known as the Hoswick Whale Case. He, and landowners including Ursula and Major Cameron of Garth, donated money to Bruce to fight the landowners' side of this dispute. On 14th September, 1888, over 300 *caain'* (pilot) whales were driven ashore by the men of Hoswick in South Mainland. The division of the spoils of such drives had been disputed by the tenant-fishermen of Shetland for over 100 years. Eighty years previously, Dr Arthur Edmondston had argued that the legalised traditional three-way division of the spoils of such a drive, between the crown, the landowner onto whose shores the whales were driven and killed, and the tenants who actually risked their boats and their lives in the drive, was unfair. He had believed that the crown had no right to a share and that even the landowner's right was based on rather flimsy arguments. However, as a compromise, he had recommended that the landowner should get a one third share and that the tenants should get two thirds. Naturally, the landowners and the crown did not agree and the traditional division was still in force when the whales were driven ashore at Hoswick.

The value of the carcasses of the whales at auction was a very substantial £450 (£29,250) and the two landowners involved vigorously pursued their one-third share. The men who had captured the whales, however, refused to pay it and the case went to the Sheriff at Lerwick who found for them and against the landowners. Money was then raised by the landowners, with the private help of Thomas the stockbroker among others, and the case was taken to the Court of Session in Edinburgh. Once again the case was found in favour of the men and that momentous decision marked the end of an almost feudal tradition. This was not just a single blow against the rights of landowners, following the Truck Commission and the Napier Commission it was the *coup de grâce* to the ancient, crumbling and one-sided tenant-landowner relationship.

Even though Thomas the stockbroker was based in London he made several, if not frequent, trips home, continuing the Edmondston interest in the wildlife on their land in Unst and specifically the protection of the *bonxie* (great skua) begun by his father, Dr Laurence at Halligarth, and his uncle, old Thomas, at the very beginning of the 19th century, then by his elder brother David, encouraged by his cousin Yankee Tom. This long family tradition of the protection of the *bonxie* on the cliff-bound peninsula and sheep farm at Herma Ness, however, had lapsed by 1876, as was explained in a letter of David's to the *Shetland News*.

"My father preserved these birds on Hermaness for a great many years, but I am sorry to say that since he ceased to do so their numbers have greatly diminished, and now there are only a very few pairs to be seen, as compared to thirty or forty which I can remember. It is indeed shameful that men who call themselves gentlemen will roam over these islands and without liberty either from landlord or tenant, shoot down and exterminate birds that are found nowhere else in Britain, and only in small numbers about the wildest and most remote hills."[15]

Thomas the stockbroker now encouraged young Laurence to take up the mantle of his late father and grandfather and protect the *bonxie* once again. Laurence responded to the challenge and employed a Shetlander, Henry Edwardson (1854-1928), as a keeper on Herma Ness. The problem of 'gentlemen' sportsmen was still very real despite the 1880 Wild Birds' Protection Act. In the *Shetland News* in 1892, Thomas the stockbroker recounted that Laurence had asked two men, who had arrived with letters of recommendation – just as had George Atkinson 60 years earlier – to wait a few days before going to watch the skuas until the birds were sitting securely on eggs, when they would be accompanied by the keeper. However, they did not wait.

"Warned off by the keeper, they laughed at his remonstrances, and proceeded to hunt for the skuas' nests. It is highly satisfactory to add that they did not find them, for the keeper, who had been joined by my nephew's shepherd, 'shadowed' them at a few paces distance ... [but] Only a few days afterwards ... two nests ... were plundered of their eggs, and there was possibility of tracing the depredators."[16]

In recognition of their conservation work over 70 years and three generations, and the appointment of Edwardson, Ursula, on behalf of the Edmondston family, received the silver medal of the Zoological Society of London in 1891.[17] Thomas the stockbroker, who revealed himself to be very knowledgeable about Shetland's birds in his correspondence with the local papers in the 1890s concerning the Wild Birds' Protection Act, of which he was highly critical in Shetland, also added two more new birds to the family list of new bird records for Shetland.

In 1899, in a response to an anonymous correspondent, A. B. L., who was critical of his late brother-in-law Dr Henry Saxby and his book, Thomas wrote a letter to the *Shetland News* in which he strongly defended the man who had given him his education in the identification and habits of Shetland's birds. Resolutely, he told A. B. L. that Henry and his book needed no defending, "His reputation is far too securely established."[18] Thomas, however, though honest in his opinion, was not as sympathetic to other of his relatives: there was a touch of his late uncle, Dr Arthur Edmondston, in him. He was not a man to bear fools easily and his criticisms, not always confined to ornithological matters, could be highly barbed. Like his late uncle, he also found himself almost penniless, though in his case, around 1893, it was because his stockbroker partner had absconded, leaving him with large debts, a wife and six young children to support. In their public correspondence in the *Shetland News*, A. B. L. had linked Thomas' reputation with that of his cousin Yankee Tom. Thomas' response was a scathing criticism of his cousin that may just have owed a little to the long family quarrel over the inheritance of the estate between his father and his uncle and American cousin.

"I beg that A. B. L. will not hold me responsible for anything in the *Glossary of the Orkney and Shetland dialect*, compiled by my late cousin and namesake, Thomas Edmondston [Yankee Tom] of Buness. The book in question is crammed with blunders in every page. My cousin, who possessed many amiable qualities and some accomplishments, had not a single qualification for the work he undertook. He was not a native of Shetland, and knew nothing of its dialect. He had no linguistic acquirements, nor any philological tastes, and it is hardly surprising in the circumstances that he produced a work which is absolutely monumental in the extent and variety of its mistakes ..."[19]

In another letter of that year, to A. H. Evans (1855-1943) the naturalist and co-author with T. E. Buckley (1846-1902) of *A Vertebrate fauna of the Shetland Islands* (1899), who had sent Thomas the proofs of a paper on the fauna of Shetland, Thomas was even more damning of his older namesake, his uncle, old Thomas the laird.[20] Evans had requested some information on Thomas' naturalist antecedents. First Thomas made it clear that although he had gone birding with Dr Henry Saxby, his brother-in-law, for eight years, he (Thomas) could take no credit for any part of Henry Saxby's book – *The Birds of Shetland*. Then he wrote of his late uncle Thomas the laird.

> "*He did nothing during his life that would in anyway interest you (or indeed anyone else), and died in 1858 at the age of 80.*"

But he was slightly kinder to his other uncle, Dr Arthur Edmondston of Lerwick, though he did not think him much of an ornithologist.

> "*He must have been an accomplished man in his day and generation, although neither good nor virtuous, and his book is still frequently referred to as an authority on the local antiquities and history of the Islands. He fancied himself an ornithologist also, but his notes are of little value.*"

And, naturally, Thomas was kindest in his opinions on his father, Dr Laurence.

> "*MacGillivray makes very frequent mention of him, and he was without doubt a keen naturalist and a very competent observer in those far away days.*"

The Politicisation of Jessie M. E.

Jessie M. E. had the restlessness, boundless energy and curiosity of her long deceased brother, Tom the botanist. Writing, although it took up much of her time, was not everything to her. One of the many causes she took up in Edinburgh was temperance, a popular liberal cause that she adopted from her parent's influence and her own Christian beliefs.[21] She was also an early feminist, not such a popular cause. Around 1886, at the time that her 17-year-old third son, Thomas (T. E.) Saxby, was just beginning medicine at Edinburgh, she travelled across Canada on behalf of Women's Emigration and also to see her fourth son, Horace Saxby, who had gone out earlier that year. Horace had settled in the Regina area where he stayed for 14 years ranching. His name appears alongside hers on a later article she wrote on her visit. Jessie M. E. travelled by sea on the Allen Liner *Norwegian* from the Clyde to the St Lawrence and then by train across Canada to Vancouver. Such a journey in the 1880s was more than just an adventure: there were physical hardships and even dangers. That Jessie M. E. should undertake it as a single woman was an indication of her gritty self-belief and determination and also a reflection that a piece of her heart was always the *Wildie* of her childhood. She loved the sea-voyage and later wrote a couple of poems about it. A verse from one – *The Spell of the Sea* – gives just an inkling of her feelings aboard ship in the Atlantic and the type of poetry popular in her day.

> "The spell of the sea!
> Does it rise from the blue waves flowing free?
> Or falls it in golden rays from blue skies?

Or shines it in sea-king's sea-blue eyes?
I know not indeed where its magic lies,
I but know it has come like a sweet surprise.
The spell of the sea! The spell of the sea!
It is over me."

When she returned to Edinburgh, like a true professional journalist, she sieved her experiences for the smallest nuggets of stories and poems and over the next six years turned them into a series of saleable articles and stories for adults and children. For the Church of Scotland magazine *Life & Work* she produced articles entitled *A Kirk in the Qu'appelle Valley* (1887), *A Sunday on the Prairie* (1888) with her son Horace, and *Heathens from Home* (1892). For *The Shetland Times*: *A Woman's Paradise* (1888), *A book and its author* (1889) and *To be or not to be … annexed* (1889) and for the *Scotsman* and *Shetland News*: *Prairie Home* (1888). For *Chambers' Journal* she wrote *The Woods of the far West* (1888) and *This year's prairie harvest* (1890). She also managed to produce a book, *Budget of Holiday Letters* (1889).

The subjects of the articles ranged hugely. *A Sunday in the Prairie* was a wholesome account of manly Canadians at their church, while *The Woods of the Far West* was a travelogue of the train journey between Quebec and the North West Territories. *A Woman's Paradise* concerned the main purpose of her visit, Canada's sore need for "respectable women … for domestic service." In Quebec and Montreal, she said, domestic servants could demand $7-10 a month and trained cooks $12, while in the western towns of the prairies and beyond servants might get $20-30 and cooks $40. In those provinces there was only one woman to every 50 men and Jessie M. E. urged young women to consider the possibilities – "To go out a servant and come back a lady – that would be an ambition indeed." *Heathens from Home*, a description of a visit she made to a refuge for Chinese women and a Chinese temple in Vancouver illustrated the compassionate side of Jessie M. E. Thousands of poor Chinese had emigrated to the west coast of North America where they lived very much as second class citizens. Jessie M. E. could not ignore the plight of anyone, whatever their race or position, was never afraid to be unconventional or controversial and she spoke up for those abandoned women in a strange land far from home.

During the latter half of the 1880s and early 1890s, when Jessie M. E. was in her mid-

Lads of Lunda *by Jessie M. E. Saxby.*

265

forties and the youngest of her boys in his late teens, she was incredibly busy, writing at least 40 articles and serialised stories for newspapers and journals and 12 children's books as well as a romance. Perhaps her most successful book of this time, that ran to three editions, was *Lads of Lunda* (1887) – Lunda Wick is a beautiful sandy bay by the ruins of a medieval church on the west coast of Unst – a book of short stories for boys, which first appeared in the *Boy's Own Paper* in 1886 and then as a book the following year. The reviews by the *Guardian* and the *Times* summed up Jessie M. E.'s particular gifts in writing for boys and her ability to conjure the distinctive Shetland culture and landscape.

> "A perfect book for boys – generous, wholesome, manly in tone and withal thoroughly young, fresh and natural. We recommend the book heartily, not only to all boys, but to everybody who knows and likes brave boys." [*Guardian*]

> "A capital series of tales. The pictures of land and sea, of life and manners, are graphically sketched by a lady who is evidently thoroughly familiar with them." [*Times*]

Jessie M. E. also encouraged her own boys to write, and besides the Canadian article she co-authored with the 15-year-old Horace, she also co-authored a story in the *Boy's Own Paper* with her youngest, Charlie Fletcher, who was just 14 at the time, entitled *Rough and Ready Chums* that was not published until 1897. Charlie was just one of the next generation to carry on the writing tradition and went on to write several books for boys under the pseudonym Argyll Saxby.

A couple of years after the Canadian journey, on the evening of 3rd October, 1888, the fortnightly meeting of the Edinburgh Orkney and Shetland Literary Association was held in the hall of Y.M.C.A. rooms in Edinburgh. Although not actually present, this occasion was one event in a series that marked the beginnings of a new career for Jessie M. E., public speaking. Jessie M. E. had been asked to provide the opening lecture for the winter meetings and since she was unable to be present, her 12-page address, later published, was read by the chairman. The paper was entitled *Shoulder to Shoulder* (1887) and it developed her long-time empathy with her Viking ancestry that could be traced back through her grandmother, Mally Sanderson of Buness. In this she was very much in tune with the attitudes of her late father and mother.

The period of this address coincided with the height of British Imperialism. The colonial Empire now stretched around the world and just a year previously its exotic and subservient representatives had attended the lavish celebrations of Queen Victoria's Jubilee in London. It was a time when British citizens could believe that they were the master race. In her address, Jessie M. E. had drawn her audience's attention to the lessons of the Jews and the Romans, and then reminded them that:

> "There is another nation of olden times to which I wish your attention drawn, – a nation whose story 'points a moral' for us more nearly than the stories of Rome and Palestine. That nation – was, and is, our <u>own</u>, – the Scandinavian race, – the Sea Kings of the North!"

Jessie M. E. suggested that:

> "Strong and demonstrative affection for one another was one of the most striking features in the Norse character. Their name has been slightly changed to suit the lands which they

colonised. We call them now Germans, Normans, Danes, Saxons, English, but these are all Northmen, bearing still the marked characteristics of the ancient Scandinavian."

Jessie M. E.'s thesis was that the bulk of the British population was Scandinavian in origin through descent from the Vikings and the Normans, it is from them, she said, that the British inherited those special genes that made Britain 'Great' and it was time that their foremost representatives in Britain, those from the northern isles of Orkney and Shetland, pulled together. Too often Shetlanders and Orcadians had been critical of each other and themselves and it was lack of co-operation that was to blame:

"... for the neglect into which our islands have fallen. Believe me, it is the want of unanimous action, the lack of generous 'brotherhood', which prevents our country from progressing as it ought."

Jessie M. E.'s enthusiasm for the Norse, as a branch of the Teutonic race, was very much part of a wider Victorian academic interest in race generally and in the origins of the sterling 'character' of the Saxons and the Celts. Yankee Tom's visitor in the 1860s, James Hunt, was an extreme exponent of these ideas. The Norse, particularly, were seen as a hardy, virtuous and freedom-loving people with whom the British could identify. Writers, such as R. M. Ballantyne in *Erling the Bold*, saw them as fighters for 'Liberty'. However, when it came to Shetlanders versus the Scots, Jessie M. E. conveniently forgot the Scottish origins of many Shetlanders, and, like Sir Walter Scott in *The Pirate*, thought of the old Norse udallers of Shetland as superior to the rapacious Scots.[22] This was to be just one of her many exhortations for the islanders to recognise and resurrect their glorious Viking past.

But, although Jessie M. E. got caught up in such romantic and mildly racist beliefs, she had a very practical attitude to helping her fellow Shetlanders in Edinburgh and in the 'little Shetland' of its contiguous neighbour, Leith. A contemporary Shetlander in Edinburgh and close friend of Jessie M. E.'s was a man called Gilbert Goudie (1843-1918), a banker by profession but an historian by nature. He too was a member of the Edinburgh Orkney and Shetland Association and a leading light in 'Shetland' activities in the capital. Another was a young man from Calback on the Buness estate on Unst, named Basil Ramsay Anderson. (1861-1888). In 1875, his mother had brought him and her other five children to Edinburgh just like Jessie M. E. had brought her boys. Except, Basil Anderson's father did not die of an illness, he was the man who had been drowned at the Unst *haaf* fishing when Basil was just five. Basil was a bright child and many years later his brother, Robert Anderson (b1859), was to say that Basil's great aptitude as a child drew the laird's (Yankee Tom) attention to him with the result that "... he charged himself with a great part of the expenses of Basil's education." Basil wanted to be a poet. Jessie M. E. was nearly twenty years older and already the author of two books of verse, so, naturally, he turned to her for support with his own work. He had been only 14 when he had arrived in Leith and he had brought with him an unquenchable nostalgia for his home. Like Jessie M. E., he wrote much of his poetry in English, but it was rather derivative of the time and place and not very original. Unlike Jessie M. E., however, his natural tongue was the Shetland dialect and it was in that which he wrote best.

Tragically, Basil Anderson died of tuberculosis in Leith in 1888, at just 27. Jessie M. E. had recognised his gifts as far superior to her own and she now collected and edited his poetry for publication, with the help and advice of Gilbert Goudie and another well known expatriate Shetlander, George Stewart (1825-1911), whose *Fireside Tales* (1877) was one of the first literary works in the Shetland dialect. If Jessie M. E. had never published anything she would still be remembered, if only for this act of homage to a fellow poet. For in the collection that she put together, entitled *Broken Lights* (1888), was the greatest poem written in the Shetland dialect.[23]

Auld Maunsie's Crö is about Magnus, an old Shetlander, the daily and seasonal rural cycles and the centre of his life, his *crö* (a small walled enclosure where kail seedlings were grown). It is very much in the Burns' tradition and, like a very few other Shetland dialect poems, deserves its place in the national pantheon because of its poetic quality and complete lack of sentimentality. The poem is composed of many stanzas and only the first and last, and one from the middle, are quoted here.

> "Oot-ower upon a weel-kent hill
> Whase waters rise to grind a mill,
> Auld Maunsie biggit him a crü,
> Ta growe him kail for mutton brü, –
> For Maunsie never thocht him hale
> Withoot sheeps' shanks an' cogs o' kail.
>
> …
>
> Whan winter skies gae ne'er a flame
> An lads were linkin' oot "fae hame,"
> Or whan da mists lay ower da hill
> Till raikin' dogs wid even will,
> Auld Maunsie's crü, set on da heicht,
> Wid tell da rodd ta left or richt,
> An' when da snaw was driftin' deep
> Da crü was soucht by cruggin' sheep,
> Whaur safe and snug dey'd buried lie
> Till fanns wir scoomed, or drifts wir by.
>
> …
>
> (Lord rest his sowl!) it cam ta geng
> By da füle name o' "Ferry-ring."
> An' so wi' age an' moss grown gray
> It waddered mony a heavy day,
> But o' da wa's 'at ance wir seen,
> Da mark an' guide ta many e'en,
> Deil stane wis left but ane or twa
> Upstaundin' whaur hill-baess could claw.
> An' later folk had mair ta dü
> Dan mind Auld Maunsie or his crü."

By 1890, Jessie M. E. was dabbling her toes in politics, but not the Tory politics of her family. She once described herself as a 'radical-imperialist', a personal observation that very accurately summed up her political brand of jingoistic passion, leavened by liberal care for the rights of the downtrodden, in whom she included women. In that year she wrote an article for the *People's Friend* that was reprinted in *The Shetland Times*, entitled *From Behind Bars*. At the beginning of the article she recalled being taken to Westminster as a young girl where:

> "The mighty gladiators of the political arena, Disraeli and Gladstone were "set for a fight," and the House, densely crowded, was hanging on their words."

The 'Bars' of the title were not the bars of a prison but the grille of the cramped Ladies Gallery in the House of Commons from where very little could be seen or heard:

> "The only place allowed to women in the House of Commons is the Cage over the Speaker's head; and the way to even that Cage is hedged about by difficulties."

Jessie M. E. was now a staunch liberal and an active member of the Liberal Association, or at least, the ladies' section and in the 1880s she resolved to return to Westminster and see if anything had changed. She noted that women were not allowed in the Stranger's Gallery or as a member of the Press and was appalled at the behaviour of the men in the absence of women and in the fact that it was so difficult for women to attend.

> "Surely, if women are encouraged to be Primrose dames and Liberal Associates, they ought to have the freedom of the House of Commons, where they can best learn of men what political life means."

Later that year she wrote an article for the *North British Advertiser*, again reprinted in *The Shetland Times*, entitled *A Hopeful Sisterhood* (1890), which was a report of her attendance at a meeting of the Women's Liberal Association that met to present an address to Mrs Gladstone whom they called their 'chief'. Like the previous article, she wrote it to bring to the attention of the ordinary woman in Scotland and Shetland just what the modern woman should be doing and saying and to take the opportunity to give the recalcitrant the edge of her tongue.

> "Not many years ago the world was want to associate the names of women who 'speak in public' with very uncomplimentary terms: such as 'blue stocking', 'bloomer', 'strong-minded nuisance' and the like … Women who were experts at pie-crust and pinafores, women whose tongues could wax eloquent in retailing gossip, or scolding servants, but considered it a virtue to be dumb when some great social question was moving the soul of the nation; women who were pretty and silly, and liked to be treated like toys – all shrugged their shoulders when they heard of a 'sister' appearing on the platform, and they spoke of her as a 'plain old thing of course', and 'quite queer, you know'. [But] What a revolution has taken place in public opinion and in women's ways during the last two decades."

And Jessie M. E., no shrinking wall-flower, was one of those in the van.

The meeting went on to endorse liberal values as those which are natural to women and Jessie M. E.'s article exhorted women to bring politics into their home; to support liberal husbands and only political policies that represented the very best of womanhood and domestic life. Like many 'feminists' of the time, Jessie M. E. was often fighting for women's rights as wives, rather than as individuals, though she was a great example herself of what a woman could then achieve.

One of the main topics of the meeting was Home Rule for Ireland, then on the liberal agenda, and Jessie M. E. gave that particular policy her full-hearted backing. Many years earlier, when she had written her first essay – on the characters of the English, Scots, Welsh and Irish – Jessie M. E. had totally disparaged the Irish character as only an upper-class child can: "That of the lower classes has hardly a virtue to adorn it." In the last decade of the 19th century she made her first visit there and came away having discarded all her prejudices and full of admiration for the struggling peasantry: "One comes away from Ireland devoutly wishing that peace and plenty may speedily visit so fair a land and so kind a people." So strong had grown her feelings for Home Rule for Ireland that she wrote, and had privately published, a little pamphlet of eight pages entitled *Home Rule apart from politics* (1891). This called for all – in the words of her hero Gladstone – "to think it out" in a dispassionate, rational manner and not to be influenced by terrorism and prejudice.

"Those who think without prejudice on this subject, soon recognise that Home Rule draws its existence from an undying source ... Deep down in the soul of every one of us dwells a passion that will not permit interference with our right to exercise free-will regarding our own affairs ... When it shapes itself into a Nation's struggle for Independence, it becomes the genius of Patriotism ... There is nothing that we Britons have fought more for than this same Home Rule, though we called it by other names."

In this pamphlet, Jessie M. E. revealed just how far, politically, she had travelled.

"*Our* nation has reached the point in life of nations where an effort to bring balance back to universal justice and brotherhood comes in ... Our leagues, and our strikes; our squabbles for religious and social equality; our demand for a more even division of wealth and work; our insistence upon individual right to the Earth for which we were made, and to which we must return – all these things find place under the banner of Home Rule ... in truth, no fierce struggle, however righteous in origin, has been carried to a victorious issue by spotless heroes only."

To admit and accept that the road to political salvation had been morally besmirched and muddied, but yet try to get on with the process peacefully, is a very modern point of view. Jessie M. E. also wrote in this pamphlet that she desired Home Rule, not only for Ireland, but for Scotland and Wales, and looked forward to a federated Britain.

In two further articles in *The Shetland Times* – *Women and Work* and *Idle Hands* – in 1892 and 1893, Jessie M. E. returned to the topic of women and their work. In the first she addressed the gulf of misunderstanding and suspicion between the woman who worked with her head or hands in a world dominated by men, and the woman who worked as a loving wife and mother. Her answer to the conflicting opinions of women as to what was the 'proper' work of women, was reconciliation – "Give *to* every woman the same generous latitude you desire to get *from* them for yourself." On the other hand, Jessie M. E. had little patience for the conventions of petty womanhood. In *Idle Hands* she devastatingly described crocheting as "sowing holes together"!

"'Where is your work?' I hear some elderly lady ask the girl who has been busy at school all day, and has seated herself beside her brother or father, to listen to their talk or tell them some incident of the day. And the poor child is sent off for some detestable piece of fancy-work, which is supposed to keep her out of mischief at all times when – duty done – her hands may be idle! She is a wise mother who comprehends that a girl's intellect does not grow while her hands are so employed. I just believe that one reason why men are more intelligent on the whole than women is because they keep their hands idle while their heads are creating and planning. I wish I could convince some women that their minds would expand much better and faster if they would sometimes leave the fancy-work upstairs and permit their fingers to lie idle."[24]

Despite those comments, Jessie M. E. herself was very competent with her hands, among many other things making fine bedcovers for her family when somehow she managed to find the time. And, although she could be disparaging about some women's attitudes, she was fierce in the defence of her sex when need be. In 1894 there was a Breach of Promise brought against her suitor by a woman in Sandness in the West Mainland.[25] The defence hinged around the courting habits of the time and *The Shetland Times* issue of the 26th May reported the comments of the lawyer and witness. To Jessie M. E.'s mind, their statements impugned the morals of Shetland's young women. She was outraged and without much thought that the case had not been resolved in court, wrote a letter to the paper two weeks later.[26] First, the feisty Jessie M. E. asked why the men of Shetland had not risen up to defend their women, then she went on to state, courageously for the time:

Bedcover by Jessie M. E.

271

Jessie M. E. dressed up in 'native' costume.

"I care nothing at all for 'conventional respectability' and despise the morality which leans on Kirk and Law for its support, but I assert that a purer and more lasting love has its home in Shetland than in any other part of 'religious' Scotland."

For publishing this comment on the ongoing trial, a case of contempt of court was brought against her and *The Shetland Times*; happily for them both, it was dismissed.

Although the men of Shetland were silent, Jessie M. E. had at least one vocal female supporter. The following week a short poem in her praise was published anonymously in *The Shetland Times* that is a worthy reflection of her standing among the women of Shetland of the time. The last verse of the poem ran:

"Sister! For that one noble word
So promptly said, so bold and true
The women of your island race
For years to come will honour you."

Jessie M. E. came from an island of remote communities where most people had little access to good literature and journalism, nor lived in conditions, even if these were available, where they could have taken much advantage of them. Jessie M. E. believed these broadened and educated the mind and she was very keen to provide such stimulation for the long winter evenings of the families of ordinary Shetlanders. She was well-meaning and wished to do this for the very best of reasons, but her zeal and her belief in her own 'superior' opinion, led her to a misjudgement. In Edinburgh, she advertised in the press for 'wholesome' books and magazines that she could have distributed to islanders. Andrew Carnegie, the great Scottish-American 'patriot and philanthropist', to whom she had dedicated her Home Rule paper, provided £10 (£670) towards the scheme and her friend, Charles Merrylees – Manager of the North of Scotland Steam Company that sailed between Leith and Lerwick – agreed to carry the material free on the steamer.[27] For all her passion to improve the lives of the disadvantaged, Jessie M. E. was not always able to shake off the views of a privileged daughter of a landed family. The scheme was seen by some Shetlanders as patronising and as a writer to *The Shetland Times* indicated, not all appreciated "this charity of cast-off magazines and cheap novels."[27] It did not last very long.

CHAPTER TWENTY

FULL CIRCLE

"Oh, the voes lie in the arms
Of the dear North Isles,
They inhale each other's charms,
They reflect each other's smiles;
The scories claug and flock
By the banks beside the sea,
And it's to the dear Old Rock
That my flauchting heart wid flee."

Jessie M. E. Saxby (1842-1940)

Rebirth of the Vikings

Although Jessie M. E. wrote many political articles promoting her Christian, liberal, patriotic, feminist and temperance beliefs, the bulk of her output was what she, herself, dismissed as "sensation story", exciting copy of controversy, adventure and romance. As Dr Joseph Bell said to her in a letter about one of her articles following her visit to Canada:

"I like your Canada paper. It has a nice fresh spring about it. Bronchoes and buckboards sound uncivilised enough for even a wild Shetlander."[1]

In reality she was being very hard-headed about her writing. There was no point in producing fine material, of which she thought she was capable, if an editor did not want to purchase it or an audience read it. Nevertheless, it hurt her that she did not get the recognition she thought she deserved. Once again, her mentor, Bell, was reassuring.

"Don't call your work unsuccessful. It has boiled the bairns' pot for many years. It would have been better work if you could have given more time to the polishing, etc. But the results are marvellous, and you are the sort of woman that does not care for fame."

Many of Jessie M. E.'s serialised stories and novels were set in Shetland. For her suburban readers she knew that an island setting would be romantic and that she should include just enough dialect to give a flavour of the culture, but not so much that the thread of a story would be lost. Sometimes her stories were pure fiction but often they were based on true events. Although she saw herself as someone who had had an avant-garde and mind-broadening upbringing and who had escaped a 'narrow' island culture, Jessie M. E. never actually rose above her 'conventional' roots. The boy-heroes of her children's stories were middle-class, the sons of doctors, lairds or ministers

Jessie M. E. in middle age.

and the stories themselves were often too obviously moralistic and melodramatic for today's tastes; but that was the genre and the times in which she wrote. The closing paragraphs in *Viking Boys* (1892) are a good example of her style. Here, the hero explains his future plans to his comrades.

> "'I want to go out and explore the world – the stars, if that were possible – and to fight all the foes of the Red Cross, and to bury all feuds, and win name and fame like a right noble and right valiant Viking.'
>
> 'You *have* done so, if you but knew it,' quoth Garth; and Harry Mitchell said, 'You will do all that, I don't doubt; and I'll follow where your flag leads, old man! I never could stand by the side of a better comrade, and I don't believe I could ever find a finer leader – so there!'
>
> 'Thank you, Harry,' Yaspard answered simply.
>
> I need not tell you of the home-coming to Moolapund, of Aunt Osla's tears and tea, of Signy's joy, of Thor's profound reflections, finished up with a sage 'Just so!' – of all the talk and enjoyment in fighting their battles o'er again.
>
> We can leave our Viking-boy at this happy stage of his career, assured (like the Yarl of Broch) that he was heard of in the world in later days."

Jessie M. E. was also rather patronising of the local people in her stories. In *The Yarl's Yacht* (1889), the fisherman's daughter who married the Yarl is referred to as "the pretty, but ignorant and uncultivated daughter of a fisherman, who was never equal to the position he gave her, and was not regretted when she died." It was only in one of her last novels of that genre, *A Camsterie Nacket: being the story of a contrary laddie ill to guide* (1894), that Jessie M. E. successfully portrayed the life of an ordinary Shetlander.[2]

Being the feminist she was, Jessie's heroes were often heroines. *A Brave Woman* (1897) was the true story of a young Shetland woman who twice rescued men from upturned boats in Bluemull Sound, the narrow but fierce tideway between Unst and Yell.

274

"A wild cry from Ellen brought Grizel out to find her sister leaning, deathly pale, against the peat stack and crying out as she pointed to the Sünd -
'There! There! I saw her whumble [capsize]. Oh Lord save them!'
Girzie looked as the trembling hand pointed and saw the boat's keel gleaming in the light as it drifted down the Sünd. She saw the men clinging there and heard their wild cries for help."

By the end of the century, Jessie had produced five more children's novels including *The Saga Book of Lunda* (1896) and *The Yarl's Yacht* (1889), a sequel to *The Lads of Lunda*, of which the *Times* critic said.

"Mrs Saxby is one of the lady writers whose books come as a blessing to the conscientious reviewer. Mrs Saxby reigns undisputably the queen of the bleak and storm-driven Shetland. Bred on those inhospitable shores, she knows all about the lives and superstitions of the sturdy natives, and can invest them with much of the romance which inspired Scott in 'The Pirate'."

The total number of children's books that Jessie M. E. wrote up to this point of her life, when she was 58, was around 30, in addition to several other books on Shetland, personal reminiscences, travel and folklore, her two collections of her own poetry, numerous articles and many speeches. This was an astonishing achievement considering she had had to support herself and her five boys since she was 32. By the mid-1890s, however, all her boys were men and looking after themselves and Jessie M. E. ceased to write any more children's books.

Throughout her writing and journalistic career she had written about Shetland, and if not expounding what she saw as Shetland's, and Britain's, manly and noble Viking heritage, she was making it the stuff of her children's novels. It was equally part of her social life in Edinburgh as a member and then honorary president of the Edinburgh Orkney and Shetland Society. Such was her standing as a Shetlander, as an author and as a speaker, that in 1892 she was invited to be the guest speaker at the first meeting of the new expatriate Orkney and Shetland society, the Viking Club in London. This was a much more academic and antiquarian body than the Edinburgh Society, with all of its members enthusiasts for the Norse past and many, such as the vice-president, William Morris (1834-1896), very prominent people of their time. Jessie M. E. became a member of the Founders Committee and editorial board of the Club's journal, *Old Lore Miscellany*, to which she contributed articles on Shetland's dialect, folklore and antiquities for several years. And, typical of Jessie M. E., in one of the first issues while she put the case for a revival of the Shetland dialect, she also pleaded:

"Would that some rousing voice could stir all classes in our Isles to the same sort of patriotism which has brought about the wonderful Keltic Renaissance."

In fact there was a literary revival and kind of Viking renaissance in Shetland in the late 19th century, partly fuelled by Jessie M. E. herself. She was just one of a number of intellectuals and writers, including the Shetland poet Basil Anderson, who helped revive Shetland's dialect and its heroic Norse past very much at the expense of the Scottish contribution to Shetland's culture and entirely ignoring, as it did not fit the myth, what the Norse had done to the original Pictish population. Interest in the dialect was given a great boost at this time by the visit to Shetland and study of its Norn roots by the Faroese scholar Jakob Jakobsen (1863-1918) in the early 1890s, who published first a doctoral dissertation on the origins of the various elements of the dialect and the classic *The Dialect and Place Names of Shetland* (1897). A great pride arose in the Shetland dialect, though there still remains a great confusion between the original Norn language bequeathed by the Norse and today's Shetland dialect, which is in reality mostly Scots and English with a liberal scattering of Scandinavian words.

Very much later, in *Shetland Traditional Lore* (1932), Jessie M. E. explained this revisionist history that was rapidly becoming the accepted truth.

"Next [After the Picts and the Finns] came the Vikings, rebels from Scandinavia, robbers and conquering heroes. Lastly the Scots, who won our Isles by fraud and violence ... When Shetland came under Scottish rule much of the Scandinavian character became coloured, of course, by the new influence, although the folk hated their oppressors. The Scots, who forced their religion, their mode of life, and their laws upon our Isles, did not change the <u>character</u> of our people, but later, grasping lairds and tyrannical clergy changed a conservative people into determined Liberals ... In this connection we must remember that under Norse rule every family owned the land they lived upon, and every man was 'as good as his neighbour' if he behaved himself ... No wonder they resented the wholesale seizure of their land which they passionately loved. No wonder they resented the insolent airs of authority and superior rank affected by the illegitimate scions of Scottish nobility who swarmed over their Isles, grasping everything from the helpless natives!"

The sort of Viking and pre-Scottish Shetlander that Jessie M. E. imagined and that remains the preferred model of celebration, was very much a wholesome hero and sea-prince, who might have sung her cheery and manly song – *Running Free* – that was set to music by a Lerwick church organist and editor of the *Shetland News*, Thomas Manson (1859-1941).

> "The gale blows wild and strong, my lads,
>   The waves are rolling high,
> And hasting to their island haunts
>   The frightened sea gulls fly,
> The shadow of a lowering cloud
>   Hangs o'er the wave its wing;
> But merrily our boat careens,
>   And merrily we sing"

With a chorus:

> "Running free, merry lads, running free!
>   Our course is clear,
>   We nothing fear,
> We love, we love the sea,
> Running free, merry lads, running free!"

A song, very like this, was written by the blind Shetland poet and Scandiavian scholar, Haldane Burgess (1862-1927), for the spectacular Shetland winter celebration of Up-Helly-Aa. This all night party, with its many traditional roots, was, in the mid-19th century, an ill-disciplined and uproarious celebration in the festive season, when young, masked men, towed burning tar barrels through the narrow streets. By the 1880s this had become a more sophisticated and controlled celebration carried out towards the end of January, involving the burning of a Viking galley built especially for the occasion. The transformation of the original rowdy and often violent celebration to the lovingly crafted galley, torchlight procession, costumed squads, Guizer Jarl and all-night, all-ticket parties of today, owes a great deal to Jessie M. E. and her fellow writers of the late 19th century. So does the romantic interpretation of Shetland's Norse era and its replacement by the "fraud and violence" of the Scots; Jessie M. E. choosing here to forget her forebears on the Edmondston side!

Return Home

All the time Jessie M. E. had been writing and bringing up her boys she had been living in Edinburgh far from her childhood home in Unst, but, busy as she was, she had always kept in close touch with all that was going on in Shetland. Now, after 25 years away, and with all

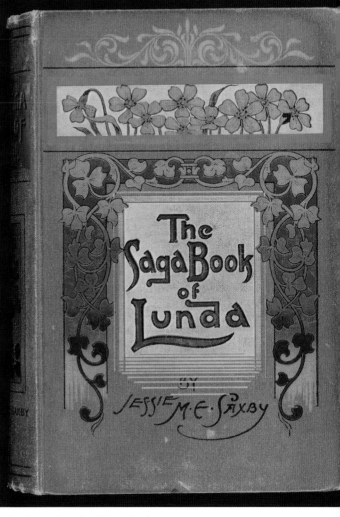

The Saga Book of Lunda *by Jessie M. E.*

the boys having grown up and left her, she found herself increasingly missing the Old Rock, her island home. Her love for Unst – the North Isles of *Summer in the Shetland Isles* – shines through her poem of the time:

> "Oh, the voes lie in the arms
>   Of the dear North Isles,
> They inhale each other's charms,
>   They reflect each other's smiles;
> The scories claug and flock
>   By the banks beside the sea,
> And it's to the dear Old Rock
>   That my flauchting heart wid flee."

Ursula Edmondston (1819-1898) in old age.

Then, in March 1898, after seven weeks' illness, Ursula died at Buness in the house where she was born and that had been her home for 78 years. David's son, Laurence, now aged 30, at last inherited the estate. Later that year he married Florence Spence (1879-1970) – granddaughter of old Thomas' and Yankee Tom's friend Dr Basil Spence of Uyea, the island at the south end of Unst – and they moved into Buness. For Jessie M. E. this was a particularly poignant event, that a Laurence Edmondston, grandson and namesake of her father, 80 years after a promise had been made, should now be fulfilling his dream: perhaps there *was* some natural justice in the world.

In her obituary in the local newspaper, Ursula was commended for the support she, and her late husband Yankee Tom, had given to the erection of a hall at Baltasound, which included the Working Men's Reading Room and Library, and to other generous acts. "She was a kind, faithful friend, and many will deplore the loss of a lady who did many charitable acts, her right hand not knowing what the left did";[3] a curious and ambiguous statement. The Reading Room and Library had actually been the idea of a self-educated Unst man, Andrew Anderson (1839-1906), who had first worked in the chromate quarry when he was thirteen and then gone to sea at nineteen when the quarry closed for a time.[4] When Yankee Tom had got wind of the project he and Ursula had generously provided the funds. After Yankee Tom's death, Ursula also built a house, Springpark, for the retiring teacher at Burrafirth, the school for which her father, old Thomas, had once provided the funds.[5] For one who had lived throughout most of the period of this story and who had played a role at the very heart of it, she left very little that tells us much about her, though snippets of her correspondence that survived suggest she was an intelligent and feisty lady. Being a woman in the 19th century, with few legal rights was bad enough, but she had also to fight to hold her place, illegitimate as it was, in the minds and hearts of her relatives. In the end though, she made sure she had the last word.

Just as the will of old Thomas had been a shock to everyone in 1858, so the 1872 joint settlement of Yankee Tom and Ursula's was a slap in the face to the rest of the family on this side of the Atlantic: that family now consisting of the new laird, Laurence, his brother and his three sisters who were all in their 30s. Then there was Jessie M. E., her brothers the Rev. Biot and Thomas the stockbroker, and her three sisters. When the will was opened after Ursula's death it was found that after the sale of all the farm stock, crops and equipment, ¾ of the net profit was to go to Laurence's younger brother Thomas and ¼ to Caroline Edmondston (Carrie, who married Charles Zogbaum) in the USA – the sister of Yankee Tom with whom their mother Mary lived until she died. Carrie also got the proceeds from the sale of all the household furniture, bedding, beds, bed and table linen. A number of American paintings and the silver also went to her, except two oil paintings, one of which was of Mally Sanderson and the other, the Raeburn painting of Eliza's grandfather, The Rev. Dr David Johnston. These went to Mary Edmondston (Coffin) and her husband Thomas the stockbroker in London. Sadly, when he was later bankrupted, they were sold to pay off debts and were lost to the family. Annuities and legacies were left to several members of the family including a £50 (£2900) annuity to Biot, a legacy of £50 (£2900) to William Sievwright's daughter, who was a good friend of Ursula's, and an additional annuity was to go to old Thomas' and Laurence's cousin, Ursula Archibald (1791-1877), daughter of their mother's sister Barbara, who had married James Archibald. Laurence got the Buness Estate all right, but the only other thing that Ursula left to him was her father's Cremona violin!

This event coincided with Jessie M. E.'s return to Unst. The trustees at Buness allowed her to build on Halligarth ground, a few hundred yards from that house, just beyond the fields, among a patchwork of flowers and outcrops of ochrous serpentine where the natural pastures slope up to the

Laurence Edmondston (1868-1915).

Florence Edmondston (Spence) at the time of her wedding.

279

peaks of Nikka Vord that shelters Balta Sound from the north. There she built the cottage of Wullver's Hool on the spot where she had sat as child and composed her first verses and stories, and where her brother Tom had done his first botanising. Her literary interests now turned to her beloved Shetland, her island home, its stories, language, folklore, antiquities and knitting. She became the Unst correspondent for *The Shetland Times*, grasped any opportunity to pass on her liberal and Christian views at public meetings, continued writing numerous articles for popular journals and, in 1913, published her memoriam to Dr Joseph Bell and a collection of sacred poems, *Leaves from a Psalmist's Life*, based on the Books of Samuel and David.

In January 1898, just prior to the death of Ursula, another circle closed. The Unst practice became vacant; the practice that had been her husband's, Dr Henry Saxby, and her father's, Dr Laurence Edmondston. Jessie M. E. immediately informed her third son in London, Dr T. E. Saxby. She told him that if he wanted to be considered she must have an immediate reply by telegraph, however, he must reply in code otherwise the local Post Office – and therefore everybody in Unst – would know. A telegraph message 'The cat jumps', duly arrived and she knew to put his name down for the vacancy. She knew because 'Tommy Kitten' had been her affectionate name for him as a wee boy! He got the position and later that year, he and his wife Maud (neé Furniss), also moved to Unst. Dr T. E. Saxby was returning to his roots, for he had been born in Ernesdaal in Baltasound 30 years previously. But it was to Halligarth, the original home of his mother, now vacated by his cousin Laurence who had moved into Buness, that he and Maud flitted. The house that had been built by old Thomas, for their mutual grandfather, now belonged to Laurence and it was to him that Dr T. E. paid the rent.

To the end, Jessie M. E. never flattered herself about the quality of her work. Late in life she wrote to her friend, the Lerwick historian E. S. R. Tait, that:

> "*I have also written a number of poems on thrilling topics of the day which have been much appreciated <u>and</u> well paid for! <u>That</u> is always the proof – to my thinking – of the popularity of poems, though it does not prove that they are high-class poetry! Most of which I have written was done under 'pressure and necessity', and was never as good as it might have been if I had had the leisure to 'amend and improve'. So perhaps it is best that much is lost.*"[6]

Dr T. E. Saxby with Lorna at Halligarth in 1906.

Much of the world's best literature has been written under 'pressure and necessity' and the best of Jessie M. E.'s work does not suggest that, had she had 'leisure', good as the best of her work was, it would have been substantially better. What was remarkable about Jessie M. E. was that she was able to produce so much good work when she had such responsibilities and pressures on her. By the end of her life she had published about 40 books and at the very least some 200 articles on a great range of topics. But Jessie M. E. should not just be remembered for her writings. She had an incredible influence, along with others, through her fascination with the Viking past, on the present Shetlanders' sense of identity with their Norse roots. She also ensured that Basil Anderson's *Auld Maunsie's Crö* survived to inspire Shetland's native dialect writers and bring pleasure to future generations. On her death, at 98, she was buried in the little graveyard at Halligarth next to her parents.

Jessie's brothers, the Rev. Biot and Thomas the stockbroker, both wrote many articles, the latter for journals such as *The Field*, and he also wrote a lively description of a day at the *haaf* fishing beyond the northern limits of the most northerly island in Britain for his parish magazine. Biot wrote several articles on Shetland for *Chambers' Journal* and combined with Jessie M. E. to write *The Home of a Naturalist* (1884). Neither of them returned to Shetland to live, but Biot returned to die. The next heir to Buness, another Laurence (1900-1987), was just six years old at the time when his grand-uncle Biot was staying at Buness in 1906. Young Laurence was being trained in table manners at breakfast one morning when his visiting grand-uncle Biot suddenly slumped forward over the table. Young Laurence, not understanding the seriousness of the situation, could not understand why, if *he* was not allowed his elbows on the table, his grand-uncle was allowed to sprawl in apparent sleep over his unfinished breakfast: Biot had died of a heart attack! Like others of the family, he was buried at Halligarth where he had been born and had spent his childhood.

Finale

It was almost exactly 100 years after the Buness estate came into the Edmondston family through the marriage of Dr Laurence Edmondston of Lerwick to Mally Sanderson and its inheritance by their son Thomas in 1800, that their great-grandson Laurence took over the estate and settled in Buness with Florence, his new wife. During the intervening period the value of the estate had increased dramatically and, as dramatically, fallen. When Laurence inherited in 1898 it was an estate with liabilities. The legacy of the profitable years of the exportation of chromate by old Thomas earlier in the century, his property in Lerwick, the bonds and cash in the bank, had all long gone through the generosity and profligacy of Yankee Tom and Ursula. Laurence had to start with a bank loan of £700 (£46,200) and hand over £900 (£59,400) at the end of the first year to his uncle, William Cameron Hamilton.[7] It was therefore a struggle from the start for him to put the estate on a sound financial footing. In 1900, Florence gave birth to their son and heir, Laurence who was to observe the death of his Uncle Biot, and two daughters quickly followed. Laurence, who had only got full control over the estate on Ursula's death, now found himself in serious debt.

Eventually, in 1913, he was forced into sequestration and the Buness estate was put up for sale to cover the liabilities. An offer of £9500 (£608,000) was made but refused. Laurence had been prevented from selling the estate 20 years earlier when he was a young man. This time there would be no return from a sale and it would be an inglorious end of the Edmondstons at Buness. On the 3rd April, 1914, a few months before the start of the First World War, the appointed trustees put the estate up for auction in two parts; Lot I – Buness at £16,000 (£992,000) and Lot II – Halligarth for £500 (£31,000). There was no bid for Lot I, but Dr T. E. Saxby – or rather his wife Maud who had the money – bought Halligarth. Thomas Saxby in turn, gave his mother, Jessie M. E., a gift of the ground and garden of Wullver's Hool.

281

For Jessie M. E. there were mixed feelings. Her father, Dr Laurence, had lived in Halligarth for many years as the tenant and only in the evening of his life had he come into its ownership. It had then passed to her brother David and then his son, and her nephew, Laurence, who had taken up residence back in Buness. This had made her feel estranged from *her* old family home. Now her son had ownership and it was a kind of closure to a family feud that had festered for as long as she could remember.

Then, before the future of the Buness estate had been settled, Laurence, like his father David, died at the early age of 47 in 1915, leaving the estate to his wife Florence who was to pass it on to her 15-year-old son. They remained in Buness under the threat of eviction all through the Great War and it was not until 1924 that the estate was again put up for auction, but once again there were no takers. Florence, however, this time found the money to pay off the debts and she brought Buness back into the Edmondston family for her son Laurence and for his descendants, with whom it still remains another 100 years on.

It is a curious quirk of fate that Buness came into the Edmondston family through a woman – Mally Sanderson, that it nearly left the family through another – Ursula Edmondston, and that it was saved for the family through yet another – Florence Spence of Uyea, none of whom were born Edmondstons. Similarly, Halligarth was bought for the Saxbys by a woman, Dr T. E. Saxby's wife, Maud.

The period of the rise and fall and resurrection of the Edmondstons at Buness was a time when other Edmondston properties that had been secured in the 16th and 17th centuries in the islands of Yell and Hascosay and elsewhere, were lost, as were the powers that the lairds and merchants had held over the tenant-fisherman. It was a time of revolutionary change just as it was for Charles and his family in North America where black slaves literally threw off *their* shackles and it was in this period that Shetland's identification with its Norse past became articulated by its intellectuals and adopted by most Shetlanders.

The Edmondstons and Saxbys, like everyone else, were haphazardly caught up in this turbulent tide. Some of them exploited its opportunities for power, influence and profit, some commented on it, yet others tried to influence its direction and rate of progress, but the majority, like ourselves, were simply driven like flotsam between the shoals. The daughters of Laurence and Mally had been unable, because of their sex, to make much of their lives outwith the narrow confines of family, but the five sons had struck out vigorously in various directions.

Of the five brothers and their spouses; Arthur was the visionary, author, doctor and knight of justice who destroyed his own talents; Thomas was the astute businessman and cornerstone of the family, who enjoyed his privileged position to the end; Henry settled for obscurity in Newcastle; Charles was the entrepreneur who lost his fortune through commercial misjudgement, but, within the slave-owning culture of Charleston, fulfilled his inner self with some integrity and generosity; Laurence, was the gifted naturalist, who lacked the mental and emotional strength of his brothers and settled instead for the position of sage and adored father; while Eliza was the devoted wife and mother who passed on her writing talents to her daughter.

Of the next generation, Tom the botanist achieved early fame, but had all his promise torn from him by a musket ball. Likewise, a fatal illness took away that of his brother-in-law, Dr Henry Saxby. The Rev. Biot and Thomas the stockbroker dabbled in natural history and literature, while David, who took over the running of the Buness Estate at a critical time, was content to be swept along by the agricultural changes that were happening all over Shetland and Scotland. But, of all this gifted family, only Jessie M. E. gave all her energy to *her* talents and was given the life, resilience and strength of purpose to fulfil them. There remains the enigma of the illegitimate Ursula and Yankee Tom the adventurer. Was it really Yankee Tom who made all the decisions in their life together, or might it have actually been Ursula, who emerged as a gritty personality after his death, who had pulled the strings?

Today, in the garden of Buness, the stone monument erected to Monsieur Jean Baptiste Biot and Captain Henry Kater by old Thomas over one hundred and eighty years ago, whose engraved letters had inspired the infant prodigy, Tom the botanist, still stands on the front lawn. From the back windows of the Haa can be seen an empty Halligarth and its little copse where Dr Laurence brought up his many children and where many of the family lie buried. Beyond, Ernesdaal is still occupied but where the land begins to climb to Nikka Vord and the Muckle Heog, Wullver's Hool, the cottage of Jessie M. E., is also empty. Looking out of the front windows, over the stone, lies the sheltered bay of Balta Sound, once the stopping place for Arctic explorers, Greenland whalers and a massive fleet of herring boats, now visited regularly only by local fishing boats and a small freighter that calls to collect talc, another derivative of serpentine. A kilometre and a half to the east can be seen the bare soils and rocks of the Keen of Hamar. There, surrounded in the early summer by the white and delicately veined flowers of young Tom's mouse-ear, lie old Thomas' abandoned chromate pits.

When all the walls have crumbled, the mouse-ear will still flower among the ochrous debris of serpentine as it did before anyone reached these islands, the *bonxie* will still lord it over intruders at Herma Ness and the *immer-gös* will still 'start' and dive into the cold green sea beyond the isle of Balta.

The story began with a letter from Laurence to his sweetheart Mally when he had to leave her in Unst and return to his practice in Lerwick. Their granddaughter, the author and poet Jessie M. E, died exactly 200 years after Laurence's birth. Of her many verses, *Da Moder Dy* – the underlying and barely detectable constant surge of the sea towards the land, discernible in the seventh wave only by the most experienced *haaf* fisherman's eye – has stood the test of time. It is a fitting tribute to a talented family and the many Shetlanders who lost their lives fishing in the seas around their islands.

> "We gaed to da haaf ae Johnsmas e'en
> Der was but a pirr o wind
> Some o wis towt dat wisna göd
> Cause he lifted an dan he linnd.
>
> …
>
> We took wir meedes an we laid our lines
> An da night drew doon ere lang
> But when morning cam, we wir baffin sair
> Mid waters baith faerce an strang.
>
> …
>
> Ye widna believe whit a stoor was dere
> Sae mad was da wind and sea
> We cut frae wir lines an we set reefed sail
> And dan shö was running free.

...
But whidder her coorse was for hame or fram
Göd only could tell, ye keen,
For da cloods hung low an da waves raise high –
Sic a tempest I never had seen.
...
Dan Maunsie he stimed weel inta da lift
An dan ipon da sea.
'Noo boys, look oot for da Moder Dy
An mark hoo shö rins,' said he.
...
Dan we took hert an we watched da sea
An we coontit da peerie dyes
And when shö wid lift da boat on her back
Da life in wir herts wid rise.
...
Yea hame we cam ta wir göd auld noost
And we tell'd o wir peril run
Dan Göd was blessed for da Moder Dy
So noo my story is done."[8]

FAMILY TREES

LAURENCE EDMONDSTON & MALLY SANDERSON
ANTECEDENTS

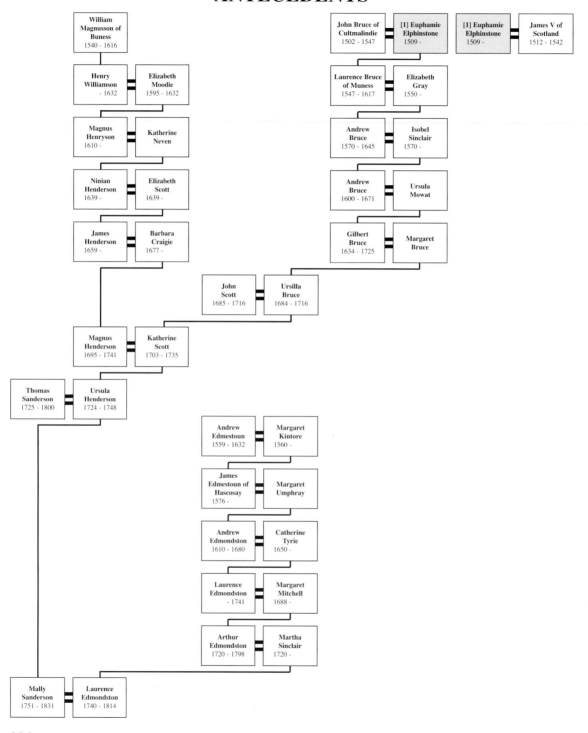

THE BROTHERS EDMONDSTON

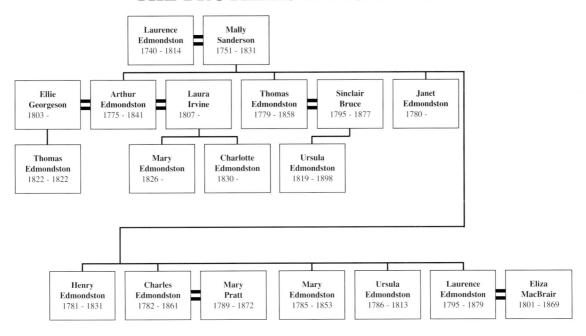

FAMILY OF LAURENCE AND ELIZA

Laurence Edmondston 1795 - 1879 === Eliza MacBrair 1801 - 1869

Thomas Edmondston 1825 - 1846

Mary Edmondston 1832 - 1898 === Andrew Symington 1824 - 1898

Biot Edmondston 1827 - 1906 === Adela Gray 1854 -

Jessie Helen Edmondston 1834 - 1841

Margaret Hamilton 1838 - 1871 === David Charles Edmondston 1837 - 1884 === Elizabeth Turner 1831 -

Isabella Edmondston 1839 - 1923

Margaret Edmondston 1841 - 1843

Jessie Margaret Edmondston 1842 - 1940 === Henry Linckmeyer Saxby 1836 - 1873

Margaret Ellen Edmondston 1845 - 1931 === William Cameron Hamilton 1847 - 1933

Thomas Edmondston 1847 - 1923 === Mary Coffin 1852 - 1924

Anne Edmondston 1863 - 1918

Margaret Edmondston 1865 -

Thomas Edmondston 1870 - 1905

Zachary Edmondston 1871 - 1871

Elizabeth Edmondston 1867 -

Henry Saxby 1860 -

Laura Saxby 1863 - 1868

Stephen Lindeman Saxby 1866 - 1941

Horace Dobell Saxby 1871 - 1959

Charles Fletcher Argyll Saxby 1873 - 1959

Thomas Edmondston Saxby 1869 - 1952 === Julie Furniss 1867 - 1939

Laurence Edmondston 1868 - 1915 === Florence Spence 1879 - 1970

FAMILY OF CHARLES EDMONDSTON

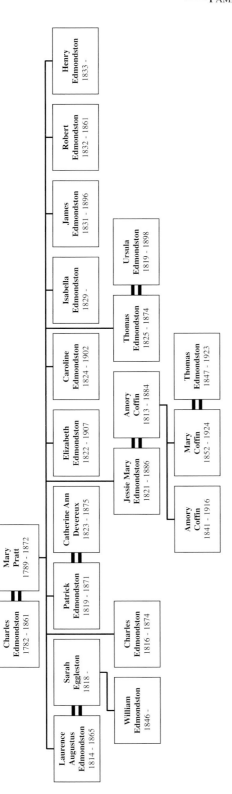

THE MOUATS AND HAMILTONS

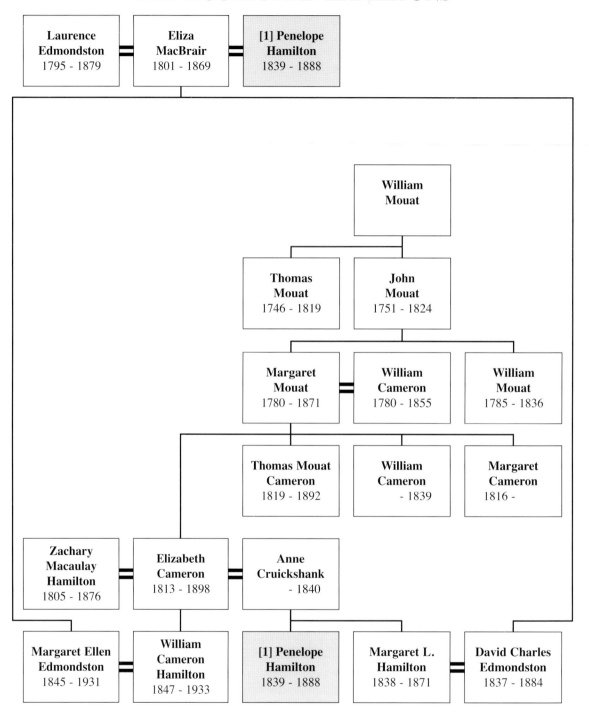

SANDERSONS, ARCHIBALDS, INGRAMS & BARCLAYS

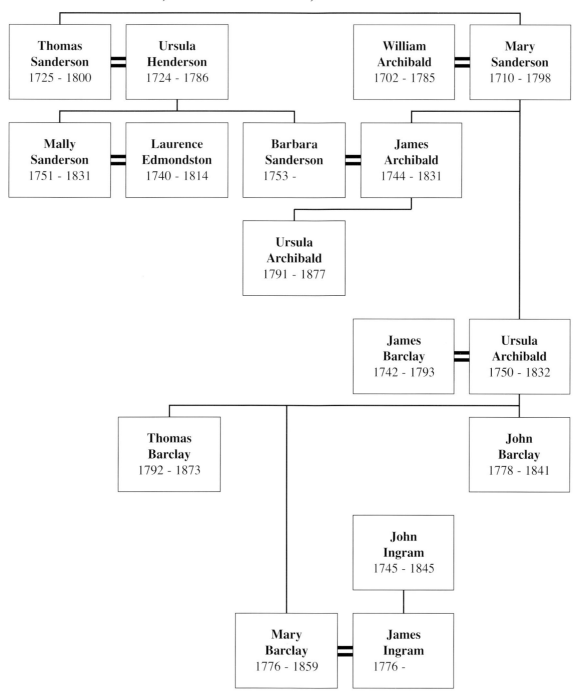

THE HAYS AND OGILVYS

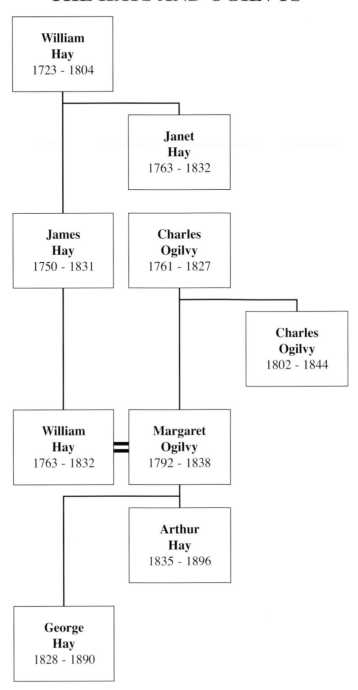

POSTSCRIPT

Jessie M. E. went on writing articles on Shetland's folklore and antiquities and contributing local news and comment to *The Shetland Times* right up to 1931. A year later, in her 90th year, she collected many of these articles together and published *Shetland Traditional Lore*. Two years later, when she was 92, she published her last work, *Threads from a tangled Skein* (1934), a collection of articles and poems.

Jessie M. E. became a Justice of the Peace, probably the first female to hold that post in Shetland. On the occasion of her 90th birthday in 1932, an illuminated address was presented to Jessie M. E. by Sir Robert W. Hamilton, grandson of the Rev. Zachary Hamilton of Bressay and MP for the County and Under-Secretary of State for the Colonies.[1] The event was held at Wullver's Hool and attended by many friends, relatives and local dignitaries. The address contained many signatories and came along with a sum of money. Typical of Jessie M. E., she used the money to erect a Memorial Cairn among the wild flowers close to Wullver's Hool, to the men of Shetland who gave their lives in the Great War, and what was left over she ensured went to the sick and needy. Jessie M. E. lived out the remaining years of her life quietly at Wullver's Hool, dying there in 1940, at the age of 98.

The ornithological tradition of the Edmondston and Saxby families continued with her son, Dr T. E. Saxby (1869-1952), who also continued the family tradition of practicing medicine, now in its fifth generation. Like his grandfather Dr Laurence Edmondston of Halligarth, T. E. Saxby also kept a weather record for the Meteorological Office for over half a century at Halligarth, and for this work the Air Ministry presented him with an inscribed barometer in 1937.[2] Between 1900 and 1929 he contributed some 21 papers to the *Zoologist*, the *Annals of Scottish Natural History* and the *Scottish Naturalist*, annotating his own copy of his father's book – *The Birds of Shetland* – with his new records. This copy was later used by the authors of the next book on the birds of Shetland – *The Birds and Mammals of Shetland* (1955) by Pat and Ursula Venables. Although T. E. Saxby pioneered motoring in Unst around 1906,[3] to help get around his practice, like his father and grandfather he was never found wanting when needed and would walk long distances in all weathers to attend his patients. In 1911 he became 'Knight, First Class, of the Royal Order of Vasa',[4] one of the highest Swedish honours and rarely bestowed on foreigners, as an acknowledgement of many years of medical ministration and care he gave to Swedish fishermen who frequented Balta Sound. In addition to his Swedish honour, T. E. Saxby was awarded an O.B.E. for his services to Unst and became, like his mother, a Justice of the Peace. On the occasion of his fiftieth year as the general practitioner, in 1948, it was said that he had never had a holiday '… except, perhaps, for a brief visit to Lerwick'.[5] He died in 1952 and was buried beside his mother and grandparents at Halligarth.

T. E. Saxby was survived by two of his brothers, Charlie Saxby (1873-1959) and Horace Saxby (1871-1959). The latter married Jane Goudie (1877-1951) of Dunrossness in the South Mainland. In 1926 they retired to the Haa at Gloup in North Yell overlooking Unst, where they stayed until 1951, when Jane died. Jane Goudie was a niece of the Shetland antiquarian, Gilbert Goudie, whom her mother-in-law, Jessie M. E. had known so well in Edinburgh. Like her uncle and mother-in-law, Jane too, had a great and enduring interest in Shetland folklore and dialect. She published a number of poems and songs in dialect and articles on Shetland folklore (under Jane

Saxby) and, on the death of Jessie M. E. in 1942, wrote an affectionate appreciation of her in *Chambers' Journal*. One of *her* poems was published in *A Shetland Anthology* (1998) alongside Jessie M. E.'s *Da Moder Dy*.

Charlie Fletcher Saxby (1873-1959), the youngest son, 'edited' and republished his uncle's – Thomas Edmondston (1825-1846) the botanist – *Flora of Shetland* (1903), and took to writing under the pseudonym Argyll Saxby. Between 1907 and 1925 he published at least 13 books for boys – very much in the style of his mother, several of which were serialised in the *Boy's Own Paper*. The second son, Stephen Lindeman (1866-1941), followed the footsteps of his great-grandfather and joined the merchant marine, eventually becoming a master mariner. He married Helen Arthur, a local girl from Burrafirth, and died in 1941.

It was Dr T. E. Saxby who was to ensure the continuation of that family connection in Unst. He and Maud had four children. The second, Ida (1900-1982), married Ian Sandison (1895-1980), whose father was a well-known merchant and landowner on Unst. They had three children, the third of whom was Ida Joy Sandison, and they lived at Houlland in Unst – where Ellen Edmondston had lived with her husband William Cameron Hamilton after they were married in 1871 – sheltered from the west by the high ridge that runs up almost the length of the west coast and terminates in Herma Ness. Joy and her brothers moved to the Scottish mainland and she became a secretary and administrator. Two other children of Dr T. E. Saxby, Lorna (1903-1994) and Stephen (1910-1994) never married and stayed in Halligarth almost right up to their deaths within months of each other in 1994: the last people to live in Halligarth. Stephen was the last of the family to contribute to our knowledge of Shetland's birds. He was a watcher on Herma Ness for a year and published several notes in the first volume of *Scottish Birds*.

Throughout this story two Shetland birds dominated the ornithological thoughts, discussions, conservation and investigation of the Edmondston and Saxby families. The first was the great northern diver and the second was the *bonxie*. While the former has markedly decreased as a visitor in recent years, the latter has steadily increased since Dr Laurence Edmondston of Halligarth persuaded his brother Thomas to give it protection on Herma Ness almost 200 years ago. In an article in the *Shetland News* in 1892, Thomas Edmondston, the London stockbroker, noted of the *bonxie* (great skua):

> "I adhere to my formerly expressed opinion that Hermaness is already stocked [with 8 pairs] to its utmost capacity, or nearly so; and, if the skuas in Unst are to be largely increased the projected area must be extended."

Thomas was writing before the gannet – the Herma Ness *bonxie's* chief victim for mugging – became established as a breeding bird there in 1917. In 1902, Dr T. E. Saxby observed in his *Notes from Shetland* in the *Zoologist*, that there were now two more *bonxie* colonies in Unst. Britain's tiny outpost of this seabird species, breeding elsewhere, principally in Faroe and Iceland, was at last secure. From then on the population steadily grew so that today there are more than 6000 pairs in Shetland as a whole, representing almost half the world's population of this species, drawing today's wildlife tourists from all corners of the globe. In international conservation terms, it is the most important bird in the islands. How proud would have been the various Edmondstons and Saxbys and Henry Edwardson, who continued as keeper, or watcher, for the Edmondstons on Herma Ness until 1911, when the RSPB took over his employment. Edwardson continued doing this job until his death in 1928. Adjacent to Herma Ness is what used to be the shore station for the Muckle Flugga lighthouse, on the former fish drying site sold by old Thomas Edmondston to the Lighthouse Commissioners. Part of the buildings are now private dwellings and part a visitor centre for the hundreds of summer visitors who come to see the skuas and the many other seabirds on what is now the National Nature Reserve of Herma Ness.

It is in the field of botany perhaps that the name of Edmondston in Shetland is most remembered, particularly in relation to Tom's mouse-ear, which after 170 years seems finally to have been recognised as a species (*Cerastium nigrescens*) in its own right. Tom had discovered his unique plant on the Keen of Hamar, but he had also discovered a second, tiny colony a short distance away. Although only half-a-mile separates the two populations, the plants of the latter site are recognised as a variation of the Keen of Hamar plant. They do not belong to a new species or even subspecies, but they neatly demonstrate the critical effect of isolation in evolution: Unst, after all, a little Galapagos!

Another curious fact, inexplicable at that time, that Tom had stumbled across among the rare arctic-alpines on the Keen of Hamar, was that the seeds of the arctic sandwort, when germinated in a different soil, produced plants strikingly different from their parents. A possible explanation for these differences was not uncovered until the middle of the 20th century by a descendant of the Spence family – a relation of Florence Spence who rescued the Buness Estate for her son. David Spence (1925-1985) was a brilliant botanist and ecologist and, like Tom, he had also explored the botany of the Keen of Hamar as a boy. From the 1950s to the 1970s he wrote a series of papers in the *Journal of Ecology* on the Keen of Hamar, identifying the odd and unique chemistry of the serpentine soil as the reason for the occurrence of certain features in many of the plants, including the arctic sandwort and Tom's mouse-ear. More recent research has indicated that it may be the porous nature of the soil which is responsible for their astonishing survival since the end of the Ice Age some 10,000 years ago. Such is the importance of soils and flora of the Keen of Hamar that it too has become a National Nature Reserve.

Tom's other contribution to our knowledge of Shetland's flora was of course his *Flora of Shetland*. Since Tom's day another list of plants of Shetland, pre-dating his, has been discovered, but it was never published. Incredibly, the next and most complete flora of Shetland, co-authored by another native Shetland botanist, Walter Scott, did not appear until 1987. Scott said of Tom's *Flora* and of his peculiar ideas on classification that he had tried to explain to his uncle Thomas,

> "Edmondston's devotion to the Shetland flora was unbounded, but it has to be admitted that his work, although remarkable for someone so young, is not without faults. The parts of Shetland outside Unst were much less well-known to him … He overlooks common species or fails to mention in his Flora ones he had quite correctly recorded in his earlier lists, perhaps as a result of the curious arrangement – a blend of the Linnaean and the 'natural' systems – adopted in the book."[6]

From our privileged position of retrospection it is easy to be critical of Tom's *Flora*, but it needs to be remembered that firstly, he was not only '*a mere lad*' in his early teens when he put most of the list together, but also a lad, to a great extent, self-taught in identification and classification. Secondly, travel in Shetland in those days was largely by boat, for the present network of roads did not exist until the meal roads were constructed during the potato famines in the 1840s. It was quite an achievement therefore for Tom to have covered so much of the Shetland archipelago.

There remains the question of the disaster of the competition at Edinburgh University when Tom was accused of cheating. One of the species he recorded for that competition was viviparous fescue, hitherto unknown in the Edinburgh area. His find was eventually confirmed on the Pentlands 156 years later in 1998[7]! This rediscovery and the fact that the plant is obviously still a rarity in that locality, speaks volumes for the assiduity of Tom's search and his discerning botanical eye in 1842, surely vindicating the authenticity of his collection.

It was Mary (Coffin) and her husband Thomas Edmondston the stockbroker who, in 1894, inherited both the portrait of Eliza's grandfather, the Rev. David Johnston by Sir Henry Raeburn and the portrait of Mally Sanderson in the style of Raeburn (possibly by George Watson), that were sold and disappeared into a Banker's Trust in America. Their third child was named Henry Saxby Edmondston (1878-1941). His second child, Mary Elizabeth Edmondston, following the family tradition, between 1944 and 1953 wrote three books for children set in Shetland, under the name Mary E. Edmondston.

In America, many of Charles and Mary's descendants dispersed from Charleston across the continent. One of those was Amory Coffin (1841-1916) who had described his very personal part in the Civil War. After the War he went into teaching and surveying and then finally found his niche in engineering, designing the structural features of many notable buildings of that period including Madison Square Garden and supervising the building of the New York Stock Exchange.

In 1984, several descendants of Charles and Mary who lived in the Charleston area, established the Charles and Mary Pratt Edmondston Endowed Scholarship Fund at the College of Charleston in their memory. The fund, with a contribution from Mary Seabrook, Charles and Mary's great-great-granddaughter, was set up to help deserving and successful students of business from across the State of South Carolina at the College of Charleston.

On the Battery, the neighbouring house on one side of the home that Charles had built, and then had to sell in the 1830s, was destroyed by Federal bombardments, while the house on the other side was destroyed by an earthquake in 1886. Charles' house, 21 East Battery, is now one of the few remaining classic antebellum mansions of Charleston and is a museum – Edmondston-Alston House – run by a non-profit making Trust.

In Shetland, the shape of the heart of Lerwick remains little changed, though the outskirts of the town have expanded enormously since Dr Arthur Edmondston's days, to now include his summer houses and the trees he planted at Seafield and Helendale. The south end of 'the Street', as it is still affectionately called in Lerwick, is still composed of the original houses – 'lodberries' (loading rocks) – that project into the sea. The majority, however, are now fronted by the harbour and the esplanade. The street remains intimate, flagged and narrow, and from it, steep, slender lanes still run up to the Hillhead between the houses, including the one on which old Thomas the laird bought his property. Just over the Hillhead is the fine County Library, originally established by Arthur's initiative. At the north end of the street Fort Charlotte, where Arthur lived and had his surgery in later life, still stands behind a high, rocky and stone-walled embankment. Today, the Street, the lanes and the Fort still retain the atmosphere of the past and it is not difficult to imagine how old Lerwick must have looked 200 years ago.

In 1994, Ida Joy Sandison inherited Halligarth on the death of her aunt and uncle, Lorna and Stephen Saxby. Joy developed a passion for Shetland's language and traditions, inherited no doubt, from her great grandmother, Jessie M E and began collecting small pieces connected with the 19th and 20th century cultural of Shetland, from toys to knitting and from Shetland words to sayings. She donated this, along with many pictures and artefacts connected with her family, particularly the books of her great grandmother and writings and drawings of Tom the botanist, to the Museum of Scotland. In 1998 Joy donated to the National Trust for Scotland her 1800 hectares of land in Unst, including Halligarth with its fields and the copse of trees that her great, great grandfather, Dr Laurence Edmondston, had planted more than 150 years previously.

His great grandson, also Laurence (1900-1987) became a Lt. Colonel in the Royal Scots and a teak forester in Burma – a colleague of Bill Williams in whose book Elephant Bill he features as H.E. In the 1930s, a visiting yachtsman, Hans Domizlaff, called in at Balta Sound and recorded1 their meeting and the traditional reception of the Edmondston family.

"We were met on the shore by a young man [Laurence] who greeted us courteously with an invitation to visit a house like a castle. I gathered from what he said that he had been born in this house, and that his father had ruled there as Laird of Unst … We were taken into the library of the Laird's house, and were received by a gracious lady [Florence] who told us of the story of the Island of Unst and of her family over a glass of whisky. Over the great bookcases hung elephant guns and hunting trophies. Everything bore witness to past glories. We learned that nowadays the old lady lived in the house alone. Her three children were scattered over the world …"

Laurence made one dramatic change to the Haa of Buness – in 1952 he blew up the large extension built by his great uncle Thomas in 1828 and the later north wing added by his great uncle Yankee Tom and great aunt Ursula, because, he said, that it was draughty and difficult to heat!

Laurence had two children, David and Geraldine. David joined the RAF as a fighter pilot, becoming a member of the Black Arrows formation aerobatic team and then pioneering the development of vertical take-off jet aircraft culminating in the Harrier 'jump-jet'. He returned to Shetland to pilot Islander aircraft on the regular services connecting all the islands, via tiny landing strips, to Mainland and to pilot the Air Ambulance Service. His wife, Jennifer, sometimes crewed with him as the qualified nurse. They settled back at Buness where David is the present laird and the fifth generation of Edmondstons to live there and have opened it as a Wolsey Lodge to summer visitors.

CHAPTER REFERENCES

Chapter One

[1]   Joy Sandison private papers
[2]   National Archives of Scotland, RS 45/9, part 1. ff. 284-5
[3]   *Zetland Family Histories* (1907), Grant, F. J., Lerwick
[4]   *A view of the ancient and present state of the Zetland Islands* (1809), Edmondston, A., Edinburgh, James Ballantyne & Co.
[5]   Ibid
[6]   Register of Edinburgh Apprentices
[7]   Shetland Archives, D 6/131/9/5
[8]   *The New Shetlander*, 54, E.S.R. Tait
[9]   SA, GD 144/141/41
[10] *A view of the ancient and present state of the Zetland Islands*
[11] National Library of Scotland, Hay of Hayfield papers, Acc. 3250 37/1
[12] Ibid
[13] SA, D 6/292/24
[14] NAS, RD 1/47, ff. 239-40
[15] SA, D 24, Box 21; NAS, RD 1/221, ff. 421; Fausti Ecclesiae Scoticanae (1915-28), Scott, H., Edinburgh; *Shetland Documents 1580-1611* (1994), Ballantyne, J.H. & Smith, B. eds., Lerwick, The Shetland Times Ltd.
[16] *Shetland Documents 1580-1611*
[17] *Zetland Family Histories*
[18] *Our Shetland Ancestry*, C.A., Pittendrigh (private papers Joy Sandison)
[19] NLS, Hay of Hayfield papers, Acc. 3250/4/1
[20] *Sons and daughters of Shetland* (1991), Robertson, M.S., Lerwick, Shetland Publishing Company
[21] SA, 2/7 E.S.R. Tait papers
[22] *Biographical notices of pharmacopola and presbyter* (1830), Edmondston, A., Edinburgh
[23] Ibid
[24] SA, D 40/59
[25] Joy Sandison private papers
[26] *Biographical notices of pharmacopola and presbyter*

Chapter Two

[1]   *A history of Scottish medicine* (2003), Dingwall, H.M., Edinburgh, University Press
[2]   *Memorials of his time* (1910), Cockburn, Sir Henry, Edinburgh
[3]   *Travellers in a bygone age* (1989), Flinn, D., Edinburgh, Scottish Academic Press
[4]   Robert Jameson and Shetland: A family history (1969), Sweet, J.M., *Scottish Genealogist* xvi, pp. 1-18
[5]   NLS, Hay of Hayfield papers, Acc. 3250, box 48, file 1 (1799-1811)

6   Comparing the purchasing power of money in GB from 1264-2002 (2004), Officer, L.H., Economic History Services, USA, Wade Forest University & What is the relative value? (2002), Williamson, S.H., Economic History Services, USA, Miami University

7   SA, D 40/59

8   Ibid

9   NLS, Hay of Hayfield papers, Acc. 3250, file 1 (1799-1811)

10 SA, D 12/153/17

11 Register of Sasines

12 NLS, Hay of Hayfield paper, Acc. 3250, Box 49, file 1 (1815)

13 *The home of a naturalist* (1888), Edmondston, B. & Saxby, J.M.E., London, Nisbet

14 Buness uncatalogued letter, June 1836

15 *The birds of Shetland* (2004), Eds. Pennington, M. et al, London, Christopher Helms

Chapter Three

1   SA, D 12/96

2   *A view of the ancient and present state of Zetland* (1809), Edmondston, A., Edinburgh, John Ballantyne & Co.

3   Ibid

4   Ibid

5   Gardie House letters no. 2015 & SA, D1/221

6   Edinburgh Review (1810), Anon, vol. xvii, pp. 135-155

7   Edinburgh University Library, Gen 1999/1/60,61,62; 129/81; 1996/15

8   EUL, Gen 129/82

9   Joy Sandison papers, ms, Jessie M.E. Saxby

10 *Slaves in the family* (1998), Ball, E., New York, Farrar, Strauss & Giroux

11 Joy Sandison papers, ms, Jessie M.E. Saxby

12 *Zetland family histories* (1907), Grant, F.J., Lerwick

Chapter Four

1   *Lines sacred to the memory of Ursula Edmondston* (1813), Edmondston, A., Privately published

2   *Memoirs of the life of Sir Walter Scott, Bart* (1893), Lockhart, J.G., London, Adam and Charles Black

3   SA, 2/7 E.S.R. Tait, draft for biography of Dr Arthur Edmondston

4   *Travellers in a bygone age* (1989), Flinn, D., Edinburgh, Scottish Academic Press

5   Ibid

6   Captain Henry Kater's Shetland journal (1966), Macmillan, D.S., *The New Shetlander*, 79, pp. 25-27 & 80, p. 24

7   EUL, Gen. 1999/1/62

8   Captain Henry Kater's Shetland journal

[9] Ibid

[10] SA, D 6/104/55

[11] *The life and correspondence of the late Samuel H. Ware* (1882), Mrs Hibbert Ware, Manchester, J.E. Cornish

[12] A letter to the chromate proprietors of the scattalds of Baliasta and Haroldswick (1839), Edmondston, T., Privately published

[13] EUL, Gen. 1996/15

[14] *The making of the Shetland landscape* (1985), Knox, S.A., Edinburgh, John Donald

[15] *The life and correspondence of the late Samuel H. Ware*

[16] Ibid

[17] A letter to the chromate proprietors of the scattalds of Baliasta and Haroldswick

Chapter Five

[1] SA, D 21/4

[2] Buness uncatalogued letter, 24th June, 1818

[3] Buness uncatalogued letter

[4] SA, D 14/222 & SC 12/53/13

[5] Buness uncatalogued letter, 13th December, 1821

[6] SA, SC 346/100/7/1861

[7] Buness uncatalogued letter, 4th May, 1821

[8] Buness uncatalogued letter, 3rd August, 1821

[9] Ibid

[10] SA, D 11/178/8

[11] SA, SC 12/6/1818/93

[12] SA, D 24/52/65/4

[13] SA, D 6/109/2

[14] SA, SC 12/6/1819/49 & SC 12/6/1821/49

[15] SA, SC 12/6/1821/44

[16] Contention Lane (1991), Strachan, D., *Shetland Life*, 123, p. 42

[17] SA, 2/7 E.S.R. Tait Draft for biography of Dr Arthur Edmondston

[18] SA, D 6/108/1

[19] SA, D 6/108/4

[20] SA, D 6/108/5

[21] SA, D 6/108/6

[22] NAS, CS 311/569 & CS 181/6419

[23] NAS, CS 1811/6417

[24] On the agriculture of the islands of Shetland (1874), Evershed, H., *Transactions of the Highland and Agricultural Society of Scotland* & SA, D 12/231/9

[25] *Two Calves in the House* (2005), Lewis, J., Ed. Bowes, H.R., Lerwick, Shetland Amenity Trust

[26] *Travellers in a bygone Shetland* (1989), Flinn, D., Edinburgh, Scottish Academic Press

[27] Ibid

[28] *Two Calves in the House* (2005), Lewis, J.

Chapter Six

[1] Middleton Place Foundation, Edmondston-Alston House papers
[2] *Charleston! Charleston! The History of a Southern City* (1991), Fraser, W.J., Charleston, University of South Carolina Press
[3] Pers. comm., Historian, Edmondston-Alston House
[4] Buness uncatalogued letter, 31st December, 1821
[5] Buness uncatalogued letter, 12th March, 1822
[6] Buness uncatalogued letter, 5th October, 1824
[7] Buness uncatalogued letter, 28th November, 1821
[8] Buness uncatalogued letter, 13th December, 1821
[9] *Shetland fishing saga* (1971), Goodlad, C.A., Lerwick, The Shetland Times Ltd.
[10] Gardie House letters
[11] SA, D 14/354
[12] SA, D 23/8/37
[13] SA, D 24/62/58
[14] Buness uncatalogued letter, March, 1822
[15] Ibid
[16] *William MacGillivray: Creatures of the air, land and sea* (1999), Ralph, R., London, Natural History Museum
[17] *The birds of Shetland* (2004), Eds. Pennington, M. et al, London, Christopher Helm
[18] *Memoirs of the Wernerian Natural History Society* (1819), vols. viii, ix and xxx, Edinburgh, Blackwood, Ballantyne etc
[19] Darwin's negro bird-stuffer (1978-79), Freeman, R.B., *Notes and Records of the Royal Society*, 33, pp. 83-86
[20] *Charles Darwin: Voyaging* (1995), Browne, J., London, Jonathan Cape

Chapter Seven

[1] *Unst, my island home* (1968), Sandison, C., Lerwick, The Shetland Times Ltd.
[2] NLS, Hay of Hayfield papers, Acc. 3250/31/1
[3] SA, D 24/11/4
[4] *A view of the ancient and present state of Zetland* (1909), Edmondston, A.
[5] Ibid
[6] Buness uncatalogued letter, 19th September, 1824
[7] Buness uncatalogued letter, 15th December, 1824
[8] Buness uncatalogued letter, 5th October, 1824
[9] Buness uncatalogued letter, 12th October, 1824
[10] Buness uncatalogued letter, 6th November, 1824
[11] *The home of a naturalist* (1888), Edmondston, B. & Saxby, J.M.E., London, Nisbet
[12] Buness uncatalogued letter, 31st December, 1821
[13] *The home of a naturalist*
[14] Sermon, prayer (undated), Edmondston, A., ms Shetland Library

15 Dr Edmondston's address to the subscribers to the Zetland County Library (1828), Privately published, Edinburgh, J. & D. Collie
16 NAS, CS 229; B/13/79
17 NAS, CS 44; 22nd January, 1828
18 Register of Sasines 1829
19 Ibid 1830
20 SA, D 6/109/10
21 SA, SC 12/6/1832/78
22 SA, SC 12/6/1832/109
23 SA, SC 12/6/1833/40a/2

Chapter Eight

1   SA, D 14/220
2   SA, 2/49 & *Shetland and its inhabitants* (1871), Cowie, R.I.
3   Adam Clarke's collected works, vol. xiii pp. 370-2 & 375
4   *Travellers in a bygone Shetland* (1989), Flinn, D., Edinburgh, Scottish Academic Press
5   Adam Clarke's collected works
6   Buness uncatalogued letter, 1831
7   Buness uncatalogued letter, June 1836
8   Ibid
9   *A narrative of certain proceedings connected with the management of the Zetland County Library* (1831), Edmondston, A., Privately published, Edinburgh, J. & D. Collie
10 *An excursion to the Shetland Islands* (1832), Atkinson, G.C., Typed copy, Shetland Library
11 A visit to Shetland in 1832 (1832), Charlton, E., *Old Lore Miscellany*, vols. iii, iv & v
12 *Shetland Fishing Saga* (1971), Goodlad, C.A., Lerwick, The Shetland Times Ltd.
13 *Journal of an expedition to Shetland in June, July and August 1834* (1834), Charlton, E., OLM vols. vi, vii & viii

Chapter Nine

1   *Travellers in a bygone Shetland* (1989), Flinn, D., Edinburgh, Scottish Academic Press
2   *The home of a naturalist* (1888), Edmondston, B. & Saxby J.M.E., London, Nisbet
3   Buness uncatalogued letter, 20th January, 1847
4   *The home of a naturalist*
5   Ibid
6   Ibid
7   Ibid
8   Ibid
9   Ibid
10 Pers. comm. Mae Sutherland
11 *The home of a naturalist*

[12] Ibid

[13] Jessie (M.E.) Saxby

[14] *The young Shetlander* (1868), Edmondston, E., Edinburgh, Mould & Todd

[15] Ibid

[16] Buness uncatalogued letter, 24th October, 1823

[17] *Notes on Norway* (1839), Hooker, W.D., Privately published

[18] Ibid

[19] Ibid

[20] Ibid

[21] *The young Shetlander*

[22] Ibid

[23] Ibid

[24] *Threads from a tangled skein* (1934), Saxby, J.M.E., Lerwick, T. & J. Manson

[25] SA, D 14/219

[26] Pers. comm. Joy Sandison

[27] *Unst, my island home* (1968), Sandison, C., Lerwick, The Shetland Times Ltd.

[28] The Unst chrome mines (1988), Ferguson, D.M., *Shetland Life*, March

[29] *Statistical account of the Shetland Islands* (1841), Ingram, J. & J.

[30] Register of Sasines

[31] Buness uncatalogued letter, 5th February, 1839

[32] Burke and Hare: A Shetland link (1963), Edmondston, L., *The New Shetlander*, 66

[33] Buness uncatalogued letter, 14th September, 1847

[34] Pers comm. Joy Sandison

[35] *Fredrick Hill: An autobiography of fifty years in time of reform* (1894), ed. Hill, C.

[36] *The young Shetlander*

[37] Ibid

[38] Ibid

Chapter Ten

[1] SA, D 24/73/3

[2] SA, TO 10/125/4

[3] SA, D 6/109/11

[4] SA, SC 12/6/1834/126

[5] SA, SC 12/6/1834/152

[6] NLS, Hay of Hayfield papers, Acc. 3250 40/1

[7] Ibid

[8] Orkney Archives, D 2/10/9

[9] Ibid

[10] Hints of a plan by which a separate Representative in Parliament may be obtained for Shetland (1863), Anderson, A., Privately published

[11] *The Shetland Times* (1831), 4th November

[12] *To the electors of Zetland* (1836), Edmondston, A., Privately published

13 OA, D 2/28/10
14 SA, D 11/10/1
15 *A letter to the chromate proprietors of the scattolds of Baliasta and Haroldswick* (1839), Edmondston, T.
16 NAS, CS 311/421
17 Private papers of Laurence Edmondston Coffin, unpublished will of Charles Edmondston
18 *America: A narrative history* (1997), Tindall, G.B. & Shi, D.E., New York, W.W. Norton & Co.
19 Middleton Place Foundation, Edmondston-Alston House archives
20 *Charleston! Charleston! The History of a Southern City* (1991), Fraser W.J., University of South Carolina Press, Charleston
21 South Carolina Department of Archives in S.C. Historical Society Charleston
22 Pers. comm. W. Saunders, Edmondston-Alston House Historian
23 *South Carolina Historical Society magazine* (1836), Charleston, Schirmer
24 *South Carolina Historical Society*

Chapter Eleven

1   Buness uncatalogued letter, 30th March, 1840
2   Buness uncatalogued letter, 21st November, 1840
3   *The young Shetlander* (1868), Edmondston, E., Edinburgh, Mould & Todd
4   Ibid
5   Ibid
6   Ibid
7   Ibid
8   Ibid
9   Ibid
10 Ibid
11 Ibid
12 Ibid
13 Ibid
14 Ibid
15 Ibid
16 Ibid
17 Ibid
18 Buness uncatalogued letter, 8th January, 1841
19 NLS, Hay of Hayfield Papers, Acc. 3250 40/1
20 SA, SA 2/49
21 SA, SC 12/6/1840/284
22 SA, SA 2/7
23 SA, D 12/101/13/21
24 *The young Shetlander*

Chapter Twelve

[1] *The young Shetlander* (1868), Edmondston, E., Edinburgh, Mould & Todd
[2] *Edmondston's Flora* (1903), Revised edition, Saxby, A.
[3] *The young Shetlander*
[4] Ibid
[5] Ibid
[6] Ibid
[7] Buness uncatalogued letter, 13th May, 1842
[8] *The young Shetlander*
[9] Ibid
[10] Ibid
[11] Buness uncatalogued letter, 29th September, 1842
[12] Buness uncatalogued letter, 4th October, 1842
[13] Ibid
[14] Ibid
[15] *The young Shetlander*
[16] Ibid
[17] Buness uncatalogued letter, 15th December, 1842
[18] *The young Shetlander*
[19] *Auld Lerwick* (1894), Saxby, J.M.E., Lerwick, Church Improvement Scheme Bazaar
[20] Ibid
[21] SA, SA 2/49
[22] The Ingrams of Unst (1967), Graham, J., *The New Shetlander* 80
[23] *Zoologist* (1843), p. 365
[24] *The Phytologist* (1843), 1 pp. 497-500
[25] Buness uncatalogued letter, 30th October, 1843
[26] Buness uncatalogued letter, 16th March, 1843
[27] *The young Shetlander*
[28] Buness uncatalogued letter, 21st August, 1844
[29] *The young Shetlander*
[30] Buness uncatalogued letter, 26th October, 1844
[31] Buness uncatalogued letter, 22nd November, 1844
[32] *The young Shetlander*
[33] Buness uncatalogued letter, 24th November, 1844

Chapter Thirteen

[1] *The young Shetlander* (1868), Edmondston, E., Edinburgh, Mould & Todd
[2] Ibid
[3] Ibid
[4] Ibid
[5] Ibid

6   Ibid

7   Buness uncatalogued letter, 26th January, 1845

8   *The young Shetlander*

9   *Phytologist* (1845), vol. ii p. 438

10 Buness uncatalogued letter, 24th March, 1845

11 Buness uncatalogued letter, 16th April, 1845

12 Buness uncatalogued letter, 17th April, 1845

13 *The young Shetlander*

14 Ibid

15 Ibid & Buness uncatalogued letter, 25th April, 1845

16 *Dictionary of British and Irish botanists and horticulturalists* (1977), Desmond, R., London, Taylor & Francis

17 *The young Shetlander*

18 Ibid

19 Buness uncatalogued letter, 2nd May, 1845

20 *The young Shetlander*

21 Ibid

22 Buness uncatalogued letter, 7th May, 1845

23 Buness uncatalogued letter, 14th May, 1845

24 Buness uncatalogued letter, 13th May, 1845

25 Buness uncatalogued letter, 14th May, 1845

26 Ibid

27 *The young Shetlander*

28 Ibid

29 Buness uncatalogued letter, 14th May, 1845

30 Ibid

31 Buness uncatalogued letter, 25th May, 1845

32 *The correspondence of Charles Darwin 1809-1882* (1983-94), Eds. Burkhardt, F.H. & Smith, S. et al., vol. 3, Cambridge, University Press

33 Buness uncatalogued letter, 14th May, 1845

34 Ibid

35 *The young Shetlander*

36 Buness uncatalogued letter, 14th May, 1845

37 Ibid

38 *The young Shetlander*

39 Ibid

40 Ibid

41 Ibid

42 Ibid

43 Ibid

44 Ibid

45 Ibid

46 Ibid

[47] *Narrative of the voyage of H.M.S. Herald during the years 1845-51* (1853), Seemann, B., London, Reeve & Co.

[48] *The young Shetlander*

[49] Log of H.M.S. Herald, Kew, Public Records Office

[50] *Narrative of the voyage of H.M.S. Herald*

[51] *Edmondston's Flora* (1903), Revised edition, Saxby, C.F.A., Edinburgh, Oliphant, Anderson & Ferrier

[52] Buness uncatalogued letter, 13th June, 1846

[53] *The young Shetlander*

[54] Ibid

[55] Ibid

[56] *The correspondence of Charles Darwin 1809-1882*

[57] On the vegetation of the Galapagos archipelago, as compared with that of some other tropical islands and of the continent of America (1851), Hooker, J.D., Trans. Act. Linn. Soc. Lond. 10, pp. 235-262

[58] *The correspondence of Charles Darwin 1809-1882*

[59] *The young Shetlander*

Chapter Fourteen

[1] Harvie Brown papers, 16/266

[2] Buness uncatalogued letter, 7th July, 1845

[3] Buness uncatalogued letter, 14th July, 1845

[4] Buness uncatalogued letter, 10th August, 1845

[5] NLS, Hay of Hayfield papers, Acc. 3250/35/1

[6] *Travellers in a bygone Shetland* (1989), Flinn, D., Edinburgh, Scottish Academic Press

[7] *The making of the Shetland landscape* (1985), Knox, S.A., Edinburgh, John Donald

[8] NAS, HD 13/15

[9] SA, HD 17/49 Highland Destitution Board

[10] NAS, HD 13/5

[11] NAS, HD 13/15

[12] Buness uncatalogued letter, 20th January, 1847

[13] Buness uncatalogued letter, 17th March, 1847

[14] Buness uncatalogued letter, undated

[15] Buness uncatalogued letter, 14th September, 1847

[16] SA, D 14/355

[17] Buness uncatalogued letter, 14th September, 1847

[18] Ibid

[19] SA, SC 12/53/12

[20] SA, D 12/128/9

[21] Buness uncatalogued letter, 15th June, 1850

[22] *Journal to the Orkneys and Shetlands* (1849), Cracroft, S., ms Cambridge, Scott Polar Research Institute

23 *Journal of a visit to the Orkneys and Shetlands* (1849), Franklin, Lady J., ms Cambridge, Scott Polar Research Institute

24 *Fatal Passage* (2001), McGoogan, K., Canada, Harper Collins

25 *Journal of a Secesh lady: The diary of Catherine Ann Devereux Edmondston 1861-1866* (1979), Eds. Crabtree, B.G. & Paton, J.W., Raleigh Division of Archives & History, Dept. of Cultural Resources, North Carolina

26 Buness uncatalogued letter, 25th April, 1848

27 Buness uncatalogued letter, 14th November, 1849

28 Private papers, Laurence E. Coffin, uncatalogued

29 Journey from New Orleans to California (1855), Edmondston, E., Edinburgh, *Chambers' Journal*, 100

30 Buness uncatalogued letter, 20th August, 1850

31 Buness uncatalogued letter, 21st April, 1853

32 Buness uncatalogued letter, 8th May, 1854

33 Buness uncatalogued letter, 30th December, 1854

34 *The lighthouse Stevensons* (1999), Bathurst, B., London, Harper Collins

Chapter Fifteen

1 *William MacGillivray: Creatures of air, land and sea* (1999), Ralph, R., London, Natural History Museum

2 Buness uncatalogued letter, 27th June, 1851

3 Buness uncatalogued letter, 12th February, 1853

4 *The correspondence of Charles Darwin 1821-1861* (1983-94), Burkhardt, F.H., Smith, S., et al., Cambridge, University Press

5 Buness uncatalogued letter, 3rd May, 1856

6 *The variation of animals and plants under domestication* (1886), Darwin, C., London, Murray

7 *The correspondence of Charles Darwin 1821-1861*

8 Ibid

9 Ibid

10 A multi-disciplinary and inter-scientific study of the Saxby Gale: October 4-5 1869 hybrid-hurricane and record storm surge (1999), Rufman, A., *CMOS Bulletin*, SCMO, vol. 27 no. 3, pp. 67-75

11 SA, D 11/20/18

12 *The home of a naturalist* (1888), Edmondston, B. & Saxby, J.M.E., London, Nisbet

13 Private papers Joy Sandison, uncatalogued

14 Private papers Joy Sandison, uncatalogued

15 Jessie M.E. Saxby: An appreciation 1842-1940 (1942), Saxby, J., Edinburgh, *Chambers' Journal*, 652, March

16 Ibid

17 Private papers Joy Sandison, uncatalogued

18 The pioneer of free press (1901), Saxby, J.M.E., Edinburgh, *Chambers' Journal* , 176

19 Buness uncatalogued letter, 26th April, 1855

20 Buness uncatalogued letter, 8th May, 1855
21 Buness uncatalogued letter, 11th March, 1856
22 Buness uncatalogued letter, 28th June, 1856
23 Buness uncatalogued letter, 6th September, 1856
24 Buness uncatalogued letter, 30th December, 1854
25 Buness uncatalogued letter, 31st March, 1857
26 SA, SA 2/49
27 Ibid
28 Buness uncatalogued letters, 14th November, 1857 & 24th December, 1857
29 Buness uncatalogued letter, 19th September, 1858

Chapter Sixteen

1   SA, D 14/213
2   Register of Sasines
3   SA, SA 2/49
4   Court of Session 346/100/7/1861
5   *The Victorian* (2002), Wilson, A.N., London, Hutchinson
6   SA, D 24/29/51
7   SA, D 24/29/52
8   NAS, CS 46 no. 100, July 1861
9   Private papers Laurence E Coffin; uncatalogued letter of Amory Coffin, 1918
10 Buness uncatalogued letter, 7th June, 1863
11 *Journal of a Secesh lady: The diary of Catherine Ann Devereux Edmondston 1861-1866*
    (1979), Eds. Crabtree, B.G. & Paton, J.W., Raleigh Division of Archives & History Dept. of
    Cultural Resources, North Carolina
12 Buness uncatalogued letter, 6th May, 1866
13 SA, D 12/116/6/6
14 Buness uncatalogued letter, 15th January, 1864
15 Buness uncatalogued letter, 7th May, 1864
16 Buness uncatalogued letter, 25th August, 1864
17 Buness uncatalogued letter, 20th February, 1866
18 Buness uncatalogued letter, 9th May, 1866
19 Buness uncatalogued letter, 6th June, 1866

Chapter Seventeen

1   *The home of a naturalist* (1888), Edmondston, B. & Saxby, J.M.E., London, Nisbet
2   SA, D 12/116/6/5
3   SA, D 12/116/6/2
4   SA, D 12/116/6/7
5   Buness uncatalogued letter, May 1863
6   Buness uncatalogued letter, 18th January, 1864

7 Buness uncatalogued letter, 17th October, 1864
8 Buness uncatalogued letter, 12th May, 1865
9 Buness uncatalogued letter, 6th May, 1866
10 Buness uncatalogued letter, 8th August, 1863
11 Buness uncatalogued letter, 6th October, 1863
12 Notes on some recent excavations in the island of Unst, Shetland (1865), Edmondston, T., *Proc. Of the Soc. Of Ant. Of Scot.*, vol. ix, pp. 283-287
13 On the discovery of large Kist-vaens on the 'Muckle Heog' in the island of Unst (Shetland) 1863-64, Roberts, G.E., *Memoir of the Anthropological Soc. Of London* vol. 1, pp. 296-7 & Report on explorations into the archaic anthropology of the islands of Unst, Bressay and the mainland of Zetland 1865-66, Hunt, J., *Memoir of the Anthropological Soc. Lond.*, vol. II, pp. 294-300
14 SA, D 12/116/6/10
15 Buness uncatalogued letter, 29th August, 1864
16 Buness uncatalogued letter, November 1866
17 *My holidays* (1867), Chambers, W.
18 Buness uncatalogued letter, September, 1863 & SA, D 12/116/6/5
19 *Birds of Shetland* (2003), Eds. Pennington, M. et al., London, Christopher Helm
20 Profiles from the past: Arthur Anderson (1959), Manson, T.M.Y., *The New Shetlander*, 50
21 Words peculiar to Shetland: Prince Louis-Lucien Bonaparte in Shetland 1858 (1996-97), R.O.S.C. *Review of Scottish Culture*, 10, pp. 108-112
22 Buness uncatalogued letter, 3rd May, 1867
23 *An Etymological Glossary of the Shetland and Orkney dialect* (1866), Edmondston, T., Edinburgh, Adam & Charles Black
24 Einar Seim farmer and folklorist (1990), Gronneburg, R., *Shetland Life*, September
25 Buness uncatalogued letters, 14th March, 5th April and 24th April, 1866
26 Buness uncatalogued letter, 10th February, 1866
27 Report of Her Majesty's Commissioners (1884), Napier Commission
28 Buness uncatalogued letter, 13th August, 1866
29 Buness uncatalogued letter, 18th August, 1866
30 SA, SA 2/49 Unst Kirk Session Minute Book 1844-1892
31 *The one wee lassie* (1875), Saxby, J.M.E., Edinburgh, Andrew Elliott
32 *Joseph Bell MD: An appreciation by an old friend* (1913), Saxby, J.M.E., Edinburgh, Oliphant, Anderson & Ferrier
34 Buness uncatalogued letter, 23rd May, 1869
35 SA, SC 12/53/12
36 SA, SC 12/53/13

Chapter Eighteen

1 *Toons and tenants* (2000), Smith, B., Lerwick, The Shetland Times Ltd.
2 On the agriculture of the islands of Shetland (1874), Evershed, H., *Trans. Of the Highland and Agricultural Soc. of Scot.* 4th series

3   *Scotsman*, 17th July, 1883, Crofter Commission Hearing
4   SA, D 12/172/7/2
5   Parliamentary Papers (1884), xxxiii, minutes of evidence, pp. 1291-5
6   On the agriculture of the islands of Shetland
7   Clearances in Unst (1986), Johnson, R.L., *The New Shetlander*, 157
8   *Toons and tenants*
9   SA, D 11/172/6/3
10   Pers. comm. Mae Sutherland
11   *Clearances in Unst*
12   *Scotsman*, 17th July, 1883, Crofter Commission Hearing
13   SA D 9/342
14   *John Walker's Shetland* (2005), Gear, W., Lerwick, The Shetland Times Ltd.
15   SA, D 12/116/6/14
16   *John Walker's Shetland*
17   Ibid
18   Buness uncatalogued letter, 18th February, 1870
19   Buness uncatalogued letter, 2nd July, 1870
20   The making of modern Shetland (1976), Smith, H.D., *The New Shetlander*, 118
21   Minutes of evidence before the Commission on the Truck System, 23rd January, 1871, Edinburgh
22   Minutes of evidence before the Commission on the Truck System, 19th January, 1872, Baltasound
23   *Joseph Bell: An appreciation by an old friend* (1913), Saxby, J.M.E., Edinburgh, Oliphant, Anderson & Ferrier
24   *Threads from a tangled skein* (1934), Saxby, J.M.E., Lerwick, T. & J. Manson
25   Buness uncatalogued letters, October & 24th November, 1871
26   Pers. comm. Joy Sandison
27   Buness uncatalogued letter, January 1867
28   Buness uncatalogued letter, 19th August, 1874
29   Buness uncatalogued letter, 8th December, 1875
30   SA, SC 2/49

Chapter Nineteen

1   SA, D 21/5
2   SA, D 11/135/3
3   *Joseph Bell: An appreciation by an old friend* (1913), Saxby, J.M.E., Edinburgh, Oliphant, Anderson & Ferrier
4   SA, D 21/5
5   Shetland and the Napier Commission 1883-1893 (1983), Smith, B. Lerwick, *The New Shetlander*, 145
6   Report of Her Majesty's Commissioners (1884), Napier Commission
7   Parliamentary Papers (1834), Napier Commission, xxxiii, p. 1334

8 Shetland phrase and idiom (1907-08), Saxby, J.M.E., *Old Lore Miscellany*, 1 pp. 268-9
9 NAS, CS 318/69/90
10 NAS, CS 46, no. 76, October 1894
11 NAS, RD 5/2613, pp. 50-60
12 NAS, CS 240 E/8/4
13 NAS, CS 249/2107
14 SA, D8/349/9
15 SA, D 4/355/6
16 SA, D 6/292/10
17 Buness uncatalogued paper, 19th March, 1891
18 *Shetland News*, 15th April, 1899
19 Ibid
20 National Museum of Scotland, J.A. Harvie-Brown Papers, 16/266
21 SA, D 21/5
22 Norse imagery in Shetland 1800-1914 (1993), Chen, B., Ph.D. thesis, University of Manchester
23 SA, D 11/135/3
24 *The Shetland Times*, 14th January, 1893
25 *Fond Hopes Destroyed* (2005), Prior, M., Lerwick, The Shetland Times Ltd.
26 *The Shetland Times*, 9th June, 1894
27 SA, D 21/5
28 Ibid

Chapter Twenty

1 *Joseph Bell MD: An appreciation by an old friend* (1913), Saxby, J.M.E., Edinburgh, Oliphant, Anderson & Ferrier
2 Norse imagery in Shetland (1983), Cohen, B., Ph.D. thesis, Manchester University
3 SA, D 21/4
4 *Heim-Laund and Heim-Folk* (1893), Saxby, J.M.E., Edinburgh, R. & R. Clark
5 SA, SA 2/49
6 SA, D 6/262/2
7 CS 318/69/90
8 *A Shetland anthology* (1998), Eds. Graham, J.G. & L.I., Lerwick, Shetland Publishing Co.

Postscript

1 Profiles from the past (1964), Saxby, L., *The New Shetlander*, 70
2 SA, D 11/21/13
3 Dr T. E. Saxby – A revered doctor in Unst (2003), Fisher, S., *Shetland Life*, February
4 SA, D 11/21/17
5 *The Shetland Times*, September 1952

[6] *The Flowering Plants and Ferns of the Shetland Islands* (1987), Scott, W. & Palmer, R., Lerwick, The Shetland Times Ltd.

[7] Pers comm. Douglas McKeen, BSBI Plant Recorder for the Pentland Hills

[8] *Dirk III: Jottings from the log and camera of a cruising yachtsman* (1937), Domizlaff, H., London, John Miles

SELECTED PUBLICATIONS BY THE FAMILY

Dr Arthur Edmondston (1775-1841)

Edmondston, A. (1802) *An account of an ophthalmia which appeared in the Second Regiment of the Argyleshire Fencibles in the month of February, March and April 1802*. London, J. Callow (Medical Bookseller).

Edmondston, A. (1806) *A treatise on the various consequences of ophthalmia*. Privately published. Edinburgh, Blackwood.

Edmondston, A. (1808) *History and laws of the Iberian Patriotic Society*. Privately published. Edinburgh, James Clarke.

Edmondston, A. (1809) *A View of the Ancient and Present State of the Zetland Islands*. 2 Vols.

Edmondston, A. (1810) Observations on the Natural and Medical Histories of the Zetland Sheep. *Memoir of the Wernerian Natural History Society*. Vol i: 258-73. Printed privately as a pamphlet.

Edmondston, A. (1810) *Dr Edmondston's reply to the strictures of Orcadensis*. Privately published. Edinburgh, Walker & Greig.

Edmondston, A. (1810) My Zetland Maid, The sailor's adieu to Zetland, Henry's Return. Edinburgh, Wallace & Greig. *NLS, S 218c. 1 (25[1-3])*.

Edmondston, A. (1811) Observation on the Natural History of the Colymbus Immer. *Memoir of the Wernerian Nat. Hist. Soc*. Vol ii: 232-7.

Edmondston, A. (1813) *Lines sacred to the memory of Ursula Edmondston*. Privately published. Newcastle, Preston & Heaton.

Edmondston, A. (1813) *Observations on the causes and probable consequences of the war in which Great Britain and the United States of America are at present engaged*. Privately published. Edinburgh, James Ballantyne.

Edmondston, A. (1820) *Observations on the Nature and Extent of the Cod Fishery*. Edinburgh, Oliver & Boyd.

Edmondston, A. (1821) Observations on the Natural History of some Species of the Genus Larus, or Gull Tribe. *Edinburgh Philosophical Journal*. Vol 5: 168-73.

Edmondston, A. (1823) *A letter to Sir William Rae, Lord Advocate of Scotland*. Privately published. Edinburgh.

Edmondston, A. (1825) *A view of the conduct of the Wesleyan preachers in the Zetland Islands (By a calm observer)*. Privately published. Leith, W. Reid & Son.

Edmondston, A. (1826) *Paraphrase of Chapter VI of the Book of Daniel*. Privately published. Leith, W. Reid & Son.

Edmondston, A. (1828) *Dr Edmondston's address to the subscribers to the General Zetland Library*. Privately published. Edinburgh, J. & D. Collie.

Edmondston, A. (1829) *Advertisement*. Privately published.

Edmondston, A. (1830) *Biographical Notices of Pharmacopola and Presbyter*. Privately published pamphlet. Edinburgh.

Edmondston, A. (1830) Situation, general appearance and climate of the Zetland Islands. Brewster, D. (ed.) In *The Edinburgh Encyclopaedia*. Vol XVIII: 105-136.

Edmondston, A. (1831) *A brief inquiry into the nature and causes of the cholera which has prevailed, and at present prevails, in the Russian armies*. Privately published. Edinburgh, John Anderson.

Edmondston, A. (1831) *A narrative of certain proceedings connected with the management of the General Zetland Library*. Edinburgh, J. & D. Collie.

Edmondston, A. (1836) *To the electors of Zetland*. Privately published.

Edmondston, A. (1837) *A few observations on the pernicious effects which result from the indiscriminate application of irritating substances*. Privately published. Wick, John O'Groat Journal.

Edmondston, A. (no date) *Sermon, Prayer and poem*. Privately published.

Edmondston, A. (n.d.) *Essay on the establishment of a Literary Society in Lerwick*. Hand written.

Edmondston, A. (n.d.) *Observations on the fisheries of Shetland*.

Edmondston, A. (n.d.) *The Zetlandic Inquirer*. (an 'introduction to an unfinished work').

Dr Henry Edmondston (1781-1831)

Edmondston, H. (1814) *Hints on Hydrophobia*. pp. vi. 44, xxii.in S. Hodgson. Newcastle-upon-Tyne.

Edmondston, H. (1828) *Observations on cowpox and on the necessity of adopting legislative measures for enforcing vaccination*. London.

Thomas Edmondston (1779-1858)

Edmondston, T. (1839) *A letter to the chromate proprietors of the scattolds of Baliasta and Haroldswick*. Privately published.

Dr Laurence Edmondston (1785-1879)

Edmondston, L. (1821) Account of a new species of Larus shot in Zetland. *Memoir of the Wernerian Nat. Hist. Soc*. Vol IV: 176-81.

Edmondston, L. (1822) Observations on the Snowy owl (Stryx Nictea; Linn.) *Memoir of the Wernerian Nat. Hist. Soc*. Vol IV: 157-60.

Edmondston, L. (1822) Additional account of the Iceland Gull. *Memoir of the Wernerian Nat. Hist. Soc*. Vol IV: 182-85.

Edmondston, L. (1822) Observations on the Immer Goose of Zetland. *Memoir of the Wernerian Nat. Hist. Soc*. Vol IV: 207-12.

Edmondston, L. (1822) Some observations on the Greenland Kittiwake Columbus Grylle. *Read to the Wernerian Nat. Hist. Soc., but not published in the Memoirs*.

Edmondston, L. (1822) List of birds observed in the Zetland Islands. *Memoir of the Wernerian Nat. Hist. Soc*. Vol IV: 271-75.

Edmondston, L. (1822) Remarks on the Larus Parasiticus or Arctic Gull; and on the Larus Risa or Kittiwake; with an account of the Greenland Kittiwake; – and on the Colymbus Grylle. *Memoir of the Wernerian Nat. Hist. Soc*. Vol 7: 90-105.

Edmondston, L. (1823) Notice of a specimen of the Larus Eburneus, or Ivory gull, shot in Zetland and further remarks on the Iceland Gull. *Memoir of the Wernerian Nat. Hist. Soc.* Vol IV: 501-507.

Edmondston, L. (1823) Observations on the Lesser Guillemot and Black-billed Auk, the Colymbus Minor and the Alca Pica of Linnaeus. *Memoir of the Wernerian Nat. Hist. Soc.* Vol V: 8-25.

Edmondston, L. (1830) *Remarks on some proposed alterations in the Course of Medical Education at the University of Edinburgh.* Privately printed pamphlet. Edinburgh, Maclachlan and Stewart.

Edmondston, L. (1836) *On the claims of Shetland to a separate representation in Parliament by a Shetlander.* Privately printed pamphlet. W. Reid & Son.

Edmondston, L. (1838) Observations on the Distinction, History and Hunting of Seals in Shetland. *Memoir of the Wernerian Nat. Hist. Soc.* Vol viii: 1-48.

Edmondston, L. (1841) General Observations on the county of Shetland. *The Statistical Account of the Shetland Islands.* Edinburgh.

Edmondston, L. (1859) *La Parabole du Semeur.* Londres.

Edmondston, L. (1863) *Notes on American Affairs.* London.

Edmondston, L. (1865) On the Manufacture of Leather from the skins of Cetaceous animals. *Prize Essay and Trans. Of Highland Soc. Of Scot.* Vol 8.

Eliza Edmondston (1801-1869)

Edmondston, E. (1844) Life in Shetland. *Chambers' Journal.* March: 145-148 & 163-165. Edinburgh.

Edmondston, E. (1855) Journey from New Orleans to California. *Chambers' Journal.* No 100.

Edmondston, E. (1856) *Sketches and Tales of the Shetland Islands.* Edinburgh, Sutherland & Knox.

Edmondston, E. (1859) Menie Henderich: a tale of Shetland. *In* Brown, C. R. (ed) *The Scottish Annual*: 250-275.

Edmondston, E. (1859) Ultima Thule. *Chambers' Journal.* 13th August.

Edmondston, E. (1861??) *The Poor Knitters of Shetland.* Paisley.

Edmondston, E. (1868) *The Young Shetlander: Shadow over the Sunshine, Life and Letters.* Edinburgh, Mould & Todd.

Edmondston, E. (n.d.) *Song of Solomon* (in Shetland vernacular) for Prince LLB. Unpublished.

Thomas Edmondston (1825-1846)

Edmondston, T., commenced 1837. *Flora Zetlandica, No 1.* Incomplete MS in the library of the British Museum (Natural History). London, Cromwell Road.

Edmondston, T. (1839) List of Plants observed in the Island of Unst, Shetland, during the summer of 1837, in Hooker, W. D., *Notes on Norway*, ed. 2: 111-117. Privately published.

Edmondston, T. (1840) The Ligneous Flora of the Shetland Islands. *The Gardener's Magazine.* 16: 102.

Edmondston, T. (1841a) List of Phanerogamous Plants together with the Cryptogamic Orders Filices, Equisetaceae and Lycopodiaceae, observed in the Shetland Islands. *The Annals and Magazine of Natural History*, 7: 287-295.

Edmondston, T. (1841b) Catalogue of the Phaneogamous plants and ferns observed in the Shetland Islands. *The Statistical Account of the Shetland Islands*. pp.150-153. Edinburgh.

Edmondston, T. (1841c) On the native dyes of the Shetland Islands. *Trans. Proc. Bot. Soc. Edinb.*, 1:123-126.

Edmondston, T. (c1842) A paper read for Mr Edmondston, jun., on the botany of Shetland. *Trans. Proc. Bot. Soc. Edin.* Vol I: 123-126.

Edmondston, T. (1843a) The Botany of Shetland. *The Phytologist*, 1: 430-432. (Repeated with slight differences, in *The Annals and Magazine of Natural History*, 11 (1843): 70-73, and in *Trans. Proc. Bot. Soc. Edinb.*, 1 (1844): 185-188.)

Edmondston, T. (1843b) Notice of a new British Cerastium. *The Phytologist*, 1: 497-500.

Edmondston, T. (1843c) Note on Cerastium latifolium. *The Phytologist*, 1: 677-678.

Edmondston, T. (1843d) Note on the Northern Diver. *Zoologist*, 365.

Edmondston, T. (1843e) Shetland locality for Cynosurus echinatus. *The Phytologist*, 1: 772.

Edmondston, T. (1844a) A fauna of Shetland. *Zoologist*, 459-67.

Edmondston, T. (1884b) Additions to the Birds of Shetland. *Zoologist*, pp. 551-52.

Edmondston, T. (1845). *A flora of Shetland: comprehending a list of the flowering and cryptogamic plants of the Shetlands*. Aberdeen.

Thomas Edmondston (1825-1874)

Edmondston, T. (1863) Notes on some recent excavations in the island of Unst, Shetland, and of the collection of stone vessels, implements etc, this obtained for the Society's museum. *Prov. of the Soc. of Ant. of Scot.* Vol ix: 283-287.

Edmondston, T. (1866) *An Etymological Glossary of the Shetland and Orkney Dialect*. Edinburgh, Adam & Charles Black.

Edmondston, T. (n.d.) Notes on a Straw Masquerade Dress still in use in some parts of Shetland, and on certain Woollen articles manufactured in Fair Isle, also of a supposed relic of the Spanish Armada. *Proc. of the Soc. of Ant. of Scot.* Vol viii: 470-2.

Biot Edmondston (1827-1906)

Edmondston, B. (1884) Seals and seal hunting in Shetland. *Chambers's Journal*. 7th June and 9th Aug.; 364-366 and 507-509. (as in *Home of a Naturalist*).

Edmondston, B. & Saxby, J.M.E. (1889) *The Home of a Naturalist*. London, Nisbet.

Edmondston, B. (n.d.) *Shetland Sketches*. Chambers' Journal.

Publications of Dr Henry L. Saxby (1836-1859)

Saxby, H. L. (1874) *The Birds of Shetland*. Edinburgh, McLaren & Stewart.

Saxby, H. L. (1859-1871) *Zoologist*, 67 papers.

Jessie M. E. Saxby (1842-1940)

Books

Saxby, J. M. E. (1868) *Lichens from the Old Rock*. (poems) Edinburgh, William Nimmo.

Saxby, J. M. E. (1874) *Glamour from Argyllshire*. (poems) Inveraray, John Rodger.

Saxby, J. M. E. (1875) *The One Wee Lass*. Edinburgh, Andrew Elliott.

Saxby, J. M. E. (1876) *Daala Mist or Stories from Shetland*. Edinburgh, Andrew Elliott.

Saxby, J. M. E. (1877) *Rock-Bound: A Story of the Shetland Isles*. Edinburgh, Thomas Gray & Co. 2 editions.

Saxby, J. M. E. (1879) *Geordie Roye or A Waif from the Greyfriars Wynd*. Glasgow, John S. Marr & Sons.

Saxby, J. M. E. (1882) *Breakers ahead or Uncle Jack's stories of great shipwrecks of recent times 1869-1880*. Edinburgh, Nelson.

Saxby, J. M. E. (1882) *Snow Dreams or Funny Fancies for Little Folks*. Edinburgh, Johnstone, Hunter & Co.

Saxby, J. M. E. (1884) *Ben Hanson: A Story of George Watson's College*. Edinburgh, Oliphant Anderson & Ferrier.

Saxby, J. M. E. (1884) *Preston Tower: or Will he no come back again*. Edinburgh, Oliphant Anderson and Ferrier.

Saxby, J. M. E. (1887) *Queen of the Isles*. London, S. W. Partridge.

Saxby, J. M. E. (1887) *Shoulder to Shoulder*. Edinburgh Orkney and Shetland Literary Assoc. Session 1888-89. pp. 1-12. and repr. *The Shetland Times* (1888, 13th October).

Saxby, J. M. E. (1887) *The Lads of Lunda*. London, James Nisbet & Co. 3 editions.

Saxby, J. M. E. (1888) *Dora Coyne*. London, S. W. Partridge & Co.

Saxby, J. M. E. (1888) *Oil on Troubled Waters*. London, Religious Tract Society.

Saxby, J. M. E. (1888) ed. *Broken Lights*. Poems and Reminiscences of Basil Ramsay Anderson.

Saxby, J. M. E. (1889) *Kate & Jean*. Edinburgh, Oliphant Anderson and Ferrier. First printed in *The Sun* (1888, 5/5 to 22/9).

Saxby, J. M. E. (1889) *The Yarl's Yacht*. London, James Nisbet & Co.

Saxby, J. M. E., Hardy, R. F. & Swann, A. S. (1889) *Vita Vinctis*.

Saxby, J. M. E. (1890) *Sallie's Boys*. London, S. W. Partridge & Co.

Saxby, J. M. E. (1890) *West-Nor-West*. London, James Nisbet & Co.

Saxby, J. M. E. (1891) *Her first place*. London, SPCK.

Saxby, J. M. E. (1891) *Milestones and other Stories*. Edinburgh, Oliphant Anderson and Ferrier.

Saxby, J. M. E. (1892) *Heim-Laund and Heim Folk*, Edinburgh, R. & R. Clark.

Saxby, J. M. E. (1892) *Viking Boys*. London, Nisbet & Co.

Saxby, J. M. E. (1893) *Lucky Lines*: or *won from waves*. Edinburgh, Oliphant Anderson & Ferrier. First printed in *The Beacon* (1992 first chapter 13th February).

Saxby, J. M. E. (1894) *A Camsterie Nacket: Being the Story of a Contrary Laddie Ill to Guide*. Edinburgh, Oliphant Anderson and Ferrier.

Saxby, J. M. E. (1894) *Auld Lerwick: A Personal Reminiscence*. Lerwick, Church Improvement Scheme Bazaar.

Saxby, J. M. E. (1894) *Tom and His Crows or Romantic Adventures in Switzerland*. London, James Nisbet & Co.

Saxby, J. M. E. (1895) *Sisters in Love*. London, S. W. Partridge & Co.

Saxby, J. M. E. (1896) *Constable AI*. London, SPCK. Penny Library.

Saxby, J. M. E. (1896) *The Saga Book of Lunda*. London, James Nisbet & Co.

Saxby, J. M. E. (1913) *"Joseph Bell, M. D." An Appreciation by an old friend*. Edinburgh, Oliphant, Anderson & Ferrier.

Saxby, J. M. E. (1914) *Leaves from the Psalmist's Life*. Edinburgh, Andrew Elliott.

Saxby, J. M. E. (1932) *Shetland Traditional Lore*. Edinburgh, Grant & Murray.

Saxby, J. M. E. (1934) *Threads from a Tangled Skein*. Poems and Ponderings. Lerwick, T. & J. Manson.

Saxby, J. M. E. (n.d.) *Tick-tock*. Edinburgh, Andrew Stevenson.

Saxby, J. M. E. (n.d.) *Winnie's Golden Key or The Right of Way*. London, The Religious Tract Society.

Saxby, J. M. E. (n.d.) *Wrecked on the Shetlands:* or *the little sea-king*. London, The Religious Tract Society. (Gilbert Goudie's copy dated 1915).

Stories, poems, articles and letters

Saxby, J. M. E. (1859) The Sea Girt Home. *In* Brown, C. R. (ed) *The Scottish Annual* and TFTS.

Saxby, J. M. E. (1859) Steen: a Shetland story. *Family Herald*, 1st October.

Saxby, J. M. E. (1860) What the Waters would Teach. *Cassell's Magazine*.

Saxby, J. M. E. (1878) The Maiden's Invocation. *Sunday at Home* (over 3 issues).

Saxby, J. M. E. (1880) Folk-lore from Unst. *Chambers' Journal* (over 4 issues) and *Leisure Hour* Vol 29 and repr. *The Shetland Times*.

Saxby, J. M. E. (1881) After rain, sunshine. *People's Friend*, 16th February.

Saxby, J. M. E. (1881) Friendship between Birds. *Leisure Hour*.

Saxby, J. M. E. (1881) Lux in tenebris. *Life & Work*, May.

Saxby, J. M. E. (1882) A Lichtsome Lindsay. *Dundee Weekly News*, First chapter, 7th October.

Saxby, J. M. E. (1882) The home of a Naturalist. *Chambers' Journal*, 11th February.

Saxby, J. M. E. (1882) The Shetland Sixern. *The Shetland Times*.

Saxby, J. M. E. (1883) Not false but free. *Dundee Weekly News*, First chapter, 24th March.

Saxby, J. M. E. (1884) A Bit of Bush Life. *The Boy's Own Paper*, July.

Saxby, J. M. E. (1884) Housekeeping under peculiar circumstances. *The Shetland Times*.

Saxby, J. M. E. (1884) The Manse boys: a Shetland story. *Life & Work,* September/October.

Saxby, J. M. E. (1885) An uncommon revenge. *Dundee Weekly News*, Xmas number.

Saxby, J. M. E. (1885) Sea Ware. *Sunday at Home*, July, August/September.

Saxby, J. M. E. (1885) Young love and old. *Dundee Weekly News*, Xmas number.

Saxby, J. M. E. (1885) The Minister's bairn. *Dundee Weekly News*, Xmas number and repr. *Shetland News* (1886) 23rd January.

Saxby, J. M. E. (1886) Folk lore of Yule in the Shetland Isles. *Leisure Hour*, December and repr. *Shetland News,* 11th December.

Saxby, J. M. E. (1886) Running free: a boating adventure in the Shetland Isles. *Boy's Own Paper,* March-July.

Saxby, J. M. E. (1886) Students to the rescue. *Life & Work*, October and repr. in *Vita Vinctus* (1887).

Saxby, J. M. E. (1886) The Bonnie Earl. *Dundee Weekly News*.

Saxby, J. M. E. (1886) The Denschman's Had: a legend of Shetland. *Chambers Journal*, 23rd October.

Saxby, J. M. E. (1886) The way to win. *Sunday at Home*, June.

Saxby, J. M. E. (1886) To my lassie: dreaming of spring; always summer; sister-crowns. *Girl's Own Paper*.

Saxby, J. M. E. (1887) A good ship. *Life & Work*, November.

Saxby, J. M. E. (1887) A kirk in the Qu'appelle Valley/A Sunday in the Prairie. *Life & Work*, June.

Saxby, J. M. E. (1887) *Crumbs from the Children's Table*. London, The Sunday School Union.

Saxby, J. M. E. (1887) Eau de Vie. *Dundee Weekly News*, Xmas number.

Saxby, J. M. E. (1887) Hot and High. *Sunday at Home*, June.

Saxby, J. M. E. (1887) *How Lady Magdalen was evolved*. Privately published. Edinburgh, E. & S. Livingstone.

Saxby, J. M. E. (1887-8) Notes on the Shetland dialect. *Saga-Book* V, pp. 65-69.

Saxby, J. M. E. (1887) Revealed at Last. *Family Herald Supplement*, 19th September.

Saxby, J. M. E. (1888) A Sea King of Whalsay (Laurence Moar and crew caught out fishing). *Boy's Own Paper*, April and repr. *The Shetland Times*, 14th April.

Saxby, J. M. E. (1888) A Sunday on the prairie. *Life & Work*, August.

Saxby, J. M. E. (1888) A visit to 'Wooden Walls'. *Girl's Own Paper*, 5/5, 12/5 and 19/5.

Saxby, J. M. E. (1888) A woman's paradise. *The Shetland Times*, 28th July.

Saxby, J. M. E. (1888) Hid in the heart. *Mother's Companion*, First chapter, January.

Saxby, J. M. E. (1888) His Finis. *Dundee Weekly News*, Xmas number.

Saxby, J. M. E. (1888) *Lindeman Brothers*. London, The Sunday School Union.

Saxby, J. M. E. (1888) Our Western limit. *The Sun*, 10/11 and 17/11.

Saxby, J. M. E. (1888) Parting Words. *Life & Work*, October and TFTS.

Saxby, J. M. E. (1888) Prairie Home. *Scotsman*, 11th July and repr. *Shetland News*, 14th July.

Saxby, J. M. E. (1888) Sun-worship. *The Sun*, 5th May and repr. *The Shetland Times*, 18th September.

Saxby, J. M. E. (1888) Tarantulae. *Young Scientist*, January.

Saxby, J. M. E. (1888) Thanksgiving. *The Sun*, 2nd June.

Saxby, J. M. E. (1888) The footsteps on the stair. *Dundee Weekly News*, Xmas number.

Saxby, J. M. E. (1888) The valley of the shadow. *Life & Work*, June.

Saxby, J. M. E. (1888) Through 'The Woods' of the Far West. *Chambers' Journal*, 27th October.

Saxby, J. M. E. (1888) *Tysties at Home*.

Saxby, J. M. E. (1889) A book and its author. *The Shetland Times*, 25th May.

Saxby, J. M. E. (1889) A daughter of sea-kings. *Life & Work*, April-June and October.

Saxby, J. M. E. (1889) A Tropical Sanatorium. (Sketch). *British Homes*, March.

Saxby, J. M. E. (1889) *Budget of Holiday Letters* (Trip to Canada). Edinburgh, Darien Press.

Saxby, J. M. E. (1889) Dad Roy/The Minister's Man. *Life and Work*, January-March.

Saxby, J. M. E. (1889) First Fit: A vision. *Now*, 27th December and repr. *Shetland News*, (1890) 4th January and *The Shetland Times*, (1890) 11th January.

Saxby, J. M. E. (1889) Light on Fair Isle. London, and *Glasgow Herald*, 10th April and repr. *The Shetland Times*, 13th April.

Saxby, J. M. E. (1889) To be or not to be ... annexed. *The Shetland Times*, 23rd March.

Saxby, J. M. E. (1890) A Hopeful Sisterhood (politics). *North British Advertiser*, 8th November and repr. *The Shetland Times*, 22nd November.

Saxby, J. M. E. (1890) Cousins. ???? May and repr. *The Shetland Times*, 26th November.

Saxby, J. M. E. (1890) From Behind Bars. *People's Friend* and repr. *The Shetland Times*, 5th July.

Saxby, J. M. E. (1890) This year's prairie harvest. *Chamber's Journal*, November.

Saxby, J. M. E. (1891) Dominion Day. *North British Advertiser, Ladies Journal* and *Shetland News*, 11th July.

Saxby, J. M. E. (1891) *Home Rule Apart from Politics*. Edinburgh, The Darien Press. Dedicated to Andrew Carnegie, and *The Shetland Times*, 13th and 22nd August.

Saxby, J. M. E. (1891) In Memoriam Robina Hardy (sketch – Edinburgh authoress). *Edinburgh Evening Despatch*, *The Shetland Times*, 29th August and *Shetland News*, 22nd August.

Saxby, J. M. E. (1891) Neil M'cara Crofter. *Sunday at Home*, January.

Saxby, J. M. E. (1891) Pi-a-Pot's reserve. *Chamber's Journal*, January.

Saxby, J. M. E. (1891) The Doctor's Laulie. London.

Saxby, J. M. E. (1891) The Last of the Sea Kings. London. *The Boy's Own Paper*, March and repr. *The Shetland Times*, 25th May.

Saxby, J. M. E. (1892) A Happy Pilgrimage. *North British Advertiser*, 17th September.

Saxby, J. M. E. (1892) Apparel. *The Shetland Times*, 5th May.

Saxby, J. M. E. (1892) Brown Jack. *Chatterbox*.

Saxby, J. M. E. (1892) For Rank's Sake. *Weekly Scotsman*, May to November.

Saxby, J. M. E. (1892) Heathens from home. *Life & Work*, May.

Saxby, J. M. E. (?) (1892) How the udallers of Shetland lost their land. *Scotsman*, 4th January.

Saxby, J. M. E. (1892) Invalidism. *The Shetland Times*, 30th April.

Saxby, J. M. E. (1892) Midnight in St Giles. *Life & Work*, May.

Saxby, J. M. E. (1892) On the Holms. *Anderson's Orkney and Shetland Almanac*.

Saxby, J. M. E. (1892) The Katyogle's haunts and ways. *The Leisure Hour*, May.

Saxby, J. M. E. (1892) The parlour lamp. *Home Messenger*, September.

Saxby, J. M. E. (1892) Women and Work. *The Shetland Times*, 16th and 23rd April.

Saxby, J. M. E. (1892) Wrecker's Holme. *Young England*, June and July.

Saxby, J. M. E. (1893) A first-rate antidote. *Girl's Own Paper*, 3/6, 10/6 and 17/6 pp. 567, 590 & 603.

Saxby, J. M. E. (1893) A peerie wird or twa. *The Shetland Times*, 12th August.

Saxby, J. M. E. (1893) Almsgiving. *The Shetland Times*, 26th August.

Saxby, J. M. E. (1893) *Birds of Omen in Shetland*. (The corbie and the catyogle). London, Inaugural address to the Viking Club, 13th October 1892. TFTS & LFOR.

Saxby, J. M. E. (1893) Clytha's fortune. *Young Women*, February.

Saxby, J. M. E. (1893) Common Civility. *The Shetland Times*, 3rd June.

Saxby, J. M. E. (1893) False Sentiment. *The Shetland Times*, 27th May.

Saxby, J. M. E. (1893) Gulls of the Northern Sea. *Chatterbox*.

Saxby, J. M. E. (1893) Her vocation. *Helping Words*, July.

Saxby, J. M. E. (1893) Idle Hands. *The Shetland Times*, 14th January.

Saxby, J. M. E. (1893) The Maids; Animal Magnetism; Selbornian. *North British Adveriser* (?).

Saxby, J. M. E. (1894) Orcadians & Shetlanders: a few foolish remarks. *The Shetland Times*, 24th February.

Saxby, J. M. E. (1894) The Voders. *Orkney and Shetland American*, May and June and *Weekly Scotsman*, 3rd August.

Saxby, J. M.E. (1895) Gossip About Gulls. *Edinburgh Orkney and Shetland Literary Assoc.* 1895-96. pp. 158-68 and *Field Naturalists' Club* (Mus. of Scot. 5480)

Saxby, J. M. E. (1895) The witches of Veesgert. *Weekly Scotsman*, 21st December.

Saxby, J. M. E. (1896) A claim on the Kirk. *Life & Work* and repr. *Shetland News*, 25th April.

Saxby, J. M. E. (1896) *A self-taught Shetlander* (Andrew Anderson). Booklet. Edinburgh, Johnston, Hunter & Co.

Saxby, J. M. E. (1896) A spring morning in the park. *The Student*, November.

Saxby, J. M. E. (1896) A trip to Ireland. *Ladies Journal*, April.

Saxby, J. M. E. (1896) An accidental shot. *Weekly Scotsman*, 11th April.

Saxby, J. M. E. (1896) By the Queen's Ferry. *Methodist Monthly*, September.

Saxby, J. M. E. (1896) Honour among thieves. *Weekly Scotsman*, 14th March.

Saxby, J. M. E. (1896) Notes on a recent trip to Ireland (political). *North British Advertiser*, 25th April and repr. *Shetland News,* 9th May.

Saxby, J. M. E. (1896) The Lamp of Lothian. *Methodist Weekly*, April.

Saxby, J. M. E. (1897) A Brave Woman. *Life & Work*, January.

Saxby, J. M. E. (1897) A Highland Elysium. *Methodist Monthly*, February.

Saxby, J. M. E. (1897) Amid the Mighty Waters. *Young England*, October.

Saxby, J. M. E. (1897) Eupham's Bairns. Edinburgh. *Life & Work* and/or *Helping Words*, July-December.

Saxby, J. M. E. (1897) Ranch Life. *Chatterbox*.

Saxby, J. M. E. (1898) Belle and her bike. *Weekly Scotsman*, 26th February.

Saxby, J. M. E. (1898) Prairie Life and Adventure. *Chatterbox* (series).

Saxby, J. M. E. (1899) Twin troubles. *Life & Work*, April-July.

Saxby, J. M. E. (1900) Aurora Borealis. Shetland Story. *Free Methodist*, 6th December.

Saxby, J. M. E. (1900) Revival of Ancient Muness Estate. *The Shetland Times*, 21st July.

Saxby, J. M. E. (1900) Rob the scavenger. *Helping Words*, August.

Saxby, J. M. E. (1900) The changeling. *Chatterbox*, Vol 13.

Saxby, J. M. E. (1901) The pioneer of a free press. *Chambers' Journal*, May and repr. *The Shetland Times,* 12th October.

Saxby, J. M. E. (1902) How she proved them and herself. *Helping Words*, July.

Saxby, J. M. E. (1902) *The Shetland Times*, 27th December and repr. (1903) Sunday in the Shetland Isles. *Family Friend Annual*.

Saxby, J. M. E. (1902) Treasure trove. *Amateur Gardening*, Xmas number.

Saxby, J. M. E. (1902) Viking relics. *Leisure Hour* pp. 481-2, and repr. *The Shetland Times*, 6th September.

Saxby, J. M. E. (1903) Diamond cut diamond. *Howood*.

Saxby, J. M. E. (1904) A Kobe diary of the War. *Scotsman* and repr. *The Shetland Times,* 10th December.

Saxby, J. M. E. (1904) Clashes frae wir toon. *The Shetland Times*, 28/4, 14/5, 4/6, 11/6, 18/6, 25/6, 2/7, 16/7, 6/8, 3/9, 17/9, 8/10 and 22/10.

Saxby, J. M. E. (1904) Interesting old Shetland couple. *Weekly Scotsman*, 17th December.

Saxby, J. M. E. (1904) The boy's mother. *Sunday at Home*, November.

Saxby, J. M. E. (1904) The "Holy-Time" in Haven. *Leisure Hour*.

Saxby, J. M. E. (1904) Wild flowers of Shetland. *Scotsman*, 13th December and repr. *The Shetland Times*, (1905) 21st January and TFTS.

Saxby, J. M. E. (1905) Sacred sites in a Shetland isle (Unst). *The Antiquarian*, April pp.133-138, *The Shetland Times*, 20th May and *Saga Book of the Viking Club*, Vol 4.

Saxby, J. M. E. (1905) Some "Aulie" Birds of Shetland. *Scotsman* and repr. *The Shetland Times*, 8th April.

Saxby, J. M. E. (1905) The boy's mother. *Leisure Hour*, pp. 38-46.

Saxby, J. M. E. (1905) The coortin' o' Maunsie Preeste's Willa. *The Shetland Times*, 11th March and TFTS.

Saxby, J. M. E. (1906) In memoriam: Andrew Anderson, Baltasound. *The Shetland Times*, 17th March.

Saxby, J. M. E. (1906) Sons of the Kirk. Edinburgh. *Life & Work*, January to December.

Saxby, J. M. E. (1906) The sister of a famous woman. *The Sunday at Home* and repr. *The Shetland Times*, 19th May.

Saxby, J. M. E. (1906) Sons of the Kirk. *Life & Work*.

Saxby, J. M. E. (1907-08) *Notes on the Shetland Dialect*. Saga-Book V pp. 65-69.

Saxby, J. M. E. (1907-08) 'Shetland Phrase and Idiom II'. *Old-lore Miscellany of Orkney, Shetland, Caithness and Sutherland*. 1: pp. 267-274 and repr. *The Shetland Times*, (1930) 22nd January and 1st March.

Saxby, J. M. E. (1907) Stray notes from Unst. *The Shetland Times*, 6th April.

Saxby, J. M. E. (1909) Shetland names for animals, etc (pt. 2). *Old-lore Miscellany of Orkney, Shetland, Caithness and Sutherland*, 2: 235-237.

Saxby, J. M. E. (1910) *The Cradle of our Race (Souvenance of a Cruise on Northern Seas)*. Edinburgh, J. & H. Lindsay Ltd.

Saxby, J. M. E. (1911) *Open letter to the Rev. James Cromarty Smith*. (pamphlet).

Saxby, J. M. E. (1912) Auld Daa's sea kist. *The Shetland Times*, 7th December.

Saxby, J. M. E. (1912) John Taylor Brown LL.D. *British Weekly*, 26th September.

Saxby, J. M. E. (1912) The Lerwick Pageant of Up-Helly-A'. *The Shetland Times*, 9th November.

Saxby, J. M. E. (1913) As some folk see us. *The Shetland Times*, 25th October.

Saxby, J. M. E. (1913) John Taylor Brown LL.D: an appreciation. *The Shetland Times*, 18th January.

Saxby, J. M. E. (1913) The Yattereens o' auld Yaspard. *The Shetland Times*, 15th February.

Saxby, J. M. E. (1914) Anderina's coo. *The Shetland Times*, 2nd May.

Saxby, J. M. E. (1914) Food of the Shetlanders Langsyne. *Old Lore Miscellany*. Vol VII, 70-8 and repr. *The Shetland Times*, (1929) 5th October.

Saxby, J. M. E. (1914) Vessiks and Goadiks. *Dunedin Magazine*, July and repr. *The Shetland Times* (1929) 14th September.

Saxby, J. M. E. (1915) Foys and fanteen. *Old Lore Miscellany*. Vol VIII pp. 22-31 and also printed for the *Viking Soc. For Northern Res.*, Univ. of London and repr. *The Shetland Times* (1929) 28th September.

Saxby, J. M. E. (1915) The Cameron Gathering. *The 79th News*, April issue and TFTS.

Saxby, J. M. E. (1916) A Cameron. *The 79th News*, July issue.

Saxby, J. M. E. (1922) A hadd for Shetland sheep. *The Shetland Times*, 7th April.

Saxby, J. M. E. (1923) Seabirds at home. *Country Life*, 2nd June.

Saxby, J. M. E. (1927) Shetland Lace. *The Bulletin* and repr. *The Shetland Times*, 17th September.

Saxby, J. M. E. (1927) The boys o' Saytir. *The Shetland Times*, 15th January.

Saxby, J. M. E. (1927) The Ghylls o' Vaalafiel. *The Shetland Times*, 7th May.

Saxby, J. M. E. (1928) The Ootsta. Britain's northern outpost. *Glasgow Herald*, 4th August and repr. *The Shetland Times*, 24th November.

Saxby, J. M. E. (1928) The Shetland knitting industry. *The Queen*, 9th May.

Saxby, J. M. E. (1928) Women knitters of Shetland. *The Bulletin*, 27th June.

Saxby, J. M. E. (1929) Some old Shetland names for nature's children. *The Shetland Times*, 2/11 and 9/11.

Saxby, J. M. E. (1929) Wir ain auld tongue. *The Shetland Times*, 23/11 and 7/12.

Saxby, J. M. E. (1930) Brochs and other ancient bields. *The Sun* and repr. *The Shetland Times* 26/4 and 17/5.

Saxby, J. M. E. (1930) Hadds and Hoiden Holls. *The Shetland Times*, 31/5 and 7/6.

Saxby, J. M. E. (1930) News from far away. *The Shetland Times*, 1st February.

Saxby, J. M. E. (1930) Odds and ends of folklore. *The Shetland Times*, 8/3 and 22/3.

Saxby, J. M. E. (1930) Tales of Trows. *The Shetland Times*, 5/4 and 12/4.

Saxby, J. M. E. (1930) The Shetlander's forebears. *The Shetland Times*, 8th February.

Saxby, J. M. E. (1930) Trows and their kindred. *The Shetland Times*, 4/1 and 11/1.

Saxby, J. M. E. (1931) An old-time skipper. *The Shetland Times*, 10th October.

Saxby, J. M. E. (1931) Auld Donal'. *The Shetland Times*, 28th March.

Saxby, J. M. E. (1931) Keety Plumper. *The Shetland Times*, 30th May.

Saxby, J. M. E. (1931) Von Staigle. *The Shetland Times*, 18th April.

Saxby, J. M. E. (1957) Bonn Hoga. *Shetland Folk Book*, Vol III. p. 70.

Saxby, J. M. E. (n.d.) *A Radical Improvement in Shetland*.

Saxby, J. M. E. (n.d.) *A Reminiscence of George Macdonald*.

Saxby, J. M. E. (n.d.) *A satisfactory discussion*.

Saxby, J. M. E. (n.d.) *A Wild Yule een. Merry and Wise*, Xmas number.

Saxby, J. M. E. (n.d.) A wird or twa frae Baltasound: Sinclair T. Duncan. *The Shetland Times*.

Saxby, J. M. E. (n.d.) *An interesting 'Social'*.

Saxby, J. M. E. (n.d.) *Athena Regina*.

Saxby, J. M. E. (n.d.) *Birth sister of Mrs Bishop's well known traveller*.

Saxby, J. M. E. (n.d.) *Britannia to her sons (Britannia's Big Sons?)*. TFTS.

Saxby, J. M. E. (n.d.) *Consecrated Knights*. TFTS.

Saxby, J. M. E. (n.d.) *Coaching Tours*.

Saxby, J. M. E. (>1900) Colonial Patriotism. Lerwick, *The Shetland Times*.

Saxby, J. M. E. (n.d.) *Dead Man's Chest*.

Saxby, J. M. E. (n.d.) *Divided Clouds*. TFTS.

Saxby, J. M. E. (>1900) Dogfish. Edinburgh, *Scotsman*.

Saxby, J. M. E. (n.d.) *Edinburgh of Today*.

Saxby, J. M. E. (n.d.) *Fule Gibbie*.

Saxby, J. M. E. (n.d.) *Hel-y-a-water*. LFOR.

Saxby, J. M. E. (n.d.) *Holiday House*.

Saxby, J. M. E. (n.d.) *In an isle of the sea: a Shetland story*.

Saxby, J. M. E. (n.d.) *John Dillon in Edinburgh*.

Saxby, J. M. E. (n.d.) *Land of Scott*.

Saxby, J. M. E. (n.d.) Look to be Found. *Morning Rays*.

Saxby, J. M. E. (n.d.) *Muness Castle*.

Saxby, J. M. E. (n.d.) Noble Service. *Morning Rays*.

Saxby, J. M. E. (>1900) Notable Shetlanders. *Australian Haim World*.

Saxby, J. M. E. (>1900) Notes on knitted lace, linen and wool. *Queen Newspaper*.

Saxby, J. M. E. (>1900) Orcadians and Shetlanders. *Christian Herald*.

Saxby, J. M. E. (n.d.) *Out in the storm*.

Saxby, J. M. E. (n.d.) *Outside the Bar*.

Saxby, J. M. E. (n.d.) *Persephone*. TFTS.

Saxby, J. M. E. (>1900) Poland's sympathy with Japan. Edinburgh, *Scotsman*.

Saxby, J. M. E. (n.d.) *Pull Together*. Words for a song with music by John C. Grieve. Edinburgh, Köhler & Son and TFTS.

Saxby, J. M. E. (n.d.) *Running Free*. Words for song with music by Thomas Manson. London, Paterson & Sons and TFTS.

Saxby, J. M. E. (n.d.) *Scout Musings*.

Saxby, J. M. E. (>1900) *Shetland Knitting*. Lerwick, Johnson and Greig. (item 82 Mus. of Scot)

Saxby, J. M. E. (>1900) Shetland's Role of Honour. Lerwick, *The Shetland Times*.

Saxby, J. M. E. (n.d.) *Signal Fire*. LFOR.

Saxby, J. M. E. (>1900) Something wrong somewhere.

Saxby, J. M. E. (n.d.) *The Beauty of Brechin*.

Saxby, J. M. E. (n.d.) *The Burden of the Lyre*.

Saxby, J. M. E. (n.d.) *The Moder Dy*.

Saxby, J. M. E. (n.d.) *The Novelist of Children*.

Saxby, J. M. E. (n.d.) *The Premier in Edinburgh*.

Saxby, J. M. E. (n.d.) *The Tug of War*.

Saxby, J. M. E. (n.d.) *The Veiled Angel*. TFTS.

Saxby, J. M. E. (n.d.) *To Queen Maud – Skoal!* TFTS.

Saxby, J. M. E. (n.d.) *Two of our Best*. J. J. Haldane Burgess and James Inkster.

Saxby, J. M. E. (n.d.) *Var da Vaigher*. TFTS.

Saxby, J. M. E. (n.d.) *Welcome Yule*.

Saxby, J. M. E. (n.d.) *Wir Boys*. TFTS.

Saxby, J. M. E. (n.d.) *Women's Organisations*.

Saxby, J. M. E. (n.d.) *Women's work in Politics*.

Saxby, J. M. E. (n.d.) *Yule Bau*.

Saxby, J. M. E. & Saxby, C. F. A. (1897) Rough and Ready Chums. *Boy's Own Paper,* February to July.

Saxby, J. M. E. and Saxby, H. D. (1888) A Sunday on the prairies. *Life & Work,* September.

Hardy, R. F., Swann, A. S. & Saxby J. M. E. (n.d.) *Live To Those Who Are Bound.*

TFTS   *Threads from a Tangled Skein.*

LFOR   *Lichens from the Old Rock.*

Publications of Thomas Edmondston (1847-1923)

Edmondston, T. (1878) The Raven. *Leisure Hour,* 167-8.

Edmondston, T. (1878) The Great Skua. *Leisure Hour,* 358-9.

Edmondston, T. (1878) A pet Cormorant. *Leisure Hour,* 572-3.

Edmondston, T. (1879) The pairing of birds. *Leisure Hour,* 230-1.

Edmondston, T. (1888-89) Deep Sea Fishing in the Shetlands. *St Saviour's Parish Magazine.*

Edmondston, T. (1893) The Great Skua. *Leisure Hour,* 139-40.

ILLUSTRATIONS ACKNOWLEDGEMENT

Reproduced by permission of University of Aberdeen
- Page 71   William MacGillivray self portrait

By permission of The British Library
- Page 192   Charles Darwin

Courtesy of Laurence Edmondston Coffin, Washington
- Page 63   Charles Edmondston and Mary Edmondston (Pratt)
- Page 182   Charles Edmondston and his sons
- Page 212   Charles Edmondston
- Page 218   Amory Coffin

Courtesy of Delgatie Castle
- Page 7   William Hay (1723-1804)
- Page 11   James Hay (1750-1831)
- Page 68   William Hay (1787-1858)

Reproduced by permission of the Denver Public Library, Colorado
- Page 185   Old Fort Laramie by William Hen Jackson

Reproduced by permission of Edinburgh University
- Page 135   Dr John Balfour
- Page 144   Dr Robert Graham

Courtesy of Mr and Mrs David Edmondston, Buness
- Page 2   Mally Edmondston (Sanderson)
- Page 10   Buness 1817, purportedly by J B Biot
- Page 19   Thomas Edmondston (1779-1858)
- Page 20   Dr Basil Spence
- Page 42   Jean Baptiste Biot
- Page 55   Lerwick 1850 by John Irvine
- Page 98   Duke of Wellington
- Page 101   Rev. John Ingram
- Page 113   William Sievwright
- Page 143   Thomas Edmondston (1779-1858)
- Page 147   Eliza Edmondston (MacBrair)
- Page 150   Rev. James Ingram
- Page 157   Robert Chambers
- Page 174   Ursula Edmondston (1819-1898)
- Page 176   Buness from Halligarth, pre 1870
- Page 190   Muckle Flugga 1858 by Frederick Schenck
- Page 195   Jessie M E

Reproduced by courtesy of the University Librarian and Director, The John Rylands University Library, The University of Manchester

Reproduced by permission of the Middleton Place Foundation, Charleston South Carolina

From Crombie, B W (1882) *Modern Athenians*, Adam and Charles Black, Edinburgh

Courtesy of Peter Stubbs from Shepherd, T H (1829) *Modern Athens*, Jones & Co., London

Reproduced by the permission of the Museum of Scotland, from the Sandison Collection,

Courtesy of *The Phytologist*
>   Page 151   Notice of a new British Cerastium, by Thomas Edmondston 1843

Reproduced by permission of the Scottish National Photography Collection, Scottish National Portrait Gallery
>   Page 33   Rev. Dr John Fleming by David Octavius Hill and Robert Adamson

Reproduced by permission of the Scottish National Portrait Gallery
>   Page 39   Sir Walter Scott by Colvin Smith

Reproduced by permission of the Shetland Library
>   Page 94   Robert Dunn at Ronas Hill from *The ornithological Guide to the islands of Orkney and Shetland*
>   Page 123   *A Laudatory and Congratulatory Epistle to Zetlandicus* 1836, attributed to the Rev. Thomas Barclay
>   Page 129   Map of the North Isles 1840 from the *New Statistical Account*
>   Page 253   Dr Joseph Bell from *An appreciation* by J M E Saxby
>   Page 265   *Lads of Lunda* by Jessie M E Saxby

Reproduced by permission of the Shetland Museum
>   Page 5   Interior of tenant's cottage
>   Page 8   Sixareens at fishermen's summer base at Fethaland
>   Page 12   Lerwick from Fort Charlotte by John Irvine
>   Page 22   Tenant's cottage
>   Page 28   Lerwick, head of Morrison's Pier 1879 by Charles McEwan
>   Page 39   Lerwick with Tolbooth 1879 by Charles McEwan
>   Page 53   Purportedly Dr Arthur Edmondston but possibly Dr Laurence Edmondston (1895-1879) by John Irvine
>   Page 60   Rev Samuel Dunn sketch, photographed by J D Rattar
>   Page 75   Hagdale chromate quarry, remains
>   Page 76   'Driving bottle-nosed whales 1891' by R H Carter
>   Page 78   Bressay Sound with boats by John Irvine
>   Page 81   Dr Arthur Edmondston (1775-1842) by John Irvine
>   Page 92   The topsail schooner *Magnus Troil* by P Henderson
>   Page 99   *Sovereign* photographed by G Robertson
>   Page 122   Rev. Thomas Barclay by John Irvine
>   Page 237   John Walker and wife

Courtesy of the Old Haa Trust, Burravoe, Yell
>   Page 112   Tom's mouse-ear on the Keen of Hamar by Bobby Tulloch

Reproduced by permission of Yale University Art Gallery, Mabel Brady Garvan Collection
>   Page 36   View of Charleston from the Harbour by S Bernard
>   Page 65   View along the East Battery by S Bernard

Courtesy of Mike Pennington from the *Manual of British Birds* (1927) by Howard Saunders and
W Eagle Clarke

Page 26   Snowy Owl by William Yarrell
Page 28   Whimbrel by William Yarrell
Page 32   Great northern diver and young by William Yarrell
Page 34   Arctic Skuas by William Yarrell
Page 88   Great Skua by William Yarrell

BIBLIOGRAPHY

Anon (1810) Review of 'A View of the Ancient and Present State of the Zetland Islands'. *Edinburgh Review. Vol XVII: 135-155.*

Anon (1850s) *Historical remarks on a refugee nobleman in Unst.* Privately Published.

Alexander, Z. (1995) *Miss Sandison: The Woman and the Collector.* Unpublished final year Dissertation, School of Scottish Studies.

Atkinson, G. C. (1832) An Excursion to the Shetland Islands. MS. Zetland County Library.

Ball, Edward. (1998) *Slaves in the Family.* Farrar, Strauss and Giroux, New York.

Ballantyne, J. H. & Smith, B. (eds.) (1994) *Shetland Documents 1580-1611.* Shetland Islands Council and The Shetland Times Ltd., Lerwick.

Ballantyne, J. H. & Smith, B. (eds.) (1999) *Shetland Documents 1195-1579.* Shetland Islands Council and The Shetland Times Ltd., Lerwick.

Barclay, Rev. J. & Mouat, T. (1792) The Statistical Account of the Island and Parish of Unst. *Statistical Account Of Scotland. 12. Vol V.*

Barnes, M. P. (1996) Jakob Jakobsen and the Norn Language of Shetland, in: Waugh, D. J. (ed.) *Shetland's Northern Links: Language and History.* Scottish Society for Northern Studies, Lerwick.

Biot, J. B. (1818) Notice of the operations undertaken to determine the figure of the earth, by M. Biot of the Academy of Science. Paris 1818. *Blackwoods Magazine.* 3: 463-470.

Bowes, H. R. (ed.) (1976) Methodism in Shetland and Orkney 1822-1852 Part 1. *New Shetlander.* 117: 20-22.

Bowes, H. R. (ed.) (1976) Methodism in Shetland and Orkney 1822-1852 Part 2. *New Shetlander.* 118: 15-17.

Brand, J. (1701) *A Brief Description of Orkney, Zetland, Pightland Firth and Caithness.* George Mosman, Edinburgh.

Browne, J. (1995) *Charles Darwin: Voyaging.* Jonathan Cape, London.

Burckhardt, F. H., Smith, S. et al. (eds.) (1990) *The Correspondence of Charles Darwin 1809-1882.* Vols 3 & 6. Cambridge University Press, Cambridge.

Cadbury, D. (2000) *The Dinosaur Hunters.* Fourth Estate, London.

Catton, J. (1838) *The History and Description of the Shetland Islands.* Wainfleet, P. I., Tuxford.

Chalmers, J. (2003) *Audubon in Edinburgh and his Scottish associates.* National Museum of Scotland, Edinburgh.

Charlton, E. (1832) Journal of a visit to and residence in the Shetland Islands in 1832. MS. National Library of Scotland, Edinburgh and *Old Lore Miscellany.*

Charlton, E. (1834) Journal of an expedition to Shetland in 1834. MS. National Library of Scotland, Edinburgh and also in *Old Lore Miscellany,* (1935-46): 55-71.

Clarke, A. (1837) *Collected Works.* Vol XIII. London

Cohen, B. (1983) *Norse Imagery in Shetland: an Historical Study of Intellectuals and their use of the past in the construction of Shetland's Identity, with particular reference to the period 1800-1914.* Unpublished PhD, Manchester University.

Coues, E. (1880) Behind the veil. *Bulletin of the Nuttall Ornithological Club.* Vol 5: 193-200.

Cowie, R. C. (1871) *Shetland: Descriptive and Historical.* John Menzies & Co., Aberdeen.

Crabtree, B. G. & Paton, J. W. (eds.) (1995) *Journal of a Secesh Lady: The Diary of Catherine Ann Devereux Edmondston*. (Third printing) Division of Archives and History, Dept. of Cultural Resources, Raleigh.

Cracroft, S. (1849) *Journey to the Orkneys and Shetlands*. MS. Library of the Scott Polar Institute, Cambridge.

Darwin, C. (1886) *The variations of animals and plants under domestication*. 2 vols. D. Murray, London.

Dasent, Sir George Webbe (1861) *The Story of Burnt Njal*. Edmonston and Douglas, Edinburgh.

Desmond, R. (1977) *Dictionary of British and Irish Botanists and Horticulturalists*. Taylor and Francis, London.

Dingwall, H. M. (2003) *A History of Scottish Medicine*. University Press, Edinburgh.

Donaldson, G. (1966) *Northwards by Sea*. Edinburgh.

Donaldson, G. (ed.) (1991) Court Book of Shetland 1615-1629. Shetland Library, Lerwick.

Doyle, A. C. (1897) Life on a Greenland Whaler. *Strand Magazine*. 13: 16-25.

Doyle, A. C. (1924) *Memories and Adventures*. Hodder & Stoughton, London.

Dunn, S. (1976) *Samuel Dunn's Shetland and Orkney Journal. 1822-25*. (ed.) H. R. Bowes, Privately printed.

Edmondston, A. (1809) *A view of the Ancient and Present State of the Zetland Islands*. John Ballantyne & Co., Edinburgh.

Edmondston, B. & Saxby, J. M. E. (1888) *The Home of a Naturalist*. Nisbet, London.

Edmondston, E. (1855) Journey from New Orleans to California. *Chambers' Journal*. No. 100.

Edmondston, E. (1868) *The Young Shetlander*. Sutherland & Knox, Edinburgh.

Edmondston, L. D. (1963) Burke and Hare: A Shetland link. *New Shetlander*. 66: 16-17 & 29.

Edmondston, T. (1845) *A Flora of Shetland*. Aberdeen.

Edmondston, T. (1866) *An Etymological glossary of the Shetland and Orkney dialect*. Adam & Charles Black, Edinburgh.

Everett, J. (1828) *Clarkeana: Collected during a trip to the Zetland Islands in 1828*. MS. Methodist Archives, John Rylands Library, University of Manchester, Manchester.

Evershed, H. (1874) On the Agriculture of the Islands of Shetland. *Trans. of the Highland & Agricultural Society of Scotland*. 4th Series. V: 187-228.

Ferguson, D. M. (1988) The Unst Chrome Mines. *Shetland Life*. March.

Flinn, D. (1989) *Travellers in a Bygone Shetland*. Scottish Academic Press, Edinburgh.

Flint, S. R. (1883) *Mudge Memoirs*. Netherton & Worth, Truro.

Forbes, Edward (1839) Notice of Researches in Shetland. British Association Report 1839.

Franklin, Lady J. (1849) *Journal of a visit to the Orkneys and Shetlands*. MS. Library, Scott Polar Institute, Cambridge.

Fraser, W. J. (1991) *Charleston! Charleston! The History of a Southern City*. University of South Carolina Press, Charleston.

Freeman, R. B. (1978-79) Darwin's negro bird-stuffer. *Royal Society Notes and Records*. 33: 83-86.

Gear, I. (1983) The Truck system in Shetland. *New Shetlander*. 143: 6-9.

Gear, W. (2005) *John Walker's Shetland*. The Shetland Times Ltd., Lerwick.

Graham, J. J. (1961) Profiles from the past XI: Basil Ramsay Anderson. *New Shetlander*. 57: 10-12.

Graham, J. J. (1967) Profiles from the past XXXIII: The Ingrams of Unst. *New Shetlander*. 80: 13-15.

Graham, J. J. (1998) *A vehement thirst after knowledge*. The Shetland Times Ltd., Lerwick.

Graham, L. (1996) Shetland Literature and the Idea of Community, in: Waugh D. J., (ed.) *Shetland's Northern Links: Language and History*. Scottish Society for Northern Studies, Lerwick.

Grant, F. J. (1907) *Zetland Family Histories*. T. & J. Manson, Lerwick

Gronneburg, R. (1982) Prince Louis-Lucien Bonaparte (1813-1891). *Shetland Life*. 18: 23.

Gronneburg, R. (1990) Einar Seim, farmer and folklorist. *Shetland Life*. September.

Hibbert, S. (1822) *Description of the Shetland Islands*. Constable, Edinburgh.

Hibbert-Ware, Mrs (1882) *The Life and Correspondence of the late Samuel H. Ware*. J. E. Cornish, Manchester.

Hill, C. (ed.) (1894) *Frederic Hill: an autobiography of fifty years in time of reform*. Publisher?

Hughson, I. (1983) The Truck system in Shetland. Part 2. *New Shetlander*. 146: 7-9.

Irvine, J. W. (1985) *Lerwick, the birth and growth of an island town*. The Shetland Times Ltd., Lerwick.

Jakobson, J. (1993) Repr. *The Place Names of Shetland*. Orcadian, Kirkwall.

Johnson, R. L. (1986) Clearances in Unst. *New Shetlander*. 157: 9-11.

Keay, J. & Keay, J. (eds.) (1994) *Collins Encyclopaedia of Scotland*. Harper Collins, London.

Keillar, I. (1982) Thomas Edmondston Ö a neglected genius. *New Shetlander*. 142: 25-27.

Lewis, J. (2005) (ed.) Bowes, H. R. *Two Calves in the House*. Shetland Amenity Trust, Lerwick.

Low, G. (1879) *A Tour through the Islands of Orkney and Shetland, 1774*.

Lyell, C. (1830) *Principles of Geology*. John Murray, London.

MacGregor (1993) pp. 40-41 Lace knitting and Saxbys in Shetland

Macmillan, D. S. (1966) Captain Henry Kater's Shetland Journal Part I. *New Shetlander*. 79: 55-57.

Macmillan, D. S. (1967) Captain Henry Kater's Shetland Journal Part II. *New Shetlander*. 80: 22-24.

Manson, T. M. Y. (1959) Profiles from the past V: Arthur Anderson. *New Shetlander*. 50: 24-26.

Manson, T. M. Y. (1991) *Lerwick during the last half century*. Community Council, Lerwick.

Matthewson, R. (1981) The capture of a sea eagle. *New Shetlander*. 137: 15-16.

Maxwell, W. H. (1860) *Wild Sports of the West*. Routledge, London.

McGoogan, K. (2001) *Fatal Passage*. Harper Collins, Toronto.

Miller, S. (1993) The 'Philological Labours' of Prince Louis-Lucien Bonaparte (1813-91). *Newsletter of the Henry Sweet Society*. 21: 2-5.

Miller, S. (1994) The 'Philological Labours' of Prince Louis-Lucien Bonaparte (1813-91) Part 2. *Newsletter of the Henry Sweet Society*. 22: 5-15.

Miller, S. (1996-97) 'Words Peculiar to Shetland': Prince Louis-Lucien Bonaparte in Shetland (1858). *Review of Scottish Culture*. 10: 108-112.

Neill, P. A. (1806) *A Tour through some of the Islands of Orkney and Shetland*. A. Constable & Co., Edinburgh.

Officer, L. H. (2004) *Comparing the purchasing power of money in G.B. from 1264-2002.* Economic History Series 2004, Wade Forest University.

Pennant, T. (1784) *Arctic Zoology (1784-87).* H. Hughes, London.

Pennington, M., Osborn, K., Harvey, P., Riddington, R., Okill, D., Ellis, P., & Heubeck, M. (2004) *The Birds of Shetland.* Christopher Helm, London.

Ployen, C. (1849) *Reminiscences of a voyage to Shetland, Orkney and Scotland in the summer of 1839.* Trans. C. Spence. T. & J. Manson, Lerwick.

Priest, J. (1994) Memories of Buness and Uyea Isle. *Shetland Life.* March: 12.

Prior, M. (2005) *Fond Hopes Destroyed.* The Shetland Times Ltd., Lerwick.

Raby, J. (1823) Letters. MS. Methodist archives, John Rylands Library, University of Manchester, Manchester.

Ralph, Robert (1999) *William MacGillivray: Creatures of the air, land and sea.* Merrell Holberton & Natural History Museum, London.

Reid, J. T. (1869) *Art Rambles in Shetland.* Edmonston & Douglas, Edinburgh.

Rendboe, L. (1985a) *The Shetland Literary Tradition: an introduction.* Odense.

Rendboe, L. (2002) Shetland Literary Tradition. *Shetland Life.* 257.

Report of Her Majesty's Commissioners of Enquiry into the Conditions of the Crofters and Cottars of the Highlands and Islands of Scotland. 1884.

Ritchie, J. A Double Centenary – two notable Naturalists, Robert Jameson and Edward Forbes. *Proceedings of the Royal Society Edinburgh, Sect. B, lxvi: 29-58.*

Robertson, B. R. (1991) A hundred years of sailing. *Shetland Life.* January: 4-7.

Robertson, M. S. (1991) *Sons and daughters of Shetland 1800-1900.* Shetland Publishing Co., Lerwick.

Rufman, A. (1999) A multi-disciplinary and inter-scientific study of the Saxby Gale: October 4-5 1869 hybrid-hurricane and record storm surge. *C.M.O.S. Bulletin.* Vol 27, 3: 67-75.

Sandison, A. (1978) *Tracing Ancestors in Shetland.* Privately published, London.

Sandison, A. (1980) *Some Inhabitants of Shetland in 1872.* ?, London.

Sandison, C. (1968) *Unst. My Island Home and Story.* The Shetland Times Ltd., Lerwick.

Sandison, R. (1997) *Christopher Sandison of Eshaness 1781-1870: Diarist in an Age of Social Change.* The Shetland Times Ltd., Lerwick.

Saxby, H. L. (1974) *The Birds of Shetland.* McLaren & Stewart, Edinburgh.

Saxby, J. (1942) Jessie M. E. Saxby 1842-1940: An appreciation. *Chambers' Journal.* 652.

Saxby, J. M. E. (1892) *Heim Launds and Heim Folk.* R. & R. Clark, Edinburgh.

Saxby, J. M. E. (1894) *Auld Lerwick: A personal reminiscence.* Church, Lerwick.

Saxby, J. M. E. (1913) *Joseph Bell, M.D.: An appreciation by an old friend.* Oliphant, Anderson and Ferrier, Edinburgh.

Schei, L. K. & Moberg, G. (1988) *The Shetland Story.* B. T. Batsford, London.

Scott, W. (1959) Notes on the flora of Shetland: Unst. *New Shetlander.* 49: 27.

Scott, W. (1962) Profile from the past. *New Shetlander.* Vol ?: 7-9.

Scott, W. (1822) *The Pirate.* Archibald Constable & Co., Edinburgh.

Scott, W. (1998) *The Voyage of the Pharos. Walter Scott's Cruise around Scotland in 1814.* Scottish Library Association, Edinburgh.

Scott, W. & Palmer, R. (1987) *The flowering plants and ferns of the Shetland Islands*. The Shetland Times Ltd., Lerwick.

Scott-Skirving, J. (1874) On the Agriculture of the Islands of Shetland, in: *Transactions of the Highland and Agricultural Society of Scotland*. 4th Series. VI: 229-264.

Seeman, B. (1853) *Voyage of H.M.S. Herald*. London.

Shirreff, J. (1814) General View of the Agriculture of Shetland.

Sinclair, J. (1943) *Unpublished letter to Peter Jamieson, 27th October, concerning croft clearances at Skaw, Unst*. Shetland Archives.

Smiley, S. (1869) Journal. MS. Friends Library, Euston Road, London.

Smith, B. (1979) "Lairds" and "Improvements" in 17th and 18th Century Shetland, in T. M. Devine, (ed.) *Lairds and Improvement in the Scotland of the Enlightenment*. 11-20.

Smith, B. (1983) Shetland and the Napier Commission 1883-1983. *New Shetlander*. 145: 6, 8-9.

Smith, B. (1987) The Tarry Kirk, The Bogus Runes and a Priestly Poker. *The Shetland Times*, 24th December, 12-13.

Smith, B. (1996) The Development of the Spoken and Written Shetland dialect: A Historian's View, in: Waugh, D. J. (ed.) *Shetland's Northern Links: Language and History*. Scottish Society for Northern Studies, Lerwick.

Smith, B. (1998) Camphor, cabbage leaves and vaccination: the career of Johnie 'Notion' Williamson, of Hamnavoe, Eshaness, Shetland. *Proc. Roy. Coll. Phys. Edin*. 28: 395-406.

Smith, B. (2000) *Toons and Tenants: Settlement and society in Shetland, 1299-1899*. The Shetland Times Ltd., Lerwick.

Smith, E. J. (1993) The Skerries Tragedy of 1842. *Shetland Life*. 155, September.

Smith, H. (1971) Life and living in 18th century Shetland. Part 1. *New Shetlander*. 97: 6-10.

Smith, H. (1871) Life and living in 18th century Shetland. Part 2. *New Shetlander*. 98: 8-10 & 13.

Smith, H. (1974) Smuggling days of long ago. Part II. *New Shetlander*. 108: 8.

Smith, H. (1974) Smuggling days of long ago. Part III. *New Shetlander*. 109: 32-25.

Smith, H. (1975) The making of modern Shetland. Part 2. *New Shetlander*. 113: 9-12.

Smith, H. (1975) The making of modern Shetland 1710-1760. Part III. *New Shetlander*. 114: 6-9.

Smith, H. (1976) The making of modern Shetland 1760-1790. Part 3. *New Shetlander*. 115: 6-9.

Smith, H. (1976) The making of modern Shetland 1790-1820. Part 4. *New Shetlander*. 116: 26-29.

Smith, H. (1976) The making of modern Shetland 1820-1840. Part V. *New Shetlander*. 117: 7-10.

Smith, H. (1976) The making of modern Shetland 1840-1870. Part VI. *New Shetlander*. 118: 11-14.

Smith, H. (1977) The making of modern Shetland 1870-1910. Part 7. *New Shetlander*. 119: 10-13.

Smith, H. (1984) *Shetland life and trade 1550-1914*. John Donald, Edinburgh.

Smith, I. J. (1974) *Selected judiciary cases 1624-1650*. Vol III. Edinburgh.

Squire, S. (1835) *Journal kept by Sarah Squire in a series of letters*. MS. Friends Library, Euston Road, London.

Stevenson, R. L. (1899) The Letters of Robert Louis Stevenson. (ed.) S. Colvin, *Scribners Mag*. 25: 41-48.

Strachan, D. (1991) Contention Lane. *Shetland Life*. January: 42.

Sutherland, G. (1993) *The Whaling Years – Peterhead 1788-1893*. Centre for Scottish Studies University of Aberdeen, Aberdeen.

Sweet, J. M. (1969) Robert Jameson and Shetland: a family history. *Scottish Genealogist* xvi: 1-18.

Tait, E. S. R. A Shetland surgeon's indentures 1745. *New Shetlander*. 54.

Ware, Mrs (1882) *The life and correspondence of the late Samuel Hibbert Ware*. J. Cornish, Manchester.

Williamson, S. H. (2002) *What is the relative value*. Economic History Series 2002, Miami University.

Wills, J. W. G. (1974) *'Of Laird and Tenant'*. Unpublished PhD Thesis, Dept. of Geog. University of Edinburgh.

Wills, J. W. G. (1984) *The Zetland Method*. in: Essays in Shetland History. (ed.) Crawford, B. E., Shetland Times, Lerwick.

Wilson, A. N. (2002) *The Victorians*. Hutchinson, London.

Wilson, G. & Geikie, A. (1861) *Memoir of Edward Forbes*. Macmillan & Co., Edinburgh.

Wilson, (1842) *Voyage Round the Coasts of Scotland and the Isles*. Vol II. Adam and Charles Black, Edinburgh.

Withrington, D. (ed.) (1983) *Shetland and the Outside World 1469-1969*. University of Aberdeen, Oxford.

INDEX